EMBODIED INJUSTICE

Black people and people with disabilities in the United States are distinctively disadvantaged in their encounters with the health care system. These groups also share harsh histories of medical experimentation, eugenic sterilizations, and health care discrimination. Yet the similarities in inequities experienced by Black people and disabled people and the harms endured by people who are both Black and disabled have been largely unexplored. To fill this gap, *Embodied Injustice* uses an interdisciplinary approach, weaving health research with social science, critical approaches, and personal stories to portray the devastating effects of health injustice in America. Author Mary Crossley takes stock of the sometimes-vexed relationship between racial justice and disability rights advocates and interrogates how higher disability prevalence among Black Americans reflects unjust social structures. By suggesting reforms to advance health equity for disabled people, Black people, and disabled Black people, this book lays a crucial foundation for intersectional, cross-movement advocacy to advance health justice in America.

Mary Crossley is a Professor of Law and John E. Murray Faculty Scholar at the University of Pittsburgh School of Law. She is a member of the Pennsylvania State Advisory Committee to the U.S. Commission on Civil Rights and is widely published on health-related inequity.

Embodied Injustice

RACE, DISABILITY, AND HEALTH

MARY CROSSLEY

University of Pittsburgh School of Law

CAMBRIDGE
UNIVERSITY PRESS

CAMBRIDGE
UNIVERSITY PRESS

University Printing House, Cambridge CB2 8BS, United Kingdom

One Liberty Plaza, 20th Floor, New York, NY 10006, USA

477 Williamstown Road, Port Melbourne, VIC 3207, Australia

314–321, 3rd Floor, Plot 3, Splendor Forum, Jasola District Centre, New Delhi – 110025, India

103 Penang Road, #05–06/07, Visioncrest Commercial, Singapore 238467

Cambridge University Press is part of the University of Cambridge.

It furthers the University's mission by disseminating knowledge in the pursuit of education, learning, and research at the highest international levels of excellence.

www.cambridge.org
Information on this title: www.cambridge.org/9781108830294
DOI: 10.1017/9781108900928

First published 2022

A catalogue record for this publication is available from the British Library.

Library of Congress Cataloging-in-Publication Data
NAMES: Crossley, Mary, author.
TITLE: Embodied injustice : race, disability, and health / Mary Crossley.
DESCRIPTION: Cambridge, United Kingdom ; New York, NY : Cambridge University Press, 2022. | Includes bibliographical references and index.
IDENTIFIERS: LCCN 2022008904 (print) | LCCN 2022008905 (ebook) | ISBN 9781108830294 (hardback) | ISBN 9781108820608 (paperback) | ISBN 9781108900928 (epub)
SUBJECTS: LCSH: Discrimination in medical care–Law and legislation–United States. | Right ot health–United States. | Health services accessibility–Law and legislation–United States. | Discrimination against people with disabilities–Law and legislation–United States. | Minorities–Medical care–Law and legislation–United States. | African Americans–Medical care–United States. | Race discrimination–Law and legislation–United States. | Hickson, Michael, 1974-2020. | Hickson, Michael, 1974-2020. | BISAC: LAW / Health
CLASSIFICATION: LCC KF3823 .C76 2022 (print) | LCC KF3823 (ebook) | DDC 344.7304/1–dc23/eng/ 2022042
LC record available at https://lccn.loc.gov/2022008904
LC ebook record available at https://lccn.loc.gov/2022008905

ISBN 978-1-108-83029-4 Hardback
ISBN 978-1-108-82060-8 Paperback

For Tom, Malcolm, and Wilson

Contents

Acknowledgments

I am grateful to many people for their support and encouragement as I worked on this book and the ideas contained in it. My thanks go to Greer Donley, Doron Dorfman, Leslie Francis, Michele Goodwin, Lisa Iezzoni, Lisa Ikemoto, Paul Lombardo, Jamelia Morgan, Kimani Paul-Emile, Elizabeth Pendo, Tomar Pierson-Brown, Robyn Powell, Charity Scott, Shira Wakschlag, Sidney Watson, Lindsay Wiley, and Ruqaiijah Yearby for their comments on various chapters of or previous work relating to this book. I offer special thanks to Brietta Clark, John Jacobi, Lois Shepherd, and Ross Silverman, who generously read and offered constructive suggestions for the entire manuscript, as well as to Lu-in Wang, who suggested that I write this book and who encouraged me throughout the process. Ongoing pep talks, guidance, and nurturance also came from Jessie Allen, Sara Goodkind, and Sheila Velez Martinez – faculty colleagues in my writing group.

I received incredible support from the University of Pittsburgh School of Law for my work on this book. Christopher Bederka, Praneeta Govil, Krista Grobelny Ebbert, Richard Haarbauer, Trisha Klan, Taylor Smith, and Jean Yesudas helped move the project forward over several years through their work as student research assistants. Linda Tashbook, law librarian extraordinaire, expertly compiled the index. LuAnn Driscoll, Vicki DiDomenico, Karen Knochel, and Darleen Mocello provided invaluable help in revising and formatting the manuscript. Dean Amy Wildermuth and the Derrick Bell Fund for Excellence at Pitt Law also provided generous support for my work on health justice for Black people and disabled people.

Finally, I thank my husband and sons for their patience as I devoted many hours to this project. More vitally, their generosity of spirit, embrace of adventure and challenge, and commitment to social justice have inspired and sustained me throughout the writing of this book.

this is what I want.

1

Introduction

On June 11, 2020, Michael Hickson died of complications of COVID-19. The father of five was forty-six years old. He had contracted the infection the previous month while in a nursing home, and he was transferred on June 2 to a hospital in Austin, Texas. A Black man, Michael Hickson had a career as an auto insurance claims estimator, a career cut short when he experienced sudden cardiac arrest at just forty-three years of age. Complications left him with quadriplegia, blindness, and brain injuries. Although he had difficulty speaking and remembering things, Michael Hickson continued to participate in his family's life, joking with his children and talking with his wife about their lives.

So far, Michael Hickson's story is unremarkable, if thick with a sense of loss. The treatment he ultimately received at the hospital, however, drew attention to his story, prompting reporting in news outlets in the United States and beyond, spurring protests by disability advocates in Austin, and prompting the filing of a complaint with the Office of Civil Rights in the US Department of Health and Human Services (HHS).

As for many people hospitalized with COVID-19, the course of Michael Hickson's disease was difficult. He developed pneumonia, a urinary tract infection, and sepsis. After Michael had been in the hospital for only three days, his medical team indicated to his family that continuing to treat him would be futile – that further treatment offered no chance of improvement – and that he should begin receiving hospice care. His sister, a physician living in Washington, D.C., agreed with the medical team's proposed shift in approach. But Melissa Hickson, Michael's wife of eighteen years, rejected the suggestion that it was time to throw in the towel on her husband's life. She agreed with the assessment that he should not be intubated but believed he had a chance to live if less invasive treatment was continued. And she refused to simply go along with what the doctors were recommending.

The following exchange (recorded by Melissa Hickson) occurred as part of a five-minute conversation in a hospital hallway, at a point when Mrs. Hickson implored her husband's doctor to continue treating him:

DOCTOR:	Cause as of right now, his quality of life – he doesn't have much of one.
MELISSA HICKSON:	What do you mean? Because he's paralyzed with a brain injury, he doesn't have quality of life?
DOCTOR:	Correct.
MELISSA HICKSON:	Who gets to make that decision … that their quality of life is not good?

* * *

MELISSA HICKSON:	I don't want him intubated, but I also don't think you should just sit him somewhere to be comfortable until he finally just drifts away.
DOCTOR:	Right.
MELISSA HICKSON:	That to me is futile too because that's saying you're not trying to save somebody's life. You're just watching him go. The ship is sailing. I mean that doesn't make any sense to me to not try. I don't get that part.

* * *

DOCTOR:	What I'm going to tell you is that this is a decision between the medical community and the state.

Over his wife's objections and as she sought to find a lawyer to represent her, the hospital withdrew treatment from Michael Hickson and put him in hospice care. After six days without any treatment for COVID-19 (accounts differ on whether he was provided nutrition and hydration), he died. Although Melissa Hickson was not able to seek legal intervention before her husband's death, two disability rights organizations subsequently filed complaints with the federal Office of Civil Rights at HHS, seeking an investigation into whether the hospital's decision to terminate treatment discriminated against Hickson because of his disability.[1] The hospital asserts that the decision was not based on disability but on the direness of Michael Hickson's medical prognosis.[2]

---

[1] Ariana Eunjung Cha, *Quadriplegic Man's Death from Covid-19 Spotlights Questions of Disability, Race and Family*, WASH. POST (July 5, 2020), https://www.washingtonpost.com/ health/2020/07/05/coronavirus-disability-death; Joseph Shapiro, *One Man's COVID-19 Death Raises the Worst Fears of Many People with Disabilities*, NPR (July 31, 2020), https://www.npr .org/2020/07/31/896882268/one-mans-covid-19-death-raises-the-worst-fears-of-many-people-with-disabilities.

[2] A Texas law establishes a procedure to be followed when a patient (or their legal representative) disagrees with a hospital on whether care should be discontinued on grounds of futility. In Michael Hickson's case, an earlier dispute between his wife and his sister about his treatment had led a court to appoint a third-party guardian to make decisions about his care. That

Michael Hickson was one of 877 people who died of COVID-19 that day in the United States, and one of more than 340,000 deaths in 2020.[3] The vast majority of those deaths were mourned by family members and friends as private tragedies, no less painful by being but one among many. Michael Hickson's treatment and death became a news story because he embodied the distinctive fears that some people attached to COVID-19. These fears were not simply the fears of becoming ill with the virus and succumbing to it. Those fears were widely held, at least among Americans who believed that the virus was not a hoax. The more particularized forebodings were of being ignored, discounted, and discriminated against by the health care providers to whom patients turned for treatment. Those fears troubled people whose communities had regularly been ignored, discounted, and discriminated against by health care professionals and who saw no reason to expect that their treatment in a pandemic would be any different. People with disabilities and Black people, while not the only groups to hold such fears, were perhaps chief among them. So a news story about a Black man with a disability dying of COVID-19 after having treatment withdrawn over his wife's objections touched a nerve for both Black people and people with disabilities, manifesting their worries in flesh and blood.

Multiple news outlets told the story of the hospital's withdrawal of treatment from Michael Hickson and his demise. But those accounts did not (and probably could not) offer a fully fleshed out description of the fullness of Michael Hickson's life, of his relationships with his wife, children, and friends. Of the work ethic that pulled him out of bed every morning to help people with car insurance claims, until his cardiac arrest left him unable to drive. Of his love of strategy games and puzzles and of engaging in spirited debate.

The accounts also did not (and could not) answer the questions we are left with. Would Michael Hickson have survived COVID-19 and gone home to his family if the hospital had treated his illness aggressively, rather than withdrawing treatment? Or would he have died even with aggressive treatment? Would the hospital have insisted on withdrawing treatment if Michael Hickson had not had cognitive and physical disabilities? Would it have insisted on withdrawing treatment, over his wife's objections, if Michael Hickson had been a White man?

Most of the news accounts of Michael Hickson's death focus on his disability – and understandably so – since the treating doctor justified the termination of treatment (at least initially) on "quality of life" grounds. But we should not ignore

guardian agreed with the hospital's recommendation to shift Michael Hickson into hospice care; thus, the law was not triggered. Margaret Nicklas, *The Case of Michael Hickson Highlights Legal and Ethical Issues around Who Receives Treatment during a Pandemic*, AUSTIN CHRONICLE (July 24, 2020), https://www.austinchronicle.com/news/2020-07-24/the-case-of-michael-hickson-highlights-legal-and-ethical-issues-around-who-receives-treatment-during.

[3] *Coronavirus in the U.S.: Latest Map and Case Count*, N.Y. TIMES, https://www.nytimes.com/interactive/2020/us/coronavirus-us-cases.html.

(as his wife did not) the possibility that race may also have played a role. One possible role is that, like many Americans, the doctors involved held implicit racial biases that led them to treat Michael Hickson less aggressively. A less direct role might lie in the potential connection between Michael Hickson's being Black and his becoming disabled. As a Black man, Michael Hickson likely was at greater risk of sudden cardiac arrest. One study found that Black Americans were, on average, six years younger than White Americans when they experienced sudden cardiac arrest and that the incidence of sudden cardiac arrest in Black men was more than twice that of White men.[4] Disparities like these are most often attributed to social and environmental factors. The point is that Black men experience the medical event that produced Michael Hickson's disabilities disproportionately and at younger ages.

Michael Hickson's death was less dramatic than George Floyd's or Ahmaud Arbery's or Daniel Prude's or Breonna Taylor's, Black persons (at least one of whom also had a disability) who died violent deaths from force involving law enforcement.[5] Michael Hickson's death was slower. It was not captured on cell phone video or police body cameras. But the disproportionate burden of illness and death experienced by Black people and people with disabilities, both during the COVID-19 pandemic and in all the years before 2020, represents its own form of violence that the state has tolerated or sanctioned, and at times directly inflicted. This is the violence of structural racism and ableism that has contributed to the documented health disparities experienced by Black people and people with disabilities in the United States.

The hashtags #SayHisName and #SayHerName reflect an insistence that the lives and individual humanity of Black persons killed by the police not go unrecognized. #SignTheirNames emphasizes including disabled people in that activism. The hashtags challenge Americans not to look away from the lives needlessly extinguished but instead to demand justice.[6]

The use of state power to end human life suddenly and violently is horrifying. But far more lives are shortened less overtly, whether through lack of access to needed medical care, neglect in the care provided, or unhealthy living conditions leading to poor health and early death. Those unhealthy conditions include not only the obvious culprits like toxic exposures or inadequate nutrition but extend as well to less direct sources of ill health like lack of education and unaffordable housing; collectively, these sources fall under the label of "social determinants of health." Structural racism and ableism also play their roles in shaping the distribution of

---

[4] Kyndaron Reinier et al., *Distinctive Clinical Profile of Black versus Whites Presenting with Sudden Cardiac Arrest*, 132 AM. HEART ASS'N J. 380, 380 (2015).
[5] Daniel Prude had mental illness and was experiencing a mental health crisis when he was killed by police. Gregory McMichael, one of several men who were found guilty of murdering Ahmaud Arbery, had been a police officer until 2019.
[6] #BlackDisabledLivesMatter may be used if the Black person killed was also disabled. The hashtag #DisabledLivesMatter is also in use but does not focus on lives lost to police violence.

those social determinants of health. And counting differences in life expectancy and mortality rates alone does not begin to measure the potential lost by people who survive but whose ability to flourish is crushed.

This book is about the health-related injustices inflicted on Black people and disabled people living in the United States. (For simplicity's sake, I will frequently use "Americans" to refer to people living in the United States.) Those injustices collectively are reflected in the data regarding health-related disparities that the next chapter describes. It begins with Michael Hickson, a disabled Black man who died of COVID-19. In a video posted on YouTube several weeks after her husband's passing, Melissa Hickson described the events leading up to his death, before stating: "Disabled people are people just like anybody else. Black people are people just like anybody else. And everybody deserves the right to live. Everybody deserves the right to be treated when they are admitted to the hospital."[7]

It would seem impossible to disagree with this statement; yet the history of encounters that Black people and disabled people have had – and continue to have – with the health care system demonstrate that these sentiments have never been uniformly accepted. I cannot say all the names of the millions of disabled and Black Americans whose lives have been shorter or filled with more suffering because of health-related injustices, but I can say the name Michael Hickson.

1.1 WHY THIS PROJECT?

I did not set out to write a book addressing the COVID-19 pandemic. The idea for this book was conceived earlier, during the attempted repeal of the Affordable Care Act (ACA) and restructuring of the Medicaid program in 2017. It was then that determined activists and protesters – including many disabled and Black Americans – played a significant role in beating back attempts by congressional Republicans and the Trump administration to shred the protections, coverage, and benefits that millions of Americans had come to rely on. It was then that I first started thinking broadly about the many ways in which Black Americans' and disabled Americans' experiences of health-related injustices bore some striking similarities.

Martin Luther King, Jr., is often quoted as saying, "Of all the forms of inequality, injustice in health care is the most shocking and inhumane." More than five decades after he made that statement, unjust health-related disparities between powerful and marginalized groups in the United States remain a stubborn fact of life. They include gaps in access to health care (a health care disparity) and in health outcomes like infant mortality or life expectancy (health disparities). These disparities are not simply the products of biological difference or patient preferences. Rather, they arise largely from a corrosive mixture of bias, discrimination, and disparities in the social and structural determinants of health. They signify the

---

[7] www.youtube.com/watch?v=P3RfoxTYqeQ&ab_channel=godsboo.

injustice that Martin Luther King decried. The COVID-19 pandemic, which emerged and raged as I wrote this book, has thrown those preexisting health-related injustices into sharp relief for all to see. But they are not new.

Embodied Injustice explores health-related disparities that Black people and disabled people in the United States experience. To be sure, they are but two of the many groups in this country who have endured inequities relating to their health. Indigenous peoples, immigrants, sexual minorities, women, Asian Americans and Pacific Islanders, and Latinx people all have stories to tell of health injustice. Many of those stories bear similarities to those told in this book. However, my more limited focus is on disability and Blackness due to three observations I have made while studying health injustice broadly over many years.

First, while commonalities might be discernible among many groups experiencing health-related disparities (for example, lower rates of insurance coverage likely produce higher rates of delayed care-seeking in many groups), commonalities between health inequities for Black people and disabled people are especially numerous and notable. I often refer to these commonalities or similarities as "parallels" in the experiences of these two groups. I believe the prominence and pervasiveness of these parallels are the result of historical (and to some degree continuing) beliefs that Black bodies and disabled bodies are innately and meaningfully different from the bodies of the White and nondisabled people, who make up the United States' dominant social, economic, and political group. As we will see, beliefs in innate bodily difference have been the basis for deeming Black people and disabled people inferior and exploiting and dehumanizing them, both within medicine and more broadly. One example is the way in which American eugenic policies in the early twentieth century sought to restrain reproduction by disabled people and Black people because of their presumed inferiority. Historical abuses perpetrated by physicians and public health officials have fed a particularly deep reservoir of distrust both in Black communities and among disabled people. Moreover, both groups consistently find themselves on the lower rungs of the United States' socioeconomic ladder, so that social and environmental factors regularly shape their health in harmful ways. And, although laws prohibit discrimination based on both race and disability, those laws have, to date, largely failed to make a dent in health-related disparities based on race or disability.

The second observation is that these parallels in health-related injustice experienced by disabled Americans and Black Americans are largely unexplored, as are the experiences of persons who are both Black and disabled. Intersectionality – the idea that an individual may encounter multiple and overlapping types of discrimination because of multiple dimensions of their identity, like race, gender, and ability – has become central to understanding and addressing issues of injustice. Legal scholar Kimberlé Crenshaw created the concept in the late 1980s to describe the barriers to justice Black women faced when bringing employment discrimination lawsuits. Courts that adjudicated these claims engaged in "single-axis thinking" that compared the plaintiff's experience to one comparator group at a time. Black women suing for race discrimination often lost because their employers could point to how they had promoted Black people (who happened to be men). And if Black women alleged sex discrimination, employers would submit that plenty of women (who just happened to be White) had been promoted.[8] Nor were feminist and critical race scholars immune to this single-axis thinking. Part of Crenshaw's original critique was that single-axis thinking around race and gender led to White women standing in for all women in analyses around gender and Black men standing in for all Black people in discussions of race. The result was that the experiences of Black women remained unaccounted for in employment discrimination law and more broadly.[9]

Applications of intersectional analysis have expanded beyond race and gender to encompass other dimensions of human identity, like sexual orientation or class. But the particular intersection of Blackness and disability in individual lives has received remarkably little attention either empirically by health researchers or in discussions of health justice. The COVID-19 pandemic offered glimpses of the virus's ferocious impact on persons who were Black and disabled. Correctional facilities, where Black people and disabled people are overrepresented, were COVID-19 hotspots.[10] And nursing homes (institutions populated primarily by disabled people) with higher percentages of Black residents suffered higher mortality rates.[11]

More generally, disability is more prevalent among Black Americans than among White Americans, for reasons connected to inequitable distribution of social, economic, and political resources. "Emergent disability" is the term some scholars use to describe disability that results when unjust social circumstances damage or degrade people's bodies or minds, leaving them disabled. The increase in cognitive disabilities among children in Flint, Michigan, after the government began supplying lead-tainted water to the predominantly Black city's residents, offers a distressing example of emergent disability. Recognizing the emergent nature of some disability entails acknowledging that the disproportionate creation of disability among Black people is unjust.

My third observation is that attending to intersectionality illuminates the potential for expanded and more effective shared advocacy for health justice. Advocates for disability rights and for racial justice have not consistently viewed each other as

---

[8] Kimberlé Crenshaw, *Demarginalizing the Intersection of Race and Sex: A Black Feminist Critique of Antidiscrimination Doctrine*, Feminist Theory and Antiracist Politics, U. CHI. LEGAL F. 139, 140 (1989).

[9] Angela Frederick & Dara Shifrer, *Race and Disability: From Analogy to Intersectionality*, 5 SOC. RACE & ETHNICITY 200, 200 (2019).

[10] Brendan Saloner et al., *COVID-19 Cases and Deaths in Federal and State Prisons*, 602 JAMA 324 (2020).

[11] Sidnee King & Joel Jacobs, *Near Birthplace of Martin Luther King, Jr., a Predominantly Black Nursing Home Tries to Heal after Outbreak*, WASH. POST (Sept. 9, 2020), https://www.washingtonpost.com/business/2020/09/09/black-nursing-homes-coronavirus.

natural allies in efforts to address health injustice. Relationships between the two movements have been limited and at times fraught. For example, the policy platform announced by the Movement for Black Lives in August 2016 was criticized for its failure to address the harms suffered by Black people with disabilities. And, both disability advocacy groups and Disability Studies scholars have been character-ized as being overwhelmingly White, producing the hashtag #DisabilityTooWhite. Acknowledging the disproportionately unjust creation of disability among Black Americans, as well as White peoples' historical equation of Blackness with disability, helps explain the distance between two movements with similar and overlapping goals. And better appreciating the reasons for that distance, along with the strategic and moral value of an intersectional approach, may open avenues of conversation and coordination between the two movements. Thus, *Embodied Injustice* argues that attending to race-and-disability intersections (at both individual and social movement levels) is critically important to achieving progress toward health equity.

1.2 SOME TERMINOLOGY AND LANGUAGE CHOICES

Language choices in writing about race and disability matter. In this book, I generally use "Black" rather than "African American" because not all persons who experience anti-Black racism in the United States are American; nor do they all claim a connection to Africa.[12] In speaking about disability, participants in the global disability rights movement hold varying views on preferred language. Some prefer to speak of "people with disabilities," a term that reflects the importance of viewing individuals as "people first." Others, however, prefer "disabled people," believing the phrase acts as a political identifier and reflects how structural barriers (rather than physical or mental impairments) disable people by preventing full inclusion.[13] To recognize the diverse views within the disability rights movement, this book employs both phrases.

At numerous points, the book refers to the roles of racism and ableism in producing health-related injustices. The precise language used to define those terms varies somewhat. Geographer Ruth Wilson Gilmore offers a definition of racism particularly apt to an examination of health-related disparities, defining it as "the state-sanctioned and/or extralegal production and exploitation of group-

---

[12] In addition, I follow the practice adopted by some publications and organizations to capitalize both "Black" and "White" as a way of recognizing that the two adjectives are not neutral descriptors of a natural state but instead convey socially constructed designations. See Kwame Anthony Appiah, *The Case for Capitalizing the B in Black*, THE ATLANTIC (June 18, 2020), https://www.theatlantic.com/ideas/archive/2020/06/time-to-capitalize-blackand-white/613159.

[13] Center for Reproductive Rights, *Shifting the Frame on Disability Rights for the U.S. Reproductive Rights Movement* 3 (2017), https://www.reproductiverights.org/sites/crr.civicactions.net/files/documents/Disability-Briefing-Paper-FINAL.pdf.

differentiated vulnerability to premature death."[14] Camara P. Jones distills the term's meaning differently, in a fashion adaptable to other -isms. Jones explains racism as:

> A system of structuring opportunity and assigning value based on the social inter-pretation of how one looks (which is what we call "race"), which unfairly disadvan-tages some individuals and communities, unfairly advantages other individuals and communities, and saps the strength of the whole society through the waste of human resources.[15]

By changing the descriptor immediately following "based on," this definition can be adapted to define other group-based structured inequity. Thus, we can use it as the foundation for a definition of ableism, which assigns value based on social interpret-ations of physical or mental impairments and unfairly disadvantages people with disabilities. Disability scholar Fiona Kumari Campbell offers another useful defin-ition of ableism as "a network of beliefs, processes and practices that produces a particular kind of self and body ... that is projected as the perfect, species-typical and therefore essential and fully human. Disability then, is cast as a diminished state of being human."[16]

As a system, racism operates on multiple levels, as does ableism. "Structural racism" describes its operation on a broad, societal level where public policies, cultural representations, institutional practices, and other norms combine, often reinforcing each other, to produce and perpetuate racial group inequity.[17] For example, Chapter 7 describes how aspects of housing unaffordability, harsh school discipline, and collateral consequences of conviction operate interactively as systems that exacerbate racial and disability-based health inequity. "Institutional racism" operates on a narrower basis, within and across institutions; it often is used to describe how institutional practices or policies that appear neutral on their faces nonetheless produce outcomes that consistently disadvantage racial minorities.[18] An example might be a hospital policy limiting admission to patients of doctors who hold staff privileges at the hospital; such a policy would consistently disadvantage racial minorities, who are more likely to receive primary care at health clinics rather than private doctors' offices. "Interpersonal" or "individual" racism describes what many people most readily think of as racism: an individual person's actions that are

---

[14] Ruth Wilson Gilmore & Golden Gulag, Prisons, Surplus, Crisis, and Opposition in Globalizing California 247 (2007).

[15] Camara P. Jones, *Systems of Power, Axes of Inequity: Parallels, Intersections, Braiding the Strands*, 10 Med. Care (Supp. 3), S71, S73 (Oct. 2014).

[16] Fiona K. Campbell, *Inciting Legal Fictions: Disability's Date with Ontology and the Ableist Body of the Law*, 10 Griffith L. Rev. 42, 44 n.5 (2001).

[17] The phrase "systemic racism" is sometimes used interchangeably with "structural racism." The Aspen Institute, *Glossary for Understanding the Dismantling Structural Racism/Promoting Racial Equity Analysis*, https://www.aspeninstitute.org/wp-content/uploads/files/content/docs/rcc/RCC-Structural-Racism-Glossary.pdf.

[18] *Id.*

motivated by conscious racial prejudice, or perhaps by unconscious (implicit) racial bias. Health care providers who invoke stereotypes of Black inferiority as a basis for coercive sterilizations, as described in Chapter 5, illustrate racism operating at the interpersonal level.

1.3 RISKS AND LIMITATIONS

Before beginning, I want to acknowledge several risks of and limitations to the project I undertake in this book. Some of them involve the book's approach, others involve its author.

By exploring parallels between the historical and contemporary experiences of Black people and people with disabilities relating to health, the book treads potentially treacherous terrain. Attempts to draw analogies between race and disability often provoke concern, and for good reasons. The histories and experiences of Black Americans and disabled Americans are different in important ways that analogies may elide and obscure. Comparisons may "reenact the conflation of race with biological deficiency," a belief historically used to justify discrimination against Black Americans.[19] Moreover, drawing analogies between groups of people risks oversimplifying reality, collapsing groups into "monolithic general categories"[20] and essentializing the experience of people in them. Doing so threatens to flatten and erase the layered inequities visited on people who experience multiple forms of inequality, for example, persons who are both disabled and Black.[21] Each person's life is shaped by multiple forces and identities; this is a central observation of intersectionality. But not everyone embraces each of their group identities. Just as experiences vary from person to person so, too, do people assign varying meanings to their experiences and their group membership.

These risks suggest a need for caution in drawing parallels but do not require abandoning the project. Analogies that are imperfect can still be illuminating if we acknowledge their limitations. Analogical thinking is pervasive in legal reasoning, extending to judicial analogies of disability and race. Justice Thurgood Marshall, the first Black justice on the United States Supreme Court, argued for greater protection of people with disabilities against state-sponsored discrimination by highlighting how people with intellectual disabilities had historically been subject to a "regime of state-mandated segregation and degradation . . . that in its virulence and bigotry

---

[19] CAROL J. GILL & WILLIAM E. CROSS, JR,. Disability Identity and Racial-Cultural Identity Development: Points of Convergence, Divergence, and Interplay, in RACE, CULTURE, AND DISABILITY: REHABILITATION SCIENCE AND PRACTICE 43 (Fabricio E. Balcazar et al. eds., 2009).

[20] Hajer Al-Faham et al., *Intersectionality: From Theory to Practice*, 15 ANN. REV. L. SOC. SCI. 247, 250 (2019).

[21] Frederick & Shifrer, *supra* note 9.

rivaled, and indeed paralleled, the worst excesses of Jim Crow."[22] Attending to parallels in the health-related experiences of Black Americans and disabled Americans also provides a natural jumping-off point for recognizing and holding up the intersectional lives of people who are both disabled and Black. With care, we can simultaneously explore parallels *and* validate intersectional perspectives.

Beyond its inaccuracy, universalizing group experience obscures the countless dimensions of individual humanity. This risk looms large in writing about health-related injustices that Black people and disabled people experience in the United States. The topic is heavy and disturbing. But the injustice a person suffers is not the total of that person's life. Michael Hickson may have died prematurely because he was Black and disabled, but he was also a person who loved his family and relished a spirited debate. Focusing solely on degradations and injustices – on what was done to Michael Hickson – risks victimization and erasure of agency by reinforcing dehumanized understandings of people whose humanity is rich and lives are full. This risk may not be entirely avoidable. Only by having data that incorporates group identity can researchers identify unjust health disparities. "No data, no problem," pithily describes the deniability of unjust disparities until data demonstrating them are marshaled. The invisibility of data about race- and disability-based disparities, and particularly the lack of attention to evidence of intersectional disparities, enables continued denial of continued injustice.

A different type of limitation to this book flows from my own limited experience. My lived experience is of being White, educated, well off, and abled. Regardless of the amount of research I do and conversations I have, I cannot write about this book's subject with the authority of lived experience. I can, however, do my best to write in a way that may both offer some new insights to readers with lived experience in the matters I write about and invite readers without that experience into new awareness of particular forms of injustice. In *So You Want to Talk About Race*, Ijeoma Oluo makes the point that White people have a responsibility not to be silent on race. Her point, I think, extends to the importance of ableds (the term some people with disabilities use to identify people who have no disability) talking about disability. Oluo cautions that when White people (like me) talk about race, we will make mistakes and will be called for it, and it will feel bad.[23] The alternative, though, is silence, which can function as acquiescence in injustice. In writing about experiences I have not lived, I am likely to fail to fully capture their dimensions. Readers with more experience can judge where I get things wrong; I run that risk consciously and with humility. But though my lived authority is limited, I can still try to be a witness. Much of my professional life has been devoted to studying health-related injustices; those years of study have enabled me to connect some dots

---

[22] City of Cleburne, Texas v. Cleburne Living Center, 473 U.S. 432, 462 (1985) (Marshall, J., concurring and dissenting).
[23] IJEOMA OLUO, SO YOU WANT TO TALK ABOUT RACE (2018).

and, more importantly, fueled my conviction that these crucial issues demand broader attention.

The book cannot help but be informed by my own process of growing awareness and understanding of health inequities based on race and disability, but this is not a navel-gazing book. I offer up what I have learned and observed in hopes that readers may find some value in it. *Embodied Injustice* describes numerous health-related inequities that have flowed, directly or indirectly, from beliefs connecting bodily difference to brokenness or lesser humanity. If we take care not to elide important differences between Black people's and disabled people's experiences, appreciating their resemblances may help build greater communion and solidarity between those groups. And that might serve as a foundation for coordinated advocacy promoting health justice.

1.4 WHAT THIS BOOK DOES: A PREVIEW

In studying health-related inequities for Black people and for disabled people, I have uncovered no sustained, thorough account of parallels (similarities) and intersections (overlaps, either in individual lives or social movements) between the groups' health-related experiences. The lacuna inhibits an understanding and leveraging of those experiences, which could potentially inform advocacy for greater equity. This book fills that void, first by illuminating parallels in historical and contemporary experiences of health inequity and then by attending to intersectionality in both lives and movements. Rather than generating new knowledge through empirical or historical research, *Embodied Injustice* draws on and synthesizes multiple forms of existing knowledge: scientific and empirical research findings; conceptual and theoretical work in fields including sociology, law, history, critical race theory, and disability studies; and accounts of the lived experiences of Black people, people with disabilities, and Black people with disabilities.

The inequities examined have multiple causes, at several levels. Causes include biased actions by individual health care providers who treat Black people or disabled people as somehow "lesser." Causes also include how health care institutions operate in response to their own institutional interests or government policies. And, crucially, causes include decisions and activities by government policy makers and corporate actors that, although occurring outside of health care settings, affect health outcomes. These actions shape social determinants of health, like education funding, neighborhood infrastructure, and food policy. The different sorts of causes often bleed together and operate in tandem. They tend to operate simultaneously, in a layered fashion, rather than in isolation.

As a result, the book's organization cannot simply be linear or sequential. Instead, after the first three chapters lay a foundation, each of the next five chapters focuses on a different aspect of similarities in the health-related inequities experienced by Black people and disabled people. As the book unfolds, later chapters highlight how people who are both Black and disabled are multiply burdened. The book's final chapters consider the importance of acknowledging, valuing, and engaging those intersectional lives to help build cross-movement alliances.

To give a bit more detailed preview: The two chapters following this Introduction summarize the evidence regarding the varied health-related disparities experienced by Black people and by people with disabilities, as well as the sources of that evidence (Chapter 2) and describe how understandings of both race and disability have evolved from biological categories to identities socially constructed by political, social, and environmental choices (Chapter 3). Nonetheless, beliefs in innate biological difference continue to influence health care providers' decisions in ways that affect the health of Black people and disabled people.

The next several chapters zoom in on several similarities in disabled people's and Black people's experiences with health care providers and the health care financing system. By describing instances of abusive experimentation and medical devaluation of their lives, Chapter 4 considers historical and present-day bases for the low levels of trust that Black people and disabled people have in health care providers and systems. Current-day manifestations of that deficit in trust (in areas ranging from support for physician-assisted suicide to use of hospice care to organ donation) bear remarkable similarities. Chapter 5 examines eugenically motivated constraints on childbearing by Black women and disabled women, focusing particularly on how physicians imposing those constraints have operated within the context of broader social policies. Chapter 6 shifts our attention to how Medicaid, the public health insurance program for low-income Americans, serves as a distinctively crucial source of health coverage for Black people and people with disabilities while also failing to meet their needs. The chapter considers how Republican attempts in 2017 to restructure the Medicaid program and decrease its funding aroused the groups' common interest in the program and prompted effective advocacy to preserve it.

The next two chapters first zoom out, and then fast forward. Chapter 7 zooms out from health-care–specific settings to flesh out social determinants' role in producing health-related disparities. Focusing specifically on housing affordability, exclusionary school discipline, and collateral consequences of conviction, it highlights these examples' similar effects on Black people and disabled people as well as their multiply concentrated impact on people who are both Black and disabled. Chapter 8 uses the context of the COVID-19 pandemic to show how eugenic thinking, patient distrust, and socially or politically produced disadvantage continue to play out in ways that have particularly harmed people who are Black, disabled, or both.

Chapter 9 builds on preceding chapters' foundation to assert the need for greater attention to documenting, understanding, and addressing intersectional (race-and-disability) health-related disparities. It also considers how the high prevalence of Black disability in the United States, much of which results from unjust social arrangements, disrupts dominant discourses of the disability rights movement. This disruption creates tensions, but it may help generate a more expansive understanding of what disability justice requires. Finally, Chapter 10 makes the case for adopting intersectional perspectives that are both race- and disability-conscious as a way of fostering coordinated advocacy for health equity. It suggests medical education, how the Medicaid program pays providers, and policies promoting affordable housing as examples of potential advocacy targets. Ultimately, it argues that joint advocacy by Black people and disabled people represents a rich – but as yet unmined – vein for promoting health equity.

Embodied Injustice does not attempt to provide a comprehensive account of all health-related inequities that people who are Black, disabled, or both have lived with. Its goal, rather, is to suggest how considering those inequities' similarities in source, impact, and implications for human flourishing might support advocacy to eliminate health injustice. Simply understanding those similarities, however, is not enough to equip advocates to address health inequities most effectively. That goal demands appreciating intersections of racial and disability identities as part of envisioning health equity in its fullest version. And that vision offers a path to unlocking the rich potential of solidarity and joint advocacy for advancing health equity.

Health Disparities Based on Race and Disability

One Saturday morning in summer 2020, I was savoring the nonurgency of getting out of bed. I eventually rolled over, checked my phone, and opened Twitter to see the latest count of local coronavirus cases; instead, something in the "trending" column caught my eye. "Chadwick Boseman, RIP." My immediate reaction was disbelief. That couldn't be. How could the young, handsome, vigorous superhero be gone? I didn't know his full body of work then, but later learned of an oeuvre that included a long list of roles. I simply knew Chadwick Boseman as T'Challa, or Black Panther. How could this embodiment of African Black Pride be returned to dust at a mere forty-three years of age?

Colon cancer was the culprit. Like millions of fans, I learned Boseman had been diagnosed four years earlier. During *Black Panther's* filming, as T'Challa evaded death after being thrown from a cliff, the real-life Boseman was undergoing surgeries and chemotherapy in an effort to pull off a similar feat in his own life. Unlike T'Challa's triumph over his foe at the movie's end, real life offered no redemptive plot twist.

A coroner would name Chadwick Boseman's manner of death as "natural," unlike the violent deaths of George Floyd and Breonna Taylor earlier the same year. But we should not assume Boseman's death was "natural" simply because it involved no physical violence. Boseman gave a human face to Black Americans' disproportionately high rates of suffering and dying from colon cancer. Black people suffer around a 20 percent higher incidence of colorectal cancer, compared to White people, and are 40 percent more likely to die from the disease.[1] Boseman's death occurred against a backdrop of these and other racial health disparities in the

---

[1] Pam Belluck, *What to Know about Colon Cancer*, N.Y. TIMES (Aug. 29, 2020), https://www.nytimes.com/2020/08/29/health/colon-cancer-chadwick-boseman.html.

United States, disparities that flow largely from social and economic factors rooted in racism.[2]

2.1 WHAT ARE HEALTH DISPARITIES AND WHY DO WE CARE ABOUT THEM?

Multiple definitions exist for the term "health disparities." One definition explains that the term "refers to a higher burden of illness, injury, disability or mortality experienced by one population group relative to another," and distinguishes health disparities from health care disparities, with the latter referring to "differences between groups in health insurance coverage, access to and use of care, and quality of care."[3] Sometimes, though, health care disparities are viewed as a subset of the umbrella category of health disparities. A more contextualized meaning appears in the federal government's decennial public health plan, *Healthy People 2020*. That document defines "health disparity" as "a particular type of health difference that is closely linked with economic, social, or environmental disadvantage... [one that] adversely affect[s] groups of people who have systematically experienced greater social or economic obstacles" based on some group trait.[4] So framed, health-related differences constitute disparities only when experienced by groups who have suffered discrimination, exclusion, or marginalization. Because these disparities are avoidable, they are unjust. They represent inequities, raising social justice concerns.[5]

"Health equity" is the mirror image of health disparities. It refers to the absence of systematic health disparities between groups at different levels in the social hierarchy.[6] In short, eliminating health disparities is central to achieving health equity. Attaining health equity is a challenging goal, however, as it "requires valuing all individuals and populations equally, recognizing and rectifying historical injustices, and providing resources according to need."[7]

---

[2] The effects of cancer and its treatment can prove disabling for some people. Although he did not publicly disclose his cancer or identify himself as disabled, Boseman might also have been regarded a person with disability due to the progression of his disease.

[3] Samantha Artiga et al., *Disparities in Health and Health Care: Five Key Questions and Answers* 2 KAISER FAM. FOUND. (Mar. 2020), https://files.kff.org/attachment/Issue-Brief-Disparities-in-Health-and-Health-Care-Five-Key-Questions-and-Answers.

[4] *Disparities*, HEALTHYPEOPLE.GOV, http://www.healthypeople.gov/2020/about/foundation-health-measures/Disparities.

[5] Paula A. Braveman et al., *Health Disparities and Health Equity: The Issue Is Justice*, 101 AM. J. PUBLIC HEALTH (Supp. 2) S149 (2011); Paula Braveman, *What Are Health Disparities and Health Equity? We Need to Be Clear*, 129 PUB. HEALTH REP. (Supp. 2), at 6 (2014).

[6] Paula Braveman & S. Gruskin, *Defining Equity in Health*, 57 J. EPIDEMIOLOGY CMTY. HEALTH 254, 254 (2003).

[7] Camara P. Jones, *Systems of Power, Axes of Inequity: Parallels, Intersections, Braiding the Strands*, 10 MED. CARE (Supp. 3), S71, S74 (Oct. 2014).

This chapter briefly examines how and why Black people and people with disabilities suffer health disparities and health care disparities. For ease of usage, going forward I will generally use the term "health disparities" to encompass health care disparities as well. Later in the book, I'll examine how disparities relating to housing, education, and criminal justice affect the health of Black people and disabled people. I use the phrase "health-related disparities" to include these disparities in social determinants of health, along with health disparities and health care disparities.

The field of disparities research and interventions is far more developed regarding racial disparities than disability-based disparities. Explanations for and effects of both types of disparities bear some similarities, however. At core, a fundamental commonality is that both Black people (as a group) and disabled people (as a group) endure disproportionate, avoidable, and unjust burdens of ill health. This chapter's account draws on what both research and lived experience tell us about health disparities for Black people and for disabled people. It consciously does not address – yet – any distinctive experiences of people who are both Black and disabled. Until recently, disparities research largely neglected the interplay of Blackness and disability in affecting health, so this evidence base remains thin. Chapters 9 and 10, however, focus squarely on what we know about that intersection and what it might teach us about progressing toward health equity.

2.2 RACIAL HEALTH DISPARITIES

Even before the COVID-19 pandemic drew the public's attention to health-related inequities for Black communities, research into and policy proposals responding to racial health disparities were something of a cottage industry, with government and philanthropy investing many millions annually. W.E.B. Du Bois was one of the earliest chroniclers of racial health disparities, documenting in 1906 that Black people in Philadelphia (and other Northern cities) suffered from some diseases at higher rates than Whites.[8] It took nearly eight more decades for the federal government to focus on these disparities, but in 1985 a Task Force on Black and Minority Health examined the health status and health needs of racial and ethnic minority populations. It identified conditions that those groups suffered from disproportionately and found higher death rates for Black people as compared to White people.[9] The 1985 *Heckler Report* (named after Margaret Mary Heckler, the Secretary of Health and Human Services who commissioned the Task Force) put racial disparities on the national health policy agenda, where it has remained for nearly four

---

[8] W.E.B. Du Bois, *The Health and Physique of the Negro American*, 1906, 93 Am. J. Pub. Health 272, 275–76 (2003).

[9] Dep't of Health, Educ. and Welfare, Report of the Secretary's Task Force on Black and Minority Health (1985).

decades. A thorough accounting of the ensuing disparities research and policy proposals would require volumes. This chapter's more modest goal is to provide a sense of how widespread and harmful racial health disparities are.

2.2.1 *Pervasiveness*

Since the *Heckler Report*, research has uncovered with devastating clarity the extent and pervasiveness of health disparities in the United States. Disparities exist along almost every imaginable aspect of health, from the prevalence and deadliness of diseases, to the length of lives, to the odds of receiving high quality, timely medical care. A 2015 Viewpoint in *JAMA* (*Journal of the American Medical Association*) succinctly sums it up: "In the United States, compared with White individuals, Black individuals have earlier onset of multiple illnesses, greater severity and more rapid progression of diseases, higher levels of comorbidity and impairment through the life course, and increased mortality rates."[10] Alongside race, place exerts a powerful influence on the gulf between Black and White health. While pervasive, disparities are not spread evenly across communities, tending instead to intensify in places where poverty, pollution, police violence, and lack of opportunity are concentrated. Chapter 7 looks closely at how several social determinants of health affect Black people and disabled people. For now, surveying a range of racial disparities illuminates how much inequity permeates the health of Black Americans.

2.2.2 *Health Status Indicators and Disease Prevalence*

"How are you doing?" This common greeting inquires as to a person's subjective experience of health (among other things). Health researchers commonly pose a similar question to probe people's perceptions of their own health. For example, a survey administered by government health researchers asks respondents: "In general, would you say that your health is excellent, very good, good, fair, or poor?" The resulting self-ratings of health have been validated as indicators useful in comparing the health of different groups.[11] In these comparisons, Black Americans' ratings of their health are consistently poorer than those of White Americans. For example, a 2013 study found that while only 14.6 percent of White men and 14.5 percent of White women rated their health as fair or poor, 22.3 percent of Black men and 26.5 percent of Black women gave that response.[12]

---

[10] David R. Williams & Ronald Wyatt, *Racial Bias in Health Care and Health: Challenges and Opportunities*, 314 JAMA 555, 555 (2015).

[11] *General Health Status*, HEALTHYPEOPLE.GOV, https://www.healthypeople.gov/2020/about/foun dation-health-measures/General-Health-Status.

[12] Audrey N. Beck et al., *Racial Disparities in Self-Rated Health: Trends, Explanatory Factors, and the Changing Role of Socio-Demographics*, 104 SOC. SCIENCE MED. 163 (2014).

Less subjective assessments, like the frequency with which specific conditions are diagnosed, also reveal numerous racial disparities. According to a 2017 report, diagnoses of chronic conditions like asthma, diabetes, high blood pressure, and stroke were all more prevalent among Black Americans as compared to White Americans.[13] Black Americans contract infectious diseases, including HIV/AIDS, shigellosis, and tuberculosis at higher rates.[14] And, of course, they have suffered higher rates of infection during the COVID-19 pandemic.[15]

2.2.3 *Health Outcomes*

Racial disparities also exist in health outcomes, including rates of mortality (death) from various causes, life expectancy, and onset of disability. We all will die, of course. But death from many treatable conditions comes earlier and more often for Black Americans compared to White Americans. In 2015, the overall ("all-cause") death rate for Black people under the age of 65 was 40 percent higher than for White people, with higher mortality rates from diabetes, cerebrovascular disease, kidney disease, and HIV infection, among others, captured in the overall figure.[16] Even those diseases less prevalent among Black people may be more likely to kill Black patients who contract them. For example, although Black adults enjoy a modestly lower prevalence of heart disease as compared to White adults (9.5 percent vs. 11.5 percent), Black heart disease patients have suffered consistently higher death rates.[17] Similarly, White people outpace their Black peers in cancer diagnoses across all age groups, but among those with some cancer diagnoses, Black patients are more likely to die, often due to delayed diagnoses. Black women are more likely to die from breast cancer than White women, and Black men are more likely to die from low-risk prostate cancer.[18]

---

[13] Timothy J. Cunningham et al., *Vital Signs: Racial Disparities in Age-Specific Mortality Among Blacks or African Americans – United States, 1999–2015*, 66 Morbidity and Mortality Wkly. Rep. 444 (2017).

[14] CDC, *Health Disparities in HIV/AIDS, Viral Hepatitis, STDs, and TB; African Americans/ Blacks*, CDC (2016), https://www.cdc.gov/nchhstp/healthdisparities/africanamericans.html; N. Adekoya, Racial Disparities in Nationally Notifiable Diseases – United States, 2002, Centers for Disease Control and Prevention (2005), https://www.cdc.gov/mmwr/preview/ mmwrhtml/mm5401a4.htm.

[15] Lily Rubin-Miller et al., *COVID-19 Racial Disparities in Testing, Infection, Hospitalization, and Death: Analysis of Epic Patient Data*, Kaiser Fam. Found., Sept. 16, 2020.

[16] Cunningham et al., *supra* note 13.

[17] *Racial and Ethnic Disparities in Heart Disease* (Apr. 2019), http://www.cdc.gov/nchs/hus/ spotlight/HeartDiseaseSpotlight_2019_0404.pdf.

[18] Bijou R. Hunt et al., *Increasing Black:White Disparities in Breast Cancer Mortality in the 50 Largest Cities in the United States*, 38 Cancer Epidemiology 118 (2014); Brandon A. Mahal et al., *Racial Disparities in Prostate Cancer-Specific Mortality in Men with Low-Risk Prostate Cancer*, 12 Clinical Genitourinary Cancer 189 (2014).

Figures regarding maternal mortality (women who die while pregnant, giving birth, or in the weeks following birth) and infant mortality (infants who die before their first birthday) tabulate stark, repeated tragedies cumulatively labeled racial health disparities. Overall, the United States performs dismally on measures of maternal and child health. An international comparison of maternal mortality published in 2020 placed it 55th overall (and dead last when compared to other comparably wealthy countries);[19] the country was ranked 33rd for infant mortality.[20] But simply bringing new life into the world is dramatically riskier for Black women and their children.[21] In 2019, Black women's maternal mortality rate was two and a half times that of White women.[22] That overall rate, shocking as it is, does not reveal the gaping disparity existing in some places. In New York City between 2011 and 2015, Black women suffered pregnancy-related deaths at a rate *eight times* that of White women.[23] Black babies born in the United States are more than twice as likely as White babies to die before their first birthdays.[24] This disparity has persisted over time and is especially large for infants born too early. Preterm infants born to Black mothers have a death rate more than three times that of babies born to White mothers.[25]

Overall life expectancy offers the highest-level view of how the health outcomes for Black and White Americans diverge. In 2020, the CDC reported that White people's life expectancy at birth (the average number of years that members of a group can expect to live at the time of birth) exceeded that of Black people by nearly four years.[26] Gaps in life expectancy narrow or widen depending on where and under what circumstances a person is born. The Ferguson Commission (an independent group of community members formed after police killed Michael Brown,

---

[19] Julia Belluz, *We Finally Have a New U.S. Maternal Mortality Estimate. It's Still Terrible*, Vox (Jan. 30, 2020), https://www.vox.com/2020/1/30/21113782/pregnancy-deaths-us-maternal-mortality-rate.

[20] International Comparison, *2018 Report, America's Health Rankings*, https://www.americashealthrankings.org/learn/reports/2018-annual-report/findings-international-comparison.

[21] Linda Villarosa, *Why America's Black Mothers and Babies Are in a Life-or-Death Crisis*, N.Y. TIMES, Apr. 11, 2018.

[22] Amanda D'Ambrosio, *U.S. Maternal Mortality Rate Climbs in 2019 – Despite National Attention, Racial Disparities Remain Vast*, MEDPAGE TODAY, Apr. 1, 2021, https://www.medpagetoday.com/obgyn/pregnancy/91888. The 2019 data showed a narrowing of the racial gap, which had been reported in 2018 as three to four times higher rates among Black women. According to Ambrosio, however, the narrowing of the gap may have simply reflected an increase in White maternal mortality.

[23] N.Y.C. DEP'T OF HEALTH AND MENTAL HYGIENE, *Pregnancy-Associated Mortality in New York City*, 2011–2015, at 5 (2020). The gap was even higher in the period 2006–2010, when Black women suffered a mortality risk twelve times that of White women.

[24] CDC, *Infant Mortality*, CDC, https://www.vox.com/2020/1/30/21113782/pregnancy-deaths-us-maternal-mortality-rate (based on 2017 data).

[25] Amanda D'Ambrosio, *CDC: Infant Mortality Drifts Lower, but Racial Disparities Persist*, MEDPAGE TODAY, Aug. 1, 2019, https://www.medpagetoday.com/obgyn/pregnancy/81347.

[26] Elizabeth Arias & Jiaquan Xu, *United States Life Tables, 2018*, 69 NAT'L VITAL STAT. REP. 1, 3 (2020).

Jr., in 2014) relied on census data to determine that a baby born in a mostly Black, lower-income suburb of St. Louis could expect to live thirty-five fewer years than a baby born several miles away in a largely White, wealthy suburb.[27] Socioeconomic factors and political choices play a central role in explaining disparities at the population level, as discussed later. That said, clear and growing evidence indicates that in the case of Black patients, substantial differences in medical diagnosis and care help explain differences in health and life span.[28]

Health care disparities comprise differences in access to and use of care as well as in the quality of the care actually received. Various metrics capture health care access and use. One set quantifies barriers to receiving care, asking: What percentage of people lack health insurance coverage? What percentage have a usual source of health care? What percentage have recently delayed seeking needed care or filling a prescription because of cost concerns or for other reasons? On all these measures, Black people fare worse than White people.[29] The passage of the Affordable Care Act and its expansion of Medicaid narrowed the racial gap on these access metrics, but they persist.[30] Thus, as a demographic cohort, Black people face more barriers to health care than White people.

Quality-of-care disparities are also undeniable.[31] The Institute of Medicine's landmark report *Unequal Treatment: Confronting Racial and Ethnic Disparities in Health Care* found the evidence of racial disparities in quality of care to be "remarkably consistent across a range of illness and healthcare services," with most disparities remaining even after socioeconomic factors and access-related factors were taken into account.[32]

One comparison method assesses how often patients in different racial groups receive a particular intervention recognized as representing high quality care. Preventive care, such as screenings, provides an example. Numerous studies have documented racial disparities in the receipt of recommended preventive care.[33] For

[27] Ferguson Commission, *Forward through Ferguson: A Path toward Racial Equity* 9 (STL Positive Change, FERGUSON COMMISSION (Oct. 14, 2015), https://forwardthroughferguson.org.

[28] Virginia Anderson, *Racism Derails Black Men's Health, Even as Education Levels Rise*, KAISER HEALTH NEWS (May 19, 2021), https://khn.org/news/article/racism-derails-black-mens-health-even-as-education-levels-rise; *Eliminating Racial/Ethnic Disparities in Health Care: What Are the Options?*, KAISER FAM. FOUND. 1 (Oct. 20, 2008), http://kff.org/disparities-policy/issue-brief/eliminating-racialethnic-disparities-in-health-care-what.

[29] Samantha Artiga & Kendal Orgera, *Key Facts of Health and Health Care by Ethnicity*, KAISER FAM. FOUND. (Nov. 12, 2019), https://www.kff.org/report-section/key-facts-on-health-and-health-care-by-race-and-ethnicity-coverage-access-to-and-use-of-care.

[30] *Id.*

[31] Kevin Fiscella & Mechelle R. Sanders, *Racial and Ethnic Disparities in the Quality of Health Care*, 37 ANN. REV. PUB. HEALTH 375 (2016).

[32] INSTITUTE OF MEDICINE, UNEQUAL TREATMENT: CONFRONTING RACIAL AND ETHNIC DISPARITIES IN HEALTH CARE 5 (Brian D. Smedley et al. eds., 2003).

[33] Heidi D. Nelson et al., *Achieving Health Equity in Preventive Services: A Systematic Review for a National Institutes of Health Pathways to Prevention Workshop*, 172 ANNALS INTERNAL MED. 258 (2020).

example, Black patients are particularly unlikely to meet the criteria for receiving lung cancer screenings, even though Black men are diagnosed with and die from lung cancer at disproportionately high rates, and Black patients receive lung cancer diagnoses at later stages of the disease.[34] Moving beyond prevention to treatment, Black patients receive the optimal standard of care for many conditions at lower rates than White patients, including the control of chronic diseases like hypertension and diabetes.[35] Black patients, however, more frequently receive undesired interventions necessitated by failures to receive good care early in the course of disease. For example, Black patients are more likely to have toes, a foot, or a leg amputated as a result of poorly controlled diabetes.[36]

Focusing on medical resources devoted to different groups offers another way to compare quality of care. In *The Death Gap: How Inequality Kills*, David Ansell describes how a skewed geographic distribution of resources in Chicago helps explain significantly higher rates of breast cancer deaths among Black Chicagoans as compared to the city's White residents.[37] Nationally, White and Black women develop breast cancer at similar rates, but Black women are 40 percent more likely to perish from the disease. One factor that contributes to Black women's higher mortality rate is the later diagnosis of their cancers, and Ansell spotlights how important it is that expert radiologists be available to read mammograms and thus make timely diagnoses possible. When he wrote, Chicago was home to fourteen hospitals with cancer programs approved by the American College of Surgeons, but only one was located in a low-income, predominantly Black Chicago neighborhood with elevated levels of breast cancer mortality. Most of the breast screening facilities in those neighborhoods employed general radiologists, not experts in breast imaging trained to spot incipient cancers. Ansell's study found that at a screening facility serving Chicago's Black community, more than half of the breast cancers appearing on mammography screens were missed by the doctors reviewing them. Ansell describes this inequality as a form of structural violence against low-income Black neighborhoods, perpetrated by decisions about where to locate resources.

2.2.4 *Explanations for Racial Health Disparities*

Reading this litany of wide-ranging disparities in the health of Black and White Americans may be exhausting. Living it can be sickening and even deadly for Black people. Indeed, as detailed below, the very experience of perceiving racial discrimination can negatively affect a person's health.

---

[34] Sandra J. Japuntich, *Racial Disparities in Lung Cancer Screening: An Exploratory Investigation*, 110 J. Nat'l Med. Ass'n 424 (2018).

[35] Fiscella & Sanders, *supra* note 31.

[36] Anna Gorman, *Diabetic Amputations a 'Shameful Metric' of Inadequate Care*, Kaiser Health News, May 1, 2019.

[37] David A. Ansell, The Death Gap: How Inequality Kills 113–21 (2017).

What explains the multitude of racial health disparities? Not surprisingly, no single factor explains the variety of documented disparities. Comprehensively surveying the explanatory theories would demand an entire book. My aim here is more limited. After briefly noting the extent to which genetic or biological factors, personal behavior, and social determinants of health might help explain disparities, this chapter explores another explanation: Black people's experience of racism, in the health care system and more broadly.

If it were true that Black people and White people were innately different biologically, or if genetic markers associated with disease propensity were connected to racial group membership, then some health status and outcome disparities might be explained. As the next chapter discusses, however, evidence that genetic variations align with racial group identity (as contrasted with group ancestry) is vanishingly small. While commonly accepted visual markers of race (like skin color) have biological bases, they are neither clear indicators of a person's racial self-identification nor do they affect a person's health. For some time now, discussions of disparities generally have rejected the premise that racial categories helpfully designate underlying genotypic differences contributing to health disparities.[38]

Early inquiries into disparities also considered whether patient preferences about medical care or other forms of personal behavior might explain some racial differences in health status and disease outcomes. For example, is it possible that mistrust of the medical system might affect some Black peoples' choices? More broadly, researchers wondered whether racial differences in so-called "lifestyle choices," like decisions about what to eat, how much to drink, and whether to exercise, had any explanatory heft. Links between diet, exercise, and substance use and the development of chronic health conditions and health outcomes are well established, so it stands to reason that individual decisions about those matters, when aggregated, might contribute to disparities.

But decisions people make in their daily lives are constrained by the *context* of their lives. The food a person eats is influenced by what kind of food is readily available and affordable, as well as by what her friends and family eat. If a person is cash-strapped and without a car, works two jobs, and has no grocery store in her neighborhood, eating the recommended diet full of fruits, vegetables, and whole grains becomes exceedingly difficult. The "choice" to eat unhealthy foods is revealed as deeply constrained. The phrase "social determinants of health" describes how the context of where people live, work, learn, play, and worship affects their health. Housing, education, and employment options are among the many social determinants that can affect health positively or negatively, a point explored more later in the book. Social determinants operate, in part, by shaping the context for individuals' health behaviors. Although the relative magnitude of different factors in

---

[38] Lundy Braun et al., *Racial Categories in Medical Practice: How Useful Are They?*, 4 PLOS MED. e271 (2007).

causing racial health disparities is still debated, studies suggest that social determinants and individual health behaviors are the primary drivers, with the former influencing the latter.[39]

Social determinants go beyond the material contexts that people live in. They include social forces like discrimination and racism at personal, institutional, and structural levels. For one thing, many social determinants that negatively affect Black health are themselves products of racial discrimination and institutional and structural racism in housing, education, employment, credit markets, and the criminal justice system.[40] But bias, discrimination, and racism – including within the health care system – act more directly on health as well.

2.2.5 *Implicit Bias and Discrimination by Health Care Providers*

Anyone who has suffered acute appendicitis knows its pain can be severe. But Black children taken to the emergency room with the condition were only one-fifth as likely to receive opioid painkillers as White children, according to researchers.[41] Numerous studies reach similar conclusions: Black patients receive less treatment for their pain than do White patients. They are less likely to receive pain medications at all, and those who receive medications tend to receive lower doses.[42] The subjective nature of pain assessments, where doctors make discretionary decisions based on what patients tell them, makes the treatment of pain particularly vulnerable to the operation of bias or misinformation. Physicians may underestimate the pain experienced by Black patients or entertain exaggerated suspicions of their drug-seeking behavior.[43] Whatever the explanations, that this disparity extends even to children confirms its noxious nature.

Racism and discrimination operating within the very system charged with promoting health are particularly pernicious, even when they are unintentional. Histories of medicine and public health are thick with racism and bias.[44] Those

---

[39] Nambi Ndugga & Samantha Artiga, *Disparities in Health and Health Care: 5 Key Questions and Answers*, KAISER FAM. FOUND. (May 2021), https://www.kff.org/racial-equity-and-health-policy/issue-brief/disparities-in-health-and-health-care-5-key-question-and-answers

[40] Brian D. Smedley, *The Lived Experience of Race and Its Health Consequences*, 102 AM. J. PUB. HEALTH 933, 934 (2012); David R. Williams et al., *Racism and Health: Evidence and Needed Research*, 40 ANN. REV. PUB. HEALTH 105, 106 (2019).

[41] Haider J. Warraich, *Racial Disparities Seen in How Doctors Treat Pain, Even among Children*, WASH. POST, July 11, 2020, https://www.washingtonpost.com/health/racial-disparities-seen-in-how-doctors-treat-pain-even-among-children/2020/07/10/265e77d6-b626-11ea-aca5-ebb63d27e1ff_story.html

[42] Kelly M Hoffman et al., *Racial Bias in Pain Assessment and Treatment Recommendations, and False Beliefs about Biological Differences between Blacks and Whites*, 113 PROCEEDINGS NAT'L ACAD. SCI. USA 4296 (2016).

[43] Oluwafunmilayo Akinlade, *Taking Black Pain Seriously*, 383 NEW ENG. J. MED. e68 (2020).

[44] See generally W. MICHAEL BYRD & LINDA A. CLAYTON, AN AMERICAN HEALTH DILEMMA: A MEDICAL HISTORY OF AFRICAN AMERICANS AND THE PROBLEM OF RACE: BEGINNINGS TO

histories live on in Black Americans' diminished trust in the medical profession, which Chapter 4 examines. The residue of racism also colors the beliefs and actions of some health professionals who, like other Americans, are subjected to culturally dominant messages about different racial groups. A growing body of evidence demonstrates how health professionals entertain explicit and implicit racial biases and beliefs and how their treatment of patients varies by race, without clinical justification. One early study asked physicians how they would manage chest pain symptoms presented by simulated patients (actually actors, including Black men and women and White men and women, with carefully scripted presentations). The researchers found that the patients' race and sex affected the likelihood of a physician referral for a cardiac catheterization, with Black women least likely to be referred.[45] Several years later, after exhaustively reviewing then-existing research on disparities, an Institute of Medicine report found compelling evidence that racial bias, discrimination, and stereotyping by providers contribute to treatment disparities.[46]

Implicit racial bias, which more recent research has identified among individual physicians, may also produce differential treatment for Black and White patients.[47] For example, in one study, physicians determined to have an implicit preference for White people and implicit stereotypes of Black people (based on administration of an Implicit Association Test) were less likely to recommend clot-busting drugs for Black patients.[48] In addition, implicit racial bias can diminish a doctor's ability to communicate effectively with a Black patient,[49] potentially negatively affecting the patient's health. Physicians' words also can convey a lack of respect or racially biased assumptions about a patient's behavior. A Black nursing professor told the story of immediately being asked about her sexual partners when she presented at an emergency room with severe abdominal pain. With her expert knowledge, she knew the question stemmed from an assumption that she was suffering from pelvic inflammatory disease, an assumption fed by stereotypes of Black women as promiscuous.[50] Even nonverbal communication can send powerful messages. In one study,

1900 (2000); W. MICHAEL BYRD & LINDA A. CLAYTON, AN AMERICAN HEALTH DILEMMA: RACE, MEDICINE AND, HEALTH CARE IN THE UNITED STATES, 1900–2000 (2001); HARRIET WASHINGTON, MEDICAL APARTHEID (2008); Kevin Outterson, *Tragedy and Remedy: Reparations for Disparities in Black Health*, 9 DEPAUL J. HEALTH CARE L. 735 (2001).

[45] Kevin A. Schulman et al., *The Effect of Race and Sex on Physicians' Recommendations for Cardiac Catheterization*, 340 NEW ENG. J. MED. 618 (1999).

[46] INSTITUTE OF MEDICINE, *supra* note 32.

[47] Kimani Paul-Emile, *Blackness as Disability?*, 106 GEO. L.J. 293, 310 n. 96 (2019).

[48] Alexander R. Green, *Implicit Bias among Physicians and Its Prediction of Thrombolysis Decisions for Black and White Patients*, 22 J. GEN. INTERNAL MED. 1231, 1231 (2007).

[49] Lisa A. Cooper et al., *The Associations of Clinicians' Implicit Attitudes about Race with Medical Visit Communication and Patient Ratings of Interpersonal Care*, 102 AM. J. PUB. HEALTH 979 (2012).

[50] Vanessa Northington Gamble, *Under the Shadow of Tuskegee: African Americans and Health Care*, 87 AM. J. PUB. HEALTH 1773, 1776 (1997).

researchers reviewed encounters between physicians and seriously ill, elderly simulated patients; other than the fact that some were Black and others White, the patients were presented identically. The researchers found that the physicians' verbal communications were similar regardless of patient race, but that they used less positive or rapport-building nonverbal cues (like open body language or standing near or touching a patient) when treating Black patients.[51]

Bias can also shape how physicians (fail to) listen to Black patients. Numerous accounts of adverse birth outcomes (or near misses) include Black women's descriptions of doctors' failing to take seriously their concerns about their pregnancy or their own health.[52] News media reported on tennis star Serena Williams' harrowing experience: the day after delivering her daughter via emergency cesarean section, Williams suspected (based on her own prior medical history) that she had developed a life-threatening blood clot, but medical providers initially ignored her concerns.[53] Hers is not an isolated case. Anthropologist Dána-Ain Davis interviewed Black mothers (as well as fathers, doulas, midwives, and obstetric and neonatal care providers) and found that obstetric racism manifested in subtle and nuanced ways. The mothers shared their experiences of feeling, for example, that medical professionals disregarded their health concerns or punished them for pursuing a nonmedicalized birth plan.[54] For Davis, the common thread from the interviews was medical racism:

> [It] exist[ed] in the crevices and creases of a conversation, in the space between a comment and a pause... [in] doctors and nurses giv[ing] dismissive looks or mak[ing] a woman feel unworthy... [or] stereotyping a patient... or setting aside a woman's concerns about the fears she [had] for her health, her newborn's health or the treatment of her partner.[55]

"Birthing while Black" is the phrase sometimes used to describe the experience.

2.2.6 *Societal Racism and Discrimination*

Racial bias in the world beyond health care settings also contributes to health disparities. Mounting evidence indicates that simply being Black in a country where racism remains a powerful force can negatively affect one's health.[56] Increased stress

---

[51] Andrea M. Elliott et al., *Difference in Physicians' Verbal and Nonverbal Communication with Black and White Patients at the End of Life*, 51 J. PAIN AND SYMPTOM MGMT. P1 (2016).

[52] Dána-Ain Davis, *Obstetric Racism: The Racial Politics of Pregnancy, Labor and Birth*, 38 MEDICAL ANTHROPOLOGY 560 (2018); Kim Brooks, *America Is Blaming Pregnant Women for Their Own Deaths*, N.Y. TIMES, Nov. 16, 2018; Villarosa, *supra* note 21.

[53] Rob Haskell, *Serena William on Motherhood, Marriage, and Making Her Comeback*, VOGUE (Jan. 10, 2018).

[54] Davis, *supra* note 52.

[55] DÁNA-AIN DAVIS, REPRODUCTIVE INJUSTICE: RACISM, PREGNANCY, AND PREMATURE BIRTH 203 (New York University Press 2019).

[56] JOE R. FEAGIN & KARYN D. MCKINNEY, THE MANY COSTS OF RACISM 65–93 (2003); Smedley, *supra* note 40; O. Kenrik Duru et al., *Allostatic Load Burden and Racial Disparities in Mortality*, 104 J. NAT'L MED. ASSOC. 89 (2012); *American Psychological Association, Fact*

from perceiving discrimination can trigger negative emotions, which in turn can contribute to physiological responses and altered health behaviors. Researchers are finding that early disease indicators (like inflammation and hardening arteries), as well as poor health outcomes (like obesity and hypertension), are positively associated with reports of experiencing discrimination.[57] Similarly, clinical settings may activate "stereotype threat," a term social psychologists use to describe the apprehension by a person from a marginalized group that she may confirm stereotypes about her group. In the health care context, stereotypes about Black patients might include presumption of unhealthy habits or failures to follow medical advice. Stereotype threat may lead to increased anxiety or impaired decision making, which can negatively affect health.[58]

Maternal and child health again offers an instructive example. Black mothers' repeated exposure to discrimination is believed to play a role in the shameful racial disparities in infant mortality noted earlier. Specifically, experiencing racial discrimination during her life increases a woman's risk of giving birth prematurely. The precise pathways from experiences of discrimination to preterm birth and other adverse outcomes have not yet been fully established. One theory is that experiencing discrimination may produce post-traumatic stress, with attendant physical manifestations.[59] Public health researcher Arline Geronimus' "weathering" hypothesis offers another possible explanation for Black women's higher likelihood of low birthweight babies, particularly in older age cohorts. "Weathering" metaphorically describes how exposure to constant stress – in this case the chronic stress of living as a Black person in a racist society – acts to eat away at health, leading to precocious health deterioration.[60] These theories help make sense of research findings that "protective factors" that reduce infant mortality among babies born to White

Sheet: Health Disparities and Stress, http://www.apa.org/topics/health-disparities/fact-sheet-stress.aspx.

[57] Williams et al., *supra* note 40; Elizabeth A. Pascoe & Laura Smart Richman, *Perceived Discrimination and Health: A Meta-Analytic Review*, 135 PSYCHOL. BULL. 531, 531 (2009); Tene T. Lewis et al., *Self-Reported Experiences of Discrimination and Health*, 11 ANN. REV. CLINICAL PSYCHOL. 407, 413 (2015).

[58] Williams et al., *supra* note 40, at 111; Diana J. Burgess et al., *Stereotype Threat and Health Disparities: What Medical Educators and Future Physicians Need to Know*, 25 J. GEN. INTERNAL MED. 169, 169 (2010).

[59] T.P. Dominguez et al., *Racial Differences in Birth Outcomes: The Role of General, Pregnancy and Racism Stress*, 27 HEALTH PSYCHOL. 194 (2008); Ann Diamond Weinstein, *Racial Disparities in US Maternal and Infant Mortality Rates*, PSYCHOL. TODAY (Mar. 6, 2020), https://www.psychologytoday.com/us/blog/the-beginning/202003/racial-disparities-in-us-maternal-and-infant-mortality-rates.

[60] Gene Demby, *Making the Case That Discrimination Is Bad for Your Health*, CODE SWITCH, NPR, Jan. 14, 2018; Arline T. Geronimus, *Black/White Differences in the Relationship of Maternal Age to Birthweight: A Population-based Test of the Weathering Hypothesis*, 42 SOC. SCI. MED. 589 (1996).

mothers (like higher educational attainment and socioeconomic status) do not similarly protect babies born to Black mothers.[61]

Evidence regarding the health impacts of racism and discrimination continues to develop, with much left to learn about exactly how and to what extent those forces contribute to racial health disparities. Well theorized, rigorous research is needed to understand the multiple pathways by which structural, institutional, and interpersonal racism operate and interact. The simultaneous operation of multiple pathways is central to the ecosocial theory of disease distribution, developed by social epidemiologist Nancy Krieger. The ecosocial theory posits that exposures to racist policies, practices, and structures pervasive in American society are akin to exposures to toxic or infectious agents in their impact on health.[62] Even historical racist practices, like Jim Crow laws, may have lingering effects on the health of Black people today, an effect that Krieger dubs "embodied history."[63] Notwithstanding the need for more research, the existing evidence has prompted a growing number of American cities and states to declare racism a public health emergency.[64]

2.2.7 *Effects of Disparities: Pernicious and Pricey*

Just as these causes of racial health disparities can be pernicious, so too are their effects. Most obvious is the human toll taken in lives lost and limited. But poorer health and shorter lives also carry an enormous financial price tag, as well as social and political costs.

According to the CDC, "age-adjusted death rates [in 2015 were] 851.9 per 100,000 Blacks and 735.0 per 100,000 Whites," reflecting a gap of 16 percent in all-cause mortality rates.[65] Technocratic presentations of disparities' impact on Black Americans, however, may obscure the human aspects of what those calculations represent. Other descriptions bring the human cost of that gap into sharper focus. In

---

[61] A.R. Gavin et al., *Racial Discrimination and Preterm Birth among African American Women: The Important Role of Posttraumatic Stress Disorder*, 11 J. HEALTH DISPARITIES RES. & PRAC. 100 (2011); Imari Z. Smith et al., *Fighting at Birth: Eradicating the Black-White Infant Mortality Gap*, SAMUEL DU BOIS COOK CENTER ON SOCIAL EQUITY AND INSIGHT CENTER FOR COMMUNITY ECONOMIC DEVELOPMENT (2018); R. Din-Dzietham & I. Hertz-Picciotto, *Infant Mortality Differences between Whites and African Americans: The Effect of Maternal Education*, 99 AM. J. PUB. HEALTH 651 (1998).

[62] Nancy Krieger, *Methods for the Scientific Study of Discrimination and Health: An Ecosocial Approach*, 102 AM. J. PUB. HEALTH 936, 941 (2012).

[63] Nancy Krieger, *Measures of Racism, Sexism, Heterosexism, and Gender Binarism for Health Equity Research: From Structural Injustice to Embodied Harm – An Ecosocial Analysis*, 41 ANN. REV. PUB. HEALTH 37, 50 (2020).

[64] As of April 2021, more than two hundred cities, counties, states, and other agencies had issued formal resolutions declaring racism a public health emergency or crisis. *State and Local Efforts to Declare Racism a Public Health Crisis – Southeastern Region Update*, NETWORK FOR PUB. HEALTH L. (Apr. 2021), https://www.networkforphl.org/resources/state-and-local-efforts-to-declare-racism-a-public-health-crisis.

[65] Cunningham et al., *supra* note 13.

2005, former Surgeon General David Satcher estimated that eliminating the mortality gap between White and Black Americans would prevent more than 83,000 premature Black deaths each year.[66] Legal scholar Dorothy Roberts offers a more dramatic illustration: "Imagine if every single day a jumbo jet loaded with 230 African American passengers took off into the sky, reached a cruising altitude, then crashed to the ground, killing all aboard."[67] Addressing racial disparities in the pandemic, legal scholar Dayna Bowen Matthew puts it bluntly: "What we politely call a 'health disparity' is killing people of color daily. It is causing people of color to live sicker and die quicker, because of the color of their skin."[68]

And though shortened lives and greater illness by themselves are devastating, racial health disparities also exact a heavy financial toll on society.[69] One study found that nearly one-third of direct medical spending on African Americans, Asian Americans, and Hispanics from 2003 to 2006 reflected "excess" spending resulting from health inequalities.[70] Its bottom line: Eliminating racial health disparities would have saved $229.4 billion in direct medical expenditures over that three-year period. When the researchers included indirect costs associated with lost work productivity, illness, and premature death, the estimated three-year cost of disparities ballooned to more than one trillion dollars. A more recent analysis estimated that eliminating racial health disparities in the United States would result in a $135 billion ($93 billion in excess medical care costs and $42 billion in lost productivity) annual increase in gross domestic product per year, a figure that does not include avoiding economic losses from premature deaths.[71] These researchers and others[72] use varying methodologies and project only estimates, but they reach the same basic

---

[66] David Satcher et al., *What If We Were Equal? A Comparison of the Black-White Mortality Gap in 1960 and 2000*, 24 Health Aff. 459 (2005).

[67] Dorothy Roberts, Fatal Invention: How Science, Politics, and Big Business Recreate Race in the Twenty-First Century 81 (2011).

[68] Tiffany N. Ford et al., *Race Gaps in COVID-19 Deaths Are Even Bigger than They Appear*, Brookings, http://www.brookings.edu/blog/up-front/2020/06/16/race-gaps-in-covid-19-deaths-are-even-bigger-than-they-appear.

[69] Ass'n State and Territorial Health Officers (ASTHO), The Economic Case for Health Equity (2012), http://www.astho.org/Programs/Health-Equity/Economic-Case-Issue-Brief ("Health equity is an economic issue as well as a social justice issue.").

[70] Thomas LaVeist et al., *Estimating the Economic Burden of Racial Health Inequalities in the United States*, 41 Int'l J. Health Servs. 231, 234 (2011) (studying costs of disparities from 2003–2006). "Excess" costs were determined by calculating, by age and gender cohorts, the expenditures that would not have occurred if a racial/ethnic group for a particular cohort had a health status equal to that of the racial/ethnic group in that cohort with the best health status. See also Timothy Waldman, *Estimating the Cost of Racial and Ethnic Health Disparities*, Urban Inst. (Sept. 2009).

[71] Ani Turner, *The Business Case for Racial Equity, A Strategy for Growth* (W.K. Kellogg Foundation and Altarum, Apr. 2018), altarum.org/publications/the-business-case-for-racial-equity-a-strategy-for-growth.

[72] Marilyn S. Nanney et al., *The Economic Benefits of Reducing Racial Disparities in Health: The Case of Minnesota*, 16 Int'l J. Env't Res. and Pub. Health 742 (2019); E.E. Bouchery et al., *Economic Costs of Excessive Alcohol Consumption in the US*, 41 Am. J. Preventive Med. 516

bottom line: Racial health disparities are responsible for enormous economic losses to society.

Pervasive health disparities also rend the social and political fabric in less obvious ways. According to the Ferguson Commission's 2015 report, racial disparities in life expectancy and health care were among the structural inequities contributing to the climate from which racial unrest arose following the police shooting of Michael Brown, Jr.[73] Higher mortality rates among Black people decrease that group's voting population, thereby lowering their political influence.[74] Similarly, their shorter life expectancy means that Black people as a group receive less in Social Security payments as a return on the payroll taxes they paid into the system.[75] More globally, because poor health hinders educational attainment and employment,[76] health disparities feed back into and reinforce lower socioeconomic status in a vicious cycle.

2.2.8 *The Persistence of Racial Health Disparities*

Dogged persistence is an unfortunate trait of racial health disparities. In 1985, the *Heckler Report* sounded a note of optimism: "It can – it should – mark the beginning of the end of the health disparity that has, for so long, cast a shadow on the otherwise splendid American track record of ever improving health."[77] The following decades witnessed government, the nonprofit sector, and researchers ramping up efforts to document racial health disparities and identify their causes. More recent efforts are exploring interventions to address disparities.[78] But, despite many millions of dollars invested in research and programming and much attention (or at least lip service) by policy makers, the goal of health equity remains elusive.[79] The 2014 *National*

(2011); CDC, *Smoking-Attributable Mortality, Years of Potential Life Lost and Productivity Losses – United States, 2000–2004*, 57 MORBIDITY AND MORTALITY WKLY. REP. 1226 (2008).

[73] Mattie Quinn, *Will Ferguson Redefine Public Health?*, GOVERNING (Nov. 17, 2015), www .governing.com/archive/gov-ferguson-report-public-health.html.

[74] David A. Graham, *A Million Missing Black Voters*, THE ATLANTIC (May 12, 2015), http://www .theatlantic.com/politics/archive/2015/05/a-million-missing-black-voters/392972.

[75] Neil Irwin, *Rich People Are Living Longer. That's Tilting Social Security in Their Favor*, N.Y. TIMES, Apr. 22, 2016.

[76] Margot I. Jackson, *Understanding Links between Adolescent Health and Educational Attainment*, 46 DEMOGRAPHY 671 (2009); Daniel Hale et al., *Adolescent Health and Adult Education and Employment: A Systematic Review*, 136 PEDIATRICS 128 (2015).

[77] DEP'T OF HEALTH, EDUC. AND WELFARE, *supra* note 9.

[78] Stephen B. Thomas et al., *Toward a Fourth Generation of Disparities Research*, 32 ANN. REV. PUB. HEALTH 399 (2011).

[79] Outterson, *supra* note 44. One pair of researchers probing the ethics of what they refer to as the "health disparities industry" ask: "Are there substantial improvements in the quality of life for vulnerable populations served by the health disparities industry? Has the mileage on the odometer changed enough to suggest that the final destination is closer than it was 20 years ago?" Mary Shaw-Ridley & Charles R. Ridley, *The Health Disparities Industry: Is It an Ethical Conundrum?*, 11 HEALTH PROMOTION PRAC. 454, 458 (2010). Ruqaiijah Yearby, *Does Twenty-*

Healthcare Quality and Disparities Report, issued by the Agency for Healthcare Research and Quality, found little improvement (and in some cases deterioration) in Black–White disparities on both measures of access and measures of quality.[80] The 2018 version of that report reported similarly disheartening conclusions, including that Black Americans received worse care than Whites on 40 percent of quality measures and that since 2000 Black–White racial disparities had narrowed for only 4 out of 56 quality measures.[81] In 2017, the CDC reported that the death rate for African Americans declined 25 percent between 1999 and 2015, narrowing the Black–White gap in mortality rates.[82] But even with that improvement, Black Americans' life expectancy remained nearly four years shorter than that of Whites. Indisputably, the *Heckler Report* did not mark the "beginning of the end" of health disparities.

In spite of the role that racial bias plays in producing and perpetuating disparities, the efficacy of civil rights laws in addressing disparities has been limited. Title VI of the Civil Rights Act of 1964 prohibits recipients of federal funding from discriminating on the basis of race, color, or national origin.[83] Because many health care actors receive federal funding, Title VI might seem a promising tool for advancing racial health equity. In fact, the anticipation of generous Medicare payments to hospitals combined with Title VI to spur the desegregation of many hospital wards in the 1960s.[84] And desegregation in that decade translated into improvements in Black health in some communities on measures like access to care and infant mortality.[85] However, any early promise of Title VI reducing disparities has faded more recently.[86] As providers' blatant, overt racial discrimination largely receded

---

Five Years Make a Difference in "Unequal Treatment"? The Persistence of Racial Disparities in Health Care Then and Now, 19 ANNALS HEALTH L. 57 (2010).

[80] AGENCY FOR HEALTHCARE RESEARCH AND QUALITY, 2014 NATIONAL HEALTHCARE QUALITY AND DISPARITIES REPORT 10. Twelve (out of 21 access measures, racial disparities improved on 2 measures and showed no change on 19), 18 (out of 165 quality measures, Blacks received worse care than Whites on 60, about the same quality of care on 85, and better care on 20), 19 (out of 148 quality measures, racial disparities improved on 13, showed no change on 126, and worsened on 9) (May 2015).

[81] AGENCY FOR HEALTHCARE RESEARCH AND QUALITY, 2018 NATIONAL HEALTHCARE QUALITY AND DISPARITIES REPORT 69–70 (Sept. 2019).

[82] Cunningham et al., *supra* note 13.

[83] 42 U.S.C. § 2000(d).

[84] DAVID B. SMITH, HEALTH CARE DIVIDED: RACE AND HEALING A NATION 121–42 (1999).

[85] Douglas Almond et al., *Civil Rights, the War on Poverty, and Black–White Convergence in Infant Mortality in the Rural South and Mississippi* (Nat'l Bureau of Econ. Research, Working Paper No. 7-04, 2006). Outterson, *supra* note 44, at 775; David Barton Smith, *The "Golden Rules" for Eliminating Disparities: Title VI, Medicare, and the Implementation of the Affordable Care Act*, 25 HEALTH MATRIX 33, 52 (2015).

[86] For fuller accountings of Title VI's inadequacies in addressing health inequality, see Ruqaiijah Yearby, *When Is Change Going to Come?: Separate and Unequal Treatment in Health Fifty Years after Title VI of the Civil Rights Act of 1964*, 67 SMU L. REV. 287 (2014); Sara Rosenbaum & Joel Teitelbaum, *Civil Rights Enforcement in the Modern Healthcare System: Reinvigorating the Role of the Federal Government in the Aftermath of Alexander v. Sandoval*, 3 YALE J. HEALTH POL'Y L. & ETHICS 215 (2003); Sidney D. Watson, *Section 1557 of the Affordable*

from view, disparities persisted, partly as a result of more subtle discrimination, implicit biases, and built-in structural features of the health care system. Title VI has proven ineffective against these forces, prompting legal scholar Dayna Bowen Matthew to conclude: "The current state of affairs is this: Anti-discrimination laws are largely unenforced or unenforceable against health care entities, while an overwhelming body of empirical evidence makes clear that discriminatory practices in health care abound."[87]

2.3 DISABILITY-BASED HEALTH DISPARITIES

Compared to racial health disparities, recognition of disability-based health disparities has lagged. One reason lies in how doctors commonly understand disability itself. According to Shane Neilson, "[M]edicine functions according to the basic idea that 'healthy' is 'normal' and 'unhealthy' is 'abnormal.'"[88] (Neilson knows what he's talking about; after becoming a physician, he earned a PhD in English and Cultural Studies and began research into disability.) His point is that, like much of the public more broadly, medicine commonly presumes that disability, as a departure from normalcy, fundamentally equates to ill health. From this perspective, social and health disadvantages that a disabled person experiences appear to be simply the "natural and direct consequences of disability."[89] As a result, even if disabled people as a group were shown to have worse health outcomes or poorer access to care, physicians could deem those misfortunes the inevitable results of people's abnormal bodies, not the sort of avoidable (and thus unjust) differences that count as health disparities. Thus, physicians and health researchers have been less likely to understand people with disabilities as a demographic group that suffers poorer health outcomes arising from sources other than their disability.[90]

2.3.1 *Conceptual Challenges*

To be sure, it can be tricky to ascertain whether health differences experienced by disabled people are avoidable, so that they should be treated as *unjust* health

Care Act: Civil Rights, Health Reform, Race, and Equity, 55 How. L.J. 855 (2012); Brietta R. Clark, *Hospital Flight from Minority Communities: How Our Existing Civil Rights Framework Fosters Racial Inequality in Healthcare*, DePaul J. Health Care L. 1023 (2005).

[87] Dayna Bowen Matthew, Just Medicine: A Cure for Racial Inequality in American Health Care 1, 28 (New York University Press 2015).

[88] Shane Neilson, *Ableism in the Medical Profession*, 192 CMAJ E411 (2020).

[89] Silvia Yee et al., Compounded Disparities: Health Equity at the Intersection of Disability, Race, and Ethnicity 6 (2016).

[90] Tawara D. Goode et al., *Parallel Tracks: Reflections on the Need for Collaborative Health Disparities Research on Race/Ethnicity and Disability*, 52 Med. Care (Supp. III) S3, S5 (2014). This traditional understanding aligns with a medical model of disability (discussed in the next chapter), which views disability as something broken or defective in a person's body and considers a medical "fix" the preferred response.

disparities. A significant overlap exists between people with disabilities and people in poor health, but the two categories are not identical. Many people with disabilities have significant medical needs. Indeed, medical conditions (like cancer, diabetes, or heart disease) may be the source of disability for some people. For example, we wouldn't classify the difference in death rates from heart disease between (1) people disabled by heart disease and (2) people not disabled by heart disease, as an unjust health disparity. Disability per se, however, need not entail poor health.[91] For example, we would not expect people who are blind, or deaf, or intellectually disabled to unavoidably experience worse health than nondisabled people. And, even for people with disabling health conditions, *health care disparities* (like differences in access to care or lower levels of receiving preventive care) are likely avoidable and thus unjust. Teasing out the elements of avoidability and injustice is at times challenging, since some (but not all) disabling conditions may produce poorer health and some (but not all) health conditions may have disabling effects.[92]

Challenges in collecting data and drawing comparisons further complicate thinking about (and research into) disability-based disparities. How do we compare the health and health care of disabled people to that of nondisabled people if we lack a single, clear definition of what constitutes disability (and, thus, who is disabled)? But government agencies and health organizations use varying definitions of disability; federal statutes alone contain dozens of definitions.[93] For example, researchers often obtain disability data from three national surveys, all of which ask about six types of disability: hearing difficulty, vision difficulty, ambulatory difficulty, cognitive difficulty, self-care difficulty, and independent living difficulty.[94] The definition of disability in the Americans with Disabilities Act of 1990 (ADA), by contrast, is more expansive. Anyone with a physical or mental impairment that substantially limits a major life activity (or who has a history of or is regarded as having such an impairment) falls within the statutory definition of an "individual with a disability."[95]

In addition, the disability population is exceptionally heterogeneous.[96] Health-related experiences of people with mobility impairments may be meaningfully different from those of people who have mental illness, sensory impairments, or chronic illness (and the list could go on).

---

[91] Donald J. Lollar & John E. Crews, *Redefining the Role of Public Health in Disability*, 24 ANN. REV. PUB. HEALTH 195, 200 (2003).

[92] Gloria L. Krahn et al., *Persons with Disabilities as an Unrecognized Health Disparity Population*, 105 AM. J. PUB. HEALTH (Supp. II) S198, S198–S202 (2015).

[93] *Id.* at S199.

[94] U.S. Census Bureau, *How Disability Data Are Collected from the American Community Survey*, http://www.census.gov/topics/health/disability/guidance/data-collection-acs.html.

[95] 42 U.S.C. § 12102.

[96] Goode et al., *supra* note 90, at S5.

2.3.2 *Recognition of Disability Disparities*

Notwithstanding these conceptual and practical challenges, the poor health status and unmet health needs of many people with disabilities gained the attention of the medical and public health establishments in recent decades. In 2000, the federal government's *Healthy People 2010* (its decennial public health blueprint) recognized people with disabilities among the groups experiencing health disparities.[97] Five years later, the Surgeon General issued a "Call to Action to Improve the Health and Wellness of Persons with Disabilities," which connected good health to disabled people's ability to participate fully in society.[98] And findings from a 2009 report by the National Council on Disability (NCD) summarized the extent of and contributors to health-related inequities for people with disabilities:

> People with disabilities tend to be in poorer health and to use health care at a significantly higher rate than people who do not have disabilities. They also experience a higher prevalence of secondary conditions and use preventative services at lower rates. People with disabilities experience more problems accessing health care than other groups, and... lack of access to health care has been associated with increased risk for secondary conditions for people with significant disabilities.
> ... People with disabilities are affected disproportionately by such barriers [to care], including health care provider misinformation, stereotypes about disability, and lack of appropriate provider training; limited medical facility accessibility and lack of examination equipment that can be used by people with diverse disabilities; lack of sign language interpreters; lack of materials in formats that are accessible to people who are blind or have vision impairments; and lack of individualized accommodations.[99]

In sum, policymakers and researchers today generally recognize that people with disabilities represent a population that experiences health and health care disparities.[100]

2.3.3 *Evidence of Disability Disparities*

Increased recognition of disabled people as a population suffering health-related disparities flows from a growing body of evidence, as researchers document

---

[97] National Center for Health Statistics. Healthy People 2010: Final Review (2012).

[98] US Surgeon Gen., U.S. Dep't Health and Human Servs., The Surgeon General's Call to Action to Improve the Health and Wellness of Persons with Disabilities V (2005).

[99] Nat'l Council on Disability, The Current State of Health Care for People With Disabilities 23 (2009) (footnotes omitted).

[100] Amy M. Kilbourne et al., *Advancing Health Disparities Research within the Health Care System: A Conceptual Framework*, 96 Am. J. Pub. Health 2113, 2115–16 (2006).

disability-based differences in health outcomes, access to care, and satisfaction with care.[101]

People with disabilities report being in poorer health and facing greater health risks than nondisabled people. They are far more likely to report being in fair or poor health.[102] They also report higher rates of risk factors (like smoking, obesity, and physical inactivity) that make it more likely their health will worsen.[103] People with disabilities (especially those with cognitive disabilities) face a heightened risk of both unintentional and violent injury.[104] Health-harming social disadvantages in education, employment, income, and transportation[105] are also more prevalent.

Disabled people also fare worse than nondisabled people on access-related and quality-related measures. Despite having rates of insurance coverage roughly comparable to nondisabled people,[106] people with disabilities still face steeper financial barriers to accessing care. Disabled adults are two and one-half times more likely than their nondisabled counterparts to say they have delayed or skipped health care because of cost.[107] Even though they report higher rates of chronic diseases than the general population, they report a lower likelihood of receiving preventive care. For example, disabled women receive Pap tests and screening mammography at lower rates than nondisabled women.[108] In one study, children with developmental disabilities were more likely than typically developing children to experience delayed treatment or have unmet health care needs.[109] Disparities in the receipt of effective therapies and mortality rates have been documented as well. Disabled persons with breast cancer and non-small cell lung cancer are significantly less likely to receive surgery and are more likely to die from their cancers.[110]

While growing, the empirical base documenting disability-based disparities in health and health care remains far more limited than the voluminous evidence of racial disparities. One reason lies in the research-design challenges associated with the heterogeneity of people with disabilities, noted earlier. Because of this diversity, research documenting disparities tends to focus on people with a particular type of disability. In addition, federal funding for disparities research focuses explicitly on

---

[101] Karen Hwang et al., *Access and Coordination of Health Care Service for People with Disabilities*, 20 J. DISABILITY POL'Y STUD. 28, 29–30 (2009).

[102] Lisa I. Iezzoni, *Eliminating Health and Health Care Disparities among the Growing Population of People with Disabilities*, 30 HEALTH AFF. 1947, 1949–50 (2011).

[103] *Id.* at 1950; Angela Senders & Willi Horner-Johnson, *Disparities in E-Cigarette and Tobacco Use among Adolescents with Disabilities*, 17 PREVENTING CHRONIC DISEASE 1 (2020).

[104] Krahn et al., *supra* note 92, at S201.

[105] *Id.* at S202; Iezzoni, *supra* note 102, at 1947.

[106] Disabled people are more likely to be covered by public insurance programs like Medicare or Medicaid. Krahn et al., *supra* note 92, at S202.

[107] *Id.* at S201.

[108] Iezzoni, *supra* note 102, at 1950–51.

[109] Jessica A. Prokup et al., *Healthcare Disparities between Children with Developmental Disabilities and Typically Developing Children in Ohio*, 12 CHILD INDICATORS RES. 667 (2019).

[110] Iezzoni, *supra* note 102, at 1950–51.

racial and ethnic disparities, which limits funding for research into disability-related disparities.[111] Despite these challenges, mounting evidence of disability-based disparities has persuaded researchers and policymakers that at least some of the health and health care differences experienced by disabled people represent avoidable inequities.

2.3.4 *Explanations for Disability Disparities*

The sources of these disparities are multiple and interacting. Because disabled people in the United States are disproportionately likely to live in poverty, receive less schooling, and be unemployed, social determinants of health doubtless play an important role. Chapter 7 illuminates how specific aspects of the housing, education, and criminal justice systems act to harm the health of many people with disabilities.

Environmental barriers to health care access clearly factor into the production of disparities, as do attitudinal barriers and misconceptions within the health care system.[112] Environmental and attitudinal barriers may amplify one another. The medical profession itself plays an outsized role. (Here I speak in generalizations, recognizing that the following does not describe all physicians.) The profession's lack of awareness of the disability experience, its stereotypes and assumptions about disability, its paternalism, and at times overt discrimination[113] all figure in the equation. So does the surprising degree of ignorance among physicians regarding what laws prohibiting disability discrimination require of them.[114]

Consider, as one example, a woman who uses a wheelchair. Physicians' practices generally have been slow to acquire medical equipment like examination tables, scales, or mammography machines accessible for people who use wheelchairs. In the absence of this equipment, women with mobility impairments receive far fewer screenings that require lying down on an examination table (to receive a pelvic examination) or standing (for a mammogram).[115] Widely held, but false, stereotypes of women with mobility disabilities as asexual may lead some physicians to conclude screenings for cervical cancer or sexually transmitted infections or discussions of fertility or birth control are unnecessary.[116] Peg Nosek, a professor of physical

[111] Goode et al., *supra* note 90, at S3.
[112] Tara Lagu et al., *The Axes of Access – Improving Care for Patients with Disabilities*, 370 NEW ENG. J. MED. 1847, 1847 (2014); see also Mari-Lynn Drainoni et al., *Cross-Disability Experiences of Barriers to Health-Care Access*, 17 J. DISABILITY POL'Y STUD. 101, 105 (2006).
[113] Elizabeth Pendo, *What Patients with Disabilities Teach Us about the Everyday Ethics of Health Care*, 50 WAKE FOREST L. REV. 287 (2015).
[114] Nicole D. Agaronnik et al., *Knowledge of Practicing Physicians about Their Legal Obligations When Caring for Patients with Disabilities*, 38 HEALTH AFF. 545 (2019).
[115] Elizabeth Pendo, *Disability, Equipment Barriers, and Women's Health: Using the ADA to Provide Meaningful Access*, 2 ST. LOUIS U. HEALTH L. & POL'Y 15, 23–24 (2008).
[116] *Id.* at 44–45; Iezzoni, *supra* note 102, at 1952.

medicine and rehabilitation and disability rights activist who used a wheelchair, described that "unfortunate stereotype" as "play[ing] out in the assumption of some physicians that we are not sexually active and that if pelvic exams or mammograms are too much trouble because of inaccessible exam tables, they can be overlooked."[117]

Thus, uninformed assumptions about how disability affects a patient's life can endanger a patient's health.[118] Similarly, assumptions that diminished cognitive capacity accompanies physical or sensory disabilities at times leads doctors or their staff to neglect communicating directly with disabled people. Angel Miles, a Black woman who uses a wheelchair, describes her frustration in not being addressed directly by medical office staff when she seeks care. "I'm often ignored. . . . I'm often spoken at, and not to. Sometimes, the person next to me is addressed instead of me. And I don't even know them half the time."[119] After enduring unhelpful and humiliating interactions with medical providers, some disabled people avoid repeating those encounters, relying instead on self-treatment.[120] And an extensive history of abuse by medical and public health professionals, which Chapter 4 details, still leads many people with disabilities to feel alienated from medicine generally.

Negative attitudes regarding disability can also skew physicians' thinking and recommendations. In numerous studies, physicians underestimated disabled persons' quality of life as compared to disabled people's self-reporting.[121] Biased underestimations of patients' quality of life can shape treatment recommendations and inflect their communications with disabled patients.[122] Recommendations against life-saving treatment for disabled patients, which are discussed in Chapter 4, provide the most chilling examples, but more mundane medical advice can also prove life-altering. Physicians sometimes devalue interventions that do not "cure" an underlying impairment but nevertheless would increase a patient's effective functioning

[117] Margaret A. Nosek, *Overcoming the Odds: The Health of Women with Physical Disabilities in the United States*, 81 Archives Physical Med. & Rehabilitation 135, 136 (2000).

[118] Tom Shakespeare et al., *The Art of Medicine: Disability and the Training of Health Professionals*, 374 The Lancet 1815, 1816 (2009).

[119] Joseph Shapiro, *People with Disabilities Fear Pandemic Will Worsen Medical Biases*, NPR (Apr. 15, 2020), http://www.npr.org/2020/04/15/828906002/people-with-disabilities-fear-pandemic-will-worsen-medical-biases.

[120] Lisa I. Iezzoni & Linda M. Long-Bellil, *Training Physicians about Caring for Persons with Disabilities: "Nothing about Us without Us!"*, 5 Disability and Health J. 136, 136 (2012); Cecelia Roscigno, *Challenging Nurses' Cultural Competence of Disability to Improve Interpersonal Interaction*, 45 J. Neuroscience Nursing 21, 22, 31 (2013).

[121] John R. Bach, *Threats to "Informed" Advance Directives for the Severely Physically Challenged?*, 84 Archives Phys. Med. and Rehab. S23, S23 (2003); Gary L. Albrecht and Patrick J. Devlieger, *The Disability Paradox: High Quality of Life against All Odds*, 48 Soc. Sci. and Med. 977 (1999); Alison Davis, *A Disabled Person's Perspective on Euthanasia*, 24 Disability Stud. Q. 1, 2–3 (2004); *A Point of View: Happiness and Disability*, BBC News (June 1, 2014), http://www.bbc.com/news/magazine-27554754.

[122] Clarissa Kripke, *Patients with Disabilities: Avoiding Unconscious Bias When Discussing Goals of Care*, 96 Am. Fam. Physician 193 (2017).

(a highly valuable result from the patient's perspective).[123] Inadequate education helps explain physicians' incomplete and skewed grasp of the lived experience of disability. Medical curricula traditionally have not included balanced and accurate information about living with disability, leaving unchallenged the societal biases and stereotypes that influence medical trainees' understanding. As a result, meager disability-oriented training leaves physicians ill-equipped to provide effective health care for disabled patients.[124]

Concrete impediments to disabled people's receipt of effective care are layered onto (and fundamentally connected with) attitudinal and interpersonal barriers.[125] Common communication barriers pose significant obstacles for patients with hearing, visual, or cognitive impairments, as well as for patients with developmental disabilities.[126] Providers commonly fail to ensure physical accessibility in their equipment and facilities.[127] Decades after the ADA's passage, lack of concern and even ignorance regarding accessibility obligations persist among health care providers, perhaps because they receive little formal training regarding those obligations.[128] More than twenty years after the ADA's enactment, a physician-researcher called more than 250 specialists, seeking to refer a hypothetical patient who was partially paralyzed, used a wheelchair, and weighed 200 pounds. The responses illuminate the pervasiveness of barriers.

> One out of five offices refused to even book an appointment. Some explained that their buildings were inaccessible to people in wheelchairs, but most refused simply because they had no equipment like height-adjustable examining tables and chairs, specially designed weight scales or trained staff members to help move the patient out of the wheelchair.

But even the offices that agreed to see the patient were not necessarily offering appropriate care. When pressed, some acknowledged that they had no plans or equipment for moving the patient. Others said that they would complete only the parts of the exam that they could – and forgo the rest. Fewer than 10 percent of these offices had appropriate equipment or employees trained to help patients with disabilities.[129] Admittedly, some questions about the ADA's precise application in health care settings remain unresolved. But refusing to book an appointment

---

[123] Lex Frieden's story in Chapter 4 is an example.
[124] Iezzoni & Long-Bellil, *supra* note 120; Pendo, *supra* note 113, at 294.
[125] Pendo, *supra* note 113, at 290.
[126] Iezzoni, *supra* note 102, at 1948.
[127] *Id.* at 1952; Elizabeth Pendo, *Shifting the Conversation: Disability, Disparities and Health Care Reform*, 6 FIU L. REV. 87, 89 (2010).
[128] Agaronnik et al., *supra* note 114.
[129] Pauline W. Chen, *Disability and Discrimination at the Doctor's Office*, N.Y. TIMES, May 23, 2013. The results of the research were published in the annals of internal medicine. Tara Lagu et al., *Access to Subspeciality Care for Patients with Mobility Impairment: A Survey*, 158 ANNALS INTERN. MED. 441, 443–44 (2013).

because a prospective patient uses a wheelchair and is paralyzed seems a clear-cut violation of the law's requirements. Respondents' seeming lack of awareness about the legal exposure created by refusing to see a disabled patient suggests that the ADA's impact in health care settings has not been robust. A small qualitative interview study published in 2019 supports this conclusion. Based on their interviews, the researchers concluded that "most physician participants exhibited a superficial or incorrect understanding of their legal responsibilities to patients with disability."[130]

Other sources confirm that disabled people seeking medical care face persistent and pervasive problems of access.[131] The extent of providers' noncompliance with the ADA's requirements for architectural alterations, auxiliary aids, and other access measures is striking. Access barriers constantly remind people with disabilities that their presence is not expected, and, implicitly, not welcomed.[132] Validating that perception, a national survey of physicians conducted in 2019–2020 revealed that just 56.2 percent of respondents agreed with the statement: "I welcome patients with disability into my practice."[133] And all these barriers to receiving optimal care coincide with disproportionate levels of poverty, unemployment, poor housing, and social isolation that compound disabled people's burden of poor health. Little wonder that disabled people (aside from the unavoidable effects of a disabling health condition) endure health disparities.

The state of research into and level of understanding of health disparities affecting people with disabilities are similar to what existed in 1985 regarding race-related health disparities. Substantial research into disability disparities remains to be done, but a path is illuminated by the racial disparities work of the last four decades.

2.4 CONCLUSION

This chapter describes evidence of how Black people and disabled people living in the United States experience worse health and inferior access to quality health care as compared to their White and nondisabled counterparts. It also highlights reasons behind those disparities, several of which will be explored in more depth in later chapters.

The amount of knowledge and data pertaining to race-based disparities far exceeds that relating to disability-based disparities. Empirical research into racial

[130] Agaronnik et al., *supra* note 114.

[131] Nancy R. Mudrick et al., *Physical Accessibility in Primary Health Care Settings: Results from California On-Site Reviews*, 5 DISABILITY AND HEALTH J. 159, 161–65 (2012); Winnie Hu, *Lawsuit Says Bronx Health Center Turns Away Patients with Physical Disabilities*, N.Y. TIMES, July 30, 2015.

[132] Jasmine E. Harris, *The Aesthetics of Disability*, 119 COLUM. L. REV. 895, 947 (2019).

[133] Lisa I. Iezzoni et al., *Physicians' Perceptions of People with Disability and Their Health Care*, 40 HEALTH AFF. 297 (2021).

health disparities, and disparities experienced by Black people specifically, has grown exponentially over the past several decades, and theoretical work applying critical lenses to evidence of disparities has flowered as well. By contrast, empirical work on disability-based disparities is far less developed, leaving more gaps in our knowledge base. Anecdotal and theoretical accounts add to our understanding of disabled people's health- and health care-related experiences, but more research is needed. That illness is a source of disability for some disabled people (but certainly not all) complicates research into health disparities experienced by people with disabilities broadly, while also making assessment of their avoidability (a question central to their unjustness) more complex.

Despite these differences, a remarkable similarity appears in how medical providers contribute to disparities for both groups. For both disabled people and Black people, provider biases play a complex role, diminishing the quality of communication and quality of care offered by providers. For both groups, patients' lack of trust in providers impedes receipt of effective care.

This chapter lays a foundation for the rest of the book both by describing the greater burdens of poor health that Black Americans and disabled Americans bear and by suggesting some questions about those inequities. To start, how do we understand the relevance (if any) of bodily distinctiveness (like skin color and other bodily signifiers of race, or physical or mental impairments) to issues of health justice? The next chapter describes parallel evolutions in understandings of biology's relevance to race and disability.

3

Biology's (In)significance

During President Barack Obama's second term, White medical students and residents at a prestigious public university participated in a research study exploring beliefs associated with racial bias in pain management, an area with well-documented racial disparities in clinical care. These highly educated doctors in training completed a questionnaire asking the extent to which they thought that fifteen factual assertions about biological differences between Blacks and Whites were true or untrue. They also read two mock medical cases about patients (one Black and one White) with a painful condition (kidney stone or ankle fracture), rated how much pain they believed the patients were in, and made recommendations for treating that pain.[1]

Researchers found that a "surprisingly high" percentage of medical students and residents endorsed false beliefs that Black people have thicker skin and less sensitive nerve endings than Whites. Moreover, participants who endorsed more false beliefs were less likely to recognize the severity of Black patients' pain. They also were less likely to make accurate treatment recommendations for Black patients. In these results, the researchers found evidence that false beliefs about racial biological differences "shape the way we perceive and treat black people."[2]

A few years before this study, a woman named Keri-Lynn went to her parents' home to celebrate her thirtieth birthday with about a dozen family members. Keri-Lynn, who was born with spina bifida, used a wheelchair, lived in a group home, and attended classes. Thirty years earlier, doctors advised her parents *not* to surgically correct the spinal opening characteristic of the condition. Had they agreed, their infant (who came to be known in court filings as "Baby Jane Doe") would have

---

[1] Kelly M. Hoffman et al., *Racial Bias in Pain Assessment and Treatment Recommendations, and False Beliefs about Biological Differences between Blacks and Whites*, 113 PROCEEDINGS NAT'L ACAD. SCI. USA 4296 (2016).

[2] *Id.*

been permitted to die from one of the infections typical in patients with uncorrected openings.[3] One doctor opined that if she lived the child would be bedbound her entire life and would be unlikely to form personal relationships or experience joy.[4] As Keri-Lynn's life at thirty showed, this prediction was wildly inaccurate. Many parents of disabled children tell stories of doctors predicting their children would be incapable of achieving physical or cognitive milestones, only to be proven wrong. And medical misperceptions exist for adults as well. Research has shown that doctors are less likely to ask women with physical disabilities (as compared to nondisabled women) about their sexual activity or offer them reproductive health screening services, apparently believing that they either cannot or do not engage in sexual activity.[5]

These stories illustrate how inaccurate perceptions of biological differences or limitations based on race and disability translate into suboptimal medical care. Both race and disability traditionally were understood as categories defined by biology, understandings that linger today. This chapter sketches the histories of scientific racism and the medical model of disability, before considering how social and political accounts of race and disability came to challenge biological accounts. Today, a fair degree of consensus exists that race is better understood as a socially created designation (rather than a biological category) and that the disadvantages experienced by persons with disabilities flow primarily from social or environmental barriers (rather than being the inevitable result of a bodily impairment). But consensus is not unanimity. Many health professionals in particular[6] hold to views attaching significant weight to bodily differences – whether real or assumed – in people with disabilities and in Black people.

3.1 RACE

3.1.1 *Biological Explanations of Race: Scientific Racism*

It may be startling to learn that some twenty-first century medical students believe Black skin is thicker than White skin, but beliefs in racial biological distinctiveness have deep historical roots.[7] Antecedents lie in racist justifications for slavery dating

---

[3] Nicole Fuller, *"Baby Jane Doe" at 30: Happy, Joking, Learning*, NEWSDAY (Oct. 13, 2013), https://www.newsday.com/news/health/baby-jane-doe-at-30-happy-joking-learning-1.6249597.

[4] Steven Baer, *The Half-Told Story of Baby Jane Doe*, 23 COLUM. JOURNALISM REV. 35, 35 (1984).

[5] Corbett Joan O'Toole, *Sex, Disability and Motherhood: Access to Sexuality for Disabled Mothers*, 22 DISABILITY STUD. Q. 81, 87–89 (2002).

[6] Other groups, including professionals like lawyers and judges, may also retain biological understandings of race and disability. I focus here on medical professionals because of their connection to the health of Black and disabled people.

[7] See ROBERT WALD SUSSMAN, THE MYTH OF RACE: THE TROUBLING PERSISTENCE OF AN UNSCIENTIFIC IDEA (2014); IBRAM X. KENDI, STAMPED FROM THE BEGINNING: THE DEFINITIVE HISTORY OF RACIST IDEAS IN AMERICA (2016).

back to the 1400s, when a papal directive authorized Portuguese traders to attack and enslave "enemies of Christ" residing in West Africa. In the late 1600s, French physician Francois Bernier was among the first to use "race" as a basis for sorting human beings into different classifications.[8] A core tenet of developing race science (the then-accepted study of the division of humans into separate races) described Black Africans as innately biologically different from, and inferior to, White Europeans. One difference, that of Africans' purported fortitude in hot, humid working conditions, bolstered claims that enslaved Africans were naturally suited to performing agricultural labor in the American South. Samuel Cartwright, a prominent expert in "Negro medicine," touted slavery's benefits to the enslaved, as it forced naturally indolent Blacks to labor, which pumped red "vital" blood to their brains.[9] An enslaved person's attempt to escape, therefore, must reflect deranged thinking; Cartwright dubbed this 'mental disorder' specific to enslaved Black persons *drapetomania*.[10] Another difference, Black people's supposed high pain threshold, excused the brutality of lashings and other castigations and justified doing surgical experiments on them, as described in Chapter 4. These and other beliefs about innate bodily differences between the enslavers and the enslaved (or as Thomas Jefferson put it "the real distinctions which nature has made")[11] supplied a moral fig leaf permitting slaveholders to argue that Black Africans and their descendants were "naturally suited" for their role in the "peculiar institution."[12]

These are examples of scientific racism, the belief that empirical evidence supports the existence of biologically based racial difference, including racial inferiority. Despite varying explanations advanced for Black people's biological distinctiveness, early theorists agreed on the group's inferiority. Race scientists sought to quantify that inferiority. Samuel Morton, a prominent physician, gathered hundreds of human skulls from around the globe and measured their shapes and sizes, a practice known as craniology. Working in the 1830s and 1840s, Morton used these measurements to claim an objective, scientific basis for ranking the cognitive capacities of racial groups.[13] His work influenced understandings of race in the emerging field of anthropology and in the scholarly community more broadly. Decades later it fed into Darwinian thinking about the naturalness and heritability of racial superiority and inferiority. Tracing the long history of the "intimate marriage of race and science," legal scholar and sociologist Dorothy Roberts' book

---

[8] DOROTHY ROBERTS, FATAL INVENTION: HOW SCIENCE, POLITICS, AND BIG BUSINESS RE-CREATE RACE IN THE TWENTY-FIRST CENTURY 6, 28–29 (2011).

[9] *Id.* at 89.

[10] *Id.* at 90.

[11] THOMAS JEFFERSON, NOTES ON THE STATE OF VIRGINIA 138 (William Peden ed., 1996).

[12] Use of the term "peculiar institution" to describe slavery in the United States is attributed to John C. Calhoun, a prominent Southern politician who served in Congress and in multiple cabinet secretary posts, and as vice president.

[13] OSAGIE K. OBASOGIE, BLINDED BY SIGHT: SEEING RACE THROUGH THE EYES OF THE BLIND 21 (2013).

Fatal Invention illuminates how scientific racism evolved as "scientists ... discovered new ways of identifying, justifying and proving race as a biological category."[14]

This abbreviated history of race science hints at medicine's role in the broader drama. Physicians endowed assertions of innate racial difference with a scientific veneer and professional credibility and thus were leaders in creating, endorsing, applying, and perpetuating these biological conceptions of race – conceptions that always have worked to advance political ends disadvantaging Black people. Over the centuries and up to today, medical "knowledge" about racial biological difference has appeared in medical and public health practice.

One example, already mentioned, is the remarkably durable but scientifically unsupported belief about Black people's lesser sensibility to pain. A similar myth involves Black women's "obstetrical hardiness," a phrase medical historian John Hoberman uses to describe racial folklore that Black women typically suffer less pain during labor and childbirth. This belief in easier labors accords with a view of Black women as primitive, even animalistic. Though neither universally accepted by physicians nor confined to Black women, obstetrical hardiness "became an influential racial folklore within medical theory and practice because it harmonized so well with the racial ideology that had already shaped Western thought about racial differences."[15]

Khiara Bridges' 2011 ethnography of a women's health clinic at a New York City hospital suggests how attending physicians may still transmit racial mythologies to impressionable medical students. Bridges unpacks her interview with a senior attending physician at the clinic to observe that this physician (who regularly teaches students in the clinic) implicitly attributes higher rates of pathology among clinic patients in part to their being non-White. When Bridges asks whether increased pathology might be nutritional in origin, the doctor responds: "I'm sure it is. I think it's cultural. Somebody coming from the middle of Africa someplace is going to have a lot more issues than somebody coming from eastern Long Island is going to have."[16]

Beliefs in innate physical difference also clustered around immunity and infectiousness. First-hand accounts of Philadelphia's 1793 yellow fever epidemic revealed a widespread view that Black people were naturally immune to yellow fever.[17] More typical, however, were physicians' views of Black people as natural victims and

---

[14] ROBERTS, *supra* note 8, at 26.

[15] JOHN HOBERMAN, BLACK AND BLUE: THE ORIGINS AND CONSEQUENCES OF MEDICAL RACISM 139–42 (2012).

[16] KHIARA BRIDGES, REPRODUCING RACE: AN ETHNOGRAPHY OF PREGNANCY AS A SITE OF RACIALIZATION 93–96 (2011).

[17] Rana Asali Hogarth, *The Myth of Innate Racial Difference between White and Black People's Bodies: Lessons from the 1793 Yellow Fever Epidemic in Philadelphia, Pennsylvania,* 109 AM. J. PUB. HEALTH 1339, 1340 (2019).

vectors of infection. Following Emancipation, Black refugees traveling without resources away from plantations suffered from a scourge of diseases. Physicians of the day attributed high rates of smallpox, tuberculosis, and other diseases to a biological inferiority of the newly freed persons and their unfitness to care for themselves.[18] But as historian Jim Downs explains, it was the lack of food, shelter, and adequate health care that caused the devastating levels of illness.[19] Views that Black bodies threatened contagion also appear in early twentieth century public health discussions. Public health strategies to control tuberculosis contributed to racial segregation in Baltimore, for example.[20] On occasion, Black communities also may have received some (albeit unequal) benefit from public health investments designed to protect White people's health.[21]

Belief in racialized diseases (that some diseases are race-specific or experienced differently by racial groups) also exemplifies medicine's historical embrace of scientific racism. The most glaring instance may be the US Public Health Service's sponsoring a study in Tuskegee, Alabama, to answer the question: "How does untreated syphilis affect Black men?" The federal government's willingness to back this study shows the credence granted to a physician's assertion that "syphilis in the negro is in many respects almost a different disease than in the White."[22] (Chapter 4 discusses this study in more depth.)

Increased schizophrenia diagnoses among Black men starting in the 1960s demonstrate the continued wedding of claims of racial pathology to attempts at social control. Jonathan Metzl, a psychiatrist with a doctorate in American studies, describes how research studies in the 1960s and 1970s increasingly "cast schizophrenia as a disorder of racialized aggression." Among other evidence, he points to an advertisement in the *Archives of General Psychiatry* for the antipsychotic drug Haldol, which depicted a Black man with a clenched Black Power fist, presumably to suggest the sort of patient "whose symptoms of social belligerence required chemical management." Mainstream White newspapers were no more subtle, describing "schizophrenia as a condition of angry black masculinity."[23] As racial unrest increased in American cities, physicians' diagnoses of "aggressive" or "militant" Black men as schizophrenic justified prescription of antipsychotic drugs or involuntary confinement to mental institutions. This racialization of a disease

[18] ROBERTS, *supra* note 8, at 86.
[19] JIM DOWNS, SICK FROM FREEDOM: AFRICAN-AMERICAN ILLNESS AND SUFFERING DURING THE CIVIL WAR AND RECONSTRUCTION (Oxford 2012).
[20] SAMUEL K. ROBERTS JR., INFECTIOUS FEAR: POLITICS, DISEASE, AND THE HEALTH EFFECTS OF SEGREGATION (2009).
[21] Isaac Chotiner, *How Racism Is Shaping the Coronavirus Pandemic*, NEW YORKER, May 7, 2020 (interviewing historian Evelynn Hammonds).
[22] Susan M. Reverby, *Special Treatment: BiDil, Tuskegee, and the Logic of Race*, 36 J.L. MED. & ETHICS 478, 480 (2008).
[23] Jonathan M. Metzl, *The Protest Psychosis*, MICHIGAN TODAY, June 9, 2010, michigantoday .umich.edu/2010/06/09/a7776/.

previously diagnosed primarily in White women thus supported social control of Black men who displayed anger.[24]

The common denominator in these examples is an ascription of innate biological difference or inferiority to Black people serving as a "scientific" basis for policy prescriptions that consolidated hierarchies of White power. Today's physicians and scientists are unlikely to explicitly invoke innate biological differences associated with race, but "the impulse to see difference rather than sameness in medical discourse and practice persists."[25] The 2016 study of racial beliefs held by medical students and residents documents this persistence. More examples of twenty-first century attachments to racialized medicine appear later in this chapter.

3.1.2 *The Social Construction of Race*

Two events, separated by a half century, pumped the scientific brakes on the concept of innate biological racial difference. In the wake of World War II, the United Nations Educational, Scientific and Cultural Organization (UNESCO) 1950 Statement on Race rejected race as biologically innate, concluding that "'race' is not so much a biological phenomenon as a social myth" and that humankind was biologically unified.[26] Five decades later, the Human Genome Project provided molecular-level confirmation of UNESCO's core message. President Bill Clinton described the import of the Project's results: "All of us are created equal. . . . [O]ne of the great truths to emerge from this triumphant expedition inside the human genome is that in genetic terms, all human beings, regardless of race, are more than 99.9 percent the same."[27]

Neither event prompted a wholesale abandonment of attachments to biological conceptions of race (whether in the medical community or society more broadly), but two conclusions from genetic advances undermine any biological basis for dividing people into races. First, an examination of the narrow sliver of genetic variability within human populations shows that genetic variations *within* racial groups exceed variations found *among* people from different racial groups. Dorothy Roberts provides an example: "A person from the Congo, a person from South Africa, and a person from Ethiopia are more genetically different from each other than [any is] from a person from France."[28] Second, genetic variations and clusterings that exist at the population level are marked by gradations stretched

[24] Dara Shifrer & Angela Frederick, *Disability at the Intersections*, 13 SOCIOLOGY COMPASS e12733 at 8 (2019).
[25] Hogarth, *supra* note 17, at 1341.
[26] *Statement by Experts on Race Problems*, UNESCO Doc. SS/1, at 3–4 (July 20, 1950), http://unesdoc.unesco.org/images/0012/001269/126969eb.pdf.
[27] *Reading the Book of Life; White House Remarks on Decoding the Genome*, N.Y. TIMES, (June 27, 2000), https://www.nytimes.com/2000/06/27/science/reading-the-book-of-life-White-house-remarks-on-decoding-of-genome.html.
[28] ROBERTS, *supra* note 8, at 52, citing JOSEPH L. GRAVES, JR., THE RACE MYTH 17 (2004).

across geographic regions, not by any definitive (or even blurry) lines supporting racial categorizations.

In refuting race as a biological fact, genetic science cleared a path for understanding race as a political and social fact: race as socially constructed, not biologically destined. It fed a movement among social scientists teasing out how racial hierarchies in society reflected social and historical contingencies, rather than the natural results of biological differences. The "social construction" of race describes how political, social, and economic forces generate the meanings that people attach to physical differences signifying race. Social constructionists interrogate why people attach particular meanings to physical appearance and how those meanings reinforce hierarchies by privileging some groups and disempowering others.[29]

Several fundamental points follow from a social constructivist perspective undergirded by genetic science. First, racial classifications do not align with meaningful biological differences. While pockets or clusterings of particular genetic variations may be found within a racial category[30] (particularly among geographically isolated populations), those variations do not appear throughout the entire racial group. For example, while research has shown that Gullah-speaking Black people living in coastal South Carolina have been shown to share a genetic marker for diabetes, Black people globally do not share that variation.[31] A person's *ancestry* (their connection to their genetic forebears) may predict their genetic makeup (and its health implications), but their racial identity does not.[32] Genetic variations across populations and social groupings of race simply are incongruent; they fail to map onto one another.

Social construction theory asserts that social forces produce both racial categories *and* racial meaning, "expos[ing] how social meanings attach to various bodies."[33] Critical race scholar Ian Haney López speaks of "racial fabrication" to describe the process by which race is formed. His phrasing is a reminder that, although constructivist accounts often point to "social forces," blame for the existence of race and racial oppression does not lie with some kind of abstract or cosmic force, but with human handiwork.[34] To a social constructivist, the inferior health, education, wealth, and power of Black Americans result from centuries of exercised power and meaning-giving, not some kind of natural order.

In a sense, racial categories and meanings have been crowd-sourced from human interactions and power plays over a span of centuries. So viewed, the way racial

---

[29] OBASOGIE, *supra* note 13, at 24–25.
[30] Ian Haney López, *The Social Construction of Race: Some Observations on Illusion, Fabrication, and Choice*, 29 HARV. C.R.-C.L. L. REV. 1, 12 (1994).
[31] Michele M. Sale et al., *Genome-Wide Linkage Scan in Gullah-Speaking African American Families with Type 2 Diabetes: The Sea Islands Genetic African American Registry* (Project SuGAR), 58 DIABETES 260 (2008).
[32] Michael Yudell et al., *Taking Race Out of Human Genetics*, 351 SCIENCE 564 (2016).
[33] OBASOGIE, *supra* note 13, at 19.
[34] López, *supra* note 30, at 27–28.

categories vary according to cultural context and morph over time makes more sense. In the early twentieth-century, immigrants from Italy and Ireland (among other European countries) to the United States were not necessarily considered White; their "racial credentials were not equivalent to those of the Anglo-Saxon 'old stock.'" Over time, though, they assumed White status.[35] Contemporary South Africa distinguishes among Black Africans, Coloured persons, and White persons, categorizing races differently from the United States. Such variability and mutability of racial categories and significance cannot readily coexist with a belief that race entails innate and categorical biological differences.[36]

Law is one social force that constructs and gives meaning to racial categories. *White by Law: The Legal Construction of Race*, by Ian Haney López, illustrates this point. López describes cases where immigrants applied to become naturalized citizens, a status largely limited up until 1952 to "white persons."[37] Immigration officials and courts considering those applications thus had to discern whether applicants from Burma and Armenia and Mexico (among others) satisfied the "white person" prerequisite and to justify their conclusions. In the first case involving an applicant from China, the judge relied on contemporary anthropological classifications of race as well as evidence of legislative intent to conclude that the applicant was not a "white person."[38] These cases provide a window on how the law and legal actors constructed race, a process that involved seeking, wielding, and maintaining power and social status.[39]

Understandings of race as a social construct rapidly took root, and sociology overtook biology as the dominant discipline for studying race. By the mid-1990s authors of a classic volume on the topic declared: "[W]e have now reached the point of fairly general agreement that race is not a biological given but rather a socially constructed way of differentiating human beings."[40] Despite its general acceptance within the social sciences, the conclusion's foothold within medicine and biology was less assured.

In 2003, competing views on biology's relevance to race appeared in a pair of articles in the august *New England Journal of Medicine*. One described race as the offspring of the "marriage of social and biologic influences" before stating: "[genetic] variation is continuous and discordant with race, systematic variation according to continent is very limited, and there is no evidence that the units of interest for

[35] MATTHEW FRYE JACOBSON, WHITENESS OF A DIFFERENT COLOR: EUROPEAN IMMIGRANTS AND THE ALCHEMY OF RACE 3 (1998).

[36] OBASOGIE, *supra* note 13, at 26.

[37] In addition to "white persons," starting in 1870 the law also permitted naturalization of persons "of African nativity, or African descent." IAN HANEY LÓPEZ, WHITE BY LAW: THE LEGAL CONSTRUCTION OF RACE 37 (10th anniv. ed. 2006).

[38] *Id.* at 38–39.

[39] *Id.* at xvi.

[40] MICHAEL OMI & HOWARD WINANT, RACIAL FORMATION IN THE UNITED STATES FROM THE 1960S TO THE 1990S, at 55 (1994).

medical genetics correspond to what we call races."[41] The counterpoint described analyses from population genetics studies as "consistently result[ing] in the delineation of major genetic clusters that are associated with racial categories."[42] Only in 2020, nearly two decades later, did medicine's dominant professional association, the American Medical Association (AMA), recognize race as a social, rather than biological, construct and proclaim that structural racism, not biological differences, produces disparities. As we'll see later in this chapter, though, conceptions of biological race continue to affect medical practice and research.[43]

3.2 DISABILITY

3.2.1 *Biological Understandings of Disability: The Medical Model*

Medical endorsement of innate biological inferiority also suffuses historical narratives of disability. Without doubt, the histories of race and disability in America differ in important ways. The history of disability has no analog for the centuries-long institution of slavery on American soil, an institution propped up in part by physicians' assertions of an innate inferiority of Black Africans and their descendants. Race science ascribed deficiency to Black people globally. By contrast, the very idea of disability as an overarching group identity is of fairly modern vintage. Historically, people viewed as blind, deaf, crippled, or daft (or various other terms no longer considered appropriate) were not seen as sharing an identity.[44] As with race, however, physicians figured centrally in supporting distinctive forms of social control over people with varying disabilities.

Segregation and detention recur across American disability history. From colonial times on, asylums were built for persons who didn't fit into "normal" society. Although asylums claimed therapeutic aims, an equally important goal was to remove disabled, deviant, or dependent persons from the community to prevent social disorder.[45] State laws permitted and in some cases even mandated this confinement. Disability-related policy at the federal level, by contrast, focused historically on disabled veterans. The pension system created for Union Civil War

---

[41] Richard S. Cooper et al., *Race and Genomics*, 348 NEW ENG. J. MED. 1166, 1167 (2003).

[42] Esteban González Burchard et al., *The Importance of Race and Ethnic Background in Biomedical Research and Clinical Practice*, 348 NEW ENG. J. MED. 1170 (2003).

[43] *New AMA Policies Recognize Race as a Social, Not Biological, Construct, Press Release* (Nov. 16, 2020), www.ama-assn.org/press-center/press-releases/new-ama-policies-recognize-race-social-not-biological-construct.

[44] PAUL K. LONGMORE & LAURI UMANSKY, Introduction, in THE NEW DISABILITY HISTORY: AMERICAN PERSPECTIVES 19 (Paul K. Longmore & Lauri Umansky eds., 2001). Some disabled people have reclaimed the word "Crip," using the former slur selectively as a form of empowerment. Andrew Pultrang, #CripTheVote: Notes on "Crip," DISABILITY THINKING, Mar. 29, 2016, https://disabilitythinking.com/disabilitythinking/2016/3/28/cripthevote-notes-on-crip.

[45] Laura Appleman, *Deviancy, Dependency, and Disability: The Forgotten History of Eugenics and Mass Incarceration*, 68 DUKE L.J. 417 (2018).

veterans initially focused on providing compensation to veterans who suffered disability because of their military service; it used a grading system to determine whether veterans' conditions were severe enough to deserve compensation. "The gatekeepers of the pension system were community doctors who examined claimants" and submitted their assessment to the federal Pension Bureau.[46] Historians Paul K. Longmore and Lauri Umansky point to the period from the late nineteenth to the early twentieth century as a "moment of major redefinition . . . [when] various state-sanctioned institutions brought many disabled people under professional supervision either to mend them into fit citizens or to sequester them permanently for society's safety."[47]

The key point for this book's purposes is the reference to "professional supervision," namely supervision by medical professionals. For much of the twentieth century, people with disabilities were understood to be inherently flawed in ways amenable to fixing, if they were at all, only by those professionals. This understanding, which came to be known as the "medical model" of disability,[48] pervaded rehabilitative efforts, social policy, and federal law for the first three-quarters of the twentieth century.

At its core, the medical model views disability as a deficit within a person. Disability resides in a person's body or mind, reflecting some sort of pathology.[49] Whatever an impairment's source or nature, the medical model understands a disabled person as somehow broken and needing medical assistance. It expects disabled persons to depend on health professionals to "fix" them, whether through treatment or prescriptions for adaptive equipment like prosthetics or orthotics. Medical professionals are heroes in this narrative, and society rightfully expects disabled people's cooperation with their curative efforts. Sociologist Talcott Parsons described this dynamic as casting disabled people in a "sick role," where they are exempted from normal social obligations like working, but only if they pursue a cure (and hence normalcy) by following medical directives.[50]

---

[46] Peter David Blanck & Michael Millender, *Before Disability Civil Rights, Civil War Pensions and the Politics of Disability in America*, 52 ALA. L. REV. 1, 14 (2000). By the early twentieth century it evolved into a general old-age pension system for Civil War veterans.

[47] LONGMORE & UMANSKY, *supra* note 44, at 22.

[48] The World Health Organization (WHO) offers the following description of the medical model:
    The medical model views disability as a problem of the person, directly caused by disease, trauma, or other health condition, which requires medical care provided in the form of individual treatment by professionals. Management of the disability is aimed at cure or the individual's adjustment and behavior change. Medical care is viewed as the main issue, and at the political level the principal response is that of modifying or reforming health care policy. WORLD HEALTH ORGANIZATION, INTERNATIONAL CLASSIFICATION OF FUNCTIONING, DISABILITY AND HEALTH 20 (2001).

[49] LONGMORE & UMANSKY, *supra* note 44, at 7.

[50] TALCOTT PARSONS, THE SOCIAL SYSTEM (1951); Rabia Belt & Doron Dorfman, *Reweighing Medical Civil Rights*, 72 STAN. L. REV. ONLINE 176, 183 (2020).

But health professionals' authority over persons with disabilities extends beyond medicine's (often illusory) promise of a cure. Society traditionally has given physicians responsibility for (with control over) validating a person's disability, a precondition to accessing any available social assistance. It falls to a physician to diagnose or categorize the cause of an impairment and to measure and document its functional impact. A person's own subjective experience of limitation is irrelevant without professional validation.[51]

The federal Social Security Disability Insurance (SSDI) program illustrates the medical model of disability in action. SSDI extends cash assistance payments to persons who have been employed and paid into the Social Security system and who then become disabled and unable to work.[52] The Social Security Administration defines disability as the "inability to engage in any substantial gainful activity by reason of any *medically determinable* physical or mental impairment which can be expected to result in death or which has lasted or can be expected to last for a continuous period of not less than 12 months."[53] This definition and agency practice accord substantial deference to physicians' objective assessments of applicants' impairments.[54] In response, the AMA developed "Guides to Evaluation of Permanent Disability" so that general practitioners could perform disability assessments.[55] Political scientist Deborah Stone describes these guides as "based on a pervading faith that a phenomenon of functional impairment, totally independent of context, can be precisely measured."[56] This approach ignores how a specific type of impairment may limit different people[57] to varying degrees. It decontextualizes disability, disregarding how physical or mental impairments interact with a person's social environment. Further wedding the SSDI program to the medical model, receipt of benefits is conditioned on a disabled person's willingness to accept treatment or rehabilitation.[58]

---

[51] Cf. SUSAN WENDELL, Toward a Feminist Theory of Disability, in FEMINIST PERSPECTIVES IN MEDICAL ETHICS 63, 72–73 (Helen Bequaert Holmes & Laura M. Purdy eds., 1992); Belt & Dorfman, *supra* note 50, at 6 n. 48.

[52] To be considered disabled for SSDI purposes, a claimant must be unable to "engage in any . . . kind of substantial gainful work which exists in the national economy." 42 U.S.C. § 423(d)(2)(A). Matthew Diller, *Entitlement and Exclusion: The Role of Disability in the Social Welfare System*, 44 UCLA L. REV. 361 (1996).

[53] U.S. Social Security Administration, *Disability Programs: Answers for Doctors and Other Health Professionals* (emphasis added), http://www.ssa.gov/disability/professionals/answers-pub042.htm.

[54] Valarie Blake, *A Physician's Guide to Social Security Disability Determinations*, AMA J. ETHICS (Dec. 2011), https://journalofethics.ama-assn.org/article/physicians-guide-social-security-disability-determinations/2011-12.

[55] DEBORAH A. STONE, THE DISABLED STATE 79–82, 110–11 (1984).

[56] *Id.* at 113.

[57] WENDELL, *supra* note 51, at 71. Harlan Hahn, *Antidiscrimination Laws and Social Research on Disability: The Minority Group Perspective*, 14 BEHAV. SCI. & L. 41, 45 (1996).

[58] STONE, *supra* note 55, at 113.

In sum, the medical model treats disability as a biological attribute setting a person apart as abnormal and wanting; it also grants the medical profession authority to identify and treat disabled persons. Under the medical model, the disabled individual is personally unfortunate because of their body or mind.[59] By ascribing disadvantages felt by disabled people to natural causes, the medical model obscures society's contributions toward – and thus responsibility for – those disadvantages. This perspective thus has significant implications for social policy regarding disability, as explored later in this chapter.

3.2.2 *The Social Model of Disability*

Building on the work of physically disabled people, British sociologist and disability rights activist Michael Oliver coined the phrase "social model of disability" to illuminate society's role in creating disability. Beginning in the 1980s, scholars associated with the emerging field of Disability Studies elaborated this model, which stood in stark contrast to the medical model. Rather than viewing limitations as flowing naturally and ineluctably from a biological defect, the social model sees disadvantages experienced by disabled people as flowing from social systems and structures. In other words, this original social model of disability believes that "contingent social conditions rather than inherent biological limitations" produce disability.[60] In this way, it parallels the social construction of race.

Drawing on feminist work, Susan Wendell explains: "Societies that are physically constructed and socially organized with the unacknowledged assumption that everyone is healthy, nondisabled, young but adult, shaped according to cultural ideals, and, often, male, create a great deal of disability through sheer neglect of what most people need in order to participate fully in them."[61] Physical environments offer a straightforward example. Constructing buildings with stairs, rather than elevators or ramps, disables people unable to climb stairs. By implicitly assuming that a building's users can climb stairs, designs relying exclusively on stairs implicitly reject non–stair-climbers. When seeking to conduct business, attend a social function, or cast a vote in a building accessible only by stairs, a wheelchair user is disadvantaged not because she cannot walk but because of the way the building is designed and constructed.[62]

Social and cultural structures can also incorporate biases and assumptions. Wendell describes how the absence of a place to sit and rest in grocery stores

---

[59] MICHAEL OLIVER, UNDERSTANDING DISABILITY: FROM THEORY TO PRACTICE 32 (1996).

[60] Michael Ashley Stein, *Disability Human Rights*, 95 CAL. L. REV. 75, 85 (2007). The social model has evolved over time in response to criticism, as discussed below.

[61] SUSAN WENDELL, THE REJECTED BODY: FEMINIST PHILOSOPHICAL REFLECTIONS ON DISABILITY 39 (1996).

[62] Ron Amundson, *Disability, Handicap, and the Environment*, J. SOC. PHIL., Spring 1992, at 105, 109.

anticipates that shoppers are strong and healthy – not easily fatigued or otherwise likely to need to rest briefly during shopping – and excludes those who do not conform to expectations.[63] Representations of disabled people in mainstream media often take the form of "inspiration porn" (which objectifies disabled people in order to tug at nondisabled people's heartstrings) or depictions of "supercrips" (which represent disabled people as extraordinary for performing activities that may be mundane or exceptional).[64] Rather than depicting disabled individuals as relatable and part of the mainstream, movie portrayals in particular often cast them as freaks, dangerous monsters, or tragic figures. All these reinforce the sense that disabled people are somehow "other," helping to perpetuate fear of or pity for disabled people.[65]

The social model does not deny atypical physiological differences in the bodies or minds of disabled people. Instead, it denies that physiological differences inevitably produce disadvantage or signify inferiority. It suggests that the very concept of normality is itself socially constructed. Rather than being cleanly divisible into ability and disability (or normality and abnormality), human functioning lies spread across a spectrum.[66] As a result, creating boundaries for disability requires drawing a line somewhere on this spectrum to differentiate "normal" ability from disability. As Lennard Davis puts it, "The construction of disability is based on a deconstruction of a continuum."[67] Drawing this dividing line demands a shared understanding of normal ability, but the idea of a "normal human being" is of relatively recent vintage. An outgrowth of the developing science of statistics, beginning in the mid-nineteenth century, "normal" evolved from a simple description of a statistical finding to a prescriptive message that normality is desirable and deviance should be avoided.[68] The perimeter of human normality has been rearranged over time and among different cultures, as seen in settings ranging from the eugenics movement's attempt to norm the population by eliminating deviants to shifts in understandings of what behaviors and temperaments are normal in schoolchildren.[69]

The social model also understands the appropriate remedy for disability differently. While the medical model seeks to mitigate disability primarily by attempting

---

[63] Wendell, *supra* note 61, at 37–38, 42–43.

[64] Sami Schalk, *Black Disability Gone Viral: A Critical Race Approach to Inspiration Porn*, 64 College Lang. Ass. J. 100 (2021).

[65] The classic reference is Rosemarie Garland-Thomson, Extraordinary Bodies (1997). For more recent inquiry, see Disability Media Studies (Elizabeth Ellcessor & Bill Kirkpatrick eds., 2017).

[66] See U.S. Commission on Civil Rights, *Accommodating the Spectrum of Individual Abilities* 87–89 (1983).

[67] Lennard J. Davis, Enforcing Normalcy: Disability, Deafness, and the Body 11 (1995).

[68] *Id.* at 24–29. Gina Maranto, *On the Fringes of the Bell Curve, the Evolving Quest for Normality*, N.Y. Times, May 26, 1998.

[69] Davis, *supra* note 67, at 30–31; Maranto, *supra* note 68; Lawrence H. Diller, *The Run on Ritalin: Attention Deficit Disorder and Stimulant Treatment in the 1990s*, Hastings Center Rep., Mar.–Apr. 1996, at 12.

to cure or rehabilitate the individual,[70] the social model prescribes "rehabilitating" the social and physical structures and systems that create disadvantages for persons with some kind of impairment. Sometimes rehabilitation may be a straightforward matter of changing the physical environment (for example, by cutting curbs or building ramps). Other times it may require modifying social systems or policies so that persons with disabilities can participate in and benefit from opportunities ordinarily enjoyed by nondisabled people.[71] Building on and politicizing the social model, the "minority group model" of disability (a phrase coined by political scientist and disability rights activist Harlan Hahn) asserts that negative and disdainful attitudes toward disabled people have translated into exclusionary and subordinating public policies.[72] Consciously drawing on the American Civil Rights movement, minority group model proponents decry patterns of hierarchy and subordination based upon physical and mental differences. Asserting a political identity, they demand political measures to eliminate barriers as a matter of disability civil rights.[73]

Over the past several decades, the social model of disability has evolved as debates over its philosophical integrity and explanatory power have revealed its limits.[74] For the purpose of this book, those disagreements do not undermine the model's usefulness in pointing out how disability is (at least partially) socially constructed.[75] The social model does not preclude acknowledging that some impairments limit what people can do regardless of the social environment[76] or that disabled people sometimes benefit from receiving medical care. Whatever the social environment, people with serious intellectual disabilities are unlikely to engage in professional pursuits requiring intense cognition. Whatever the social environment, people with chronic, energy-sapping health conditions are unlikely to engage in activities requiring intense physical effort. In the daily reality of living in their bodies, some disabled persons experience limitations or physical pain independently of any disabling social

---

[70] Gary L. Albrecht, The Disability Business: Rehabilitation in America (1992).

[71] Robert L. Burgdorf, Jr., *The Americans with Disabilities Act: Analysis and Implications of a Second-Generation Civil Rights Statute*, 26 Har. C.R.-C.L. L. Rev. 413, 460 (1991).

[72] Harlan Hahn, *Antidiscrimination Laws and Social Research on Disability: The Minority Group Perspective*, 14 Behav. Sci. & L. 41, 45, 53 (1996).

[73] Jonathan C. Drimmer, *Cripples, Overcomers, and Civil Rights: Tracing the Evolution of Federal Legislation and Social Policy for People with Disabilities*, 40 UCLA L. Rev. 1341, 1355–57 (1993). In a similar vein, Elizabeth Barnes argues that disability (despite its socially constructed nature) provides an organizing framework for people engaged in a civil rights struggle. Elizabeth Barnes, The Minority Body: A Theory of Disability 7 (2016).

[74] Tom Shakespeare, Disability Rights and Wrongs (2006).

[75] Elizabeth Barnes refers to the social model as the "most familiar social constructionist approach to disability," but disputes that it offers a fully satisfactory philosophical explanation of disability. Barnes, *supra* note 73, at 25–27.

[76] Elizabeth Emens, *Against Nature*, 52 Evolution & Morality 293, 301 (2012). As discussed in Chapter 9, disability can also be "socially constructed" when social or environmental factors cause a person to suffer a physical or mental change, injury, or degradation that proves disabling.

environment.[77] Contemporary disability scholars expand on the social model to characterize disability as representing the interplay between people's bodily impairments and the world they live in, with all its social, environmental, and cultural barriers.[78] Even if many disadvantages experienced by disabled people are socially constructed, bodies still matter to disability. So viewed, disability is dynamic and evolving; changes in either society *or* a person's body may alter the experience of and disadvantage associated with disability.

Acknowledging that disability is not purely socially constructed does not dilute the social model's core insight. Its revelation that most disadvantages endured by disabled people flow more from social decisions than from biological impairments has influenced federal legislation and crept into the public consciousness. And it has helped discredit the traditional medical model that urged medical fixes as the preferred way to improve the lot of people with disabilities.[79] As we'll see, though, the medical profession has been slow to embrace the social model.

3.3 SOCIALLY BUILT PARALLELS

The preceding discussion highlights parallels in how understandings of race and disability have evolved. Historically, both mechanisms of human classification pointed to biological inferiority or defectiveness as explaining disadvantage and legitimating control and inequality.[80] And the medical profession was deeply involved in those projects. Today, social constructionist understandings of race and disability predominate in shaping academic research, public discourse, and public policy making. But the similarities between evolving understandings of race and disability, while notable, are not complete. Briefly teasing out several parallels and divergences may be instructive.

To start, contrasting understandings of race and disability have political dimensions. Political progressives typically adopt social models of group identity and disadvantage and dispute the stance (more often associated with conservatives) that group identity has some kind of innate basis, or what Elizabeth Emens calls "nature talk."[81] Likewise, progressives seeking a rearrangement of social and institutional structures often highlight how systems of power and privilege reap material, social, and political benefits from categorizing others as innately inferior. Examples lie in some proposed policy interventions to address the medical and social structures contributing to race- and disability-based health disparities.

---

[77] Caroline J. Huang & David Wasserman, Chronic Pain as a Challenge for Disability Theory and Policy, in DISABILITY, HEALTH, LAW AND BIOETHICS (I. Glenn Cohen et al. eds., 2020).
[78] Belt & Dorfman, *supra* note 50, at 8.
[79] Emens, *supra* note 76, at 302–03.
[80] Shifrer & Frederick, *supra* note 24.
[81] Emens, *supra* note 76.

3.3.1 *Physical Features and Social Meanings*

Even as social constructionists reject beliefs in socially meaningful bodily differences, they cannot avoid bodily difference entirely. Race is not divorced from the
human body; physical features typically signal to others a person's racial identity. As
with race, visual salience has also mattered to biological understandings of disability.
Socially produced meanings attach to disabled bodies, as they do to Black bodies.[82]
Historically, those meaning have at times been connected. Historian Douglas
Baynton details how arguments supporting slavery and other means of anti-Black
social oppression attributed disability to Black people.[83] For example, a common
antebellum argument took physical difference and weaponized it, politically and
socially. The argument was that Black Africans' inferior intellects and weak consti-
tutions rendered them and their offspring incapable of caring for themselves or
participating in society on an equal footing with Whites.

Americans' fascination with bodies that visibly depart from the "normal" body also
demonstrates a tendency to objectify difference. This fascination with both non-
White and disabled bodies is evidenced by nineteenth and twentieth century
sideshows (or "freak shows") that displayed persons from Africa and persons with
unusual physical disabilities, often side by side.[84] "[T]he cardinal principle of
enfreakment," according to humanities and disability studies scholar Rosemarie
Garland-Thomson, is "that the body envelops and obliterates the freak's potential
humanity" in a "social process of making cultural otherness from the raw materials
of human physical variation."[85] Obliterating the humanity of Black people or
disabled people smooths the paths for the political, social, and economic decisions
that produce disadvantage.

3.3.2 *Binary or Not*

Another similarity is that, for both Blackness and disability, law and society often
have ignored obvious gradations of race (and color) and (dis)ability, instead
endowing binary classifications with legal force.[86] Segregationist Jim Crow regimes

---

[82] Beth Omansky Gordon & Karen E. Rosenblum, *Bringing Disability into the Sociological
Frame: A Comparison of Disability with Race, Sex, and Sexual Orientation Statuses*, 16
DISABILITY & SOCIETY 5 (2001); OBASOGIE, *supra* note 13, at 32.

[83] DOUGLAS C. BAYNTON, Disability and the Justification of Inequality in American History, in
THE NEW DISABILITY HISTORY: AMERICAN PERSPECTIVES 37 (Paul K. Longmore & Lauri
Umansky eds., 2001).

[84] HARRIET A. WASHINGTON, MEDICAL APARTHEID: THE DARK HISTORY OF MEDICAL
EXPERIMENTATION ON BLACK AMERICANS FROM COLONIAL TIMES TO THE PRESENT,
Ch. 3 (2007).

[85] ROSEMARIE GARLAND-THOMSON, EXTRAORDINARY BODIES: FIGURING PHYSICAL DISABILITY IN
AMERICAN CULTURE AND LITERATURE 59–60 (1997).

[86] RUTH COLKER, HYBRID: BISEXUALS, MULTIRACIALS, AND OTHER MISFITS UNDER AMERICAN
LAW (1996).

applied the infamous "one drop rule," which decreed that having a single Black ancestor, no matter how far back in the family tree, made a person legally "Negro" (in the language of the time). Offspring from unions of Black and White parents (and their descendants) had no option to be "some of both." Despite the difficulties of policing racial boundaries, Jim Crow officially recognized no racial gradations.[87] The racial prerequisite cases that Ian Haney López dissects reflect a similar binary. The immigration laws required officials to decide whether would-be immigrants belonged in the "white person" bucket or "not white person" bucket.[88]

The law and society often treat disability as dichotomous as well.[89] Either a person is or is not disabled. Doctors are called on to assess whether applicants for disability benefits meet the criterion of having a "medically determinable . . . impairment" that prevents employment. If not, benefits are denied.[90] Only a person meeting the ADA's statutory definition of an "individual with a disability" (for which courts may demand medical validation) can claim that law's protections.[91] Judicial enthusiasm for narrowing the boundaries of "disability" led to the dismissal of a large percentage of ADA cases in the law's early decades, requiring Congress to pass the ADA Amendments Act of 2008 to clarify that "disability" should be construed broadly.[92] In fact, disability occurs along a spectrum and is fluid: An impairment's effects on a person may vary over time and by context. Attempts to create strict binaries in situations where gradations are pervasive and palpable reinforce the conclusion that any dividing line between Black and White or disabled and nondisabled reflects social choices, not simply biology.

3.3.3 *Divergences in the Relevance of Biology*

In some respects, though, the parallels between Blackness and disability with respect to biology's significance break down. When an accident injures a person's spinal cord, for example, their body becomes vulnerable to disabling barriers like stairs. Because bodies and minds can change over time, either suddenly or gradually, anyone can become disabled. Referring to nondisabled people as "temporarily able bodied," as some disabled people do, rhetorically reminds us of that point.[93] By

---

[87] Daniel J. Sharfstein, *Crossing the Color Line: Racial Migration and the One-Drop Rule, 1600–1860*, at 91 MINN. L. REV. 592 (2007).

[88] LÓPEZ, *supra* note 37.

[89] Recognizing gradations in and fluidity of disability is distinguishable from a universal view of disability that asserts that everyone has some kind of impairment or imperfection and that proclaims, "We are all disabled." DORON DORFMAN, The Universal View of Disability and Its Danger to the Civil Rights Model, in DEFINING THE BOUNDARIES OF DISABILITY 37 (Licia Carlson & Matthew C. Murray eds., 2021).

[90] Blake, *supra* note 54.

[91] Belt & Dorfman, *supra* note 50.

[92] Carol J. Miller, *EEOC Reinforces Broad Interpretation of ADAAA Disability Qualification: But What Does "Substantially Limits" Mean?*, 76 MO. L. REV. 43 (2011).

[93] ROBERT MCRUER, Compulsory Able-Bodiedness and Queer/Disabled Existence, in THE DISABILITY STUDIES READER, 2D ED. 301 (Lennard J. Davis ed., 2006).

contrast, race is generally understood as a lifelong, durable category that physiological changes do not disrupt. Instances of people "passing" or changing their racial self-identification reinforces the point that a transition between races for an individual reflects social choice, not biological imposition. People with disabilities may also try to "pass" by hiding their impairment (for example, by developing strategies for hiding their limited vision or suppressing aberrant behavior),[94] but corporeal realities can make that infeasible.

This divergence between Blackness and disability suggests another one. Despite the entrenchment of anti-Black prejudice and yawning racial disparities in health, wealth, justice system involvement, and social and political power in the United States, no serious thinkers today assert that Blackness is inherently and innately bad (meaning entirely apart from disadvantages flowing from social meanings assigned to Blackness). By contrast, in the early twenty-first century a debate emerged within bioethics over whether disability should be understood as a "mere" difference or a "bad" difference. Without plumbing the debate's finer philosophical points, the basic question is whether disability is inherently bad, in the sense of making disabled people worse off, or whether disability has no more negative value than differences like eye color.

This "bad difference" versus "mere difference" debate reveals a divergence between disability and race with respect to how comprehensively disadvantage is tied to social, rather than biological, causes. Even Elizabeth Barnes, a leader in the "mere difference" camp, acknowledges that many disabilities entail some kind of "pathology" for which a person might sensibly seek medical care. While arguing that such "pathology" does not make those disabilities normatively bad, Barnes concedes that for many disabled people biology matters along with social meanings.[95] By contrast, social constructionists are unified in rejecting the idea that phenotypic traits read as "Black" entail any negative value. While Black Americans endure pervasive health disparities, those disparities are the product of *racism*, not innate, race-linked, biological differences. In short, Black people as a group are not innately biologically different from or inferior (or superior, for that matter) to White people as a group in any meaningful way, but many people with disabilities are biologically different from nondisabled people in some meaningful sense.

For what it's worth, disability rights advocates (many of whom have lived experience with disability) are more likely to describe disability as a "mere" difference. Philosophers and health professionals are less willing to accept that being disabled is neutral with respect to a person's well-being.[96] Though social constructionist

---

[94] DISABILITY AND PASSING: BLURRING THE LINES OF IDENTITY (Jeffrey A. Brune & Daniel J. Wilson eds., 2013).

[95] ELIZABETH BARNES, Disability, Health, and Normal Function, in DISABILITY, HEALTH, LAW AND BIOETHICS 6 (I. Glenn Cohen et al. eds., 2020).

[96] BARNES, *supra* note 73, at 54–55; ANI B. SATZ, Healthcare as Eugenics, in DISABILITY, HEALTH, LAW & BIOETHICS 20 (I. Glenn Cohen et al. eds., 2020).

understandings are now firmly established in the social sciences and humanities, significant pockets of belief in biology's relevance to explaining difference seem to persist within medicine and the biological sciences. Medicine is a profession accustomed to receiving social status and political power based on its practitioners' ability to fix bodily ills, and it may be loath to admit an erosion of its domain.[97] Perhaps some doctors are ambivalent about acknowledging that a patient's main difficulties from being disabled result from social choices and exceed their curative power. The next sections explore several areas where aspects of the medical model and notions of biological race endure within the medical profession.

3.4 MEDICINE'S ABIDING ATTACHMENT TO BIOLOGICAL UNDERSTANDINGS

3.4.1 *Defaulting to the Medical Model ... in Medicine*

The broad acceptance of social constructivist explanations of disadvantage experienced by Black people and people with disabilities is not universally held. Some within the medical profession and health care system continue to understand disability as a problem, a "bad" difference to vanquish or eliminate when possible. Many health professionals reflexively default to trying to fix or alter a disabled patient's body, rather than addressing social barriers (including their own prejudices and preconceptions) or deploying aids to increase patient functioning. Without undervaluing medicine's ability to cure or manage disease, many disabled people assign high value to improving their functional ability.

Legal scholar Ani Satz characterizes medicine's emphasis on preventing or curing disability as negative eugenics. She argues that both medical care and health insurance promote certain human traits by preferring typical means of human functioning (for example, walking) over equally effective atypical methods (for example, wheeling).[98] To illustrate, Satz points to medical education, which typically addresses deviations from typical function as a pathology without addressing social construction of disability or exposing medical students to the lived experiences of people with disabilities.[99] Medical education regarding hearing loss and cochlear implants is an example. Surgically implanting a cochlear implant in the brain permits persons who are deaf or hard-of-hearing (DHH) to perceive some level of sound; implants thus reflect a push toward normalization. Satz questions whether implants offer the best functional outcome for everyone with hearing impairments, because a *noncurative* adaptation – the use of sign language – may expand their

---

[97] PAUL STARR, THE SOCIAL TRANSFORMATION OF AMERICAN MEDICINE (1982).

[98] SATZ, *supra* note 96.

[99] Mary Crossley, *Disability Cultural Competence in the Medical Profession*, 9 ST. LOUIS U. J. HEALTH L. & POL'Y 89 (2015).

social and cultural opportunities.[100] Communication and language researcher Tom Humphries further points out that cochlear implant surgeries do not always produce good results. He emphasizes the need to expose children who are deaf or hard-of-hearing to sign language as a way to promote early language acquisition and cognitive development. Humphries worries, though, that "sign languages and the acquisition of sign language are rarely, if ever, included as essential topics for medical students," who are more likely to be instructed in technologies like cochlear implants and hearing aids.[101]

Another example of bias in medical practice and research towards normalizing function is found in efforts to restore walking after a spinal cord injury. Cutting-edge treatments to attain the "holy grail" of recovery from paralysis include surgery, electronic brain stimulation, and robotic exoskeletons.[102] Some disabled people advocate strongly for this research, including Christopher Reeves (the late actor known to many as Superman), who was paralyzed after falling from a horse. A social model perspective, however, contends that ensuring that wheelchair users can go wherever they want makes more sense than setting the restoration of walking (through grueling, expensive, and often painful treatments and rehabilitation) as a presumptive goal. Some research, as well as anecdotal accounts, indicate that many disabled people value accessibility and independence over the pursuit of a "cure."[103] Physicians often underestimate the high value that people with disabilities place on assistive measures that enable functioning in an atypical fashion. And because of their professional authority, doctors' own conceptions of what's best for disabled patients can determine the interventions those patients receive.[104] Finally, most health insurance is more likely to pay for medical or surgical interventions designed to restore normal functioning (or a close approximation of it), but not for measures like quality wheelchairs that support atypical functioning.[105]

The disability community has also raised concerns that prenatal testing for disabling or potentially disabling conditions such as Down syndrome, spina bifida, and achondroplasia (dwarfism) often treats disability as a bad biological difference. Prenatal testing has become widespread; a study conducted in 2012 found that testing for Trisomy 21 (the genetic anomaly that causes Down syndrome) occurred

---

[100] SATZ, *supra* note 96, at 25–26.

[101] Tom Humphries et al., *What Medical Education Can Do to Ensure Robust Language Development in Deaf Children*, 24 MED. SCI. EDUCATOR 409 (2014).

[102] Steven Novella, *Helping the Paralyzed Walk*, SCIENCE BASED MEDICINE, Sept. 2, 2015, https://sciencebasedmedicine.org/helping-the-paralyzed-walk.

[103] Harlan D. Hahn & Todd L. Belt, *Disability Identity and Attitudes Toward Cure in a Sample of Disabled Activists*, 45 J. HEALTH & SOC. BEHAVIOR 453 (2004); Andrew Pulrang, *Disabled People's Feelings about Cures Are More Complex Than You May Think*, FORBES (Sept. 7, 2020), https://www.forbes.com/sites/andrewpulrang/2020/09/07/disabled-peoples-feelings-about-cures-are-more-complex-than-you-may-think/?sh=4d53d72a36c6.

[104] SATZ, *supra* note 96, at 26.

[105] *Id.* at 26–27.

in around 70 percent of pregnancies.[106] Some people undergo testing to be prepared for any special medical needs or disability their infant might have. The majority who receive results indicating the presence of Trisomy 21, however, choose to terminate the pregnancy.[107] A recent spate of state laws prohibit abortion in cases of prenatally identified Down syndrome;[108] such prohibitions limit pregnant people's autonomy and devalue their agency and health.[109]

But even pro-choice advocates can recognize that choices about whether to continue or terminate a pregnancy are made within and shaped by societal and medical contexts.[110] Society's failures to remove barriers to disabled people's full inclusion and to provide adequate supports to families raising children with disabilities are part of that context.[111] So are physicians, many of whom hold negative views of disabled life and who at times use offensive language when describing disabled persons.[112] The medical context also encompasses prenatal counseling of expectant mothers, counseling that often presents medicalized and negative views of disability that tend to steer recipients toward termination.[113] According to a 2018 article, "Many parents report feeling badgered into getting an abortion and judged if they decline to do so."[114] Counseling that casts disabled life as flawed, undesirable, and avoidable by medical intervention reflects a medical model of disability.

Doctors and other health professionals can be valuable partners in enhancing health and functioning for people with disabilities, but only if they reject the premise that disabled life is flawed and that they know best what people with disabilities should want or need from them. Valorizing long-shot and expensive initiatives to cure or fix disabilities risks distracting medicine from developing or

---

[106] Glenn E. Palomaki et al., *Screening for Down Syndrome in the United States*, 137 ARCHIVES PATHOLOGY & LABORATORY MED. 921, 921 (2013).

[107] Jaime L. Natoli et al., *Prenatal Diagnosis of Down Syndrome: A Systematic Review of Termination Rates (1995–2011)*, 32 PRENATAL DIAGNOSIS 142, 142 (2012).

[108] Ruth Graham, *Choosing Life with Down Syndrome*, SLATE, May 31, 2018, https://slate.com/human-interest/2018/05/how-down-syndrome-is-redefining-the-abortion-debate.html.

[109] The ethical, social, and political issues raised by prenatal testing have at times divided feminists (who have emphasized the importance of women's unfettered autonomy regarding their pregnancies) and disability justice advocates and disability studies scholars (who are troubled by practices designed to prevent the existence of people with disabilities). Erik Parens & Adrienne Asch, *Special Supplement: The Disability Rights Critique of Prenatal Genetic Testing Reflections and Recommendations*, 29 HASTINGS CENTER REP. S1 (1999).

[110] Adrienne Asch, *Prenatal Diagnosis and Selective Abortion: A Challenge to Practice and Policy*, 89 AM. J. PUB. HEALTH 1649 (1999).

[111] Shifrer & Frederick, *supra* note 24, at 10.

[112] Lisa I. Iezzoni et al., *Physicians' Perceptions of People with Disability and Their Health Care*, 40 HEALTH AFF. 297 (2021); Nicole Agaronnik et al., *Exploring Issues Relating to Disability Cultural Competence Among Practicing Physicians*, 12 DISABILITY & HEALTH J. 403 (2019).

[113] Anne C. Madeo et al., *The Relationship between the Genetic Counseling Profession and the Disability Community*, 155 AM. J. MED. GENETICS 1777 (2011).

[114] Graham, *supra* note 108. Legislation at both the federal and state levels seeks to ensure that expectant parents receive more informative and balanced information about disability, but its effect remains unclear.

supporting interventions that disabled people often value more highly. When it defaults to the medical model of disability, the healthcare system continues to situate the problem of disability in deviant bodies rather than in discriminatory structures and attitudes.

3.4.2 *Medicine's Enduring Reliance on Race*

In July 2020 Randy Vince, a urologic oncologist, shared a story from his medical training with the readers of *JAMA*. He was a medical student in the early 2010s (one of only five Black students in his class) when a professor instructed the class about Black men's greater risk of dying from prostate cancer as compared to White men. Vince was familiar with the social determinants of health, having grown up in economically stressed circumstances. He approached the professor after class to ask about how Black men's lack of access to care could explain the heightened mortality. But his professor was having none of it. "[T]he professor's response was clear and emphatic, 'No, it's the tumor biology.'"[115]

Vince's experience is not unique. Shifting our focus from disability to race reveals persistent beliefs that race involves innate biological differences. Belief in biological race has a remarkable stickiness for some physicians and medical scientists. It shows up in biological explanations of racial health differences, as in Vince's story. It also shows up in the clinical setting where decisions are made for patients and in medical and pharmaceutical research. In all these settings, when attention is paid to purported biological race, there is a risk that the adverse impacts of racism and other structural determinants of health will be obscured. Historian Rana Hogarth suggests that "we might consider viewing disparities as a function of how Black people's bodies have been regarded by the medical profession – shifting our efforts away from trying to understand what might be different about a Black person's body to trying to understand the contexts in which that body exists."[116]

Hogarth uses the CDC's website regarding racial disparities in maternal mortality as an example. Black women are three to four times as likely as White women to die in connection with being pregnant. Despite a prevailing (by 2019) understanding that chronic stresses from racial discrimination likely contribute to the disparity, the word "racism" was entirely absent from the CDC's discussion. By failing to even mention racism, the government agency missed an opportunity to "shift our attention to larger structural problems both inside and outside the realm of medicine and away from any potential innate biological reason for the disparity."[117]

---

[115] Randy A. Vince, Jr., *Eradicating Racial Injustice in Medicine – If Not Now, When?*, 324 JAMA
    451 (2020).
[116] Hogarth, *supra* note 17.
[117] *Id.* at 1340–41.

3.4.2.1 Biological Race in Clinical Decisions (by Doctors and Computers)

"I am a racially profiling doctor" declared psychiatrist Sally Satel in a 2002 *New York Times Magazine* article. In it, Satel relied on her experience practicing at a drug clinic to take issue with prominent physicians' disavowals of the validity of using race in medical practice.[118] Satel described why she initially prescribed the antidepressant Prozac at a lower dosage for her Black patients than for her White patients: "[B]ecause clinical experience and pharmacological research show that blacks metabolize antidepressants more slowly... [so that] levels of the medication can build up and make side effects more likely." Asserting that 40 percent of Black people are slow metabolizers, Satel justifies starting all her Black patients on a lower dose: "[T]he risk of provoking side effects like nausea, insomnia or fuzzy-headedness in a depressed person – someone already terribly demoralized who may have been reluctant to take medication in the first place – is to worsen the patient's distress and increase the chances that he will flush the pills down the toilet."

In defending racial profiling, Satel also relies on colleagues' clinical experiences and published research finding correlations between patients' race and physiological and epidemiological differences. Stopping short of a claim that race can be defined with biological or genetic precision, Satel nonetheless calls it an "imprecise clue" providing a helpful and efficient aid to clinical decision making. Her argument is benign on its face, claiming beneficial payoffs for her Black patients. Given medicine's historical role in advancing race science, however, we should think twice about taking statements about race in medicine at face value.

Satel's use of "racial profiling" is a hat tip to the more widely recognized practice of racial profiling in law enforcement. The phrase refers to targeting a member of a certain racial group based on a belief that people in that group share particular behaviors or traits, rather than basing actions on individual, nonracial information. "Driving while Black" describes the experience of Black men pulled over by police for no reason (aside from skin color) or specious reasons. Race also creeps into decisions about which pedestrians police should "stop and frisk," leading a federal judge to rule that NYPD's "unwritten policy of targeting 'the right people' for stops" was a form of unconstitutional racially discriminatory profiling.[119] Racial profiling in law enforcement also has been condemned as contributing to mass incarceration, leading to unjust arrests and convictions, and being ineffective in controlling crime and making neighborhoods safer.[120]

Is racial profiling in medicine any more defensible? Doctors who practice racial profiling may believe it helps diagnose and treat their patients. But the evidence base

[118] Sally Satel, *I Am a Racially Profiling Doctor*, N.Y. TIMES, May 5, 2002.
[119] Floyd v. City of New York, 959 F. Supp. 2d 540, 561 (S.D.N.Y. 2013).
[120] David A. Harris, *Racial Profiling: Past, Present, and Future?*, A.B.A., https://www.americanbar .org/groups/criminal_justice/publications/criminal-justice-magazine/2020/winter/racial-profil ing-past-present-and-future.

for racial assumptions is limited and weak; Satel makes her case based largely on anecdotes from a colleague and her own experience treating patients. In 2006 she admitted that racial differences in salivation rates, an example she had touted for its clinical value, lacked a scientific basis.[121] Using race in clinical decisions without scientific validation permits an irrelevant factor to influence patient care and may lead to serious medical errors.[122] Even if a particular physiological or genetic trait (for example, sickle cell trait)[123] appears more frequently in a racial group, relying on a statistical probability of its presence is a sorry substitute for inquiring about a specific patient's family history, environmental exposures, or social factors relevant to health.

Justifications for racial profiling can reflect stereotypes. A majority of Satel's Black patients with depression received a suboptimal dosage of Prozac because she believed that 40 percent were slow metabolizers. She described starting patients on lower-than-recommended doses to avoid having some of them "flush the pills down the toilet" if they experienced side effects. Satel appears to worry that Black patients experiencing side effects may not take prescribed medicines. This concern sounds reasonable, but it is hard to disentangle from the widely held medical stereotype that Black patients are noncompliant, that they are less likely than White patients to follow medical advice.

Racial profiling in clinical care can also reinforce questionable or false beliefs. Doctors who use race as a basis for diagnosis without an established scientific basis can produce a "self-reinforcing truth."[124] Clinicians relying on race may overdiagnose a disease in their Black patients; their inaccurate diagnoses will be incorporated in epidemiological data that track disease incidence among racial groups; the epidemiological data may then be read as supporting the use of race in diagnosing the disease because of its high incidence among Black people.[125] A similar circular reinforcement of inaccurate beliefs about the level of crime committed by Black people occurs in law enforcement.

Finally, racially profiling patients can reinforce unfounded beliefs in innate racial differences and long-held prejudices (like beliefs in Black infectiousness and non-compliance), while diverting attention and resources away from the social and

---

[121] Sally Satel, *I Am a Racially Profiling Doctor (Erratum?)*, https://sallysatelmd.com/articles/2002/i-am-a-racially-profiling-doctor.

[122] Lundy Braun et al., *Racial Categories in Medical Practice: How Useful Are They?*, 4 PLoS Medicine 1423 (2007).

[123] The prevalence of the sickle cell gene is between 6,500 and 7,000 per 100,000 among self-identified Black Americans and only 250 per 100,000 self-identified White Americans. The gene is most prevalent among people tracing their ancestry to West Africa, India, and the Middle East. Angela Saini, Superior: The Return of Race Science 197 (2019).

[124] Thomas V. Perneger et al., *Diagnosis of Hypertensive End-Stage Renal Disease: Effect of Patient's Race*, 141 Am. J. of Epidemiology 10 (1995).

[125] Mary Crossley, *Infected Judgment: Legal Responses to Physician Bias*, 48 Vill. L. Rev. 195, 204–05 (2003).

economic determinants most responsible for the worse health outcomes suffered by Black people. I'll return to that point shortly.

Beyond individual doctors' developing rules of thumb based on their own experience, organized medicine has long endorsed more formal algorithms to help physicians apply voluminous medical knowledge to a patient's symptoms. Clinical guidelines promulgated by medical societies are one example. Increasing scrutiny has focused on the flimsy evidentiary base for using race in medical algorithms,[126] particularly as development of artificial intelligence (AI)-powered medical algorithms render the inclusion of race less visible and, thus, less contestable. Because medical AI builds on knowledge created by medical research and real-world medical practice, it incorporates and replicates the biases (conscious or unconscious) that suffuse those practices. Biased input leads to biased output, influencing treatment and reinforcing disparities.[127]

For example, in 2019 scientists detected "racial bias" in an AI application widely used to predict which patients would benefit most from additional medical support. Health systems use these predictions to attempt to lower the chances of expensive and harmful complications by enrolling the patients identified in "high-risk care management" programs.[128] To make its predictions, the algorithm relied on data regarding care previously received by the patient to generate a risk score regarding the patient's predicted future cost of health care. In essence, it used a patient's past medical costs to forecast future medical costs. That approach sounds reasonable, but reliance on a patient's past medical spending introduces a well-documented health care disparity into the process: Statistically, Black people receive less health care than White people with comparable health needs. The researchers measured that difference and found: "At a given level of health . . ., Blacks generate lower costs than Whites – on average, $1801 less per year."[129] As a result, review of the algorithm's operation revealed that Black patients identified as priority recipients of additional support were much sicker than White patients similarly identified. The algorithm espouses no racist ideology, but it effectively reinforces a preexisting inequity by identifying White patients to receive intensive support over sicker Black patients. Sociologist Ruha Benjamin reminds us why Black people use less health care: "Black patients do not 'cost less,' so much as they are valued less."[130]

---

[126] Darshali A. Vyas, *Hidden in Plain Sight – Reconsidering the Use of Race Correction in Clinical Algorithms*, 383 NEW ENG. J. MED. 874 (2020).

[127] Nancy Krieger, *Measures of Racism, Sexism, Heterosexism, and Gender Binarism for Health Equity Research: From Structural Injustice to Embodied Harm – An Ecosocial Analysis*, 41 ANN. REV. PUB. HEALTH 37, 48 (2020); Dhruv Khullar, *A.I. Could Worsen Health Disparities*, N.Y. TIMES, Jan. 31, 2019.

[128] Ziad Obermeyer et al., *Dissecting Racial Bias in an Algorithm Used to Manage the Health of Populations*, 366 SCIENCE 447 (2019).

[129] *Id.* at 450.

[130] Ruha Benjamin, *Assessing Risk, Automating Racism*, 366 SCIENCE 421 (2019).

3.4.2.2 Racialized Scientific Research Redux

The scientific racism described at the beginning of this chapter is a matter of some historical embarrassment. But less explicitly value-laden strains have endured into the twenty-first century.[131] Growing interest in precision medicine (also called "personalized medicine"), where treatments are crafted to meet a patient's individual genetic profile, and the development of race-specific pharmaceutical patents have prompted research that seeks to explain socially induced health disparities as the results of biological differences connected to racial groups.[132] Financial incentives spur pharmaceutical companies to find the tiny sliver of genetic difference among humans and then to mine it for profit. Because individualized gene mapping remains expensive, researchers may turn to race as a proxy for clusters of genetic variation.[133]

The FDA's approval of the drug BiDil to treat heart failure in self-identified Black patients is instructive. BiDil combines into a single pill two generic drugs long used to treat cardiovascular problems. Trials conducted in the 1980s showed the combined generics to be effective in treating heart failure in a multiracial cohort. Nearly a decade later, though, the FDA denied a new drug application for BiDil because reanalysis of data from the 1980s trials failed to show sufficiently powerful statistical evidence of the drug's efficacy.[134] Jay Cohn, the researcher holding the patent on BiDil took a new tack, publishing a paper claiming that the combination drug was more effective in Black patients and obtaining a new race-specific patent for BiDil. Cohn licensed the renewed patent to NitroMed, a pharmaceutical company, which conducted a new clinical trial that enrolled *only* self-identified Black subjects. That trial confirmed that BiDil was effective in reducing mortality from cardiac causes among its enrollees. But because it included only Black subjects, it could not claim superior effectiveness in that population as compared to others. Nonetheless, NitroMed persuaded the FDA to grant its first race-specific drug approval in 2005.[135]

After studying this tale, legal scholar Jonathan Kahn concluded that Cohn's and NitroMed's exclusive focus on Black patients was commercially rather than scientifically driven. No scientific proof of biological differences between races or even racial differences in drug efficacy supported the race-specific approval of the generic combination. For Kahn, BiDil's approval offers a model for drug development that

---

[131] Saini, *supra* note 123.

[132] Anthony Ryan Hatch, Blood Sugar: Racial Pharmacology and Food Justice in Black America 62 (2016).

[133] Saini, *supra* note 123, at 196–97. The cost of genome sequencing likely exceeds $1,000 per genome, once associated costs are considered. Katharina Schwarze et al., *The Complete Cost of Genome Sequencing*, 22 Genetics Med. 85 (2020).

[134] Roberts, *supra* note 8, at 169–70.

[135] Jonathan Kahn, *Exploiting Race in Drug Development: BiDil's Interim Model of Pharmacogenomics*, 38 Soc. Stud. Sci. 737, 738–39 (2008).

"exploits race to gain regulatory and commercial advantage, while ignoring its power to promote a regeneticization of racial categories in society at large."[136]

Kahn highlights shaky scientific underpinnings as one problem with race-based pharmaceuticals like BiDil. Another lies in their resurrection of scientific racism. BiDil may well help Black cardiac patients who take it, but "its approval sanctions the dangerous idea that congestive heart failure is a different disease in Black people than in White people for biological reasons."[137] Developers of race-linked biotechnologies will not control how they are used, either practically or ideologically.[138] For example, White nationalist groups have latched onto research into a genetic trait associated with the ability to digest lactose. Research has shown the trait to be more common in White people, leading White nationalists to engage in milk-chugging displays as proof of their Whiteness.[139]

Moreover, suggesting that genetic interventions can reduce racial heath disparities may obscure and divert resources and attention away from known social determinants of health inequity. Medical elites have been slow to reckon with racism's impact on health. A 2021 analysis of articles published over three decades (1990–2020) in the world's top four medical journals confirms that while medical researchers have eagerly investigated the biological significance of *race*, top journals have shied away from empirical research into *racism* and health. Of 226,305 articles published during that time span, only 1,213 referred to "racism" at all. And more than 90 percent of those articles were commentaries or opinion pieces rather than scientific research studies.[140] In an interview, one researcher recalled that when she submitted her research into high pregnancy death rates among Black women, an editor at *JAMA* deleted the word "racism" from her manuscript before rejecting it entirely.[141] The authors of the study into journals' publishing records reflected: "Ignorance is neither neutral nor benign, especially when it cloaks evidence of harm."[142]

In a 2007 episode of the Oprah Winfrey show, Oprah presented (with Dr. Mehmet Oz's endorsement) the so-called "slavery hypothesis," which attributes Black Americans' high hypertension rates to a genetic predisposition toward salt retention that evolved as an adaptation to the slave trade's brutal conditions.

---

[136] *Id.*

[137] Hogarth, *supra* note 17, at 1441.

[138] Obasogie, *supra* note 13, at 6.

[139] Amy Harmon, *Why White Supremacists Are Chugging Milk (and Why Geneticists Are Alarmed)*, N.Y. Times (Oct. 17, 2018), https://www.nytimes.com/2018/10/17/us/white-supremacists-science-dna.html.

[140] Nancy Krieger et al., *Medicine's Privileged Gatekeepers: Producing Harmful Ignorance about Racism and Health*, Health Affairs Blog (Apr. 20, 2021), www.healthaffairs.org/do/10.1377/hblog20210415.305480/full/.

[141] Apoorva Mandavilli, *Medical Journals Blind to Racism as Health Crisis, Critics Say*, N.Y. Times (June 2, 2021), www.nytimes.com/2021/06/02/health/jama-racism-bauchner.html.

[142] Krieger et al., *supra* note 140.

Sociologist and legal scholar Osagie Obasogie wrote in the *L.A. Times* to lay out the scientific flaws in the hypothesis. He reflected: "[I]n a world with finite resources, it's regrettable that we continue to invest millions of research dollars... looking for genes to explain racial disparities in health, when so many causes lie simply in how we treat one another."[143]

3.5 CONCLUSION

Days after George Floyd's murder, lawyer and social justice activist Bryan Stevenson responded to a question about the frustration fueling widespread protests of police brutalizing Black people. He said: "The great evil of American slavery wasn't the involuntary servitude; it was the fiction that black people aren't as good as white people, and aren't the equals of white people, and are less evolved, less human, less capable, less worthy, less deserving than white people."[144] Stevenson's statement could be addressed to medicine as well. We could also adapt it to address the fiction that disabled people aren't as good, or worthy, or deserving as nondisabled people.

This chapter has highlighted how beliefs in innate, biological inferiority of Black people and disabled people have given way to understandings that social, political, and economic choices have constructed those categories and produced their disadvantage. It has also discussed strains of biological thinking regarding both groups that persist within medicine and health care. These beliefs may be transmitted as racial folklore, buried in algorithms, or touted as offering targeted benefits to Black patients. Mythologies of inferiority also undergird medicine's continued failure to consistently provide high quality, patient-centered care for disabled people and its tolerance of ableist prenatal screening practices.

The roles of social construction in producing race and disability are not identical. A disabled person's body or mind typically has some physical or mental feature that affects functioning. Even if we ascribe disability-based disadvantages to social causes, function-limiting bodily features may strike many observers as meaningful differences in ways that skin color no longer does. And for people whose disability lies in a disease or otherwise compromises their health, medical assistance may be beneficial.

Whether thinking about Blackness or disability, repudiation of spurious beliefs in innate biological difference and inferiority does not require rejection of the body's centrality as the site of a person's existence in this world; people's bodies matter to them. The impairments that disabled people have may shape their daily experience of the world, sometimes as sources of pain or challenge, sometimes as the wellspring

---

[143] Osagie K. Obasogie, *Oprah's Unhealthy Mistake*, L.A. TIMES, May 17, 2007.

[144] Isaac Chotiner, *Bryan Stevenson on the Frustration behind the George Floyd Protests*, THE NEW YORKER, June 1, 2020.

of disability pride. Black pride celebrates Black bodies even as Black people with natural hair styles and dark skin still endure discrimination.

Of course, bodies can also be sites of oppression. Racism can produce bodily imprints that human evolution did not. For much of American history, physical brutality left scars on the bodies of enslaved Black people. Today, exposures to discrimination, toxic environments, and unjust social structures may be absorbed by Black bodies, with harmful effects. Experiencing the social, economic, and environmental manifestations of racism produces "embodied inequality." Social epidemiologist Nancy Krieger's reference to embodiment is literal,[145] and it provides an added dimension to understanding race as a social construct. (The same point pertains with regard to the impact of ableism on disabled people's bodies, though the evidence base there is less developed.)

The ecosocial theory means that, although race is not a biological fact, racism can produce enduring physiological impacts on Black bodies. When working to understand and address racial health disparities, we must recognize that higher rates of obesity, hypertension, and infant mortality in Black communities may involve bodily differences resulting not from variant genetic makeups but from unjust social structures. Thus, race is divorced from biology, but racism is not. We need to make sure our causal arrows are pointed in the right direction. Innate biological differences do not create race, but racism can produce distinctive harms to Black bodies.

---

[145] Krieger, *supra* note 127. Note that Krieger's work is not confined to racism, but also encompasses other isms associated with injustice. At this point the evidence base for the impact of racism is more thoroughly developed.

4

Medical Mistrust

Its Roots and Some Fruits

4.1 INTRODUCTION

Distrust of the health care system or providers can affect a patient's decisions concerning whether to seek medical care, how openly to share health concerns, and how closely to follow a provider's advice. A person's health literacy and understanding of disease can also shape their interactions with medical professionals. Some analyses of racial health disparities have considered how patient "preferences" and behavior might contribute to those disparities or provide a basis for doctors' stereotypes of Black patients as "noncompliant."[1] Various initiatives have sought to increase the trust that Black people or those from other marginalized communities place in medicine, approaching patients' low trust levels as if they were a vitamin deficiency that needed correcting.

Recently, though, the narrative around trust has begun to shift. Conversations today are more likely to identify the problem as a dearth of trustworthiness on the part of the medical and scientific community rather than one of patient noncompliance. Identifying this professional community as the source of trust issues helps to focus remedial steps, such as efforts to make medicine demonstrably more trustworthy to communities whose history with medicine has been troubled.

This chapter offers an overview of encounters with medical practitioners, researchers, and other health care professionals that Black people and those with disabilities have experienced. These encounters are both historical and modern; they include use of persons as involuntary research subjects and devaluation of their lives and freedom in various ways. These interactions have undermined the trustworthiness of medicine and the health care system in the eyes of many Black people

---

[1] INSTITUTE OF MEDICINE, UNEQUAL TREATMENT: CONFRONTING RACIAL AND ETHNIC DISPARITIES IN HEALTH CARE (Brian D. Smedley et al. eds., 2003).

and disabled people. They have lowered the odds that individuals in those groups will view medical providers as concerned foremost with their welfare and understanding of their concerns.

The chapter then describes several areas where weakened trust helps explain ways that medically related views or actions of disabled people and Black people vary from those of White and nondisabled majorities in the United States. These areas include physician-assisted suicide, hospice care, and organ donation. The thread tying these together is their connection to medical decisions about how life ends and a shared wariness of giving doctors authority (or perceived authority) to end life prematurely.

Views of and decisions about how one wishes to die are complex. They involve a host of fears, beliefs, values, and attitudes that may be grounded in religious doctrine or cultural understandings. My claim is not that impaired trust on its own explains views held more broadly by people with disabilities and those in the Black community. I do think it plays a role, though. The similar roots of a shared distrust of medicine reflect a parallel in how health injustice plays out for Black people and disabled people.

4.2 "MEDICAL APARTHEID"

"Apartheid" refers to a system of institutionalized racism in South Africa that required segregation of non-White people and legal and economic discrimination against them. "Medical apartheid" is the term author and medical ethicist Harriet Washington uses in her sweeping history of medical experimentation on and mistreatment of Black people in America.[2] Some of the book's narrative force derives from its stories of suffering and indignities endured by Black individuals who became subjects of experimentation. The narrative also reveals a longstanding and pervasive willingness among scientists, doctors, and the government, among others, to exploit Black bodies to further White goals that included a tangled mix of medical knowledge, power, and profit. Readers learn that the better-known stories, like the Tuskegee study, are not isolated, but rather they are emblematic.

This section briefly describes two notorious episodes of medical exploitation – one that occurred when Black people were enslaved and one from the Jim Crow era. It then describes a more recent episode of ethically problematic research on Black children, as well as how more mundane encounters with the health care system undermine Black people's trust. Taken together, these descriptions begin to suggest why many Black people deem the medical establishment untrustworthy.

---

[2] Harriet A. Washington, Medical Apartheid: The Dark History of Medical Experimentation on Black Americans from Colonial Times to the Present (2007).

4.2.1 *Betsey, Anarcha, and Lucy*

In recent years, stories about the removal of statues of Confederate generals and politicians appeared regularly on the evening news. A statue removed in April 2018 from New York City's Central Park, by contrast, lauded its subject not for military or political exploits, but instead for inventing the speculum and wielding a scalpel. This statue depicted J. Marion Sims, who some call the "Father of Modern Gynecology."

Betsey, Anarcha, and Lucy were three of the enslaved women on whom Sims performed experimental surgeries during the mid-nineteenth century. The goal of the surgeries was to figure out how to repair vesico-vaginal fistulas – injuries from childbirth that caused uncontrollable incontinence. Sims also operated on other Black women (probably nine or ten, total), but Betsey, Anarcha, and Lucy were the only ones named in Sims's accounts of the surgeries. The first time Sims operated on Lucy, he invited other Alabama doctors to watch and learn. In front of about a dozen observers, he operated on Lucy – positioned on a tabletop on her hands and knees – for more than an hour. Without anesthesia. Ether was not yet in common usage in the 1840s, so none of the enslaved women subjected to Sims's experimental surgeries received any anesthesia, nor did Sims take other steps to try to reduce their pain. He developed his surgical technique through trial and error, operating on Anarcha at least thirty times.[3]

The vociferous debate in recent decades about the ethics of Sims's experimental surgeries has a Rorschach-test quality to it. Apologists for Sims laud how the knowledge developed through his experimentation ultimately helped women. They portray Sims as a product of his time who cannot fairly be faulted for his racist views and practices. Critics denounce Sims for personally profiting from pain he caused enslaved women powerless to withhold their consent or seek medical care for their condition. Both positions reflect some truth. In the midst of the controversy over Sims's statue, medical historian Deirdre Cooper Owens wrote: "James Marion Sims was a product of his time, but this fact does not detract from his role as a man who participated in a system that reduced human beings to movable property, one that was built on violence, terror, and white supremacy."[4]

Whether Sims was a hero or villain, the bigger point is that his career exemplifies a broader pattern of White men (and doctors in particular) assuming control over Black women's bodies for their own purposes. Other examples include enslavers use

---

[3]   Megan Flynn, *Statue of "Father of Gynecology," Who Experimented on Enslaved Women, Removed from Central Park*, Wash. Post (Apr. 18, 2018), https://www.washingtonpost.com/news/morning-mix/wp/2018/04/18/statue-of-father-of-gynecology-who-experimented-on-enslaved-women-removed-from-central-park.

[4]   Deirdre Cooper Owens, *More than a Statue: Rethinking J. Marion Sims' Legacy*, Rewire News (Aug. 24, 2017), https://rewirenewsgroup.com/article/2017/08/24/statue-rethinking-j-marion-sims-legacy.

of Black women's reproductive capacity for their own enrichment, sales of children as chattel, and involuntary sterilization of Black women by twentieth-century doctors for eugenic ends (discussed in Chapter 5). The instrumental use of Black female bodies seemed unremarkable and unquestioned – whether justified as serving the professional or economic benefit of White men, the health dividends to White women, or the purported benefit to society more broadly. "[I]t is this ordinariness that is noteworthy,"[5] one journalist recently wrote of the common practice of operating on enslaved women. The statue of J. Marion Sims that once stood in Central Park now resides in Green-Wood Cemetery in Brooklyn, near Sims's grave. It bears a sign explaining its history, but it still provokes controversy.

4.2.2 Tuskegee

Sometimes a single word can summon up an entire chapter in history; "Tuskegee" is such a word.

In 1932, the US Public Health Service partnered with the Tuskegee Institute and other local agencies to begin the "Tuskegee Study of Untreated Syphilis in the Negro Male." The purpose was to learn about how the serious, sexually transmitted disease progressed without treatment and how it caused death. The researchers went to rural Macon County, Alabama, and enrolled 399 men diagnosed as having syphilis (the study group) and 201 who were not (the control group). Those men were mostly uneducated and poor; rarely had they seen a doctor. Researchers told them that for being part of the study they would receive treatment for "bad blood" (a phrase local residents used to refer to a variety of ailments, including syphilis) and get free medical exams, free meals, and burial stipends.[6] The experiment continued for forty years. That meant that the men in the study group had untreated syphilis for decades, even after an effective treatment became available.[7] Some men undoubtedly passed the disease to their wives, who may then have transmitted it to children in utero. As late as 1969, the federal government decided against providing treatment to the men still in the study.[8]

In 1972, the American public finally learned that for forty years the federal government had deceived these Black men about their participation in a study of the natural progression of syphilis and refused to treat them when effective therapy became available. That disclosure led to Senate hearings, a federal investigation, a

[5] Sarah Zhang, *The Surgeon Who Experimented on Slaves*, THE ATLANTIC (Apr. 18, 2018), https://www.theatlantic.com/health/archive/2018/04/j-marion-sims/558248/.
[6] Stephen B. Thomas & Sandra Crouse Quinn, *The Tuskegee Syphilis Study, 1932 to 1972: Implications for HIV Education and AIDS Risk Education Programs in the Black Community*, 81 AM. J. PUB. HEALTH 1498 (1991).
[7] US Public Health Services Syphilis Study at Tuskegee, *The Tuskegee Timeline*, CENTERS FOR DISEASE CONTROL AND PREVENTION, https://www.cdc.gov/tuskegee/timeline.htm.
[8] JAMES JONES, BAD BLOOD: THE TUSKEGEE SYPHILIS EXPERIMENT – A TRAGEDY OF RACE AND MEDICINE 193–96 (1981).

lawsuit with a $10 million settlement in 1974, and in 1997 – twenty-five years after the public disclosure – a formal apology by President Clinton. Disclosure of the Tuskegee study also reinforced Black Americans' distrust of the federal government and health professionals.

In the Tuskegee study, glaring ethical lapses were layered upon racist medical assumptions that syphilis in Black men was a distinctive disease. Researchers enrolling Black men for the study did not accurately describe to them the study's purpose or its risks, thus failing to obtain the men's informed consent to participate. And their misdeeds went beyond incomplete disclosure. According to historian Susan Reverby, "Deception was deemed necessary by the researchers to make the men believe they were being helped: the diagnostic lumbar punctures were called 'special treatment' and the aspirins and iron tonics were purported cures for their 'bad blood.'"[9] But, since the experiment studied "untreated syphilis," the researchers worked to keep the men from getting any actual treatment, even once penicillin emerged as an effective therapy for syphilis. Today, continuing to deprive research subjects of an effective treatment would be considered unethical; studies investigating potential disease therapies must be terminated once an effective treatment is discovered.[10]

After its revelation, the Tuskegee Study became notorious for its ethical failures and racist foundations. In the process of going from news story to investigative report to cultural legend, the popular narrative of Tuskegee acquired details unsupported by the historical record, including the claim that researchers actually injected study participants with syphilis.[11] The idea that the US government would infect Black Americans with a deadly disease spread like a contagion in many Black communities. Over time, "Tuskegee" became "a metaphor for the dangers of racism and unchecked government and medical power in clinical trials."[12]

4.2.3 *Baltimore's Black Children*

Ethically questionable research on Black Americans persists.[13] In 2001, Maryland's highest court reinstated a lawsuit filed against the Kennedy Krieger Institute (KKI), a

---

[9]   Susan M. Reverby, *Listening to Narratives from the Tuskegee Syphilis Study*, 377 THE LANCET 1646 (2011).

[10] US Public Health Services Syphilis Study at Tuskegee, *supra* note 7.

[11] Early in the AIDS epidemic, an academic included the "purposeful exposure" idea in a widely read essay. Harlon L. Dalton, *AIDS in Blackface*, 118 DAEDALUS 205, 220–21 (1989).

[12] Reverby, *supra* note 9, at 1646.

[13] Ethically problematic research on Black people outside the United States has continued. In 2009, the Second Circuit Court of Appeals ruled that a group of Nigerian children and their guardians could sue Pfizer in the United States for conducting experimental drug trials on 200 children suffering from meningitis without obtaining their consent. Pfizer was testing Trovan, an experimental antibiotic, during a 1996 meningitis epidemic in Nigeria [Rabi Abdullahi v. Pfizer, Inc., 562 F.3d 163 (2d Cir. 2009)]. Plaintiffs in the lawsuit alleged that

pediatric clinic and research center affiliated with the Johns Hopkins University, that alleged researchers failed to obtain valid informed consent from parents before enrolling their children in a study exposing them to residential lead paint, a known toxin that irreversibly impedes children's neurological development. Specifically, each family enrolled (most of whom were Black and low-income) would be placed in an apartment and the children's blood lead levels would be monitored during the research. A majority of the families were placed in apartments with a level of lead dust known to be dangerous to children's developing brains. Eighty percent of the apartments were in older buildings that had lead-based paint in them at some point. Of those older apartments, three of four still had a considerable amount of lead dust present, but each had undergone one of three levels of partial abatement. The goal of the research was to identify a level of partial abatement that would be relatively safe but still economical for landlords. Although the trial court initially dismissed the complaint, the appellate court issued a scathing opinion that compared the research to the Tuskegee study and other instances of researchers' abuse of vulnerable subjects.[14]

The court's comparisons sparked controversy within the research community, with some deeming them hyperbolic and misguided.[15] Because ensuring lead-free housing in low-income urban neighborhoods seemed economically and politically infeasible, they argued that partial abatement measures (which might be feasible) would benefit the Black children participating in the study by *lowering* their exposure to lead. These assertions echo justifications of troubling experimentation in the past. Defenders of the lead abatement study assert that children in the study were moved from apartments with unabated lead to apartments that had undergone partial abatement measures, and thus could be expected to benefit (even as they were still exposed to unsafe lead levels). J. Marion Sims's defenders argue that his enslaved subjects may have received some therapeutic benefit from his surgical experiments. Questions arise about whether experiments such as the lead abatement study would *ever* be performed on White, middle-class children. The factually accurate retort that White, middle-class children no longer live in lead-riddled housing stock simply confirms our society's willingness to impose environmental hazards disproportionately on people of color and people with low incomes. In short, a "pragmatic understanding of justice"[16] permits rationalizing conducting

---

Pfizer's actions caused the deaths and serious disabilities of many children. The case was ultimately settled for $75 million, in 2011.

[14] Grimes v. Kennedy Krieger Inst., Inc., 782 A.2d 807 (Md. 2001).

[15] See David Rosner & Gerald Markowitz, *With the Best Intentions: Lead Research and the Challenge to Public Health*, 102 AM. J. PUB. HEALTH e19 (Nov. 2012); David R. Buchanan & Franklin G. Miller, *Justice and Fairness in the Kennedy Krieger Institute Lead Paint Study: The Ethics of Public Health Research on Less Expensive, Less Effective Interventions*, 96 AM. J. PUB. HEALTH 781 (2006).

[16] Buchanan & Miller, *supra* note 15, at 786.

painful, risky, or degrading research on Black people or members of other marginalized groups.

4.2.4 *Discrimination and Disregard Undermine Trust*

Stories of unethical (or at least ethically questionable) research on Black people are regularly cited as the reason for Black Americans' mistrust of medicine and public health. The Tuskegee study may be blamed most often, but researchers are skeptical of assigning blame to any single historical incident.[17] Physician and scholar Vanessa Northington Gamble describes numerous instances of medical untrustworthiness occurring before the abuses of Tuskegee came to light.[18] In addition to Sims's gynecological experiments on enslaved women, Gamble points to experiments performed on an enslaved man to assess remedies for heat stroke. The common practice of robbing graves at Black cemeteries to provide cadavers for White medical students supported the post-Reconstruction Black community's folk belief in "night doctors," who might steal their bodies (living or dead) for use in medical experiments.[19] Eugenically inspired sterilization abuses of Black women and girls, the "Mississippi appendectomy" described in Chapter 5, often involved coercion or deception.

Apart from such instances of medical exploitation, Black people have long undergone more mundane devaluation and discrimination in medical settings. During the Jim Crow era, Black people in many parts of the country were denied access to hospitals, clinics, or doctors' offices or confined to segregated wards. Facilities for "colored only" were small and underequipped.[20] Even decades after civil rights laws ended de jure discrimination, many Black Americans receive health care in facilities that continue to be de facto segregated, partly because of continuing high levels of residential segregation.[21] A 2005 study found that four in five Black Medicare recipients suffering an acute heart attack received treatment in just 20 percent of hospitals, while 40 percent of hospitals had no Black heart attack patients.[22]

---

[17] Aaron E. Carroll, *Did Infamous Tuskegee Study Cause Lasting Mistrust of Doctors among Blacks?*, N.Y. TIMES (June 17, 2016), https://www.nytimes.com/2016/06/18/upshot/long-term-mistrust-from-tuskegee-experiment-a-study-seems-to-overstate-the-case.html.

[18] Vanessa Northington Gamble, *Under the Shadow of Tuskegee: African Americans and Health Care*, 87 AM. J. PUB. HEALTH 1773 (1997).

[19] *Id.* at 1773–74.

[20] KAREN KRUSE THOMAS, DELUXE JIM CROW: CIVIL RIGHTS AND AMERICAN HEALTH POLICY, 1935–1954, at 36 (2011).

[21] Zinzi D. Bailey et al., *Structural Racism and Health Inequities in the USA: Evidence and Interventions*, 389 THE LANCET 1453, 1458 (2017); David Barton Smith, *Racial and Ethnic Health Disparities and the Unfinished Civil Rights Agenda*, 24 HEALTH AFF. 317–24 (2005).

[22] Amitabh Chandra et al., *Challenges to Reducing Discrimination and Health Inequity through Existing Civil Rights Laws*, 36 HEALTH AFF. 1041 (2017).

More workaday forms of disregard and disrespect likely occur daily in teaching hospitals across the country, as doctors in training hone their skills. In 1973, David Satcher, who would later become the US Surgeon General, wrote of how White doctors exploited the power imbalance with Black patients: "Black patients... are frequently exploited for teaching sessions. One black woman related to me that she had had nine pelvic examinations by physicians and students and had never been told whether her pelvis was normal or abnormal."[23] A physician in training, writing in 2015 to describe the "silent curriculum," suggested that not much may have changed: "I learned that white women are allowed to refuse my involvement at the birth of their child, while poor immigrants are given less space to turn me down. I learned I am more likely to be asked by a resident or attending to try a new procedure when there is a language barrier or a power dynamic that will prevent a family from understanding, refusing, or complaining."[24] The perception that power-less patients (a category that aligns substantially with low-income patients of color) are the most fitting for trainees to practice on reflects diminished respect for those patients and regard for their well-being.

Black people today regularly experience that health care professionals treat them differently than they do White people – less attentively, less respectfully, less effectively, less promptly, less thoroughly, less aggressively.[25] In a 2020 survey, seven in ten Black Americans said the health care system treats patients unfairly based on their race or ethnicity either very or somewhat often. One in five Black adults reported experiencing racial discrimination when getting health care for themselves or a family member in the past year.[26] A firsthand account shares what this feels like. A medical student recently described accompanying her mother (a Black woman) to her first oncology appointment after receiving a cancer diagnosis. Rather than explaining her mother's diagnosis or prognosis or addressing her fears about having cancer, the oncologist launched into a pitch for the patient – whom she had just met – to enroll in a clinical trial of a new chemotherapy regimen. The reaction? "Unbeknownst to her, the doctor had already lost our trust.... To [my mother], it seemed that the oncologist saw her as a body whose value resided in the contribu-tion it could make to future scientific discovery, not a patient in need of care."[27] Reading this account, we cannot know whether the oncologist was elevating an interest in research over patient-centered care; perhaps enrolling in a clinical trial actually offered the patient her best chance to access the most effective treatment.

[23] David Satcher & Charles R. Drew, *Does Race Interfere with the Doctor-Patient Relationship*, 223 JAMA 1498 (1973).

[24] Katherine C. Brooks, *A Silent Curriculum*, 313 JAMA 1909 (2015).

[25] Gamble, *supra* note 18, at 1776.

[26] Liz Hamel et al., *KFF/The Undefeated Survey on Race and Health*, KAISER FAM. FOUND. (2020), https://www.kff.org/report-section/kff-the-undefeated-survey-on-race-and-health-main-findings/#HealthCareSystem.

[27] Shakkaura Kemet, *Insight Medicine Lacks – The Continuing Relevance of Henrietta Lacks*, 381 NEW ENG. J. MED. 800 (2020).

The point is that contemporary experience layers onto histories of exploitation and devaluation to give Black Americans reason to be suspicious of doctors and the health care system.

4.2.5 *An Absence of Trust: Framing and Effects*

According to the 2003 report Unequal Treatment: Confronting Racial and Ethnic Disparities in Health Care:

> Racial and ethnic disparities in care may emerge, at least in part, from a number of patient-level attributes. For example, minority patients are more likely to refuse recommended services . . . , adhere poorly to treatment regimens, and delay seeking care . . . . These behaviors and attitudes can develop as a result of a poor cultural match between minority patients and their providers, mistrust, misunderstanding of provider instructions, poor prior interactions with healthcare systems, or simply from a lack of knowledge of how to best use healthcare services.[28]

Framing mistrust as a patient-level variable typifies much of the analysis suggesting that Black patients contribute to their own health care disparities. It has prompted a critique that focusing on Black patients' mindset and conduct is a form of victim blaming. A swelling chorus of advocates and researchers emphasize the need to recognize and address the many ways that the racist actions of health care actors have shown them to be untrustworthy. The remedy for distrust within the Black community toward health care institutions requires not a focus on patient behavior but an uprooting of racist structures and practices embedded in those institutions.[29]

However framed, Black Americans' low levels of trust in the medical profession are real and can be consequential. Notwithstanding some variations based on geography and socioeconomic status, the Black community overall expresses lower trust levels than the White community.[30] This distrust generally reflects less a skepticism of doctors' technical competence than suspicions about whether White doctors will be honest, respectful, and caring when treating Black patients.[31] Research documenting better health outcomes when Black patients are treated by Black doctors gives credence to such suspicions. A stunning example can be seen in a 2020 study finding that the mortality rate for Black babies was cut in half when

---

[28] INSTITUTE OF MEDICINE, *supra* note 1, at 7.

[29] Laura Specker Sullivan, *Trust, Risk, and Race in American Medicine*, 50 HASTINGS CTR. REP. 18, 19 (2020).

[30] Katrina Armstrong et al., *Racial/Ethnic Differences in Physician Distrust in the United States*, 97 AM. J. PUB. HEALTH 1283 (2007).

[31] Katrina Armstrong et al., *Differences in the Patterns of Health Care System Distrust between Blacks and Whites*, 23 J. GEN. INTERNAL MED. 827 (2008).

Black doctors cared for those infants, an effect that showed up even more strongly in complicated cases.[32]

A lack of trust can interfere with effective care and thus negatively affect health. Mistrust seems to affect when and how Black people pursue care for their health needs. For example, research has found correlations between medical mistrust and lower rates of using preventive services and higher rates of visiting emergency departments.[33] Fewer visits to primary care providers can translate to delayed diagnoses of serious health conditions. When seeking care, wary Black patients may not fully follow treatment recommendations. A doctor may view such a patient as noncompliant or perhaps even less intelligent.[34] Descriptions of patients as noncompliant can suggest they are somehow deficient. Sociologist Ruha Benjamin asserts that the "trope of the 'noncompliant (Black) patient' is yet another way that hospital staff stigmatize those who have reason to question medical authority."[35] From a patient's perspective, doubts about whether a doctor's orders really reflect her best interests – combined perhaps with the cost and inconvenience of recommended treatment – may contribute to a rational choice.

Novel diseases and medical research may heighten wariness, as was apparent when researchers sought to recruit participants for vaccine trials and other studies during the COVID-19 pandemic.[36] Decades earlier, many Black Americans voiced suspicions as Black communities battled high rates of HIV infection and AIDS. In 1991, researchers urged public health professionals to "recognize that Blacks' belief in AIDS as a form of genocide is a legitimate attitudinal barrier rooted in the history of the Tuskegee Syphilis Study."[37] In a 2010 study, one in five Black men who were prescribed antiretroviral (ART) medications believed that people taking HIV medications were treated like "human guinea pigs"; nearly as many believed that ART was a poison.[38] In 2016, researchers reported that Black people with HIV infection

---

[32] Tonya Russell, *Mortality Rate for Black Babies Is Cut Dramatically When Black Doctors Care for Them after Birth, Researchers Say*, WASH. POST (Jan. 13, 2021), htttps://www.washingtonpost.com/health/black-baby-death-rate-cut-by-black-doctors/2021/01/08/e9f0f850-238a-11eb-952e-0c475972cfc0_story.html.

[33] M.J. Arnett et al., *Race, Medical Mistrust, and Segregation in Primary Care as Usual Source of Care: Findings from the Exploring Health Disparities in Integrated Communities Study*, 93 J. URB. HEALTH: BULLETIN OF THE N.Y. ACAD. MED. 456 (2016).

[34] William J. Hall et al., *Implicit Racial/Ethnic Bias among Health Care Professionals and Its Influence on Health Care Outcomes: A Systematic Review*, 105 AM. J. PUB. HEALTH e60 (2015), https://www.ncbi.nlm.nih.gov/pmc/articles/PMC4638275.

[35] Ruha Benjamin, *Assessing Risk, Automating Racism*, 366 SCIENCE 421, 422 (2019).

[36] Jan Hoffman, *"I Won't Be Used as a Guinea Pig" for White People*, N.Y. TIMES (Oct. 7, 2020), www.https://nytimes.com/2020/10/07/health/coronavirus-vaccine-trials-african-americans.html.

[37] Stephen B. Thomas & Sandra C. Quinn, *The Tuskegee Syphilis Study, 1932 to 1972: Implications for HIV Education and AIDS Risk Education Programs in the Black Community*, 81 AM. J. PUB. HEALTH 1498, 1503 (1991).

[38] Laura M. Bogart et al., *Conspiracy Beliefs about HIV Are Related to Antiretroviral Treatment Nonadherence among African American Men with HIV*, 53 J. ACQUIRED IMMUNE DEFICIENCY SYNDROME 648 (2010).

had death rates 13 percent higher than White people's, a disparity the researchers chalked up in part to delayed diagnoses and poor adherence to treatment regimens involving ART medications.[39]

4.3 DEVALUING LIFE WITH A DISABILITY

Like Black people, people with disabilities also have a history of being subjected involuntarily to medical research. In many cases, that research was conducted in state-run institutions, where disabled residents had no power to refuse to participate and where degradation and mistreatment of residents were endemic. In addition, government-sponsored eugenic policies sought historically to segregate and limit reproduction by disabled people. In more modern times, physicians have endorsed withholding treatment from infants with disabilities to permit their premature deaths. Disabled people also offer accounts of how the medical system discounts the value and quality of their lives, accounts increasingly documented by research- ers. This section describes these episodes and how they contribute to a mistrust of medicine that is common among disabled people.

4.3.1 *American Eugenics as Inspiration for German Atrocities*

In the early twentieth century, many states passed laws authorizing the involuntary sterilization of people deemed to be hereditarily unfit and socially burdensome. Chapter 5 recounts the story of these laws and the broader American Eugenics movement of which they were part.

Historians have traced how, in the period following World War I, Germans advancing theories of racial purity turned to America for both ideological contribu- tions and a model for Germany's own sterilization law, which was enacted in 1933.[40] That law fed into the Third Reich's increasing propaganda against disabled people, which described their lives as burdensome and worthless. The Nazis ultimately adopted a program of systematically killing disabled people. The killing began in 1939 with infants and children, when the Third Reich ordered doctors, nurses, and midwives to report newborns and young children who showed signs of severe disability.[41] Children who were reported were removed from their parents, admitted to "clinics," and killed. The Euthanasia Program ripened into a regime of medical

---

[39] Seth C. Kalichman et al., *Race-Based Medical Mistrust, Medication Beliefs and Treatment Adherence: Test of a Medication Model in Persons with HIV/AIDS*, 39 J. BEHAV. MED. 1056 (2016).

[40] STEFAN KÜHL, THE NAZI CONNECTION: EUGENICS, AMERICAN RACISM, AND GERMAN NATIONAL SOCIALISM (1994).

[41] *Nazi Persecution of the Disabled: Murder of the "Unfit"*, US Holocaust Memorial Museum, https://www.ushmm.org/information/exhibitions/online-exhibitions/special-focus/nazi-persecu tion-of-the-disabled.

killing that led to the deaths of approximately 300,000 people with physical or mental disabilities; it was a less recognized parallel to the mass killings of Jews, Roma, and others at extermination camps. By reporting disabled children and later by identifying disabled adults as incapable of working, physicians played a critical role in implementing the program.[42]

American history does not include the intentional and systematic murder of disabled people, but neither is the United States historically innocent of the impulse to prevent disabled people from being part of its society. These histories have long shadows, as evidenced by more recent stories of physicians' roles in terminating treatment for or experimenting on disabled people. Antecedents for the distrust that many Americans with disabilities feel for the medical profession can be found in the profession's historical complicity in treating their lives as burdensome and expendable. Some examples of medical devaluation of the lives of people with disability illuminate the wellspring of medical distrust among people with disabilities.

4.3.2 *Babies Doe*

In the 1980s, examples of American doctors deciding that some disabled infants' lives were not worth saving became public. In 1982, media spotlighted the short life of Baby Doe, a boy born with Down syndrome. After learning that their newborn had an esophageal blockage, then consulting with their doctors, the baby's parents decided against routine surgery to correct the blockage. As a result, he was unable to take in nutrition orally and died of starvation when he was days old.[43] A year later a similar case arose when a baby girl, known as Baby Jane Doe, was born with spina bifida and hydrocephalus. Her parents refused surgery that would have closed the spinal column opening that causes spina bifida, but would not prevent disabilities often associated with this condition. The parents' decision came after physicians advised that, without treatment, the baby would die more quickly.[44]

At the time it was not uncommon for parents of infants with disability to withhold essential treatment on the advice of doctors, thus ensuring their child's rapid death. Some pediatricians in the 1970s sought to establish criteria for "selective

---

[42] Michael S. Bryant, Confronting the "Good Death": Nazi Euthanasia on Trial 1945–1953, at 39 (2005); Olga Khazan, *Remembering the Nazis' Disabled Victims*, The Atlantic (Sept. 3, 2014), https://www.theatlantic.com/health/archive/2014/09/a-memorial-to-the-nazis-disabled-victims/379528; Holocaust Encyclopedia, *Euthanasia Program and Aktion T4*, US Holocaust Memorial Museum, https://encyclopedia.ushmm.org/content/en/article/euthanasia-program.

[43] George F. Will, *"The Killing Will Not Stop"*, Wash. Post (Apr. 22, 1982), https://www.washingtonpost.com/archive/politics/1982/04/22/the-killing-will-not-stop/7c69c6b7-b3fd-401c-8344-9a7d24c994d2/.

[44] Adrienne Asch, Disability, Bioethics, and Human Rights, in Handbook of Disability Studies (Gary L. Albrecht et al. eds., 2001). Ultimately, the infant's spinal column opening healed on its own. As described in Chapter 3, Keri-Lynn (Baby Jane Doe's actual name) celebrated her thirtieth birthday with family and friends in 2013.

nontreatment" of infants born with congenital anomalies and their acceptance of parental decisions not to treat those infants.[45] A survey published in 1977 showed significant support among Massachusetts pediatricians for withholding treatment from newborns deemed "defective."[46] One pediatrician argued that rather than simply "letting nature take its course," actively killing infants with myelomeningocele (a severe form of spina bifida) would reflect the "highest form of medical ethic."[47]

The Baby Doe cases catapulted issues surrounding selective nontreatment from the privacy of labor and delivery suites and neonatal intensive care units into the public forum. Lawsuits unsuccessfully sought to compel treatment of infants whose parents and physicians refused to provide it. The federal government responded, first by treating selective nontreatment as a civil rights issue and then as a child welfare issue. Regulations providing that hospitals' withholding "nourishment or medically beneficial treatment . . . from handicapped infants" would violate disability discrimination law were struck down by the Supreme Court for lack of an evidentiary foundation.[48] In the meantime, Congress entered the public debate. The Child Abuse Amendments of 1984 characterized selective nontreatment (with narrow exceptions) as a form of medical neglect, and therefore properly within the jurisdiction of state child welfare agencies charged with protecting children from abuse and neglect.[49] Disability rights advocates supported these government actions to protect disabled infants, arguing that selective nontreatment decisions reflected the medical profession's devaluing of and discriminating against disabled people.[50]

Fast forward to 2020, when disability rights activists protested an appearance by philosopher Peter Singer, a chaired professor at Princeton, for endorsing what they

---

[45] See, e.g., Raymond S. Duff & A.G.M. Campbell, *Moral and Ethical Dilemmas in the Special-Care Nursery*, 289 NEW ENG. J. MED. 890, 891 (1973) (reporting that over a two-and-a-half-year period, 43 of 299 deaths in the special care nursery of Yale–New Haven Hospital resulted from the withdrawal of treatment); John Lorber, *Early Results of Selective Treatment of Spina Bifida Cystica*, 4 BRIT. MED. J. 201, 203 (1973) (examining list of contraindications to acute therapy for infants with spina bifida cystica); Anthony Shaw et al., *Ethical Issues in Pediatric Surgery: A National Survey of Pediatricians and Pediatric Surgeons*, 60 PEDIATRICS 588, 591–92 (1977) (finding that 19.9 percent of pediatric surgeons and 43.7 percent of pediatricians would recommend surgery for Down syndrome infant with duodenal atresia).

[46] I. David Todres et al., *Pediatricians' Attitudes Affecting Decision-Making in Defective Newborns*, 60 PEDIATRICS 197, 201 (1977).

[47] John M. Freeman, *Is There a Right to Die – Quickly?*, 80 J. PEDIATRICS 904, 905 (1972).

[48] Bowen v. Am. Hosp. Ass'n, 476 US 610 (1986).

[49] Pub. L. No. 98-457, 98 Stat. 1749 (codified as amended at 42 U.S.C. §§ 5101–5106), § 5106(b) (10).

[50] Anti-abortion advocacy groups also urged legal responses to the Baby Doe cases, drawing an analogy between nontreatment decisions and pregnancy termination decisions. Leading disability rights advocates rejected the abortion analogy for its failure to account for the role of women's agency over their bodies. See ADRIENNE ASCH & MICHELLE FINE, Shared Dreams: A Left Perspective on Disability Rights and Reproductive Rights, in WOMEN WITH DISABILITIES: ESSAYS IN PSYCHOLOGY, CULTURE, AND POLITICS 297 (Michelle Fine & Adrienne Asch eds., 1988).

called "selective infanticide." Singer's 1979 book *Practical Ethics* argued that parents should be permitted to euthanize infants with certain disabilities,[51] an argument he has not retracted. In the twenty-first century, stories still arise about doctors declining to treat infants diagnosed with severe developmental disabilities. *The Hill* reported on a case in 2013 where doctors entered a DNR order for an infant with Trisomy 18 without the parents' knowledge and withheld nutrition until his death.[52] The point I make here is not that all infants with disability must receive maximal medical interventions, no matter how dire their short-term prognosis is or how invasive and painful treatment might be. In such cases, parents face wrenching decisions. Rather, I aim to underscore how medical advice (along with other influential voices) that may be biased against disability can sway or even displace parental decisions.

4.3.3 *Willowbrook, Institutions, and Experimentation*

In 1947, the New York Department of Mental Hygiene opened the Willowbrook State School for children with intellectual disabilities on an isolated 375-acre "campus" on Staten Island. Designed to accommodate 4,000 children, it eventually housed more than 6,000 children, many of whom had severe disabilities.[53] Its isolation, combined with the stigma that many parents of disabled children felt at the time, permitted Willowbrook to evade public scrutiny of its operations. Although Robert Kennedy visited the institution in 1965 and described it as a "snake pit," only when a young Geraldo Rivera visited Willowbrook with a hidden camera in 1972 did the public witness the horrific living conditions of its child residents. In over-crowded, squalid quarters, some children were completely naked or left to sit on the floor in feces, urine, and other filth. Residents lacked toothbrushes and were not regularly bathed. Disease outbreaks occurred frequently, and one doctor told Rivera on camera that 100 percent of children contracted hepatitis within six months of arriving at Willowbrook.[54]

The high incidence of hepatitis at Willowbrook was the impetus for Dr. Saul Krugman's experiments on disabled children. A faculty member at New York University's Medical School, Krugman began conducting research at Willowbrook

---

[51] Naaman Zhou, *Peter Singer Event Cancelled in New Zealand after Outcry over Disability Stance*, THE GUARDIAN (Feb. 8, 2020), https://www.theguardian.com/world/2020/feb/19/peter-singer-event-cancelled-in-new-zealand-after-outcry-over-disability-stance.

[52] Rachel Bovard, *States Are Right to Act toward Preventing an Alfie Evans in the US*, THE HILL (May 5, 2018), https://thehill.com/opinion/international/386907-states-are-right-to-act-toward-preventing-an-alfie-evans-in-the-us. Trisomy 18 is a genetic abnormality typically associated with slow growth, congenital heart defects, delayed development, and other complications. *Trisomy 18* (also known as Edwards Syndrome), MINN. DEPT. HEALTH https://www.health.state.mn.us/diseases/cy/trisomy18.html.

[53] Matt Reimann, *Willowbrook, the Institution that Shocked a Nation into Changing Its Laws*, TIMELINE (June 15, 2017), https://timeline.com/willowbrook-the-institution-that-shocked-a-nation-into-changing-its-laws-c847acb44e0d.

[54] *Willowbrook: The Last Great Disgrace* (WABC television broadcast Jan. 6, 1972).

searching for a cure or vaccine for hepatitis. Krugman's research method provoked controversy. He extracted hepatitis virus from the feces of six infected Willowbrook residents and used it to infect other Willowbrook children by putting the virus in their food.[55]

Some scholars defend Krugman because he obtained consent from parents of the child subjects and independent reviews from other experts. Krugman's research contributed to the development of the Hepatitis B vaccine, which dramatically reduced the incidence of hepatitis at Willowbrook. Other ethicists, however, argue that no amount of knowledge gained can justify intentionally infecting disabled children with a potentially deadly virus. One critic wrote to the British medical journal *The Lancet*, "If Krugman and [colleagues] are keen to continue their experiments, I suggest that they invite the parents of the children involved to participate. I wonder what the response would be."[56] Critics also questioned the validity of the parental consent Krugman obtained, suggesting that parents consented to ensure their children would be admitted to Willowbrook, which was already full.[57] Notwithstanding its defenders (who sound eerily like the defenders of Sims's experimental surgeries), Krugman's research intentionally caused harm to children with disabilities.

The story of Elsie Lacks offers another glimpse into experimentation and conditions at institutions for disabled people in the mid-twentieth century. Accounts of medical abuse of Black people often describe how White doctors used cells taken in a biopsy from Henrietta Lacks, a poor, Black woman they were treating for cervical cancer, to create a highly profitable cell line widely used in medical research, without obtaining Lacks's consent.[58] Less well known is the story of Elsie Lacks, Henrietta's oldest daughter, who was nonverbal and likely had some mental disability. On the advice of a doctor, Henrietta sent Elsie to an institution founded as The Hospital for the Negro Insane (and later renamed Crownsville State Hospital) when the girl was ten years old. Within five years, Elsie was dead.[59]

As a poor, disabled, Black girl who lived and died in Jim Crow Maryland, Elsie Lacks exemplified what scholars mean when they talk of a person having an intersectional life or being multiply marginalized. Few details of Elsie's life are known, but available evidence portrays life in the institution as grim and brutal.

---

[55] WALTER M. ROBINSON & BRANDON T. UNRUH, The Hepatitis Experiments at the Willowbrook State School, in THE OXFORD TEXTBOOK OF CLINICAL RESEARCH ETHICS 80–86 (Ezekiel J. Emanuel et al. eds., 2011).

[56] Stephen Goldby. *The Willowbrook Letters*, THE LANCET (Apr. 10, 1971), https://science .jburroughs.org/mbahe/BioEthics/Articles/WillowbookLetters.pdf.

[57] ALLEN M. HORNBLUM ET AL., AGAINST THEIR WILL: THE SECRET HISTORY OF MEDICAL EXPERIMENTATION ON CHILDREN IN COLD WAR AMERICA 99 (2013).

[58] The book whose popularity brought Henrietta Lacks's story to the general public is REBECCA SKLOOT, THE IMMORTAL LIFE OF HENRIETTA LACKS (2010).

[59] Michael Gill & Nirmala Erevelles, *The Absent Presence of Elsie Lacks: Hauntings at the Intersection of Race, Class, Gender, and Disability*, 50 AFRICAN AM. REV. 123 (2017).

Photos show residents, including children, chained to a wall, or strapped to a chair.[60] Doctors at the institution conducted nonconsensual experiments on disabled residents. As at Willowbrook, some residents were injected with hepatitis. Some were injected with malaria. Residents were also subjected to experiments on their brains. These included inserting metal rods into their brains to stimulate nerves and a painful procedure called pneumoencephalography, which involved drilling holes in the skull, draining the cerebrospinal fluid that cushions the brain, and replacing it with oxygen or helium so that the brain appears clearly on x-rays.[61] A local historian who has studied Crownsville conjectures that because Elsie was diagnosed with epilepsy and cerebral palsy she likely was subjected to this procedure.[62] Any knowledge about what being institutionalized did to Elsie comes from Rebecca Skloot, whose book about Henrietta Lacks made her story famous. Skloot describes a photo of Elsie discovered in her file at Crownsville:

> Her . . . eyes bulge from her head, slightly bruised and almost swollen shut. She stares somewhere just below the camera, crying, her face misshapen and barely recognizable, her nostrils inflamed and ringed with mucus; her lips – swollen to nearly twice their normal size – are surrounded by a deep, dark ring of chapped skin; her tongue is thick and protrudes from her mouth. She appears to be screaming. Her head is twisted unnaturally to the left, chin raised and held in place by a large pair of white hands.[63]

Although the number of disabled people living in institutions has decreased substantially, those residing in institutions today may still be treated as research subjects without their consent. In 2019, journalists reported on a Department of Justice investigation into practices at the Glenwood Resource Center, a state-run home for people with intellectual disabilities in Iowa.[64] The investigation concluded a year later, with the Justice Department finding reasonable cause to believe that Glenwood residents had been subjected to uncontrolled and harmful experimentation. An Assistant Attorney General involved in the investigation reminded the public: "Individuals with disabilities are not human guinea pigs, and like all persons, they should never be subject to bizarre and deviant pseudo-medical 'experiments' that injure them."[65]

---

[60] Tom Marquardt, *Tragic Chapter of Crownsville State Hospital's Legacy*, CAPITAL GAZETTE (June 5, 2013), https://www.capitalgazette.com/cg-tragic-chapter-of-crownsville-state-hospitals-legacy-20140730-story.html?outputType=amp.

[61] *Id.*; Gill & Erevelles, *supra* note 59.

[62] Marquardt, *supra* note 60.

[63] SKLOOT, *supra* note 58, at 272–73.

[64] Mitch Smith, *Justice Department Investigates Experiments on People with Disabilities*, N.Y. TIMES, Dec. 13, 2019.

[65] Press Release, US Dept. of Justice, Justice Department Alleges Conditions at Iowa Institution for Individuals with Disabilities Violate the Constitution (Dec. 22, 2020), https://www.justice.gov/opa/pr/justice-department-alleges-conditions-iowa-institution-individuals-disabilities-violate.

Recent research on interventions for very premature infants, a vulnerable population at risk of experiencing disability, has also prompted ethical questions.[66] For example, in 2013 federal officials claimed researchers conducting a study involving more than 1,300 extremely premature infants failed to provide parents with adequate information about foreseeable risks of the treatments investigated. Without knowledge of risks, the parents' consent to participation could not be truly informed.[67] These examples raise troubling ethical questions about failures to obtain truly informed consent to research participation for people who are or may become disabled.

4.3.4 *Medical Devaluing of Life with Disability*

As with Black people, mundane medical interactions are sites of discrimination and disregard for disabled people. Biases against disabled people remain pervasive in American society, and physicians carry them as well. Many still view disability as a flaw needing medical correction and signaling a diminished quality of life. Beliefs about low quality of life implicitly support beliefs that disabled life has lesser value – to the disabled person, as well as to their family and society broadly. Disabled people describe how doctors still express these beliefs. And many doctors openly subscribe to myths about disabled life.

Seeking medical care routinely entails indignities that erode people with disabilities' confidence in the health care system. As described in Chapter 2, more than three decades after the ADA's passage, the medical equipment and physical premises of many providers' offices remain inaccessible. If they do get in to see a doctor, disabled people may find they aren't treated respectfully, as autonomous agents. Angel Miles, a health policy analyst, describes an experience shared by others: "I'm often ignored. . . . I'm often spoken at, and not to. Sometimes the person next to me is addressed instead of me."[68]

4.3.4.1 Medical Care Undervaluing Assisted Functioning and Continued Life

A disabled person's experience of life can be significantly enhanced by having access to equipment, treatment, or personal assistance enabling them to engage in daily activities. Medical care may be needed to maximize functioning and health.

---

[66] Laura I. Appleman, *The Captive Lab Rat: Human Medical Experimentation in the Carceral State*, 61 B.C. L. Rev. 1, 36–38 (2020).

[67] Richard Knox, *Feds Fault Preemie Researchers for Ethical Lapses*, NPR (Apr. 10, 2013), https://www.npr.org/sections/health-shots/2013/04/10/176811809/feds-fault-preemie-researchers-for-eth ical-lapses.

[68] Joseph Shapiro, *People with Disabilities Fear Pandemic Will Worsen Medical Biases*, NPR (Apr. 15, 2020), https://www.npr.org/2020/04/15/828906002/people-with-disabilities-fear-pan demic-will-worsen-medical-biases.

Disabled people, however, speak of how physicians regularly undervalue medical interventions that support daily functioning, but do not "fix" a patient's disability. The care Lex Frieden received for a crushed hip provides an example. In 1967, Frieden became paraplegic from a spinal cord injury during a car wreck. Nearly forty years later, another wreck sent Frieden to the emergency room with a crushed hip bone. His doctor elected not to perform surgery to repair the broken hip, apparently reasoning: "Why incur the resources and risk of surgery when this man will never walk again anyway?" The failure to repair Frieden's broken hip, however, has meant that he is in pain when he uses his wheelchair. That result limits his ability to get around.[69]

Bill Peace's story illustrates how physicians may also fail to appreciate the value of continued life to a disabled person. An anthropologist and disability rights advocate who used a wheelchair, Peace wrote about his encounter with a physician when he was hospitalized with a life-threatening wound infection. Peace was medically stable but was vomiting and had a high fever when a physician he had never met visited him at 2 a.m. Alone in the room with Peace, the physician detailed the medical, social, and financial challenges of continuing to treat Peace's wound. Then, the physician told Peace he could discontinue the antibiotic treatment needed to save his life and assured him that, if he chose that option, he could be made very comfortable.[70]

Over the course of his life with a disability, Peace had learned to navigate medical settings, and he rejected the suggestion that he choose a comfortable death. Later, after recovering from his wound, he described that night: "My fear was based on the knowledge that my existence as a person with a disability was not valued. Many people – the physician I met that fateful night included – assume disability is a fate worse than death.... In a visceral and potentially lethal way, that night made me realize I was not a human being but rather a tragic figure. Out of the kindness of the physician's heart, I was being given a chance to end my life."[71] Peace insisted that his suspicion and fear were not unique. "Most people with a disability fear even the most routine hospitalization. We do not fear any of the commonplace indignities those without a disability worry about when hospitalized. Our fear is primal – will our lives be considered devoid of value?"[72]

4.3.4.2 Medical Opinions of Low Quality of Life with Disability

Physicians express views supporting this unflattering portrait of medical professionals who devalue life with disability. Research going back decades documents medical

---

[69] *Id.*

[70] William J. Peace, *Comfort Care as Denial of Personhood*, 42 HASTINGS CTR. REP. 14 (July–Aug. 2012).

[71] *Id.* at 15.

[72] William J. Peace, *Disability Discrimination: The Author Responds*, HASTINGS CTR. BIOETHICS F. (July 27, 2012), https://www.thehastingscenter.org/disability-discrimination-the-author-responds/.

discounting of disabled people's quality of life. Physicians tend to believe that disability causes diminished enjoyment of or satisfaction with life, when, in fact, surveys of people with varying disabilities show them to be about as satisfied with their lives as nondisabled people.[73] Confirming the persistence of these erroneous assumptions, 82.4 percent of physician respondents in a recent national survey indicated they believed that people with significant disability generally have a worse quality of life than nondisabled people.[74] Although the study did not test whether those beliefs translated into care disparities, the researchers concluded: "It seems reasonable to expect that explicit bias would work similarly [to implicit racial biases' demonstrated effect on care], with deleterious effects on care equity for people with disability."[75]

Some physicians recognize the potential for biased evaluations of disabled patients. As one wrote in *American Family Physician*: "Physicians should be careful to avoid making assumptions about patients' quality of life, especially those who rely on external assistance . . . [and] avoid reinforcing patient or caregiver fears and misconceptions about living with disability."[76] But many in the medical profession fail to acknowledge the corrosive and potentially dangerous consequences of dis-counting the quality of life with disability.

In 2016, a publication entitled "States Worse than Death among Hospitalized Patients with Serious Illnesses" described researchers' asking hospitalized patients with serious illnesses about a series of "states of debility" and how the patients would compare those conditions to being dead. Fewer than 10 percent of the patients thought that using a wheelchair would be as bad as or worse than death, but nearly 70 percent thought that relying on a breathing machine or having bowel or bladder incontinence would be that bad. These responses reflect how members of the public discount the quality of life with disability. The premise of the research also raises concerns: The investigators, their funding organization, and an Institutional Review Board approved of asking nondisabled hospital patients whether they find death preferable to experiencing circumstances (e.g., using a wheelchair, being incontin-ent, or requiring assistance with breathing) that many disabled people live with for

---

[73] See, e.g., John R. Bach, *Threats to "Informed" Advance Directives for the Severely Physically Challenged?*, 84 Arch. Phys. Med. Rehabilitation S23 (2003); D. Lule et al., *"Life Can Be Worth Living in Locked-In Syndrome"*, 177 Progress in Brain Research 339, 341–43, 346–47 (2009); Gary L. Albrecht & Patrick J. Devlieger, *The Disability Paradox: High Quality of Life against All Odds*, 48 Soc. Sci. & Med. 977 (1999).

[74] Lisa I. Iezzoni et al., *Physicians' Perceptions of People with Disability and Their Health Care*, 40 Health Aff. 297 (2021). The question regarding quality of life referred simply to "persons with significant disability." The survey also included different questions about respondents' experi-ence treating patients with significant chronic mobility limitations, significant vision limita-tions, significant hearing limitations, comorbid serious mental illness, and significant intellectual disability.

[75] *Id.* at 303.

[76] Clarissa Kripke, *Patients with Disabilities: Avoiding Unconscious Bias When Discussing Goals of Care*, 96 Am. Fam. Physician 193, 195 (2017).

years or decades. The authors suggested that the study's results "should challenge . . . those who develop quality measures to formulate and use new metrics such as the avoidance of states worse than death."[77] The logical consequences of this suggestion are immensely troubling. Using nondisabled people's fear of disability as a basis for assessing quality of care could introduce dangerous incentives. Two geriatricians responded to the article based on their experience caring for patients who are incontinent, unable to get out of bed, or experience dementia or constant confusion. They reported it was "vanishingly rare" for their patients in "states of debility" to express a preference for being dead.[78]

4.4 WARINESS OF MEDICAL AUTHORITY OVER LIFE-SHORTENING DECISIONS AMONG DISABLED PEOPLE AND BLACK PEOPLE

So far, this chapter has offered historical, empirical, and anecdotal evidence of medicine's past and continuing exploitation and devaluation of Black people and people with disabilities in the United States. The stories about Blackness and disability that this assemblage portrays are not identical. They have a similar effect, though, of indicating that Black people's and disabled people's shared wariness of medical practitioners and researchers is a sensible response to unspoken and explicit messages conveyed over decades and centuries. The remainder of this chapter describes several situations involving choices near life's end where this wariness shapes disabled people's and Black people's attitudes and decisions.

Attitudes regarding these topics – physician-assisted suicide, hospice care, and organ donation – are neither simple nor uniformly shared among people with disabilities or Black people. The following sections do not attempt to address fully the complexity of either personal choices or policy positions regarding these matters. The only purpose here is to highlight a similarity in how weakened trust in the medical system among marginalized groups manifests in the twenty-first century. Racism and ableism are sometimes described as sharing roots in White supremacy. With shared roots it is not surprising that experiences of racism and ableism in medicine would produce similar fruits.

4.4.1 *Physician-Assisted Suicide*

4.4.1.1 Activism by People with Disabilities

Negative experiences with the health care system (historical and personal) have led to disabled people and organizations representing them being among the strongest

[77] Emily B. Rubin et al., *States Worse than Death among Hospitalized Patients with Serious Illnesses*, 176 JAMA INTERNAL MED. 1557 (2016).
[78] Stephanie Nothelle & Tom Finucane, *States Worse than Death*, 177 JAMA INTERNAL MED. 593 (2017).

voices opposing legalization of physician aid in dying, also known as physician-assisted suicide. (The term used varies, largely depending on whether the speaker is a supporter of the practice, advocating for "physician aid in dying," or a critic, warning against "physician-assisted suicide." To avoid taking sides, this chapter uses both.) Whatever the semantics, the practice permits patients to request and receive a lethal prescription from a physician, which the patient can then take.

Since the 1990s, public support for legalizing physician aid in dying has grown, with opinion polling showing that by 2018 a majority of Americans supported it.[79] In 1997, Oregon became the first state to legalize the practice, and eight states and Washington, D.C., have followed suit. State laws permitting doctors to assist patients seeking to die typically include safeguards meant to prevent abuse, such as limiting availability to patients diagnosed as terminally ill, requiring multiple requests from the patient, and imposing a waiting period before the lethal medication can be dispensed.[80]

Despite an apparent rising tide of approval, support for legalized physician-aided dying is not uniform. Disability rights advocates have tried to stem the tide, with mixed success. Although some prominent individual disability rights advocates have argued for the ability to choose assistance in dying,[81] a range of major organizations representing and advocating for people with disabilities have consistently opposed legalization.[82] Their resistance stems from the perceived risk that, despite being promoted as increasing patient autonomy, legalizing physician-assisted suicide could create new avenues to abuse disabled patients. Social, cultural, and economic factors feed the deep skepticism of disability rights advocates that "safeguards" in assisted suicide legislation would in fact prevent abuse of disabled people. To start, because most people with disabilities are not financially well off, financial pressures may distort their choices.[83] Pressures could come from health insurers seeking to cut

---

[79] Megan Brenan, *Americans' Strong Support for Euthanasia Persists*, GALLUP (May 31, 2018), https://news.gallup.com/poll/235145/americans-strong-support-euthanasia-persists.aspx (finding 65 percent supported physician-assisted suicide).

[80] Paula Span, Aid in Dying Soon Will Be Available to More Americans. Few Will Choose It., N.Y. TIMES (July 8, 2019), https://www.nytimes.com/2019/07/08/health/aid-in-dying-states.html.

[81] See Drew Battavia & Hugh G. Gallagher, *Gallagher and Batavia on Physician-Assisted Suicide – An Open Letter to People with Disabilities*, INDEP. LIVING INST., https://www.independentliving.org/docs1/gallbat.html; see also ANITA SILVERS, Protecting the Innocents from Physician-Assisted Suicide: Disability Discrimination and the Duty to Protect Otherwise Vulnerable Groups, in PHYSICIAN ASSISTED SUICIDE EXPANDING THE DEBATE 133 (M. Pabst Battin et al. eds., 1998).

[82] NATIONAL COUNCIL ON DISABILITY, THE DANGER OF ASSISTED SUICIDE LAWS 39 (2019). In January 2015 the Disability Rights Legal Center launched the End of Life Liberty Project (ELLP) under the leadership of Kathryn Tucker, a leading advocate for legalization of physician aid-in-dying and physician-assisted suicide. In 2016, both Tucker and the ELLP left the Disability Rights Legal Center, moving eventually to an affiliation with U.C. Hastings College of the Law. End of Life Liberty Project now at UC Hastings, Bioethics.net (Jan. 3, 2018), https://www.bioethics.net/2018/01/end-of-life-liberty-project-now-at-uc-hastings.

[83] NATIONAL COUNCIL ON DISABILITY, *supra* note 82, at 28–29.

costs. The cost of lethal medications is low compared to most medical interventions meant to sustain life. While insurers are legally obligated to cover "medically necessary" care, stories of patients being forced to fight insurers' denials of coverage are common. The prospect of such a fight could play a role in steering a patient toward assisted suicide.[84]

More fundamentally, American society fails to adequately support disabled people's ability to live independently. Most commercial insurance does not pay for long-term services and supports for independent living. In theory, Medicaid covers those supports, but much variation exists in what benefits states cover and most states' funding is inadequate to meet demand. Many doctors (who must order supports for them to be reimbursable) are neither well informed about the range of supports nor empathic regarding their value. People with disabilities may face impossible choices between living in an institution or remaining in the community without their basic needs being met.[85]

Another source of concern for disabled opponents of legalization is that messages devaluing disabled life, whether from medical providers or society more broadly, may demoralize some disabled people about their lives. Pervasive messaging that "dignity" requires living without needing assistance unmistakably signals to many disabled people that their lives are undignified.[86] Proponents of legalization often cast lack of dignity as an accepted basis for choosing death. In 2020, a proposed "death with dignity" bill was reintroduced in the New Hampshire legislature. Its preamble asserted the rights of "terminally ill patients [who] experience severe unrelenting suffering, mental anguish over the prospect of losing control and independence, *and/or embarrassing indignities* for long periods."[87] During the debate over Washington, D.C.'s proposed Death with Dignity Act, one proponent (in an echo of the "states of debility" argument described earlier) told *The Washington Post*: "If I find myself in a situation where I can't go to the bathroom on my own, where someone has to change my diapers, where I can't feed myself, where I can't care for the people around me, where other people have to move me around to keep me from having bedsores, I would then submit, 'Is that really living?'"[88] Arguments like that led one disability rights organization to call the (then) proposed D.C. legislation a "death before disability bill." A post on the Not Dead Yet blog dubbed it the "extreme ableism of assisted suicide."[89]

[84] Marilyn Golden & Tyler Zoanni, *Killing Us Softly: The Dangers of Legalizing Assisted Suicide*, 3 DISABILITY & HEALTH J. 16 (2010).
[85] Michael Ogg, *Remaining at Home with Severe Disability*, 38 HEALTH AFF. 1046 (June 2019).
[86] NATIONAL COUNCIL ON DISABILITY, *supra* note 82.
[87] HB 1659-FN, https://www.deathwithdignity.org/wp-content/uploads/2015/10/2020-NH-HB1659.pdf.
[88] Liz Szabo, *'Death with Dignity' Laws and the Desire to Control How One's Life Ends*, WASH. POST, Oct. 24, 2016.
[89] Diane Coleman, *The Extreme Ableism of Assisted Suicide*, NOT DEAD YET BLOG (Jan. 28, 2020), https://notdeadyet.org/2020/01/the-extreme-ableism-of-assisted-suicide.html. The blog post quotes a letter from the organization Second Thoughts Massachusetts to the D.C. Council.

Disabled people are acutely aware that some nondisabled people fear disability intensely and believe a quick death seems more attractive than receiving assistance with activities of daily living from personal assistants, family members, and technology. The reality that many people with disabilities lead happy and productive lives while relying on supports seems incredible to some people, especially when popular films like *Million Dollar Baby* and *Me Before You* dramatize and valorize a desire to die rather than live with quadriplegia. The disability community roundly condemned both films as reinforcing prejudices about life with disability.[90]

Aid in dying laws typically give doctors important gate-keeping roles, a pattern that amplifies disability community objections. Laws modeled on Oregon's original Death with Dignity Act require two physicians to confirm terminal illness (meaning death is expected within six months) on the part of a patient requesting lethal medication. A physician who suspects a mental condition is affecting the patient's judgment must refer the patient for a psychological examination.[91] Although proponents hail these steps as guarding against patients with treatable conditions ending their lives, disabled opponents see them as authorizing physicians to validate and encourage choices that align with negative views of disabled life. Projections of how long a person will live are not reliable and may be infected by bias.[92] Physicians may misjudge complex disabilities as constituting a terminal illness; physician Clarissa Kripke warns that misjudgment is a "common confusion [that] can result in premature withdrawal of life-preserving care."[93] If a disabled patient is depressed by his life prospects and requests lethal medication, the large majority of doctors who believe that significant disability produces poor quality of life may view the request as supremely rational and fail to recognize the patient's depression.

Moreover, some proponents now argue for expanding the right to obtain physician-assisted suicide by removing the requirement of terminal illness. In 2021, Canada's Parliament approved legislation expanding the right to patients with nonterminal conditions if their physical or psychological suffering is "grievous and irremediable."[94] Disabled opponents of assisted suicide view such expansions as

---

[90] *Million Dollar Baby Built on Prejudice about People with Disabilities*, DISABILITY RTS. EDUC. & DEF. FUND (Feb. 2005), dredf.org/archives/mdb.shtml; Emily Ladau, *Spare Me, "Me Before You": Hollywood's New Tearjerker Is Built on Tired and Damaging Disability Stereotypes*, SALON (May 24, 2016), https://www.salon.com/2016/05/24/spare_me_this_tearjerker_romance_ me_before_you_is_the_latest_in_an_endless_line_of_disability_objectification.

[91] THADDEUS POPE, IMPLEMENTATION AND PRACTICE OF PHYSICIAN-ASSISTED DEATH: SAFEGUARDS IN PHYSICIAN-ASSISTED DEATH: SCANNING THE LANDSCAPE: PROCEEDINGS OF A WORKSHOP 75, 77 (2018) (ebook).

  Hawaii's 2018 legislation authorizing physician-assisted suicide requires all patients seeking a lethal prescription to be referred for counseling. HAW. REV. STAT. ANN. § 327L-6 (LexisNexis 2020).

[92] Golden & Zoanni, *supra* note 84, at 21.

[93] Kripke, *supra* note 76, at 193.

[94] Mark S. Komrad, *Oh, Canada! Your New Law Will Provide, Not Prevent, Suicide for Some Psychiatric Patients*, PSYCHIATRIC TIMES (June 1, 2021), https://www.psychiatrictimes.com/view/

highly dangerous, as they would open the door for disabled people who are not terminally ill, but whose lives in nursing homes are intolerable, to succumb to society's message that their lives are not worth living.

Mistrust of medicine and the health care system, situated within the broader web of society's failure to ensure that disabled people have needed food, housing, and personal assistance, thus undergirds the disability community's opposition to legalizing physician-assisted dying. Many disabled people do not trust nondisabled people, especially those with power and privilege, to value disabled lives. Carol Gill, a psychologist and Disability Studies scholar, warns of how privilege threatens to obscure the risks of legalization:

> Many of the key spokespersons in favor of assisted suicide . . . are familiar with ideals such as independence, control, and freedom because they are by and large from the dominant sector of society that has had access to those experiences. . . . They have enjoyed a good deal of control, know exactly what they have to lose, and are determined to retain it until death. Unfortunately, viewing the world from a position of privilege may limit one's insight into the consequences of a policy change whose greatest impact could fall on socially marginalized groups.[95]

4.4.1.2 Black People's Doubts about Physician-Assisted Suicide

Given Black Americans' historical and contemporary experiences of medical exploitation and discrimination, it is not surprising that they too have been slower to endorse physician-assisted suicide. Evidence of organized Black opposition to legalization is less clear than disability organizations' near universal condemnation. Nevertheless, a 2013 opinion poll conducted by the Pew Research Center reported that while 53 percent of White respondents approved of laws allowing physician-assisted suicide for terminally ill patients, only 29 percent of Black respondents favored such laws.[96] An earlier survey sought to discern whether legalization would negatively affect patients' trust in their doctors. It found that by a margin of three to one more adults disagreed than agreed that allowing doctors to "help patients die" would lessen their trust in their own doctors. Black respondents were less sanguine.

---

canada-law-provide-not-prevent-suicide; Harold Braswell, *Canada Is Plunging toward a Human Rights Disaster for Disabled People*, WASH. POST (Feb. 29, 2021), https://www.washingtonpost .com/outlook/canada-is-heading-toward-a-human-rights-disaster-for-disabled-people/2021/02/19/ 01cbfca4-7232-11eb-85fa-e0ccb3660358_story.html.

[95] Carol J. Gill, *No, We Don't Think Our Doctors Are Out to Get Us: Responding to the Straw Man Distortions of Disability Rights Arguments against Assisted Suicide*, 3 DISABILITY & HEALTH J. 31, 36 (2010).

[96] *Views on End-of-Life Medical Treatments*, PEW RES. CTR. (Nov. 21, 2013), https://www .pewforum.org/2013/11/21/views-on-end-of-life-medical-treatments. Earlier studies from the 1990s produced similar findings of lower support among Black Americans. Patricia A. King & Leslie E. Wolf, *Empowering and Protecting Patients: Lessons for Physician-Assisted Suicide from the African-American Experience*, 82 MINN. L. REV. 1015 (1998).

Only 41 percent of them (as compared to 58 percent in the full sample) disagreed that legalization would result in diminished personal trust, suggesting a more tenuous faith in their doctors.[97]

Reasons for Black Americans' muted enthusiasm for physician aid in dying are complex. Spiritual beliefs and distrust of government likely play roles, but so does an unwillingness to give doctors the power to "play God" by making life-and-death decisions.[98] As with the disability community, wariness of medicine seems tightly bound up with a larger fabric of distrust and suspicion that the political elite neither identify with nor share Black people's concerns. Terri Laws, a Religious Studies scholar who focuses on Black religious experience, expressed this perspective, observing that physician-assisted suicide is "supported by Americans with resources, political power, and privilege. Health and healthcare are not simply the apt use of medical knowledge, but a sociocultural process in which culture, including religious beliefs, and social position are too often overlooked[.] . . . Physician-assisted suicide, then, becomes a healthcare choice for the cultural one percent."[99] Laws's emphasis on the privilege enjoyed by leading proponents of legalization, together with their inattention to the importance of social position, echoes Carol Gills's expression of disability concerns.

This point is important. Pro legalization rhetoric commonly extols autonomy and control at life's end. It valorizes getting what you want (a quick, painless, "dignified" death) and avoiding the dying you fear. But, to steal from the Rolling Stones, many Black Americans don't even get what they need when it comes to health care. The litany of racial health disparities includes both higher mortality rates from several cancers and inadequate attention to pain management. That combination means Black Americans disproportionately suffer painful deaths from cancer, a paradigmatic case that physician-assisted suicide proponents point to as justifying the practice.[100] They are also more likely than White Americans to live in poverty and less likely to have comprehensive insurance coverage, all of which may make more attractive the "choice" of lethal medications. Black opponents of legalization question whether giving people who consistently receive less and lower quality medical care the option to "choose" a quick and painless death truly respects autonomy in a robust, contextualized sense of the word. A Washington, D.C., community activist worried that the lack of financial means to pursue aggressive

[97] Mark Hall et al., *The Impact on Patient Trust of Legalising Physician Aid in Dying*, 31 M. MED. ETHICS 693 (2005).

[98] Cindy L. Cain & Sara McCleskey, *Expanded Definitions of the "Good Death"? Race, Ethnicity, and Medical Aid in Dying*, 41 SOC. HEALTH & ILLNESS 1175, 1184 (2019).

[99] Terri Laws, *How Race Matters in the Physician-Assisted Suicide Debate*, RELIGION & POLITICS. RELIGION & POL. (Sept. 3, 2019), https://religionandpolitics.org/2019/09/03/how-race-matters-in-the-physician-assisted-suicide-debate.

[100] Cf. Lydia S. Dugdale, *Will Black Lives Matter to Death with Dignity Act?*, THE HILL (Jan. 23, 2017), https://thehill.com/blogs/pundits-blog/healthcare/315731-will-black-lives-matter-to-death-with-dignity-act.

care for a terminal illness might lead low-income Black elders to a premature death. She concluded of the District's measure legalizing physician aid in dying: "It's really aimed at old black people. It really is."[101]

4.4.2 *Black People's Hesitancy Regarding Hospice Care and Organ Donation*

Attention to risks for marginalized groups posed by legalizing physician-assisted dying is where similarities between Black people's and disabled people's mistrust of medicine is most visible. Manifestations of mistrust show up in other areas as well; racial disparities relating to use of hospice care and to organ transplantation are two examples where these groups' weak or nonexistent trust plays a role.

4.4.2.1 Choosing Hospice

Hospice care seeks to meet the emotional, psychosocial, and spiritual needs of terminally ill patients and their families and to minimize the patient's physical pain. It offers an alternative (often provided in a patient's home) to medical interventions seeking cure or prolongation of life.[102] Hospice care has in recent decades become an accepted alternative to aggressive life-prolonging treatment. For the first time in more than a half century, more Americans died at home in 2019 than in hospitals.[103] In a 2017 survey, 85 percent of Americans who had heard of hospice care reported a favorable opinion of it, with nearly half saying their opinion was very positive.[104]

In the same survey, however, much higher percentages of Black Americans said that living as long as possible was extremely important to them personally and that the health care system places too little emphasis on preventing deaths and extending lives as long as possible.[105] According to a 2021 review, "overwhelming evidence

---

[101] Fenit Nirappil, *Right-to-Die Law Faces Skepticism in Nation's Capital: 'It's Really Aimed at Old Black People'*, WASH. POST (Oct. 17, 2016), https://www.washingtonpost.com/local/dc-polit ics/right-to-die-law-faces-skepticism-in-us-capital-its-really-aimed-at-old-black-people/2016/10/17/ 8abf6334-8ff6-11e6-a6a3-d50061aa9fae_story.html.

[102] Hospice care is a specialized type of palliative care, which focuses on providing relief from the symptoms and stress of a serious (but not necessarily terminal) illness.

[103] Gina Kolata, *More Americans Are Dying at Home than in Hospitals*, N.Y. TIMES (Dec. 11, 2019), https://www.nytimes.com/2019/12/11/health/death-hospitals-home.html.

[104] Liz Hamel et al., *Views and Experiences with End-of-Life Medical Care in the U.S.*, KAISER FAM. FOUND. (Apr. 27, 2017).

[105] *Id.* An extreme example these views can be seen in the case of Jahi McMath, a Black teenager whom doctors declared brain dead following post-operative complications. Her family rejected the declaration of death, believing instead that Jahi was profoundly disabled. They continued mechanical ventilation and other measures to maintain Jahi's bodily functions for years. Reporting connected the family's reaction to their belief that doctors failed to listen to their concerns about Jahi's bleeding after surgery. Rachel Aviv, *What Does It Mean to Die?*, NEW YORKER (Jan. 29, 2018).

reveals that non-Hispanic Black patients are less likely to use hospice and more likely to die in the hospital than their non-Hispanic White counterparts."[106] That disparity means older Black people are more likely to have untreated pain at the end of life and their families are less likely to receive hospice's supportive services.[107]

As with physician aid in dying, Black Americans' less favorable attitudes towards hospice are complex. Religious beliefs, family-centered decision making, a lack of familiarity with hospice care, physicians' lack of cultural competence in talking with Black patients about hospice, and hospice providers' lack of diverse staff may all contribute.[108] Mistrust of medical providers also appears on lists of possible explanations. A causal relationship between Black Americans' wariness of the medical system and lower hospice usage has not yet been clearly established, but its logic is apparent. Filtered through awareness of historical abuses and contemporary medical inequities, suggestions of hospice services may sound like a doctor doesn't think a terminally ill Black patient deserves an all-out effort. Patients may also hear suggestions of hospice care as signifying an insurance company's attempt to save money.[109] Either message can trigger protective responses by patients and their families, like demanding aggressive life-sustaining care.[110]

The story of Sarah Johnson, an eighty-six-year-old Black woman in New Orleans, provides concrete grounding for such suspicions. Before becoming sick with COVID-19, Johnson was frail, but she still lived in her own home (which she bought with cash earned working as a hospital nurse). When she became sick and too weak to get out of bed, she was admitted to the hospital with a COVID-19 diagnosis. Less than 24 hours later, the hospital – at the time overwhelmed with COVID-19 patients – informed Johnson's children that doctors could do nothing more for her: Even though she was breathing on her own, her kidneys were failing. If they wanted to bring her home, according to the hospital, hospice could make sure she would be comfortable. In fact, once her children brought Sarah Johnson

---

[106] Mohsen Bazargan & Shahrzad Bazargan-Hejazi, *Disparities in Palliative and Hospice Care and Completion of Advance Care Planning and Directive among Non-Hispanic Blacks: A Scoping Review of Recent Literature*, 38 AM. J. HOSPICE & PALLIATIVE MED. 688, 691 (2021).

[107] Ramona Rhodes, *Racial Disparities in Hospice: Moving from Analysis to Intervention*, 8 AMA J. ETHICS 613 (2006); Tim Pittman, *Hospice Use Lower among African Americans*, DUKE HEALTH (Jan. 15, 2018), https://physicians.dukehealth.org/articles/hospice-use-lower-among-afri can-americans.

[108] Sarah Varney, *A Racial Gap in Attitudes toward Hospice Care*, N.Y. TIMES (Apr. 11, 2020), https://nyti.ms/1J9wmyq; Kimberly S. Johnson, *Racial and Ethnic Disparities in Palliative Care*, 16 J. PALLIATIVE MED. 1329 (2013); Angela D. Spruill et al., *Barriers in Hospice Use among African Americans with Cancer*, 15 J. HOSPICE & PALLIATIVE NURSING 136 (2013); Rochaun Meadows-Fernandez, *The Ways Inequality Affects Black Americans at the End of Life*, NEXT AVENUE (blog post) (Nov. 2, 2018), https://www.nextavenue.org/end-of-life-inequal ity-black-americans.

[109] Varney, *supra* note 108.

[110] Sarah Varney, *A Matter of Faith and Trust: Why African-Americans Don't Use Hospice*, KAISER HEALTH NEWS, May 5, 2015.

home, they were largely left alone with her for thirteen days until she died, because hospice providers were limiting in-person visits due to the pandemic. Later external scrutiny of Johnson's records suggested the hospital's assessment of her condition as hopeless relied on questionable medical judgments and failed to consider improvements in her kidney function. It concluded that Sarah Johnson would have had good odds of survival if she had continued to receive aggressive hospital care.[111]

Johnson's story is disturbing on several levels. According to reporting by *ProPublica*, the hospital Johnson went to departed from standard practice by sending patients sick with COVID-19 back home to be cared for by family members, who were unlikely to have proper protective equipment. Reporters interviewed the families of about two dozen patients who sought care for the coronavirus at New Orleans hospitals, and who were discharged before they died. All of these patients were Black. Family members of eight of those patients described feeling pressured by hospital staff to transition their loved one into at-home hospice care, even as they questioned the suggestion. The hospital network where Johnson received care denied that it ever rationed care and would not discuss her case. But stories like Sarah Johnson's give credence to wariness Black patients and their families express regarding hospice care.[112]

4.4.2.2 Choosing Organ Donation

Decisions whether to consent to organ donation for transplantation are technically questions about postmortem treatment of a body. For many Black people, though, invitations to consider organ donation provoke concerns about their premortem medical treatment.[113]

A couple of points about the organ transplantation ecosystem are worth highlighting. First, organ transplantation is a big business, generating billions in revenues annually. But the enterprise relies on human altruism for its key raw material – transplantable organs. In the US, offering any kind of monetary compensation to a person (or their family members) in return for donating organs is illegal. The wisdom of this prohibition has been debated, but it generally remains intact.[114]

---

[111] Annie Waldman & Joshua Kaplan, *Sent Home to Die*, PROPUBLICA (Sept. 2, 2020), https://www.propublica.org/article/sent-home-to-die.

[112] *Id.*

[113] People with disabilities have expressed a different type of concern about the operation of the organ transplantation system, specifically pointing to instances of disabled people being categorically excluded from organ waiting lists. NATIONAL COUNCIL ON DISABILITY, ORGAN TRANSPLANT DISCRIMINATION AGAINST PEOPLE WITH DISABILITIES (Sept. 25, 2019), https://ncd.gov/sites/default/files/NCD_Organ_Transplant_508.pdf.

[114] Richard Weinmeyer, *The Racially Unequal Impact of the US Organ Procurement System*, 16 AM. MED. ASS'N J. ETHICS 461 (2014). Michele Goodwin provides an in-depth examination of this approach's problematic nature and the resulting international black market for organs in BLACK MARKETS: THE SUPPLY AND DEMAND OF BODY PARTS (2006).

Chronic scarcity of transplantable organs is also a reality. Eighteen people, on average, die every day while waiting for an organ to become available.[115]

White people on transplant waiting lists are more likely than their Black counterparts to receive a transplant. According to federal government data from 2019, transplants were performed on 25.8 percent of the Black patients awaiting transplants, while 47.6 percent of the White patients received transplants.[116] Because Black Americans suffer higher rates of chronic diseases like diabetes, kidney disease, and hypertension, they are disproportionately likely to suffer organ failure and are disproportionately represented on organ waiting lists.[117] Because the chances of transplant success increase if the donor has tissues that "match" the recipient, shared ancestry within racial and ethnic groups means that increasing the number of Black donors will increase the number of suitable organs for Black patients on the waiting list.[118]

For that reason, public health initiatives have sought to increase the number of Black people choosing to donate organs. To be clear, Black people are *not* generally less likely to donate their organs. Following campaigns focused on increasing transplantation awareness and donation rates among Black Americans, donation rates in 2010 among Black Americans exceeded those of other racial and ethnic groups.[119] Higher donation rates still would help meet the greater need. Donation decisions can occur either when a person registers as a prospective donor, for example when obtaining a driver's license, or when family members are approached by an organ procurement organization (OPO) asking them to donate their loved one's organs. Thus, individuals' understandings about what may happen to their body in some unknown future are relevant to attempts to increase donation rates, as are families' perceptions about the fate of a loved one who may have just been declared dead or whose death is imminent.

Many Black people are skeptical about whether medical professionals will work hard to save the lives of patients who are organ donors. This skepticism is not unique

---

[115] UNOS (2019). National data. Retrieved from https://unos.org/data.

[116] *Organ Donation and African Americans*, OFF. MINORITY HEALTH, US DEP'T OF HEALTH & HUM. SERVS., https://minorityhealth.hhs.gov/omh/browse.aspx?lvl=4&lvlid=27. This is one of multiple transplant-related disparities that Black Americans face. Todd Park et al., *The Costly Effects of an Outdated Organ Donation System, Inequity in Organ Donation*, BLOOMWORKS, https://bloomworks.digital/organdonationreform/Inequity.

[117] According to 2019 figures published by the federal Office of Minority Health 28.7 percent of the candidates on waiting lists for any type of organ were Black, in contrast to their 12.7 percent share of the general population. Organ Donation and African Americans. Moreover, because Black patients often face delays in being referred to transplantation waitlists, their representation on those lists likely does not reflect the actual level of need. Park et al., *supra* note 116.

[118] Dana H.Z. Robinson & Kimberly R. Jacob Arriola, *Strategies to Facilitate Organ Donation among African Americans*, 10 CLINICAL J. AM. SOC'Y NEPHOLOGY 177 (2015).

[119] Clive O. Callender et al., *Organ Donation in the United States: The Tale of the African-American Journey of Moving from the Bottom to the Top*, 48 TRANSPLANTATION PROC. 2392, 2392 (2016).

to the Black community. Educational campaigns seeking to increase organ donation generally have had to counter beliefs that when faced with a patient in extremis doctors might be less motivated to take aggressive life-saving measures if the patient is an organ donor. After all (so the thinking goes), why would one take heroic measures, fighting against the odds to save a single life, when an organ donor's death might translate into multiple lives saved? Fear of encouraging a premature death is an obstacle to organ donor registration generally.[120]

Black Americans also have distinctive misgivings about organ donation. As with decisions about hospice care, multiple factors (including religious beliefs and concerns about preserving the integrity of a deceased person's body) may influence their decisions. Mistrust, however, presents an especially salient impediment to increasing organ donation.[121] Recent research employing focus groups of Black Americans unpacked layers of distrust. Historical and current-day experiences of societal oppression and discrimination influenced participants' beliefs that Black donors are likely to be mistreated or, in the words of one participant, "be disposable parts for people."[122] Participants pointed to historical bases (ranging from slavery to the Tuskegee study) for skepticism that either the government or medical institutions could be trusted to protect Black organ donors from abuse.

Contemporary disregard for Black life also fuels skepticism. Recent research finds that within the Black community suspicions persist that black market sales of donated organs incentivize premature retrieval and that waiting lists are rigged to favor wealthy and White recipients.[123] The latter suspicion is grounded in stories like that of Bruce Tucker, a Black man who was rushed to the hospital following a head injury in 1968. After doctors declared him brain dead, the hospital removed Tucker's heart without contacting his family or obtaining any consent and transplanted the heart into a White businessman.[124] In the late 1990s, investigative reporting uncovered that the Los Angeles County coroner's office was harvesting and selling corneas from bodies at local morgues. Over 80 percent of the "donors" were Black or Latino.[125] Sinister rumors of contemporary organ trafficking involve killings of young Black men as part of a system of organ harvesting, with funeral homes receiving victims' bodies with organs missing.[126] Twenty-first century beliefs about stealing and

---

[120] Susan E. Morgan et al., *Facts versus "Feelings": How Rational Is the Decision to Become an Organ Donor?*, 13 J. HEALTH PSYCHOL. 644 (2008).

[121] Lillie D. Williamson et al., *African-Americans' Perceptions of Organ Donation: 'Simply Boils Down to Mistrust!'*, 45 J. APPLIED COMMUN. RES. 199, 200 (2017) (citing 2013 Gallup survey results).

[122] Lillie D. Williamson et al., *A Qualitative Examination of African Americans' Organ Donation-Related Medical Mistrust Beliefs*, 30 HOW. J. COMM. 430 (2019).

[123] Williamson et al., *supra* note 121.

[124] CHIP JONES, THE ORGAN THIEVES: THE SHOCKING STORY OF THE FIRST HEART TRANSPLANT IN THE SEGREGATED SOUTH (2020).

[125] Michele Goodwin, *Rethinking Legislative Consent Law?*, 5 DEPAUL J. HEALTH CARE L. 257 (2002).

[126] Williamson et al., *supra* note 121.

selling organs from Black bodies so that White patients can live parallel the nineteenth-century "brisk trade in dead black people"[127] for dissection by White medical students.

Finally, suspicions specific to organ donation exist in the context of rampant health disparities experienced by Black Americans. After delving into the history, data, and mythology around organ donation by Black people, journalist Patia Braithwaite summed up her thinking: "I'm asked to donate to an organ registry that might exclude me. I'm asked to participate in a healthcare system that is five times more likely to amputate my limb, or deny me pain medication given to white Americans. It is hard to understand why I should give the gift of my organs when, while alive, I am systematically denied resources and opportunities that could prolong and improve my quality of life."[128]

4.5 CONCLUSION

"Trust life, and it will teach you, in joy and sorrow, all you need to know."[129] James Baldwin's advice recognizes that lived experience is a trusted teacher – more trusted than professions that assume trust as their due. Lessons that Black Americans and disabled Americans have learned from their lived experiences with the medical profession – both historically and currently – influence their thinking and choices. This chapter has sought to explain the way lessons of untrustworthiness resonate, particularly for choices about how life ends. Increasingly, health care providers and systems are recognizing that the trust deficit they face with Black and disabled patients is the result of systemic racism and ableism. The failing lies within them, not with their mistrustful patients; the prescription is thus fitting: "Physician, heal thyself."

---

[127] Angela Saini, Superior: The Return of Race Science 30 (2019).

[128] Patia Braithwaite, *Why Black People Don't Want to Donate Their Organs*, VICE (Mar. 29, 2017), https://www.vice.com/en/article/mgd584/why-black-people-dont-want-to-donate-their-organs.

[129] James Baldwin, The White Man's Guilt, in James Baldwin: Collected Essays 727 (1998).

5

Maligned Mothers

5.1 MOTHERHOOD MYTHS

5.1.1 *Idealized Mothers*

Motherhood is often idealized. The dominant imagination admires idealized mothers for being loving, self-sacrificing, and nurturing. They are wise in discerning their children's needs and supportive and generous in meeting them. Idealized mothers are strong and sensible, but always stand ready to offer a warm embrace. Television viewers may recognize the idealized mother in the iconic June Cleaver, whether they watched *Leave It to Beaver* in its original run during the 1950s and 1960s or in reruns.[1] This traditional ideal is firmly grounded in twentieth century, middle-class, White, heterosexual norms of domestic motherhood.[2] The ideal of good motherhood has evolved to admit the possibility that women who work outside the home might qualify as good mothers. But recent years have seen a resurgence of the traditional ideal of intensive mothering (which expects mothers to focus their energy and resources on child-rearing) and even competitive mothering (which describes antagonism between different approaches to mothering, often displayed in blogs or social media).[3]

Critiquing idealized motherhood is easy. Feminists like Nancy Chodorow and Adrienne Rich have theorized idealized motherhood as a patriarchal mechanism for

---

[1] Mark Memmott, *In the Hall of Fame for TV Moms, Where Does 'June Cleaver' Rank?*, NPR (Oct. 17, 2010), https://www.npr.org/sections/thetwo-way/2010/10/17/130625402/great-tv-moms.

[2] Lisa C. Ikemoto, *The Code of Perfect Pregnancy: At the Intersection of the Ideology of Motherhood, the Practice of Defaulting to Science, and the Interventionist Mindset of Law*, 53 OHIO ST. L.J. 1205, 1210 (1992).

[3] Jenna Abetz & Julia Moore, *"Welcome to the Mommy Wars, Ladies": Making Sense of the Ideology of Combative Mothering in Mommy Blogs*, 11 COMMUNICATION, CULTURE & CRITIQUE 265 (2018).

limiting women's participation in public life and their political power.[4] Valorizing women *as mothers* ties their ability to achieve status to their reproductive capacity. Properly performed, motherhood surrenders to men the field of public life. So understood, the myth of ideal motherhood historically has served to subordinate women.

The mythology of idealized motherhood also entails assumptions about class, sexual orientation, ability, and race. Performing ideal motherhood requires either independent wealth, financial support from a bread-winning partner, or the ability to go without sleep to both tend to children and earn money. Its empirical divergence from the lives of most actual mothers – reflecting neither their struggles nor the richness of their experiences in having and raising children – suggests that the ideal is largely a fiction.[5] The myth bears no resemblance to low-income mothers raising their children without support from another parent; their need to feed, clothe, and shelter their children may require working multiple jobs and rarely seeing their children.[6] The myth is utterly foreign to a woman who faces eviction with her children and has nowhere secure to go.[7] The myth likely seems fantastical to a mother whose disability requires her reliance on others for support in performing daily activities, the very type of support she is supposed to give her children, according to the ideal.

Numerous institutions and actors play roles in sustaining the myth of ideal motherhood. Lawmakers, prosecutors, the child welfare system, and popular media all figure in. So do medicine and the health care system. Most women who become mothers go through pregnancy and childbirth, processes that have become intensely medicalized in American culture. Medicalization risks dehumanizing and wresting agency from women[8] and may have worse effects for Black women and disabled women. Cultural stereotypes depict them as inadequate or even malign mothers, deviating radically from the mythological ideal. By infecting health care providers' views, those stereotypes have created barriers to bearing children for Black women and disabled women.

When a woman wishes to become a mother, the effects of gender's intersection with race or disability or both can present challenges. (Though my focus is race and disability, gender's intersection with immigrant status, identification as LGBTQ,

---

[4] NANCY CHODOROW, THE REPRODUCTION OF MOTHERING (1978); ADRIENNE RICH, OF WOMAN BORN: MOTHERHOOD AS EXPERIENCE AND INSTITUTION (1976).

[5] Ikemoto, *supra* note 2, at 1304–05.

[6] In her memoir, Patrisse Cullors-Khan (one of the founders of Black Lives Matters) describes how rarely she saw her mother on weekdays because of her mother's multiple jobs. PATRISSE CULLORS-KHAN & ASHE BANDELE, WHEN THEY CALL YOU A TERRORIST: A BLACK LIVES MATTER MEMOIR (2018).

[7] See MATTHEW DESMOND, EVICTED: POVERTY AND PROFIT IN THE AMERICAN CITY (2016).

[8] REBECCA KUKLA & KATHERINE WAYNE, Pregnancy, Birth, and Medicine, STANFORD ENCYCLOPEDIA OF PHILOSOPHY (Edward N. Zalta ed., Spring 2018 ed.), https://plato.stanford .edu/archives/spr2018/entries/ethics-pregnancy.

and other marginalized identities can also create challenges.) The practice and politics of motherhood presents an intersectional roller derby of sorts, where multiple aspects of a woman's identity collide repeatedly. As the realities of a woman's life diverge from White, nondisabled, and other ideals, her path to motherhood may become increasingly difficult.[9] She may face barriers to having children, including disproportionate medical or legal threats if she becomes pregnant. This chapter examines barriers (historical and contemporary) that Black women and disabled women have faced.

5.1.2 *Stereotyped Mothers*

Just as the mythic "good mother" reflects dominant cultural ideals, stereotypes about women with disabilities and Black women distance them from those ideals. At first glance, common stereotypes of Black women appear diametrically opposed to those of women with disabilities. But these stereotypes lead to a common destination, even as they travel from different directions: Black women and disabled women are commonly supposed to be bad mothers.

So what are these stereotypes? Women with disabilities – particularly those with physical disabilities – are often viewed as asexual and unsuitable for motherhood. Such views generate assumptions that disabled women are unable or unlikely to reproduce.[10] While the dominant culture views nondisabled woman as deviant if they fail to reproduce, it views women with disabilities as deviant if they do. Health professionals entertain this fallacy as well. They too often assume that having a disability overwhelms a woman's interest in sex or in becoming a mother.[11] (Or they may believe a contrary stereotype, specific to women with cognitive disabilities, that they are sexually uninhibited and aggressive.[12] Whether viewed as undersexed or oversexed, disabled women are commonly believed to miss the Goldilockean "just right" ideal.) Judgments that women with physical, mental, or intellectual disabilities are unlikely mothers are belied by estimates that more than 160,000 women with physical disabilities become pregnant annually[13] in the US and by findings that

---

[9] Ikemoto, *supra* note 2, at 1305.

[10] See Mary Ann McColl et al., *Physician Experiences Providing Primary Care to People with Disabilities*, 4 HEALTHCARE POL'Y e129 (2008); Lisa Iezzoni et al., *"How Did That Happen?" Public Responses to Women with Mobility Disability during Pregnancy*, 8 DISABILITY & HEALTH 380 (2017); LESLIE FRANCIS ET AL., Women with Disabilities: Ethics of Access and Accommodation for Infertility *Care*, in ETHICAL ISSUES IN WOMEN'S HEALTHCARE: PRACTICE & POLICY (Lori d'Agincourt-Canning & Carolyn Ells, eds., 2019).

[11] FRANCIS ET AL., *supra* note 10.

[12] MICHAEL L. PERLIN & ALLISON J. LYNCH, SEXUALITY, DISABILITY, AND THE LAW: BEYOND THE LAST FRONTIER (2016).

[13] FRANCIS ET AL., *supra* note 10.

disabled women are just as likely as nondisabled women to wish to and plan to have children.[14]

By contrast, common stereotypes of Black women include hypersexuality and hyperfecundity. One recent study surveyed undergraduate students to examine stereotypes of Black American women and found that various caricatures of Black womanhood, including the "jezebel" and the "welfare queen," remain strong.[15] The "jezebel" stereotype, which predates Emancipation, depicts Black women as "immoral, sexually promiscuous, and sexually available." Of more recent vintage, the "welfare queen" stereotype conjures the image of a single, poor Black woman who has baby after baby to increase her welfare benefits.[16] Conservative policy-makers during the Reagan era repeatedly invoked the welfare queen stereotype to build public support for cutting welfare programs.

Despite their differences, these stereotypes of disabled women and Black women contribute in startlingly similar ways to impediments to childbearing. Beliefs about the inadequacy of Black mothers and disabled mothers help justify numerous policies constraining the ability of the women in both groups to become mothers in the first place.

5.2 EUGENIC ROOTS OF DEVALUED MOTHERHOOD

These stereotypes grow from deep historical roots, particularly for Black women. For enslavers, the productive value of Black African women lay not simply, or even primarily, in their capacity to toil. Instead, their ability to reproduce, creating new chattels, was of critical value. Especially after the international slave trade ended, an enslaved woman's capacity to produce offspring enriched her enslaver. Dorothy Roberts explains that when pregnant enslaved women were punished, they were made to lie prone on the ground, with their bellies (containing valuable assets) protectively cradled in a trench while their backs were scourged.[17] After Emancipation made trafficking in Black children illegal, the dominant White culture no longer viewed Black women's reproductive capacity as an asset. Instead, by the early twentieth century, it viewed Black women's fertility as a liability, feeding into the eugenics movement. The similarities in eugenics-era controls on disabled women's and Black women's reproduction foreshadow modern-day child-bearing constraints experienced by those groups.

---

[14] Shandra et al., *Planning for Motherhood: Fertility Attitudes, Desires and Intentions among Women with Disabilities*, 46 PERSPECTIVES ON SEXUAL & REPRODUCTIVE HEALTH 203 (2014).

[15] Lisa Rosenthal & Marci Lobel, *Stereotypes of Black American Women Related to Sexuality and Motherhood*, 40 PSYCHOLOGY OF WOMEN Q. 414 (2016). The study involved undergraduates from a northeastern US university.

[16] *Id.*

[17] DOROTHY ROBERTS, KILLING THE BLACK BODY: RACE, REPRODUCTION, AND THE MEANING OF LIBERTY 39–40 (2d ed. 2017).

5.2.1 *Eugenicists' Premises*

The guiding principle of the eugenics movement was to improve society by sorting people into categories of "superior" and "inferior" stock, encouraging people of superior stock to reproduce more, and limiting reproduction by people of inferior stock. This principle claimed a supposedly scientific basis in genealogical studies from "hereditary science" of the inheritable nature of traits such as poverty, criminal conduct, laziness, feeble-mindedness, and sexual immorality; those studies found those traits clustering in poor families.[18] Mainstream scientists and public figures alike endorsed the beliefs that most human traits passed from one generation to the next as a matter of genetic heredity[19] and that they could improve the human race by urging the "'better classes' to mate and breed liberally" while intervening to curtail the fertility of those on the lower rungs of society.[20] In short, they sought to accelerate a process they viewed as "natural selection."

Eugenicists' rhetoric about promoting public health and alleviating social ills cloaked a desire to limit public responsibility for addressing those ills. Progressives who advocated for eugenics saw it as a way "to delegate the control of social welfare programs to a professionally trained class of experts."[21] Those experts' preferred scientific theories, however, exploited theories of biological racial difference relying on heritable inferiority and superiority.[22] Eugenics "helped transform the familiar discourses of bigotry and nativism into biological 'fact.'"[23] By offering an ostensibly scientific justification for preventing dilution of the White race, the emerging movement appealed to Whites who felt threatened by increasing immigration and a Black birth rate exceeding their own.[24]

5.2.2 *Compulsory Sterilization Laws*

These theories bore fruit in state and federal laws designed to prevent the replenishment of "inferior stock." Purportedly as a way to address social problems like poverty, illiteracy, and unemployment, states enacted laws targeting persons identified as bearers of unhealthy, dangerous, and societally expensive traits, seeking to cut off the

---

[18] Paul A. Lombardo, Three Generations, No Imbeciles: Eugenics, The Supreme Court, and Buck v. Bell 8–9 (2008).

[19] Judith Daar, The New Eugenics: Selective Breeding in an Era of Reproductive Technologies 33 (2017).

[20] Lombardo, *supra* note 18, at 7.

[21] *Id.* at 17.

[22] Roberts, *supra* note 17, at 61.

[23] Laura Appleman, *Deviancy, Dependency, and Disability: The Forgotten History of Eugenics and Mass Incarceration*, 68 Duke L.J. 417, 441 (2018).

[24] Osagie K. Obasogie, *More than Love: Eugenics and the Future of Loving v. Virginia*, 86 Fordham L. Rev. 2795, 2797–98 (2018).

propagation of degenerate lines.[25] The most notorious examples of these laws authorized compulsory surgical sterilization of persons deemed "defective." A majority of states passed such laws, resulting in the surgical sterilization of approximately 65,000 people in the US between 1907 and 1979.[26] States also adopted measures segregating "defective" persons in custodial colonies, away from mainstream society.[27] A leading eugenicist defined "the socially inadequate classes" capaciously to include persons who were (using his terms) feeble-minded, insane, epileptic, diseased, blind, deaf, deformed, and crippled.[28] Thus, people who had (or were thought to have) some kind of disability were prime targets for involuntary sterilizations.

Carrie Buck, a poor White teenager in Virginia who became pregnant after being raped, has come to represent compelled eugenic sterilizations. Although historical research has revealed no evidence that Carrie Buck had any intellectual impairment, she was identified as being feeble-minded, consigned to the Virginia Colony for Epileptics and Feeble-Minded, and surgically sterilized without her consent.[29] Carrie Buck's tragedy, of being physically invaded and robbed of her ability to have children, was personal. It is also emblematic of how powerful actors can misattribute intellectual disability to certain groups of people as a mechanism of social control and oppression. More broadly, Carry Buck's violation has resounded for nearly a century, in the words of Supreme Court Justice Oliver Wendell Holmes, Jr. In rejecting a challenge to Virginia's Eugenical Sterilization Law of 1924, Justice Holmes' opinion in *Buck v. Bell*[30] endorsed state-compelled sterilizations as pro-social, public health measures. His opinion's indelible conclusion still echoes: "Three generations of imbeciles are enough."

5.2.3 *Preventing the Dilution of Whiteness*

American eugenicists saw threats wherever "unfit" people multiplied and threatened to overwhelm the society of "superior" people. Their conception of "unfitness" was expansive, extending to race. In addition to attempting to prevent hereditary transmission of impairment or degenerate conduct, eugenic policies sought to prevent corruption of the White race by darker-skinned immigrants. As states passed laws permitting involuntary sterilizations, Congress passed the 1924 Immigration Restriction Act. Believing that immigrants from Southern and Eastern Europe were more fertile than Americans, but of inferior stock, lawmakers acted to stem the

---

[25] Seema Mohapatra, *Politically Correct Eugenics*, 12 FIU L. Rev. 51, 54 (2016).

[26] Lombardo, *supra* note 18, at 293–94. Daar, *supra* note 19, at 42.

[27] Daar, *supra* note 19, at 43.

[28] *Id.* at 43, quoting from Harry Laughlin, The Legal Status of Eugenical Sterilization 65 (1907).

[29] Lombardo, *supra* note 18.

[30] Buck v. Bell, 274 U.S. 200 (1927).

"rising tide of defective germ plasm."[31] President Calvin Coolidge's statement supporting the law couldn't be clearer: "America must be kept American [because] biological laws show . . . that Nordics deteriorate when mixed with other races."[32]

By supplying a purported public health justification, the White racial superiority thread of the eugenics movement breathed new life into state efforts to prevent racial mixing. Laws prohibiting interracial marriage traced their origins to the colonial period. Some states repealed their bans after Emancipation, only to enact new ones during the eugenics movement, thus medicalizing what had been purely racist laws.[33] In the mid-1920s a majority of states had such laws on their books. They were part of Jim Crow's regime of legally enforced separation, but they also advanced eugenic ends by prohibiting interracial mating to keep "superior" White stock unsullied.[34]

Despite professing public health rationales, both compulsory sterilization laws and antimiscegenation laws embodied social prejudices and sought to keep the "fittest" (namely nondisabled Whites) numerically, socially, and politically dominant. These laws expressed potent messages. They associated poverty with biological inferiority, degeneracy, and immorality.[35] By setting up disabled people and non-White people as morally degraded, they justified marital segregation of some people and even surgical invasion of their bodies. They dehumanized the very human desire to have children and form a family, instead treating human reproduction by Black and disabled people purely instrumentally. Legal scholars Michele Goodwin and Erwin Chemerinsky put it poignantly: "The state tilled women's and girls' bodies like a farmer clears the land, moving offending species in order to avoid their recurrence. In this case, snipping the Fallopian tubes of little girls was taken as lightly as pruning weeds."[36] Americans' ardor for overtly eugenic measures appeared to cool after World War II and the exposure of the Nazis' eugenically justified program of mass murder, but eugenic thinking was never entirely uprooted from American political and social thinking. Beliefs that for the 'benefit' of society women from some groups should not reproduce, have remained remarkably hardy and influential.

The legal landscape is different today. Laws criminalizing interracial marriage or compelling involuntary sterilization of disabled women have been declared unconstitutional or repealed. But even without legal mandates, Black women and disabled

---

[31] Paul A. Lombardo, *Medicine, Eugenics, and the Supreme Court: From Coercive Sterilization to Reproductive Freedom*, 13 J. CONTEMP. HEALTH L. & POL'Y 1, 5 (1996).

[32] DAAR, *supra* note 19, at 36, quoting DANIEL J. KEVLES, IN THE NAME OF EUGENICS 97 (1985).

[33] *Id.* at 38.

[34] Obasogie, *supra* note 24; cf. Paul A. Lombardo, *Miscegenation, Eugenics, and Racism: Historical Footnotes to Loving v. Virginia*, 21 U.C. DAVIS L. REV. 421 (1988).

[35] MICHAEL B. KATZ, The Biological Inferiority of the Undeserving Poor, in BEYOND BIOETHICS: TOWARD A NEW BIOPOLITICS (Osagie I. Obasogie & March Darnovsky eds., 2018).

[36] Michele Goodwin & Erwin Chemerinsky, *Pregnancy, Poverty, and the State*, 127 YALE L.J. 1270, 1316 (2018).

women have encountered policies and practices – by states and private actors – that have limited their reproduction, either purposefully or by effect. Justifications for these constraints often invoke broader social goals, signaling that these women's procreative freedoms are subordinated to the majority's beliefs about its own welfare. This chapter focuses on three types of constraint: bodily interference with women's fertility; policies that limit reproduction by segregating women from sexual partners; and practices limiting access to assisted reproductive technology.

5.3 BIOLOGICAL INTERFERENCE WITH WOMEN'S FERTILITY

5.3.1 *Sterilizing Women and Girls without Their Consent*

5.3.1.1 Sterilization for Disabled Women and Girls

The Supreme Court has not overruled *Buck v. Bell*. Nor has it directly addressed the rights of intellectually disabled women regarding fertility, bodily integrity, or their reproductive futures. This silence leaves state courts and legislatures to address these questions, with varied answers. The law sometimes permits family members or guardians to choose surgical sterilization for an intellectually disabled woman. Typically, states require judicial involvement if a third party seeks sterilization for an intellectually disabled woman or girl. Courts presented with sterilization requests may establish procedural protections like appointment of a guardian ad litem to represent the female's interest. They may also apply substantive criteria, like requiring the judge to find that sterilization is in her "best interests" or is the "least restrictive alternative" for preventing pregnancy.[37] The bottom line, though, is that women with intellectual disabilities can still be sterilized without giving consent. As recently as 2012, the National Council on Disability reported that eleven states still had statutes permitting some form of involuntary sterilization for persons.[38]

Petitions by family members seeking judicial authorization of sterilization for a disabled daughter or sister often cite concerns about her inability to provide appropriate care for a child. In addition, self-interest may motivate family members. In one case, parents of a 6-year-old girl named Ashley subjected their daughter, who had profound intellectual and developmental disabilities, to a hysterectomy, a double mastectomy, and high doses of estrogen meant to stunt her growth. The parents justified these invasive interventions – none of which was medically necessary – as enabling them to care for Ashley at home as they aged. Physicians at the

---

[37] MARTHA A. FIELD & VALERIE A. SANCHEZ, EQUAL TREATMENT FOR PEOPLE WITH MENTAL RETARDATION: HAVING AND RAISING CHILDREN 15 (1999); Elizabeth S. Scott, *Sterilization of Mentally Retarded Persons: Reproductive Rights and Family Privacy*, 1986 DUKE L.J. 806 (1986).

[38] NATIONAL COUNCIL ON DISABILITY, ROCKING THE CRADLE: ENSURING THE RIGHTS OF PARENTS WITH DISABILITIES AND THEIR CHILDREN 40 (2012).

Children's Hospital of the University of Washington performed those interventions without seeking court authorization.[39] Once publicized, Ashley's case generated significant criticism from disability rights advocates and an investigation into the hospital's failure to seek judicial involvement. Some commentators expressed support for the parents' prerogative, and the case caught the attention of parents of other disabled children. Evidence indicates that severely disabled children have undergone similar interventions in the US and abroad.[40] Despite professions by parents (like Ashley's) of a sincere belief that these interventions are best for their daughters, I find them troubling. For one thing, parents often justify sterilization in part based on fear that sexual abuse might produce a pregnancy. Given high rates of sexual abuse against disabled people this fear is rational, but it demonstrates how society's failure to provide sufficient protections for intellectually disabled women shapes parents' choices. Moreover, pursuit of these invasive and extreme interventions may sometimes elevate familial convenience in caretaking over their disabled relative's bodily integrity.[41]

Laws requiring judicial involvement do not guarantee robust protection of a disabled person's reproductive liberty, bodily integrity, and best interests. In some cases (like Ashley's), medical providers and family members may simply flout those requirements, proceeding without involving the courts. In other cases, judges who consider the petitions may be easily persuaded that sterilization is a sensible way to protect against unwanted pregnancies. Influenced by stereotypes of intellectually disabled women as sexually promiscuous, judges may sympathize with family members, without seriously considering less invasive alternatives and critically assessing sterilization's impact on the disabled person, who should properly be the center of inquiry.[42]

5.3.1.2 Sterilization of Black Women and Girls

The Relfs were a Black family living in Montgomery, Alabama, in the early 1970s. A social services organization assisted Mr. and Mrs. Relf and their three adolescent daughters in moving into public housing when they moved to Montgomery; it also

---

[39] Alicia Ouellette, *Growth Attenuation, Parental Choice and the Rights of Disabled Children: Lessons from the Ashley X Case*, 8 Hous. J. Health L. & Pol'y 207 (2008).

[40] Genevieve Field, *Should Parent of Children with Severe Disabilities Be Allowed to Stop Their Growth?*, N.Y. Times, Mar. 22, 2016.

[41] Patricia J. Williams, *Babies, Bodies and Buyers*, 33 Colum. J. Gender & L. 11 (2016).

[42] Lombardo, *supra* note 18, at 267–68. Some states are more stringent in their oversight when parents seek the sterilization of minor girls with intellectual disabilities, but according to Field and Sanchez, "[C]ourts frequently approve sterilizations of minors and even twelve-year-olds." Field & Sanchez, *supra* note 37, at 107. The potential for judicial biases and fragility of judicial protections are also evident in cases where courts have authorized abortions for cognitively disabled women who, though deemed legally incompetent to make their own decisions, had expressed their desire not to have an abortion. See Mary Crossley, *Reproducing Dignity: Race, Disability, and Reproductive Controls*, 54 U.C. Davis L. Rev. 195, 220–21 (2020).

arranged for the involuntary sterilization of two of their daughters. Minnie Lee and Mary Alice Relf were 14 and 12 years old, respectively, when they along with their mother were picked up by a family planning nurse employed by the organization. The nurse told the Relfs she was taking them for "some shots," but they were taken to the hospital. Mrs. Relf, who was illiterate, signed an "X" to a consent form she could not read. It was a consent form for surgical sterilization, but no one informed Mrs. Relf that the girls were to be sterilized. Their older sister, Katie, avoided that fate only by locking herself in her bedroom to avoid going with the nurse.[43]

Katie, Minnie Lee, and Mary Alice Relf were not unique, but they were unusual because their story is known. They were the lead plaintiffs in a 1973 federal class-action lawsuit alleging that the federal government, by providing funding for surgical sterilizations without adequate protections for patient autonomy, was funding involuntary sterilizations. The trial court found that Minnie Lee and Mary Alice were among 100,000 to 150,000 poor women that programs funded by the federal government sterilized *each year*.[44] According to one study, almost half of the women sterilized were Black.[45]

Eugenics-era reasoning persisted well past World War II, as demonstrated by doctors' and legislators' endorsement of sterilizing poor women to limit spending for public assistance. Dorothy Roberts' book, *Killing the Black Body: Race, Reproduction, and the Meaning of Liberty*, unflinchingly details how Black women have been prevented from bearing children.[46] Nonconsensual sterilizations were shockingly common from the 1940s through the 1970s. Lingering eugenic sentiments were clearest in the sterilization of women committed to state institutions. But such sentiments also lurked behind "Mississippi appendectomies," the name Black civil rights activist Fannie Lou Hamer gave to nonconsensual hysterectomies that doctors performed on poor women (often, but not always, Black) who had just given birth or were receiving other medical care.[47] Some doctors openly embraced a eugenic justification for intervening to prevent recipients of public assistance from further burdening society. In one South Carolina county, mothers receiving welfare for their children faced a difficult "choice" if they became pregnant again. The sole obstetrician in the county who took patients covered by Medicaid (the public program that covers many low-income pregnant women) would deliver their baby only if the women "agreed" to being sterilized following the delivery.[48] These

---

[43] LISA C. IKEMOTO, Infertile by Force and Federal Complicity: The Story of Relf v. Weinberger, in WOMEN AND THE LAW STORIES (Elizabeth M. Schneider & Stephanie M. Wildman eds., 2011).

[44] Relf v. Weinberger, 372 F. Supp. 1196, 1199 (D.D.C. 1974), vacated, Relf v. Weinberger, 565 F.2d 722 (D.C. Cir. 1977).

[45] DOROTHY ROBERTS, KILLING THE BLACK BODY: RACE, REPRODUCTION, AND THE MEANING OF LIBERTY 93 (2d ed. 2017).

[46] *Id.* at 61.

[47] ROBERTS, supra note 17, at 93.

[48] *Id.* at 92.

"vigilante population control"[49] sterilizations were not secret or taboo. Legislators in about a half-dozen states proposed laws permitting the compulsory sterilization of unmarried welfare recipients if they gave birth.[50]

The Relfs' lawsuit led to regulations enhancing procedural requirements for sterilizations provided through federally funded programs, but their effectiveness in ending abusive sterilizations of poor women of color has been unclear. Some women freely choose sterilization as an effective birth control method. A 2015 study, though, found Black women undergoing sterilization at rates higher than White women (36 percent as compared to 30 percent).[51] Given the history of abusive sterilization practices, the higher rate of sterilizations among Black women merits further scrutiny.[52]

5.3.2 *Coercive Contraception*

5.3.2.1 Black Women and Constrained Contraceptive Choices

Sterilizations without voluntary consent provide the starkest reminders of our eugenic past, but nonpermanent contraception used without interruption has the same effect. "Encouraging" Black women and girls to use long-acting reversible contraception (LARC) raises concerns about coerced contraception. Research into how women are counseled about IUDs (one form of LARC) has found that providers are more likely to recommend IUDs to low-income Black and Latina women than to low-income White women.[53] Having access to a highly effective and long-acting contraceptive device enhances a woman's ability to plan her future by controlling her fertility. But when reversibility depends on going to a doctor, as is the case with IUDs and other forms of LARC, control may shift out of the woman's hands. What are we to make of providers' greater likelihood of recommending IUDs to low-income Black women than low-income White women? Widening our frame helps put that question in context.

The claim that the early birth control movement, with Margaret Sanger at its helm, was a eugenic effort to stem Black population growth has often been repeated. Dorothy Roberts paints a more complicated picture of Sanger's own motives, concluding that Sanger attributed social problems to poor people having too many children, but *not* to any innate racial or genetic inferiority. Roberts agrees, however,

---

[49] Ikemoto, *supra* note 43, at 197.
[50] ROBERTS, *supra* note 17, at 94.
[51] Karina M. Schreffler et al., *Surgical Sterilization, Regret, and Race: Contemporary Patterns*, 50 SOC. SCI. RESEARCH 31 (2015).
[52] ROBERTS, *supra* note 17, at 97.
[53] Christine Dehlendorf & Kelsey Holt, *The Dangerous Rise of the IUD as Poverty Cure*, N.Y. TIMES (Jan. 2, 2019), https://www.nytimes.com/2019/01/02/opinion/iud-implants-contraception-poverty.html.

that early efforts to expand birth control in Black communities facilitated eugenicists' goals.[54] More recent examples of coerced contraception that devalues Black
women's reproductive autonomy are easy to find. Darlene Johnson's experience
offers an example. In 1991, Johnson, a poor, Black woman with four children, was
charged with child abuse, and she agreed to a plea deal that included one year in jail
and a three-year term of probation. The judge in the case, thinking it would be
better for her not to have more children, attached a condition of his own: Johnson
had to agree to be implanted with Norplant. At the time, Norplant (a form of LARC
that is surgically implanted in a woman's arm) was newly approved by the FDA.
What some hailed as innovative sentencing many condemned as coercive. Rachael
Pine of the ACLU's Reproductive Freedom project called the threat of a longer
prison term a "block of cement over [Johnson's] head," making her plea deal
unavoidably coercive.[55]

Johnson's case is not unique, nor is it simply a relic of enthusiasm for a new
technology during a less enlightened time. In 2017, a Tennessee judge offered
inmates a 30-day sentence reduction in return for being implanted with LARC
(for women) or undergoing a vasectomy (for men).[56] Judges have tended to "pre-
scribe" contraception in cases involving low-income minority women,[57] forcing
those defendants to choose between physical freedom and reproductive freedom.
These cases reflect judges' belief that curtailing people's fertility is a suitable way to
address social issues. Using contraception as a sentencing tool also revitalizes the
eugenic dogma tying criminality to biological inferiority. Bioethicist George Annas
reflected on Darlene Johnson's case: "A lot of people have given up on social policy,
on taking care of poor women, and there is an increasing undercurrent that since we
don't really know what to do about crack addicts, people with AIDS and child
abusers, we should stop them from having kids."[58]

The thinking that society would be better off if irresponsible women (often
imagined as dark skinned) would stop having babies they could not afford has
appeared repeatedly in both mainstream media and health publications. Almost as
soon as the FDA approved Norplant in 1990, a *Philadelphia Inquirer* editorial
suggested that offering welfare recipients financial incentives to use the implant
might lower the number of "Black children living in poverty" and "reduce the
underclass."[59] The ensuing firestorm prompted a quick apology; today proponents of

---

[54] ROBERTS, *supra* note 17, at 72–81.
[55] Tamar Lewin, *Implanted Birth Control Device Renews Debate over Forced Contraception*, N.Y.
TIMES, Jan. 10, 1991.
[56] Kalhan Rosenblatt, *Judge Offers Inmates Reduced Sentences in Exchange for Vasectomy*, NBC
NEWS (July 21, 2017), https://www.nbcnews.com/news/us-news/judge-offers-inmates-reduced-
sentences-exchange-vasectomy-n785256.
[57] Dorothy E. Roberts, *Crime, Race, and Reproduction*, 67 TULANE L. REV. 1945, 1968 (1993).
[58] Lewin, *supra* note 55.
[59] ROBERTS, *supra* note 17, at 106 (quoting *Poverty and Norplant – Can Contraception Reduce the
Underclass*, PHILA. INQUIRER, Dec. 12, 1990, at A18).

the basic idea are likely to choose their words more carefully. Public health experts, for example, may begin by noting that using LARC could help "at risk" populations like adolescent women of color by preventing unwanted pregnancies, but also point to reducing Medicaid and welfare spending as benefits.[60] A 2014 headline on *Forbes'* website made no attempt at subtlety: "Can the IUD Prevent Poverty, Save Taxpayers Billions?"[61]

Praise for the social benefits of expanded LARC usage typically ignores an issue that girls and women who have been implanted are all too aware of. A woman who experiences bothersome side effects or decides she would prefer another form of contraception or would like to become pregnant may have a difficult time finding and paying a doctor to remove the implant. Women have reported that some clinicians are reluctant to remove LARC methods, and some state Medicaid programs have restricted payment for removals.[62] To be fair, some providers, sensitive to the history of coercive controls on Black women's reproduction, emphasize the proper goal of contraceptive counseling is to empower girls and women.[63] But providers, public health experts, and policy makers do not consistently address linked histories of procreative control and Black women's lingering suspicion that choosing LARC today could limit their choices tomorrow

5.3.2.2 Contraception for Disabled Women

Do contemporary contraceptive practices of disabled women raise similar concerns about coercion and lingering eugenic sentiments? Curiously, what little we know on the topic indicates that disabled women are *less* likely than nondisabled women to use highly or moderately effective forms of nonpermanent contraception (including LARC) and *more* likely to use less effective forms or none at all. These findings are for women with physical disabilities and sensory disabilities (like blindness and deafness) as well as women with cognitive or developmental disabilities.[64] By

---

[60] See Aline C. Gubrium et al., *Realizing Reproductive Health Equity Needs More than Long-Acting Reversible Contraception (LARC)*, 106 AM. J. PUB. HEALTH 18 (2016) (responding to J.L. Northridge & S. Coupey, *Realizing Reproductive Health Equity for Adolescents and Young Adults*, 105 AM. J. PUB. HEALTH 1285 (2015)). See, e.g., Caitlin Parks & Jeffrey F. Peipert, *Eliminating Health Disparities in Unintended Pregnancy with Long-Acting Reversible Contraception (LARC)*, 214 AM. J. OBSTETRICS & GYNECOLOGY 681 (2017).

[61] Carrie Sheffield, *Can the IUD Prevent Poverty, Save Taxpayers Billions?*, FORBES (Oct. 5, 2014), https://www.forbes.com/sites/carriesheffield/2014/10/05/can-the-iud-prevent-poverty-save-taxpay ers-billions/#74f7750c3291.

[62] Julia Strasser et al., *Access to Removal of Long-Acting Reversible Contraceptive Methods Is an Essential Component of High-Quality Contraceptive Care*, 27 WOMEN'S HEALTH ISSUES 253 (2017).

[63] See Christine Dehlendorf & Kelsey Holt, *The Dangerous Rise of the IUD as Poverty Cure*, N.Y. TIMES, Jan. 2, 2019.

[64] See Justine Wu et al., *Use of Reversible Contraceptive Methods among U.S. Women with Physical or Sensory Disabilities*, 49 PERSP. ON SEXUAL & REPROD. HEALTH 141 (2017); Justine

contrast, disabled women undergo sterilization at disproportionately high rates; recent research shows a prevalence nearly double that of nondisabled women. Females with cognitive disabilities have especially high sterilization rates[65] and undergo the procedure at a younger age.

Painting with too broad a brush is unwise, as disabled women have diverse experiences. Childbearing constraints that women with physical or sensory disabilities encounter are likely different from those encountered by cognitively disabled women. In many cases, women in the latter group may have decisions made *for them* by family members or guardians. In an echo of eugenic sterilizations of "feeble-minded" women, third-parties' pursuit of permanent contraception (i.e., sterilization) for women with intellectual disabilities may reflect a premise that they are incapable of deciding for themselves (and certainly are incompetent to become mothers). In some cases, a woman's cognitive disability may be so profound that she would be unable to parent a child, even with supports. But (as I discuss further below) nondisabled people's thinking about parental capacity regularly fails to contemplate how disabled persons *might* parent effectively. Notwithstanding the need to avoid overgeneralizations about disabled women, a striking paradox appears between higher rates of sterilization and lower rates of using effective (but nonpermanent) contraception. Could it be that nondisabled decision makers and medical providers prioritize ensuring disabled women don't have children over providing them with support and contraceptive counseling?

5.4 ASSISTED REPRODUCTION

Infertility presents a different sort of impediment to childbearing for some women. Use of assisted reproductive technology (ART) to address that impediment represents another area where some parallels exist between Black women's and disabled women's experiences. Fertility clinics, endocrinologists, and other providers in the fertility services industry are less likely to treat Black women and disabled women than White and nondisabled women. The reasons behind these disparities aren't entirely clear but multiple causes are likely. One cited by scholars and commentators is that this industry, despite its "Brave New World" sheen, still reflects our history of eugenics. How doctors are trained, how they decide which patients to

---

Wu et al., *Provision of Moderately and Highly Effective Reversible Contraception to Insured Women with Intellectual and Developmental Disabilities*, 132 OBSTETRICS & GYNECOLOGY 565 (2018).

[65] Justine P. Wu et al., *Female Sterilization Is More Common among Women with Physical and/or Sensory Disabilities than Women without Disabilities in the United States*, 10 DISABILITY & HEALTH J. 400 (July 2017); William Mosher et al., *Contraceptive Use by Disability Status: New National Estimates from the National Survey of Family Growth*, 97 CONTRACEPTION 552 (2018); Henan Li et al., *Female Sterilization and Cognitive Disability in the United States, 2011–2015*, at 132 OBSTETRICS & GYNECOLOGY 559 (2018).

serve, and how the industry pursues profits all appear to interact with Black and disabled women's desires for pregnancy to produce disparate access to services.

5.4.1 *ART's Unavailability to Disabled Women*

Infertility is a famously difficult experience. Addressing it medically entails physical, emotional, and financial burdens for women. Being disabled adds distinctive challenges. Because adoption agencies often screen out prospective parents with disabilities, seeking medical assistance may be the only option for a disabled woman experiencing infertility.[66] But if she decides to employ assisted reproductive technologies, a disabled woman has a good chance of finding inexperienced and biased providers. Medical education has long fallen short in providing trainees with instruction about disability and clinical experiences with disabled patients. As a result, doctors, including fertility specialists, often are technically unprepared for disability-related issues and are personally uncomfortable interacting with a disabled patient. Unfamiliarity may prompt providers to avoid disabled patients, out of fear of adverse outcomes and potential liability. Many medical offices still lack accessible medical equipment, like examination tables, despite the ADA's passage more than three decades ago. And fertility services may be financially inaccessible for many women with disabilities who are insured by Medicaid, which typically does not pay for assisted reproduction services.[67]

Adding to these factors, some ART providers express misgivings about whether some disabled women should have children at all. When deciding whether and how to treat patients, some fertility specialists consider not just the (prospective) patient's health but also the welfare of a potentially resulting child. A survey of ART programs suggests some skepticism about the ability of parents who have a sensory, psychiatric, or intellectual disability to parent a child safely and appropriately.[68] Disabled people seeking fertility services often face provider refusals or discriminatory treatment, according to the National Council on Disability.[69]

Given the paucity of disability-oriented training, it is unsurprising that ART providers share common biases against disabled people as parents. Nondisabled parents readily rely on supports like daycare, assistance from family members, and tutoring to manage the demands of parenting. Doctors (and society more broadly), however, often suffer a lack of imagination regarding supports that would permit disabled people to parent successfully. This unevenness in supporting parents reflects an ableist inability (or unwillingness) to view disabled people as equally deserving of a desired family life. The lesser willingness to support disabled parents

---

[66] See NATIONAL COUNCIL ON DISABILITY, *supra* note 38, at 181–82.

[67] FRANCIS ET AL., *supra* note 10, at 8–12.

[68] Kimberly M. Mutcherson, *Disabling Dreams of Parenthood: The Fertility Industry, Anti-Discrimination, and Parents with Disabilities*, 27 L. & INEQUALITY 311, 316–17 (2009).

[69] NATIONAL COUNCIL ON DISABILITY, *supra* note 38, at 171–72.

stems from the same lineage as eugenics-era sterilizations.[70] These historical deprivations are essential context for assessing the legitimacy of denying fertility services based on assumptions about the parenting capacity of disabled women.

5.4.2 *Black Women's Limited Pursuit of ART*

Women of color experience higher rates of medical infertility than White women. Potential explanations include higher rates of medical conditions (like uterine fibroids) and environmental exposures to reproductive toxins, among others.[71] Despite this disparity, women of color are less likely to seek medical assistance for help in having a baby.[72]

As with disabled women, many factors help explain Black women's low rates of seeking fertility services. Their disproportionate reliance on Medicaid coverage (compared to White women) creates a financial barrier to access. Policy makers' unwillingness to cover treatment for infertility as part of Medicaid follows logically from disapproval of poor women reproducing. Lingering mistrust of medicine, fed by awareness of White gynecologists' exploitation of Black women, also likely plays a role.[73] Moreover, some evidence suggests a woman's race influences referrals for infertility treatment, with gynecologists associating endometriosis (which can cause infertility) with White women and not Black women. One expert explained that gynecologists are more likely to diagnose Black women's symptoms as pelvic inflammatory disease, which would not lead to an infertility work up.[74] Inaccurate diagnoses can contribute to Black women being slower to seek fertility services, and that delay helps explain why Black women who use ART have worse outcomes (including lower fertilization rates, lower pregnancy rates, and lower live birth rates).[75]

Moreover, the fertility industry has made little effort to court Black women. Research from the 2010s into the location of clinics and clinic websites supports a theory of industry targeting. From their location in affluent, predominantly White neighborhoods to online marketing that features mostly images of White babies as their "product," fertility clinics' preferred patient is not hard to discern.[76] L'Oreal

---

[70] Francis et al., *supra* note 10, at 7, 12.

[71] Daar, *supra* note 19, at 80–81.

[72] *Id.* at 82–83; Roberts, *supra* note 17, at 246–93.

[73] Vanessa N. Gamble, *Under the Shadow of Tuskegee: African Americans in Health Care*, 87 Am. J. Public Health 1773 (1997). Dierdre Cooper Owens, Medical Bondage: Race, Gender, and the Origins of American Gynecology (2017).

[74] Roberts, *supra* note 17, at 255–56.

[75] Press Release, *IVF Treatments Not as Successful in African American Women*, Am. Society for Reproductive Medicine (Oct. 8, 2018), https://www.asrm.org/news-and-publications/news-and-research/press-releases-and-bulletins/ivf-treatments-not-as-successful-in-african-american-women; see also Daar, *supra* note 19, at 82–84; see also Molly Quinn & Victor Fujimoto, *Racial and Ethnic Disparities in Assisted Reproductive Technology Access and Outcomes*, 105 Fertility & Sterility 1119, 1121 (2016).

[76] Daar, *supra* note 19, at 97–98.

Thompson Payton, a Black woman who sought treatment for infertility, describes her experience: "Literally, we are the only Black couple in the waiting room. You look at the photos of the babies on the wall and don't see any melanin anywhere, not even a speck. It takes this already isolating experience and makes it so much worse."[77] Enduring stereotypes also reappear. Black women with infertility reported feeling uncomfortable when seeking treatment because doctors made assumptions about their sexual promiscuity, weight, or ability to pay.[78] Little wonder that Black women respond accordingly. Consequently, "the profile of people most likely to use IVF is precisely the opposite of those most likely to be infertile."[79]

The racial disparity in usage of ART may have deeper cultural and historical roots as well. The stigma often attached to infertility in Black communities probably deters some women from seeking professional help.[80] Dorothy Roberts also suggests that the legacy of eugenics plays a role; she connects White couples' willingness to endure expensive and physically demanding ART regimens to the premium they attach to genetic connection to their children. The same history, she reckons, explains Black people's tendency to be "skeptical about any obsession with genes." Still, given the broader context of attempts to curtail Black women's childbearing, Roberts finds the racial disparity in ART usage troubling: "What does it mean that we live in a country in which White women disproportionately undergo expensive technologies to enable them to bear children, while Black women disproportionately undergo surgery that prevents them from being able to bear any?"[81]

5.5 INSTITUTIONAL SEGREGATION AND ABSTINENCE

So far, this chapter has examined how sterilization and contraception practices, particularly but not exclusively of medical providers, have functioned as impediments to childbearing by Black women and disabled women. The purpose of sterilization and contraception is to prevent pregnancy; their role in inequitable constraints on childbearing is thus highly salient. But less obvious mechanisms for curtailing reproduction also exist. Disabled women and Black women have been subject to policies disproportionately impeding their sexual activity and pursuit of pregnancy. I refer to policies producing disparate levels of institutionalization, a term I use broadly to encompass residence in a nursing home, psychiatric hospital, or similar setting as well as involuntary confinement in a correctional institution.

---

[77] Usha Lee McFarling, *For Black Women, the Isolation of Infertility Is Compounded by Barriers to Treatment*, STAT (Oct. 14, 2020), https://www.statnews.com/2020/10/14/for-black-women-isolation-of-infertility-compounded-by-barriers-to-treatment.

[78] *Id.*

[79] ROBERTS, *supra* note 17, at 252.

[80] McFarling, *supra* note 77.

[81] ROBERTS, *supra* note 17, at 261, 267, 285.

Women with disabilities are disproportionately found in the former, Black women in the latter. Eugenic undercurrents can be detected in both.

5.5.1 *Eugenic Undertones of Medicaid's Institutional Bias*

As already noted, disabled women are more likely than nondisabled women to have health coverage through Medicaid. This public insurance program is biased towards providing services to disabled people in institutional settings, as Chapter 6 discusses in depth. Effectively, states can choose to cover home and community-based services (HCBS) as part of their Medicaid programs, but are not legally required to. In recent decades, many states have increased their funding for services provided in community settings, consistent with disabled people's desires. But demand for accessible and affordable community-based housing still far exceeds supply. As a result, many disabled Medicaid recipients have little choice but to continue residing in institutional settings.[82]

Living in an institution can limit a disabled woman's ability to engage in sexual activity or become pregnant.[83] Women with cognitive disabilities, psychiatric disabilities, or severe physical disabilities are more likely to reside in institutions or other congregate settings (like group homes) and thus to face such limits. Doors that don't lock. Single beds in residents' rooms. Institutional arrangements like these can function as surveillance techniques and barriers to women's privacy and sexual expression. Women with intellectual disabilities have voiced frustration with their families or service agencies limiting their social activities with men and interfering with displays of physical affection.[84] High rates of sexual violence against disabled people justify some institutional measures to protect against sexual predation.[85] Attempts to prevent all sexual intimacy by disabled people living in institutional

---

[82] Mary Crossley, *Threats to Medicaid and Health Equity Intersections*, 12 ST. LOUIS U. J. HEALTH L. & POL'Y 311 (2018); Jessica Schubel, *Medicaid Is Key to Implementing Olmstead's Community Integration Requirements for People with Disabilities*, CTR. ON BUDGET & POL'Y PRIORITIES (June 22, 2018), https://www.cbpp.org/blog/medicaid-is-key-to-implementing-olm steads-community-integration-requirements-for-people-with.

[83] LAURA HERSHEY, Women with Disabilities: Health, Reproduction, and Sexuality, in 1 ROUTLEDGE INTERNATIONAL ENCYCLOPEDIA OF WOMEN: GLOBAL WOMEN'S ISSUES AND KNOWLEDGE 385 (Cheris Kramarae et al. eds., 2000).

[84] Donna J. Bernert, *Sexuality and Disability in the Lives of Women with Intellectual Disabilities*, 29 SEXUALITY & DISABILITY 129 (2010); Pierre Pariseau-Legault & Dave Holmes, *Mediated Pathways, Negotiated Identities: A Critical Phenomenological Analysis of the Experience of Sexuality in the Context of Intellectual Disability*, 22 J. RES. NURSING 599 (2017); Natalie M. Chin, *Group Homes as Sex Police and the Role of the Olmstead Integration Mandate*, 42 N.Y.U. REV. L. & SOC. CHANGE 379 (2018).

[85] Jasmine E. Harris, *Sexual Consent and Disability*, 93 N.Y.U. L. REV. 480, 497–98 (2018). For some people with disabilities, legitimate questions exist as to their ability to consent to sexual activity, so that protective measures may be needed. Rates of sexual violence against people with disabilities are much higher than against nondisabled people, and persons with intellectual disabilities are particularly likely to be victims. *Id.* at 491 & n.39.

settings, however, likely reflect beliefs that sexual activity by people with mental disabilities is taboo and immoral and stereotypes that women with physical disabilities are uninterested in sex and motherhood.[86]

Appreciating how institutional life constrains a disabled woman's ability to be sexually active reveals an unstated assumption of Medicaid's preference for institutional care: namely, that publicly funded medical and supportive services can effectively be conditioned on disabled recipients' surrendering opportunities for sexual activity and childbearing. Limiting support for independent living restricts the ability of women with disabilities to have children. Thus, Medicaid's bias implicitly dismisses and devalues disabled women's childbearing interests.

5.5.2 *Mass Incarceration's Eugenic Nature*

Institutionalization of a different ilk – mass incarceration – complicates Black women's childbearing. Discussions of mass incarceration often focus on Black men, but Black women are also disproportionately incarcerated; in 2016, they were incarcerated at twice the rate of White women. High incarceration rates translate to lower fertility rates among affected groups. Imprisonment often occurs during prime childbearing years, but sex-segregated prisons may prohibit inmates' sexual contact with visitors. Incarceration suspends a person's constitutionally protected liberty interest in childbearing. And mass incarceration may dull the family-creation desires of Black women living in the community, as they face thinned ranks of prospective Black fathers.

Thus, mass incarceration acts to constrain Black women's ability to have children, even depressing reproduction rates for Black Americans. Sociologist James Oleson argues that this effect is eugenic. "Black hyper-incarceration operates as a contemporary iteration of an earlier eugenic logic."[87] Or as Dorothy Roberts puts it: "A concern for the incarceration rate of Black men, ... without attention to the control of Black women's reproduction, will miss a critical technique of racial subordination."[88]

Viewing mass incarceration side-by-side with Medicaid's bias towards institutionalization reveals a haunting parallel: Both exist as contemporary incarnations of the eugenics-era colonies that segregated "inferior" persons to keep them from degrading the germ pool. In examining how historical policies for disabled persons shaped the growth of mass incarceration, Laura Appleman reflects: "Segregation and detention have always served to control those on the margins: [T]he poor ... minorities ... and the disabled."[89] Today, Black women and disabled women are disproportionately confined in institutions that curtail their freedom to have children.

---

[86] PERLIN & LYNCH, *supra* note 12.
[87] James C. Oleson, *The New Eugenics: Black Hyper-Incarceration and Human Abatement*, 5 SOC. SCI. 66 (2016), https://doi.org/10.3390/socsci5040066.
[88] Roberts, *supra* note 57, at 1977.
[89] Appleman, *supra* note 23, at 419.

5.6 PERILOUS PREGNANCY

5.6.1 *Medical Risks*

5.6.1.1 Excessive Maternal Mortality and Other Risks for Black Women

Of course, many Black women and disabled women become pregnant and have children. But pregnancy poses greater risks for them than it does for White, nondisabled women. These risks include heightened odds of disrespectful treatment, complications, and even death. Black women, moreover, are more likely to have their pregnancies policed, both by health professionals and law enforcement.

For much of human history, pregnancy and childbirth were death-defying acts. Just over a century ago, for every 1,000 live births in the US, 6 to 9 women died of complications relating to pregnancy or birth.[90] By the end of the twentieth century that rate had declined almost 99 percent to less than 0.1 death per 1,000 live births.[91] Even with this dramatic improvement, the US still ranks poorly on international rankings of maternal mortality, as noted in Chapter 2. In recent years, moreover, maternal mortality rates in the US have been climbing.[92] And the variation in death rates among different demographic groups of women is alarming.

Pregnant Black women face especially grave risks. A 2019 report showed a Black maternal mortality rate more than tripling the White rate, with a rate four to five times higher for Black women aged 30 or older.[93] This savage disparity persists across class and education levels, indicating that poverty and low socioeconomic status cannot alone explain it. Instead, pregnancy's exaggerated peril for Black women appears to be the product of multiple factors. Lesser access to and quality of health care likely play a role. Racial stereotyping and implicit bias in the health care system can influence the care pregnant Black women receive, a reality acknowledged by the American College of Obstetricians and Gynecologists.[94] Simply living in a racist society also appears to be a factor. The "weathering" hypothesis posits that repeated stresses from discrimination and racism contribute to Black women's poorer overall

---

[90] Centers for Disease Control and Prevention, *Achievements in Public Health, 1900–1999: Healthier Mothers and Babies*, MMWR WEEKLY, Oct. 1, 1999.

[91] *Id.*

[92] Nina Martin & Renee Montagne, *U.S. Has the Worst Rate of Maternal Deaths in the Developed World*, NPR (May 12, 2017), https://www.npr.org/2017/05/12/528098789/u-s-has-the-worst-rate-of-maternal-deaths-in-the-developed-world.

[93] Emily E. Petersen et al., *Racial/Ethnic Disparities in Pregnancy-Related Deaths – United States, 2007–2016*, 68 MORBIDITY & MORTALITY WEEKLY REP. 762 (2019), https://www.cdc.gov/mmwr/volumes/68/wr/mm6835a3.htm.

[94] Committee on Health Care for Underserved Women, *Committee Opinion No. 649, Racial and Ethnic Disparities in Obstetrics and Gynecology*, 126 OBSTETRICS & GYNECOLOGY 130 (2015).

health, which helps determine their maternal mortality rates.[95] In effect, experiencing racism repeatedly during her lifetime increases the odds a Black woman will not survive bringing new life into the world.

Being Black and pregnant exaggerates nonlethal medical risks as well. Researchers have found that during pregnancy, childbirth, and the postpartum period, Black women are more likely to report being disregarded, verbally mistreated, or subjected to nonconsensual or even violent medical interventions.[96] One Black woman reported:

> The doctor... refused to test me for an amniotic fluid leak and instead tested me for an STD test I had already received during the pregnancy. I believe his assumption that I was leaking something due to an STD rather than a pregnancy complication was due to race... I went a week leaking fluid after I had went in to get it checked out.[97]

A doula described to a researcher how, after one of her Black clients delivered her baby, "the doctor aggressively 'went in' to remove [blood] clots" as the woman screamed "Stop! Stop!"[98]

5.6.1.2 Medical Risks for Disabled Women

Do women with disabilities face similarly sobering medical risks when they become pregnant? The lack of pan-disability data collection prevents a precise answer. As with Black women, disabled women's poorer overall health may increase pregnancy-associated risks; potentially disabling chronic health conditions like hypertension or diabetes can elevate a woman's risk of pregnancy complications and maternal death.[99] In studies involving women with various disabilities, researchers have found their subjects were more likely than nondisabled women to delay prenatal care, experience pregnancy complications, give birth early, deliver by cesarean section, suffer intimate partner violence while pregnant, and suffer symptoms of postpartum

---

[95] Petersen et al., *supra* note 93; Cristina Novoa & Jamila Taylor, *Exploring African Americans' High Maternal and Infant Death Rates*, CTR. FOR AMERICAN PROGRESS (Feb. 1, 2018), https://www.americanprogress.org/issues/early-childhood/reports/2018/02/01/445576/exploring-african-americans-high-maternal-infant-death-rates.

[96] Saraswathi Vedam et al., *The Giving Voice to Mothers Study: Inequity and Mistreatment during Pregnancy and Childbirth in the United States*, 16 REPRODUCTIVE HEALTH 77 (2019); Dána-Ain Davis, *Obstetric Racism: The Racial Politics of Pregnancy, Labor, and Birthing*, 38 MEDICAL ANTHROPOLOGY 560, 569 (2018) (analyzing birth stories of Black women in the US).

[97] Vedam et al., *supra* note 96.

[98] Davis, *supra* note 96, at 560.

[99] Centers for Disease Control and Prevention, *Pregnancy Mortality Surveillance System*, CTRS. FOR DISEASE CONTROL AND PREVENTION (Oct. 10, 2019), https://www.cdc.gov/reproductive health/maternalinfanthealth/pregnancy-mortality-surveillance-system.htm. Cf. Lisa Iezzoni et al., *General Health, Health Conditions, and Current Pregnancy among U.S. Women with and without Chronic Physical Disabilities*, 7 DISABILITY & HEALTH J. 181 (2014).

depression.[100] Even without data indicating disabled women are more likely to die from pregnancy or childbirth, these disparities in receiving prenatal care, experiencing complications, and suffering physical and emotional harm demand attention.

Explanations for these disparities are layered. As noted, some chronic illnesses increase the risk of pregnancy complications. But for many disabled women, pregnancy-related risks flow from a wicked brew of social and economic stresses mixed in with medical biases and stereotypes. Doctors generally remain woefully ignorant of the health needs and risk factors associated with perinatal care for disabled women. Obstetric providers typically have received little or no training specific to caring for women with mobility or other impairments, and evidence-based guidelines for maternity care are lacking. Women with disabilities have described health providers unprepared to manage their pregnancies and deliveries. They've also described being subjected to providers' negative stereotypes about their suitability for motherhood. Little wonder that some disabled women hesitate to seek prenatal or postpartum care.[101]

5.6.2 *Legal Risks: The Criminalization of Pregnancy*

Threats to health and life are not the only hazards a pregnant woman faces. Some also risk facing criminal prosecution for alleged harm to their fetuses. The "criminalization of pregnancy" refers to prosecutors' use of criminal sanctions to punish pregnant (or formerly pregnant) people for actions viewed as harmful to their own pregnancies. It encompasses prosecutions for an array of behaviors, ranging from use of illegal drugs to failure to wear a seatbelt to alleged attempts at suicide. The common thread in these prosecutions is an expectation that a pregnant woman is responsible for ensuring her fetus's welfare – even at the cost of her own welfare or

---

[100] Justine Wu et al., *Use of Reversible Contraceptive Methods among U.S. Women with Physical or Sensory Disabilities*, 49 PERSP. ON SEXUAL & REPROD. HEALTH 141 (2017); Blair Darney, *Primary Cesarean Delivery Patterns among Women with Physical, Sensory, or Intellectual Disabilities*, 27 WOMEN'S HEALTH ISSUES 336 (May–June 2017); Monika Mitra et al., *Maternal Characteristics, Pregnancy Complications, and Adverse Birth Outcomes among Women with Disabilities*, 53 MED. CARE 1027, 1031 (Dec. 2015).

[101] Francis et al., *supra* note 10; Suzanne C. Smeltzer et al., *Obstetric Clinicians' Experiences and Educational Preparation for Caring for Pregnant Women with Physical Disabilities: A Qualitative Study*, 11 DISABILITY & HEALTH J. 8 (2018); Monika Mitra et al., *Barriers to Providing Maternity Care to Women with Physical Disabilities: Perspectives from Health Care Practitioners*, 10 DISABILITY & HEALTH J. 445 (2017); Lorraine Byrnes & Mary Hickey, *Perinatal Care for Women with Disabilities: Clinical Considerations*, 12 J. FOR NURSE PRACTITIONERS 503, 508 (2016); Suzanne C. Smeltzer et al., *Labor, Delivery, and Anesthesia Experiences of Women with Physical Disability*, 44 BIRTH 315 (2017); Monika Mitra et al., *A Perinatal Health Framework for Women with Physical Disabilities*, 8 DISABILITY HEALTH J. 499 (2015).

freedom – and that she deserves criminal sanction if she comes up short.[102] Feminists have pointed out how elevating "fetal interests" serves to obscure and subordinate pregnant women.[103]

Not all pregnant people feel the threat of criminal prosecutions equally. Instead, prosecutions have fallen disproportionately on low-income and Black women, despite evidence that drug use during pregnancy (the most common factual basis for prosecution) extends across class and racial lines. The exact number of prosecutions is unknown. A comprehensive study of cases where pregnant women were arrested or forced to undergo medical interventions found that 71 percent of cases involved women whose low income entitled them to indigent defense, and 52 percent involved Black women.[104]

But how does the behavior of low-income and Black pregnant women come to the attention of prosecutors, enabling this lopsided pattern of prosecutions? Is there a "stop and frisk" policy that racially profiles pregnant women? Such a seemingly absurd proposition may not be so far from the truth. Sociologist and legal scholar Khiara Bridges has described how reliance on publicly funded prenatal care exposes poor women to closer scrutiny and greater censure than middle-class women.[105] In many cases, medical providers actively inform law enforcement of conduct like drug use or suspected self-harm.

In one egregious example, in 1989 doctors and nurses at the Medical University of South Carolina in Charleston began collaborating with local law enforcement. Medical providers would perform nonconsensual drug screening on pregnant women and report positive tests to law enforcement.[106] In *Policing the Womb: Invisible Women and the Criminalization of Motherhood*, Michele Goodwin details

---

[102] Amnesty International defines the phrase as "[t]he process of attaching punishments or penalties to women for actions that are interpreted as harmful to their own pregnancies ... includ[ing] laws that punish actions during pregnancy that would not otherwise be made criminal or punishable ... [and] other laws not specific to pregnancy ... [that] are either applied in a discriminatory way against pregnant women and/or have a disproportionate impact on pregnant women ...." Amnesty International, *Criminalizing Pregnancy: Policing Pregnant Women Who Use Drugs in the USA* 5 (2017), https://www.amnesty.org/download/Documents/AMR5162032017ENGLISH.pdf; LINDA C. FENTIMAN, BLAMING MOTHERS: AMERICAN LAW AND THE RISKS TO CHILDREN'S HEALTH 3 (2017).

[103] Ikemoto, *supra* note 2, at 1304.

[104] FENTIMAN, *supra* note 102, at 114, 141; Amnesty International, *supra* note 102, at 8; MICHELE B. GOODWIN, POLICING THE WOMB: INVISIBLE WOMEN AND THE CRIMINALIZATION OF MOTHERHOOD 82, 97 (2020); Lynn M. Paltrow & Jeanne Flavin, *Arrests of and Forced Interventions on Pregnant Women in the United States, 1073–2005: Implications for Women's Legal Status and Public Health*, 38 J. HEALTH POLITICS, POL'Y & L. 299, 311 (2013).

[105] KHIARA BRIDGES, REPRODUCING RACE: AN ETHNOGRAPHY OF PREGNANCY AS A SITE OF RACIALIZATION 36 (2012).

[106] ROBERTS, *supra* note 17, at 164–65. In Ferguson v. City of Charleston, 532 U.S. 67, 71–72 (2001), the Supreme Court held that the Medical University, by conducting nonconsensual drug testing, had engaged in unreasonable searches and thus violated the pregnant women's Fourth Amendment rights.

the problems with health professionals acting as "hospital snitches and police informants."[107] Professionals who covertly report on pregnant patients breach fiduciary duties and obligations of confidentiality. Moreover, casting them as "deputized interpreters of the law" may encourage providers to elevate "the exercise of their legal judgment over that of their medical judgment."[108] Medical personnel may be ill equipped to assess whether or not the conduct of a pregnant patient is illegal. And even health justifications for reporting (like fetal welfare) are, on balance, unconvincing. Medical and public health experts caution that reports to law enforcement engender distrust among pregnant patients, discouraging them from seeking prenatal care and leading to worse pregnancy outcomes for both mother and child.[109]

Health professionals who report pregnant women to law enforcement occupy a patently conflicted role, raising the question as to what might lead a health care provider to break patient confidentiality? Racial bias may provide an answer; twenty-six of the twenty-seven women that Charleston's Medical University referred to law enforcement were Black. (And according to her medical record, the twenty-seventh woman had a Black boyfriend.) In an echo of earlier eugenic sentiments, a nurse who was central to the program's operation shared her view that most Black women should undergo tubal ligations.[110] Subordination of women's health to other goals is not limited to Black women; White women's pregnancies have also been criminalized. But disproportionate criminalization of low-income and Black women, often enabled by medical policing, signals their devaluation as persons and as mothers.

5.7 POST-PREGNANCY RISKS AND CONCLUSION

In this chapter, my focus has been the uncertain and contested path to motherhood for many Black women and disabled women, with particular attention to challenges associated with medicine and health care. Other challenges arise once motherhood is attained. Those challenges lie outside my focus here, but I conclude by noting briefly that Black mothers and disabled mothers cannot rest easy on an expectation that they will be left to raise their children in peace. Compared to nondisabled

---

[107] GOODWIN, *supra* note 104.

[108] *Id.* at 81.

[109] Michelle Oberman, *Thirteen Ways of Looking at Buck v. Bell: Thoughts Occasioned by Paul Lombardo's Three Generations, No Imbeciles*, 59 J. LEG. EDUC. 357, 377 (2010); Amnesty International, *supra* note 102, at 61. Positive drug tests of pregnant patients, new mothers, or newborns may also prompt reports to local child welfare agencies, triggering civil investigations and potential removal of a drug-exposed infant from maternal custody. Child abuse reporting laws in many states require or encourage these reports. Marian Jarlenski et al., *Characterization of U.S. State Law Requiring Health Care Provider Reporting of Perinatal Substance Use*, 27 WOMEN'S HEALTH ISSUES 264 (2017). Like fears of criminal prosecution, fears of having their babies taken away may deter pregnant women from seeking medical care.

[110] ROBERTS, *supra* note 17, at 174–75.

White women, they are at greater risk of losing their child, either to death or the child welfare system.

The United States' infant mortality rate (the measure of how many babies die before their first birthdays) exceeds those of most other developed countries. As with maternal mortality, stark racial disparities exist. Babies born to Black mothers are twice as likely to die before their first birthday as are babies born to non-Hispanic White mothers.[111] And, as with maternal mortality, data regarding infant mortality among babies born to disabled woman are scarce. Some research, however, suggests that women with certain disabilities may be more likely to suffer adverse birth outcomes or infant death.[112]

Parallels in disrupted maternal bonds are clearer regarding the way the child welfare system threatens Black mothers and disabled mothers with loss of custody. Whether temporary or permanent, removing a child from parental custody can produce enduring effects on both parent and child. Mothers with disabilities encounter discrimination in the child welfare system.[113] Child welfare workers' decisions can reflect stereotyped assumptions about a disabled mother's inability to meet her child's needs. Combined with ignorance of supports available to assist disabled parents, these assumptions of inadequacy create profound custodial precarity for disabled mothers.[114] Black parents are overrepresented in the system, with racial disparities existing in decisions made at various stages of the child welfare process.[115] Medical biases may contribute to these disparities. Evidence indicates that when Black or Hispanic children (as compared to White non-Hispanic children) are brought to the emergency room with minor head trauma, staff are more likely to suspect child abuse and make reports.[116] For both Black and disabled

---

[111] Novoa & Taylor, *supra* note 95.

[112] For example, one study suggests that women with intellectual and developmental disabilities (IDD) are more likely to experience adverse birth outcomes including preterm births, low birthweight babies, and stillbirths. The researcher suggests that the higher rate of adverse birth outcomes may result from the intersection of disadvantage (including SES, race, and comorbidities) that typifies many women with IDD, but that the higher risk of adverse outcomes persisted even when accounting for covariates. Ilhom Akobirshoev, *Birth Outcomes among US Women with Intellectual and Developmental Disabilities*, 10 DISABILITY & HEALTH J. 406 (2017). See also Mitra et al., *Barriers to Maternal Care, supra* note 101.*supra* note 100.

[113] NATIONAL COUNCIL ON DISABILITY, *supra* note 38, at 40; Samuel R. Bagenstos, *Disability and Reproductive Justice*, 14 HARV. L. & POL'Y REV. 273 (2020).

[114] Robyn M. Powell, *Safeguarding the Rights of Parents with Intellectual Disabilities in Child Welfare Cases: The Convergence of Social Science and Law*, 20 CUNY L. REV. 127 (2016); Robyn M. Powell, *Family Law, Parents with Disabilities, and the Americans with Disabilities Act*, 57 FAM. CT. REV. 37, 39 (2019).

[115] Office of Child Welfare Serv., Admin. of Children and Families, *Racial Disproportionality and Disparity in Child Welfare* (Nov. 2016), https://www.childwelfare.gov/pubpdfs/racial_disproportionality.pdf.

[116] Stephanie Clifford & Jessica Silver-Greenberg, *Foster Care as Punishment: The New Reality of "Jane Crow"*, N.Y. TIMES, July 21, 2017.

women, maternity that deviates from idealized norms – whether because of poverty, impairment, cultural factors, or inadequate social supports – may be cut off.

This chapter has explored how many Black women and disabled women have faced impediments to becoming a mother, impediments often connected to a lingering taint of eugenic prejudices regarding who should reproduce. Striking parallels emerge from this examination. One common theme is a devaluation of women's individual and maternal worth and competency, often springing from persistent stereotypes of Black and disabled women. A second parallel lies in the involvement of the medical profession and the broader health care system in making the path to motherhood more difficult. Both Black women and disabled women face constraints on childbearing; the intersection of those identities seems certain to compound challenges. Among the first to call out disability's role in intersectionality, Eddie Glenn described the impact of being Black, disabled, and a woman as a "'triple jeopardy' syndrome" carrying multiple layers of stigma.[117] Moreover, the stresses of living in poverty exacerbate a woman's risk of facing degrading constraints on childbearing, and both Black women and disabled women are disproportionately represented among people with low incomes.[118]

Fuller consideration of how acknowledging these and other parallels might yield valuable health equity returns for Black people and people with disabilities will be offered in the book's final chapter. Before moving on, though, I'll offer a final observation about medicine's role in devaluing and disempowering Black and disabled maternity. Advances in medicine and public health over the past century should be lauded for dramatically decreasing the risks women face when they become pregnant. But those advances have come at a cost. The medicalization of pregnancy and childbirth grants medical professionals authority over pregnant patients and diminishes women's agency. That loss of agency heightens women's vulnerability to the sorts of eugenically informed justifications for intrusions on procreative freedom examined in this chapter. This cost is exaggerated for Black women, whose egregiously excessive maternal mortality rates reveal how they have profited less than White women from the tradeoff between maternal agency and maternal survival. The health care system, then, has too often served as a channel for mistreatment of Black women and women with disabilities. It did not birth racism or ableism, but it has claimed increasing power over women's reproductive

[117] Eddie Glenn, *African American Women with Disabilities: An Overview, in Disability and Diversity: New Leadership for a New Era* 66 (1995), https://books.google.com/books?id= TXtv5jaXjcMC&pg=PA66&lpg=PA66&dq=eddie+glenn +disability&source=bl&ots=482oO8Nsqr&sig=ACfU3U38X9KNbr2wBSW9JaFqapKQaADM- xQ&hl=en&sa=X&ved=2ahUKEwjYsZaMhffnAhUVZDUKHT- SC8wQ6AEwBHoECAoQAQ#v=onepage&q=eddie%20glenn%20disability&f=false.
[118] Nanette Goodman et al., *Financial Inequality: Disability, Race and Poverty in America*, NATIONAL DISABILITY INSTITUTE (2017), https://www.nationaldisabilityinstitute.org/wp-con tent/uploads/2019/02/disability-race-poverty-in-america.pdf.

opportunities and choices. Structural biases in the system become apparent when disabled women and Black women are deprived of agency or are subjected to mistreatment. The growing demand by Black women for nonmedicalized pregnancy and childbirth options, which midwives, doulas, and birthing centers provide, can be seen as an effort to right that balance.[119] True equity for all women who seek to bear children still seems an elusive end.

---

[119] Alice Proujansky, *Why Black Women Are Rejecting Hospitals in Search of Better Births*, N.Y. TIMES (Mar. 11, 2021), https://www.nytimes.com/2021/03/11/nyregion/birth-centers-new-jersey .html?referringSource=articleShare.

6

Medicaid Preservation

A *Shared Priority*

On July 28, 2017, Senator John McCain walked onto the floor of the Senate Chamber and into the middle of an intense congressional debate over the future of health care in the United States. Since earlier that year, a Republican majority in Congress had been pushing proposals to repeal the Affordable Care Act (ACA) and make fundamental changes to the Medicaid program. Although McCain previously had expressed his opposition to the ACA, at the time of the vote, his support for the repeal legislation was in question. McCain entered the chamber as voting was underway. Instead of heading to his seat on the Republican side of the chamber, he paused before the Senate chair and extended his arm. Then came McCain's dramatic gesture: Thumb's down on the bill. With that simple motion, McCain upended Republican efforts to scuttle a central piece of President Obama's legacy. He also preserved the existing structure of Medicaid against Republican efforts to weaken and shrink it, efforts that posed especial threats to Black Americans and disabled Americans.[1]

The media replayed McCain's vote repeatedly, but his action was only part of the story of the repeal's defeat. In the months leading up to that vote, media regularly reported on public protests and political agitation by activists and nonactivist citizens concerned about losing their health coverage and protections against health status discrimination. The protesters included all sorts of people, but Black people and disabled people were among the most vocal and engaged. They demanded that Congress not dismantle the ACA or eviscerate Medicaid. These events highlighted both groups' shared concerns with preserving Medicaid and its expansion under the ACA. The joint federal-state program of health coverage for low-income Americans is especially important to Black people and people with disabilities, in part because health disparities they experience leave them with significant health care needs and

---

[1] A video of the dramatic moment is available at https://www.youtube.com/watch?v=hT2pp_KrJGg.

the expenses that accompany them. For Black Americans, undoing the ACA's Medicaid expansion would likely have widened the Black–White disparity in health insurance coverage, with effects on health care access and outcomes. People with disabilities also worried about losing the Medicaid expansion, but they had another, distinctive concern: that draconian cuts to Medicaid funding would force them out of their homes and into nursing homes in order to receive services. For both disabled people and Black people, protecting Medicaid was a matter of health justice. By examining their shared and distinctive interests in Medicaid, this chapter shifts to the realm of health care financing and health policy and their health equity implications. It offers an example of how common goals can support effective advocacy.

6.1 REPUBLICANS' ATTEMPT TO TRANSFORM MEDICAID

A basic description of Medicaid will help set the stage for discussing the events of 2017. Congress created Medicaid in 1965 as a public health insurance program providing coverage for certain categories of low-income Americans. Though a creature of federal law, Medicaid is administered at the state level. States help fund Medicaid, but if a state's program abides by certain conditions established by the federal law, the federal government will match the state's financial contributions. The result is that each state has leeway to shape its Medicaid program to meet its specific needs, even as each state's program must conform to basic parameters.

How did the Medicaid program end up in Republicans' crosshairs in 2017, alongside the ACA? Conservative lawmakers have never had affection for Medicaid. Despite preserving substantial discretion for states, Medicaid effectively creates a federally mandated, open-ended entitlement to covered services for eligible enrollees. In short, no predetermined limit on the federal government's obligation to fund Medicaid exists. Anyone eligible for Medicaid is legally entitled to receive covered benefits.[2] That federally funded entitlement has long been a bitter pill for conservatives, who for decades have floated proposals to shift greater control to the states and to end the open-ended nature of the federal government's obligations by transforming Medicaid into a block grant program, where a predetermined amount of federal funds would be provided for Medicaid with few conditions attached.[3] The ACA's expansion of Medicaid eligibility to include virtually all nonelderly adults with sufficiently low incomes (which I discuss more below) simply aggravated

---

[2] Victoria Wachino et al., *Financing the Medicaid Program: The Many Roles of Federal and State Matching Funds*, KAISER COMM'N ON MEDICAID & THE UNINSURED (Jan. 2004), https://www.kff.org/wp-content/uploads/2013/01/financing-the-medicaid-program-the-many-roles-of-federal-and-state-matching-funds-policy-brief.pdf.

[3] See FRANK J. THOMPSON, Medicaid Rising: The Perils and Potential of Federalism, in MEDICARE AND MEDICAID AT 50: AMERICA'S ENTITLEMENT PROGRAMS IN THE AGE OF AFFORDABLE CARE 196 (Keith A. Wailoo & Julian E. Zelizer eds., 2015).

conservatives' objections to the program. By the time a Republican-dominated Congress and White House assumed power in 2017, proponents of limited federal government sought not only to repeal the ACA (including its Medicaid expansion) but also to fundamentally restructure Medicaid by shifting more control to states and slashing future federal funding.[4] The health care bills that Congress debated over the spring, summer, and fall of 2017 shared key elements relating to Medicaid.

First, reflecting Republicans' antipathy to the ACA, the proposals either cut federal funding for the Medicaid expansion or terminated it altogether.[5] For example, the American Health Care Act (AHCA), passed by the House in March 2017, would have cut off the chance to expand Medicaid for states that had not yet done so.[6] It also called for ending enhanced federal funding for covering Medicaid enrollees who became eligible via the expansion. Under the AHCA, rather than paying 90 percent of costs for those enrollees (as the ACA requires), the federal government would pay only its regular federal Medicaid match,[7] an average of 56 percent. That cut would force states that had expanded their Medicaid programs either to shoulder far more of the cost of covering newly eligible enrollees or to retighten eligibility standards and eliminate their coverage.[8] From the perspective of low-income Americans who had gained health coverage through Medicaid's expansion, this proposal threatened their ability to stay covered.

Republican proposals also sought to shift more authority regarding Medicaid eligibility, coverage, and operations to the states while capping federal spending on each state's Medicaid program. Such a funding cap would have departed sharply from the historic model where the federal government matches (according to a formula) each state's Medicaid spending with no predetermined limit.[9] To consider the implications of this change, imagine federal funding as a water supply for Medicaid. Since Medicaid's creation in 1965, the federal funding faucet has continued to flow to match states' spending their own funds on Medicaid recipients' health needs. By contrast, Republican proposals would have transformed federal

---

[4] Maggie Haberman & Robert Pear, *Trump Tells Congress to Repeal and Replace Health Care Law "Very Quickly,"* N.Y. TIMES (Jan. 10, 2017), https://www.nytimes.com/2017/01/10/us/repeal-affordable-care-act-donald-trump.html; Shefali Luthra, *Everything You Need to Know about Block Grants – The Heart of GOP's Medicaid Plans,* KAISER HEALTH NEWS (Jan. 24, 2017), https://khn.org/news/block-grants-medicaid-faq.

[5] Edwin Park et al., *Ctr. on Budget & Pol'y Priorities, House Republican Proposals to Radically Overhaul Medicaid Would Shift Costs, Risks to States* 1 (2017), https://www.cbpp.org/sites/default/files/atoms/files/2-24-17health2.pdf.

[6] H.R. 1628, 115th Cong. (2017).

[7] Julia Paradise, *Restructuring Medicaid in the American Health Care Act: Five Key Considerations,* KAISER FAM. FOUND. 2 (2017), https://www.kff.org/medicaid/issue-brief/restructuring-medicaid-in-the-american-health-care-act-five-key-considerations.

[8] Matt Broaddus & Edwin Park, *Ctr. on Budget and Pol'y Priorities, House Republican Health Bill Would Effectively End ACA Medicaid Expansion* 1 (2017), https://www.cbpp.org/research/health/house-republican-health-bill-would-effectively-end-aca-medicaid-expansion.

[9] Park et al., *supra* note 5, at 5.

funding into a yearly bucket of water for each state that when depleted would remain empty until delivery of the following year's bucket. And, to continue the metaphor, the resulting drought (i.e., the gap between the states' water needs and federal water supplies) predictably would have worsened over time, as Medicaid enrollment increased and the health care inflation rate exceeded that of general inflation. Legislative proposals in 2017 consistently limited the growth in annual federal allotments to a predetermined inflation rate, regardless of states' future needs. The projected result: $834 billion less in federal Medicaid spending from 2017 to 2026,[10] a huge number that would likely translate over time into fewer Medicaid-eligible persons and some enrollees being unable to obtain needed care.

To sweeten the prospect of reduced federal funding, Republicans touted proposals to restructure Medicaid as giving states greater latitude to tailor their Medicaid programs with respect to benefits, payments to providers, and eligibility, including the ability to impose work requirements or drug testing on recipients.[11] Federal dollars would be capped but would come with fewer strings attached. Critics saw the trade-off differently. They worried about how capped funding would constrain states' ability to address changing needs, such as the increased demands for treatment associated with the opioid addiction epidemic, natural disasters, or an aging population.[12] Given Republicans' control of both houses of Congress and the White House, enacting the proposed legislation should have been a straightforward task. Yet repeated attempts at passage failed. Many factors were at play, but sustained vocal protests targeting more moderate Republicans doubtless played a role. People with disabilities figured prominently among protesters, along with people of color and others.

To aid understanding of why Medicaid has particular importance to disabled Americans and Black Americans, a bit more background regarding the program's history and nature is needed.

6.2 MEDICAID'S EVOLUTION

"[A] program for the poor will always be politically vulnerable, underfunded, and generally inadequate"[13] was how health law scholar Timothy Jost described

---

[10] Congressional Budget Office, Cost Estimate H.R. 1628 American Health Care Act of 2017 tbl.3 (2017), https://ww.cbo.gov/system/files/115th-congress-2017-2018/costestimate/hr1628aspassed.pdf.

[11] Gary Claxton et al., *State Flexibility to Address Health Insurance Challenges under the American Health Care Act, H.R. 1628*, KAISER FAM. FOUND. 1–3 (2017), https://www.kff.org/health-reform/issue-brief/state-flexibility-to-address-health-insurance-challenges-under-the-american-health-care-act-h-r-1628.

[12] Haeyoun Park, *Republicans' Changes to Medicaid Could Have Larger Impact than Their Changes to Obamacare*, N.Y. TIMES (Mar. 7, 2017), https://www.nytimes.com/interactive/2017/03/07/us/politics/medicaid-reform-impact-on-states.html?auth=login-smartlock.

[13] TIMOTHY JOST, DISENTITLEMENT?: THE THREATS FACING OUR PUBLIC HEALTH-CARE PROGRAMS AND A RIGHTS-BASED RESPONSE 178 (2003).

Medicaid in 2003. As a program for poor people that depends partly on state tax revenues, Medicaid has consistently faced thin political support and funding shortfalls during economic downturns when low-income residents need the program the most.[14] Medicaid disproportionately covers marginalized populations, including poor people, disabled people, and people of color, even as it has evolved during the fifty-plus years since its creation into much more than a program of "welfare medicine."[15]

6.2.1 *Medicaid's Origins as "Welfare Medicine"*

Congress created Medicaid in 1965, along with its legislative twin, Medicare. Descended from the Elizabethan Poor Laws, Medicaid's purpose was to provide coverage for the "deserving poor." This phrase was used to describe people who could not be expected to work because they were too old, sick, or disabled. Their poverty, so the thinking goes, was not their own fault (and neither was their lack of health insurance).[16] Initially, Medicaid covered only persons who, by virtue of their poverty, were eligible for cash assistance programs based on old age or blindness, or who had a minor child in their household. The creation in 1972 of Supplemental Security Income (SSI), a new, purely federal cash assistance program for the aged, blind, and disabled, added persons with disabilities to these "categorically eligible" groups. In this original incarnation, Medicaid eligibility derived from a person's receipt of cash welfare benefits – hence the original conception of Medicaid as "welfare medicine."[17]

Medicaid also followed in the path of the Kerr–Mills program, which provided states with federal funding to pay for medical care provided to "medically indigent" senior citizens. Under Kerr–Mills, states had broad latitude to determine eligibility and benefits, within limited federal constraints.[18] Lawmakers incorporated this division of financial responsibility and administrative authority into Medicaid, giving states substantial flexibility to adapt the program to state-level needs as long as they would comply with federal program requirements. This devolution of authority permitted the creation of fifty different Medicaid programs, each responding to

---

[14] Judith D. Moore & David G. Smith, *Legislating Medicaid: Considering Medicaid and Its Origins*, 27 Health Care Financing Rev. 45, 45 (2005); Stan Dorn et al., Kaiser Commission on Medicaid and the Uninsured, *Executive Summary on Medicaid, Schip and Economic Downturn: Policy Challenges and Policy Responses* 5 (2008).

[15] *Medicaid: No Longer the Welfare Medicine Afterthought*, Columbia U. Mailman Sch. Pub. Health (July 9, 2015), https://www.mailman.columbia.edu/public-health-now/news/medicaid-no-longer-welfare-medicine-afterthought.

[16] David Orentlicher, *Medicaid at 50: No Longer Limited to the "Deserving" Poor?*, 15 Yale J. Health Pol'y, L. & Ethics 185 (2015).

[17] Jill Quadagno, The Transformation of Medicaid from Poor Law Legacy to Middle Class Entitlement?, in Medicare and Medicaid at 50: America's Entitlement Programs in the Age of Affordable Care 78 (2015); Thompson, *supra* note 3, at 193–94.

[18] Moore & Smith, *supra* note 14, at 45.

state-level needs and priorities but reflecting state values and prejudices. The retention of significant control at the state level assuaged concerns of lawmakers from
Southern states, where many objected to what they perceived as federal government
overreach on racial issues in the 1960s. The history of Medicaid thus shows the role
racial politics played in its creation.[19]

Over several decades, Congress drew more groups under Medicaid's eligibility
umbrella, including low-income pregnant women and, with the creation of the
State Children's Health Insurance Program (CHIP) in 1997, more low-income
children and their uninsured parents. These expansions weakened the link between
welfare programs and Medicaid, both programmatically and in the minds of the
public.[20] Despite these incremental expansions, however, a taint of welfarism could
still be discerned in aspects of states' tight-fisted Medicaid implementation. For
example, many states established income eligibility thresholds well below the
poverty level for low-income parents. In Arkansas, the threshold in 2009 was 17
percent of the federal poverty level. Though theoretically eligible for coverage,
parents of a child covered by Arkansas's Medicaid program would be deemed too
well off to receive Medicaid coverage if they earned more than $3,113 annually.[21]
Another example is the notoriously low rates that states pay for health care providers
who treat Medicaid enrollees. Bargain-basement fees cause some physicians to stop
treating patients covered by Medicaid, leaving some localities with a dearth of
physicians that will provide services.[22] By concentrating the treatment of enrollees
in a small number of physician practices and stoking resentment among those
providers, low payment rates reinforce a perception of Medicaid as second-tier
health care.

Even with this perception, Medicaid's role in providing some access to care for its
enrollees has been important, and it has played a particularly critical role for people
with disabilities. Because disabled people were included among the initial categories of eligible low-income people, Medicaid's range of covered benefits has been
broader than those of health plans that employers typically offer. As we'll see,

---

[19] *Id.* at 45–48; Julian E. Zelizer, The Contentious Origins of Medicare and Medicaid, in
Medicare and Medicaid at 50: America's Entitlement Programs in the Age of
Affordable Care 3, 9 (2015).

[20] In the 1980s, Congress initially gave states the option of covering children and pregnant women
with incomes too high to receive welfare benefits. Congress later proceeded to require states to
cover those groups as well. Thompson, *supra* note 3, at 195. Quadagno, *supra* note 17, at 79–80.

[21] *Medicaid Income Eligibility Limits for Parents, 2002–2018*, Kaiser Fam. Found., https://www
.kff.org/medicaid/state-indicator/medicaid-income-eligibility-limits-for-parents/?currentTimefra
me=0&sortModel=%7B%22colId%22:%22Location%22,%22sort%22:%22asc%22%7D; 2009
HHS Poverty Guidelines, U.S. Dep't Health & Hum. Servs. (Dec. 1, 2009), https://aspe.hhs
.gov/2009-hhs-poverty-guidelines.

[22] Jayne O'Donnell & Laura Ungar, *Medicaid Turns 50 Mired in Controversy*, USA Today
(July 15, 2017), https://www.usatoday.com/story/news/2015/07/15/medicaid-expansion-effect-on-
patients-taxpayers-states-hospitals/25612707; Nicole Huberfeld, *The Universality of Medicaid at
Fifty*, 15 Yale J. Health Pol'y, L. & Ethics 67, 71 (2015).

though, accessing those services has often come at high price for disabled Medicaid enrollees.

Between eligibility expansion by federal policies and devolution of significant policy and implementation authority to the states, a lack of clarity regarding the program's nature marked Medicaid's first forty-five years. In short, how did policies loosening eligibility standards in order to cover more people fit with the program's hard-to-shake image as welfare medicine, an image that states remained free to bolster? However ambiguous Medicaid's nature at the beginning of the twenty-first century, the program's key role in the United States' health care system soon became undeniable. Health reform's enactment in 2010 promised to reinforce and transform Medicaid's role by making it the ACA's "key mechanism to move [the U.S.] toward universal coverage."[23]

6.2.2 *Medicaid as a Stepping Stone toward Universal Coverage*

As enacted, the ACA required states to extend Medicaid eligibility to all nonelderly adults with a family income of up to 138 percent of the federal poverty level, without regard to traditional eligibility categories. This "expansion" was a condition of each state's continued participation in Medicaid. It thus compelled states that subjected parents to miserly pre-ACA income eligibility thresholds to raise them to the ACA-required level.[24] It also meant that low-income, childless adults in all states for the first time would become eligible for Medicaid. To ensure coverage for newly eligible enrollees would be meaningful, the ACA directed states to cover ten categories of essential health benefits.[25] And, the mandate wasn't unfunded. To make its strong medicine more palatable, the ACA required the federal government to pay for the vast majority of the cost of covering the expansion population.[26] The goal was to make Medicaid coverage available to almost anyone whose income was low and who didn't receive health coverage through another source.

That was the plan, anyway. A judicial challenge to the Medicaid expansion's constitutionality, however, disrupted the plan before it ever went into effect. In *National Federation of Independent Businesses (NFIB) v. Sebelius*, the Supreme Court held the ACA's expansion mandate unconstitutionally coercive because a

---

[23] Quadagno, *supra* note 17, at 78.

[24] Huberfeld, *supra* note 22, at 72.

[25] Patient Protection and Affordable Care Act § 1302, 42 U.S.C. § 18022.

[26] Under the ACA, for the first three years of the expansion (2014–2016), the federal government would be responsible for 100 percent of the costs of Medicaid for newly eligible enrollees. After 2016, the federal share would decline to 90 percent in 2020. By contrast, the federal government pays a much smaller share of the Medicaid costs of traditional enrollees, paying 73 percent of Medicaid costs in the poorest states, with the national average of federal cost-share falling between 57 percent and 60 percent. *Policy Basics: Introduction to Medicaid*, CTR. ON BUDGET & POL'Y PRIORITIES (Aug. 16, 2016), https://www.cbpp.org/research/health/policy-basics-intro duction-to-medicaid.

state that refused to expand would risk losing all federal funds for its entire Medicaid program. The judicial disruption was not complete, though. The Court did not entirely strike down the ACA's mandatory expansion provision but instead recast it as optional.[27] In short, post-*NFIB*, each state has been free to choose whether or not to implement the Medicaid expansion.

It is a choice that carries far-reaching implications. Most obviously, uninsured low-income persons who would gain coverage are affected by their state's decision whether to expand. A growing body of research supplies evidence associating Medicaid expansion with improved measures of health care access and better health outcomes among low-income persons.[28] States that expand Medicaid may help mitigate health care disparities, as disproportionately uninsured groups gain coverage and, with it, access to testing and care.[29] Expanding Medicaid can also advance health equity in less obvious ways. For example, expanding Medicaid in California was associated with a decrease in evictions. And because negative health outcomes are among the many "devastating long-term consequences [of evictions] for . . . burdened low-income families"[30] (a point the next chapter will explore), decreasing the number of evictions can improve health outcomes.

Because expanding Medicaid increases the number of low-income patients who can pay for the care they need, states' expansion decisions are also consequential for health care providers. Studies have found that hospitals and clinics in expansion states have experienced reductions in uncompensated care costs.[31] The converse is true in states that have not expanded. The crisis of rural hospital closures has been most acute in nonexpansion states, which include the eight states with the largest number of rural hospital closures over the past decade.[32]

---

[27] National Federation of Independent Businesses v. Sebelius, 567 U.S. 519 (2012).

[28] Heidi Allen & Benjamin D. Summers, *Medicaid Expansion and Health: Assessing the Evidence after 5 Years*, 322 JAMA 1253 (2019). For example, states that expanded Medicaid saw a trend towards fewer deaths from end-stage liver disease, especially in racial minorities. John Gever, *ACA's Medicaid Expansion Tied to Reduced Liver Disease Mortality*, MEDPAGE TODAY, Nov. 16, 2020.

[29] One study found an association between expanding Medicaid and a significant increase in testing for HIV. Yunwei Gai & John Marthinsen, *Medicaid Expansion, HIV Testing, and HIV-Related Risk Behaviors in the United States, 2010–2017*, 109 AM J. PUB. HEALTH 1404 (2019). Increased testing provides an opportunity to address the spread of HIV and to provide early treatment to those diagnosed with an infection. According to the CDC, in 2018, 42 percent of new HIV diagnoses were in Black Americans, who made up only 13 percent of the American population. *Impact on Racial and Ethnic Minorities*, HIV.gov, https://www.hiv.gov/hiv-basics/overview/data-and-trends/impact-on-racial-and-ethnic-minorities.

[30] Heidi L. Allen et al., *Can Medicaid Expansions Prevent Housing Evictions?*, 38 HEALTH AFF. 1451, 1456 (2019).

[31] Rachel Garfield & Madeline Guth, *The Effects of Medicaid Expansion under the ACA: Updated Findings from a Literature Review KFF* (2020), https://www.kff.org/medicaid/report/the-effects-of-medicaid-expansion-under-the-aca-updated-findings-from-a-literature-review.

[32] Eyal Press, *A Preventable Cancer Is on the Rise in Alabama*, THE NEW YORKER, Apr. 6, 2020.

As of early 2021, twelve states remained adamant in refusing to expand their Medicaid programs.[33] It is reasonable to ask why a state would reject an offer of millions of federal dollars to provide health coverage for its low-income residents and thereby bolster the solvency of its hospitals and other providers. Politicians in nonexpansion states point to expansion's impact on state coffers and question the reliability of the federal commitment to shoulder the vast majority of expansion costs. (However, some analyses indicate that expanding Medicaid might offer states substantial economic benefits.[34]) But politics and ideology also play a role. Not surprisingly, states refusing to expand are "red" states, with Republican-dominated statehouses or governors.[35] Most are also states whose uninsured residents living in or near poverty (the people who would benefit from expanding Medicaid) are disproportionately Black and Brown.[36] As described below, states' expansion decisions raise racial equity issues, as does the Court's opinion in *NFIB* itself.

6.3 MEDICAID'S FOUNDATIONAL ROLE

The brief history provided above gives the context for the strong public reaction to proposals in 2017 to fundamentally restructure Medicaid and cut its funding. With the expansion, Medicaid pays for 45 percent of births in the United States and for 51 percent of long-term care services provided to elderly and disabled people.[37] It helps fund safety-net health care providers like community health clinics. For millions of Americans of limited means it makes the difference between the ability to seek needed medical care and going without. In short, Medicaid is important to all sorts of people. This section, though, focuses on its distinctive importance to Black Americans and disabled Americans.

---

[33] *Status of State Medicaid Expansion Decisions*, KAISER FAM. FOUND. (June 7, 2021), https://www .kff.org/medicaid/issue-brief/status-of-state-medicaid-expansion-decisions-interactive-map.

[34] The benefits would accrue from a combination of federal expansion funding, savings from the elimination of preexisting state programs for medically indigent persons, and state tax revenues flowing from the infusion of additional Medicaid dollars into a state's economy. For examples, see Gov. Edwards, *LDH Unveil Economic Impact of Medicaid Expansion*, OFFICE OF THE GOVERNOR, Apr. 10, 2018, https://gov.louisiana.gov/news/gov-edwards-ldh-unveil-economic-impact-of-medicaid-expansion (Louisiana); David J. Becker & Michael A. Morrisey, *An Economic Evaluation of Medicaid Expansion in Alabama under the Affordable Care Act*, Nov. 5, 2012, https://jointhehealthjourney.com/images/uploads/channel-files/UABStudy.pdf.

[35] See Thompson, *supra* note 3, at 204, 207.

[36] Rachel Garfield et al., *The Coverage Gap: Uninsured Poor Adults in States That Do Not Expand Medicaid*, KAISER FAM. FOUND. 3 (2018), https://www.kff.org/medicaid/issue-brief/the-coverage-gap-uninsured-poor-adults-in-states-that-do-not-expand-medicaid.

[37] Olivia Pham & Samantha Artiga, *Medicaid Initiatives to Improve Maternal and Infant Health and Address Racial Disparities*, KAISER FAM. FOUND. (2020), https://www.kff.org/racial-equity-and-health-policy/issue-brief/medicaid-initiatives-improve-maternal-infant-health-address-racial-disparities; Erica L. Reaves & MaryBeth Musumeci, *Medicaid and Long-Term Services and Supports: A Primer*, KAISER FAM. FOUND. (Dec. 2015), https://www.kff.org/medicaid/report/medicaid-and-long-term-services-and-supports-a-primer.

When the court decided *NFIB*, the idea that the Tenth Amendment's preservation of powers to the States could prevent the federal government from requiring states to enforce or adopt federal law (sometimes referred to as the "anti-commandeering doctrine") was not new; it had been established in the early 1990s.[49] But by recognizing the Tenth Amendment as a limit on Congress's spending power, *NFIB* broke new ground in the "Federalism Revolution."[50] Robust articulations of federalism can easily bleed over into rhetoric about "states' rights," a rhetoric historically used to maintain states' ability to discriminate and pursue White supremacist policies.[51] Historian Tomiko Brown-Nagin describes how New Deal social welfare legislation preserved implementation discretion for states, an approach she characterizes as "amount[ing] to an imprimatur to discriminate against disfavored groups, including Blacks and others deemed unworthy of charity because of color or perceived moral failing."[52]

I do not mean to suggest that the plurality opinion in *NFIB* was an endorsement of states' rights, with all that concept's historical racial baggage. Justices Breyer and Kagan, who are regularly characterized as being part of the Court's liberal wing, joined Chief Justice Roberts to form the plurality adopting the unconstitutional coercion theory. Nor do I argue that explicitly recognizing the predictable disparate racial impact of leaving expansion decisions to the states necessarily would have compelled the Court to reach a different conclusion. Brown-Nagin's point, I believe, is to cast Chief Justice Roberts' reasoning regarding coercion in a new light, reminding us of the link between states' historical insistence on having discretion in implementing social welfare programs and White supremacy.

The impact on low-income and disproportionately Black residents of nonexpansion states goes beyond exclusion from Medicaid. People of color in nonexpansion states also have fallen disproportionately into the "coverage gap," a term that describes the situation created by the *NFIB* decision of low-income persons who are ineligible for Medicaid (because their state has not expanded) *and* unqualified to receive federal subsidies for buying private insurance on ACA exchanges (because their income falls below the federal poverty level). The gap exists because when Congress enacted the ACA, there was no need to subsidize private insurance purchases by people falling below the federal poverty line, since the ACA as enacted required all states to cover those persons by expanding Medicaid. As a result, many poor people in nonexpansion states are left without any of the ACA's coverage-

---

[49] Steven Schwinn, *Symposium: It's Time to Abandon Anti-commandeering (but Don't Count on this Supreme Court to Do It)*, SCOTUSBLOG (Aug. 17, 2017), www.scotusblog.com/2017/08/symposium-time-abandon-anti-commandeering-dont-count-supreme-court.

[50] Huberfeld et al., *supra* note 46, at 47–48.

[51] Desmond King, *Forceful Federalism against American Racial Inequality*, 52 GOVERNMENT & OPPOSITION 356 (2017).

[52] Tomiko Brown-Nagin, *Two Americas in Healthcare: Federalism and Wars over Poverty from the New Deal-Great Society to Obamacare*, 62 DRAKE L. REV. 101, 110 (2014).

related benefits.[53] Southern states that opted out of Medicaid expansion have left their uninsured Black adults more than twice as likely to fall into the coverage gap, as compared to both Whites and Hispanics.[54]

Is the greater negative impact of nonexpansion on Black people purely coincidental? Or did race somehow shape those decisions? Policymakers in nonexpanding states are unlikely to explicitly express their unwillingness to provide health coverage to racial others, but researchers have uncovered some evidence of race's influence. Scholars who analyzed public opinion in nonexpanding states found evidence that public opinion regarding the expansion was racialized. More specifically, they found that states' decisions tended to reflect the level of White support (or nonsupport) for expansion. These researchers posit that large non-White populations combined with low White support for expansion may have produced "racialized backlash" against expanding in some states.[55]

In *Dying of Whiteness: How the Politics of Racial Resentment Is Killing America's Heartland*,[56] Jonathan Metzl (a psychiatrist with a doctorate in American culture) shares what racially inflected opposition to the expansion sounds like. In a chapter exploring why Tennessee became a Medicaid expansion holdout, Metzl describes listening in 2016 to focus groups of White men talk about health care reform. In objecting to expanding government-funded health care, one man invoked the welfare queen stereotype described in Chapter 5: "[T]here's a lot of people that use welfare, the welfare department and stuff that needs to get jobs, quit having children, and really get buckled down now. I mean, I'm not saying everybody; I'm just saying there's people that have ten and twelve kids. There ought to be a cutoff point somewhere there."[57] Another focused on not wanting to have to pay for undocumented immigrants (who are not actually eligible for Medicaid under the ACA's expansion): "[T]he worst thing is, is that what really pisses Americans off is that we are pocketing all the Mexicans, all the, all the illegal, mother, mothertruckers, their houses, their cars, their food stamps, everything they want, we're paying for it." Another finished the thought: "Yeah, if they're illegal, they'll go to the Medicaid

[53] See Rachel Garfield et al., *The Coverage Gap: Uninsured Poor Adults in States that Do Not Expand Medicaid*, KAISER FAM. FOUND. (June 12, 2018), https://www.kff.org/medicaid/issue-brief/the-coverage-gap-uninsured-poor-adults-in-states-that-do-not-expand-medicaid.

[54] Samantha Artiga et al., *The Impact of the Coverage Gap for Adults in States Not Expanding Medicaid by Race and Ethnicity*, KAISER FAM. FOUND. (Oct. 2015), https://www.kff.org/racial-equity-and-health-policy/issue-brief/the-impact-of-the-coverage-gap-in-states-not-expanding-medicaid-by-race-and-ethnicity; *Issue Brief: The Impact of the Coverage Gap in States Not Expanding Medicaid by Race and Ethnicity*, KAISER FAM. FOUND. (Dec. 2013), https://kaiserfamilyfoundation.files.wordpress.com/2013/12/8527-the-impact-of-the-coverage-gap-in-states-not-expanding-medicaid.pdf.

[55] Colleen M. Grogan & Sunggeun (Ethan) Park, *The Racial Divide in State Medicaid Expansions*, 42 J. HEALTH POL., POL'Y & L. 539, 558 (2017).

[56] JONATHAN M. METZL, DYING OF WHITENESS: HOW THE POLITICS OF RACIAL RESENTMENT IS KILLING AMERICA'S HEARTLAND (2019).

[57] *Id.* at 149.

system."[58] After these focus groups, Metzl concluded that having a common enemy in health care reform offered White men group cohesion and affirmed the value of their Whiteness, even as it deprived them of access to needed health care. A community organizer described the same antiexpansion dynamic in Texas using less academic terms: "I think Republicans were pretty good at . . . [p]itting communities against each other and using a lot of dog whistle politics . . . like, 'Medicaid equates to Black freeloading people.'"[59]

6.3.2 *Medicaid's Distinctive Importance for People with Disabilities*

Medicaid also holds special value for people with disabilities. As with Black Americans, they have greater than average health needs and are disproportionately likely to live in poverty and unlikely to receive employer-sponsored health coverage. As explained below, the types of services Medicaid covers are what make the public program crucially important for many disabled people.

It's helpful to unpack a bit more why Medicaid coverage is not only more common for people with disabilities but often preferable. Considered the epitome of the "deserving poor," disabled people with very low incomes have been among the persons eligible for Medicaid since its early years. Eligibility for SSI, the federal cash assistance program for low-income persons deemed "totally and permanently disabled," carries with it eligibility for Medicaid. In 2015, more than 10 million nonelderly persons with disabilities (or almost one in six Medicaid enrollees) qualified for Medicaid based on their disability. But SSI is not the only Medicaid "eligibility pathway" for disabled persons. Elderly persons living in poverty qualify for Medicaid based on age and income, but they may also be living with a disability.[60] Younger people who qualify for Medicaid because of low income may have a physical or mental impairment that negatively affects their ability to work, even if it doesn't leave them totally and permanently disabled.

The Medicaid expansion enhanced disabled people's ability to achieve and maintain Medicaid coverage. For starters, by extending eligibility to any nonelderly adult with an income less than 138 percent of the federal poverty level, it eliminated

---

[58] *Id.* at 150–51.

[59] HEATHER MCGHEE, THE SUM OF US: WHAT RACISM COSTS EVERYONE AND HOW WE CAN PROSPER TOGETHER 59 (2021).

[60] See Molly O'Malley Watts et al., *Medicaid Financial Eligibility for Seniors and People with Disabilities in 2015*, KAISER FAM. FOUND. 1, 10 (2016), http://files.kff.org/attachment/report-medicaid-financial-eligibility-for-seniors-and-people-with-disabilities-in-2015; *Health Care Experiences of Adults with Disabilities Enrolled in Medicaid Only: Findings from a 2014–2015 Nationwide Survey of Medicaid Beneficiaries*, MEDICAID.GOV 1–2, 14 (2017), https://www.medicaid.gov/medicaid/quality-of-care/downloads/performance-measurement/namcahpsdisabilitybrief.pdf; cf. L. Krause et al., *Rehabilitation Research & Training Center on Disability Statistics & Demographics*, 2017 DISABILITY STATISTICS ANNUAL REPORT 2 (2018), https://disabilitycompendium.org/sites/default/files/user-uploads/2017_AnnualReport_2017_FINAL.pdf (finding that 35.2 percent of persons aged sixty-five or older had a disability in 2017).

the need to prove total disability to gain access to Medicaid through SSI. In addition, raising the income eligibility threshold made it less likely that finding work would lead to a disabled person's losing their Medicaid eligibility. Some evidence indicates that expanded Medicaid has been associated with increased employment among people with disabilities.[61] As of 2019, well over half of the nearly 6 million nonelderly adult disabled Medicaid enrollees were *not* SSI recipients, indicating that the ACA's Medicaid expansion provided an important eligibility pathway to coverage for many disabled people.[62]

Medicaid covers benefits that are vitally important to many people with disabilities but not available through commercial insurance plans and even Medicare.[63] These benefits aid persons needing assistance with activities of daily living because of a disability, chronic health condition, or aging. These "long-term services and supports" (LTSS) complement treatments for acute or short-term medical needs – the kind of services that private health insurance covers. LTSS include facility-based care but also encompass a variety of services that help support independent living. These range from occupational therapy to meal delivery to assistance with dressing and bathing. The list of covered LTSS benefits varies somewhat from state to state, but all Medicaid programs cover some of these services.[64] Thus, though some may view Medicaid as second-class health coverage, for many disabled people Medicaid is superior to other insurance.

There's a catch to Medicaid's coverage of LTSS, though, as illustrated by the story of Lois Curtis and Elaine Wilson. Each woman had been diagnosed with a mental disability as an adolescent. Their diagnoses led to separation from families and friends, as they were placed in institutional settings. For years, each woman was in and out of different hospitals, institutions, and other facilities. When Lois Curtis reached her mid-twenties, she already had spent much of her life in Georgia's state-

---

[61] Jean P. Hall et al., *Medicaid Expansion as an Employment Incentive Program for People with Disabilities*, 108 Am. J. Pub. Health 1235 (2018). By contrast, another study using earlier data did not find evidence that expanding Medicaid significantly affected the employment of disabled adults. Purvi Sevak & Jody Schimmel Hyde, *The ACA Medicaid Expansions and Employment of Adults with Disabilities*, J. Disability Pol'y Studies (2020), https://doi.org/10 .1177/1044207320943554.

[62] MaryBeth Musumeci & Kendal Orgera, *People with Disabilities Are at Risk of Losing Medicaid Coverage without the ACA Expansion*, Kaiser Fam. Found., Nov. 2, 2020, https://www.kff.org/ medicaid/issue-brief/people-with-disabilities-are-at-risk-of-losing-medicaid-coverage-without- the-aca-expansion. Because of these multiple eligibility pathways and the lack of consistent data collection regarding recipients' disabilities, stating with confidence the percentage of Medicaid recipients who have some disability is difficult. Relying on the 2019 American Community Survey, the study just cited estimated that 24 percent of nonelderly, noninstitutionalized adults enrolled in Medicaid (or 5.9 million people) had a disability. But that number does not include the sizable number of elderly disabled Medicaid enrollees or those residing in institutions.

[63] Robin Rudowitz & Rachel Garfield, *10 Things about Medicaid: Setting the Facts Straight*, Kaiser Fam. Found. 4–5 (2018), http://files.kff.org/attachment/Issue-Brief-10-Things-to-Know- about-Medicaid-Setting-the-Facts-Straight.

[64] Reaves & Musumeci, *supra* note 37.

run institutions. Elaine Wilson was admitted to thirty-six institutions. Both women wanted a chance to live in the community. Though Georgia's Medicaid program paid for institution-based treatment, the women's health care providers agreed that community-based treatment would meet their needs. But no space was available in Medicaid-funded community settings. As a result, Curtis and Wilson had no option but to stay in a facility.[65]

Like Curtis and Wilson, many people with disabilities depend on LTSS but do not want to live in a facility like a nursing home, preferring to live in their own home or some other community setting. Even with severe disabilities, most disabled people can live in noninstitutional settings provided they can receive appropriate home and community-based services (HCBS). However, spaces in Medicaid-funded HCBS programs are not equally available in all states. This variability results from Medicaid's structural preference for nursing home care over community-based care, a preference resulting from the distinction between "mandatory" and "optional" Medicaid benefits. Federal law requires coverage of certain "mandatory" services as a condition of a state's participation in Medicaid. It also gives states the freedom to cover a wide range of "optional" services as well as an opportunity to receive waivers of certain statutory requirements. This general framework ensures a baseline of covered services, while giving each state some flexibility to tailor its Medicaid program to its needs. Of relevance to the current discussion, services provided to adults in nursing facilities are mandatory services. By contrast, most home and community-based services (like personal attendant services, habilitation services, transportation support, and case management) are optional.[66]

Independent living advocates have long pushed for more resources and structures to support community-based living. Federal Medicaid policy has responded, increasing the number of ways that states can cover a range of HCBS to support independent living.[67] In 2013, for the first time, a majority of Medicaid LTSS dollars went to HCBS rather than institutional care.[68] But the innovations permitting this redirection of funds generally remain optional for states, resulting in "a patchwork that varies substantially from state to state."[69] All states have opted to cover some HCBS, but most limit their financial exposure by limiting how many Medicaid recipients can participate. The result has been long waiting lists of persons seeking Medicaid-

---

[65] *Sue, Lois, and Elaine, Olmstead Rights,* https://www.olmsteadrights.org/iamolmstead/history.

[66] Sidney D. Watson, *From Almshouses to Nursing Homes and Community Care: Lessons from Medicaid's History,* 26 GA. ST. L. REV. 937 (2010).

[67] Laura D. Hermer, *Rationalizing Home and Community-Based Services under Medicaid,* 8 ST. LOUIS U. J. HEALTH L. & POL'Y 61 (2014); Sara Rosenbaum, *Using the Courts to Shape Medicaid Policy: Olmstead v. L.C. by Zimring and Its Community Integration Legacy,* 41 J. HEALTH POLITICS, POL'Y & L. 585 (2016).

[68] Mary Sowers et al., *Streamlining Medicaid Home and Community-Based Services: Key Policy Questions,* ISSUE BRIEF, KAISER FAM. FOUND. (2016), http://www.kff.org/report-section/streamlining-medicaid-home-and-community-based-services-key-policy-questions-issue-brief.

[69] Hermer, *supra* note 67.

covered services in the community. In 2015, more than 640,000 disabled people were on waiting lists, where they spent more than two years on average.[70]

Litigation under the ADA has been a crucial advocacy tool for expanding HCBS offerings. A disability activist involved in the ADA's 1990 passage observed that the law's "statutory findings ... make it as plain as it could be that the primary evil addressed in the ADA was the segregation that continues to impose an isolated, denigrated existence upon persons with disabilities."[71] And institutionalization was one aspect of that segregation.[72]

Here we return to the story of Lois Curtis and Elaine Wilson. They used the ADA to challenge their continued institutionalization. Specifically, their lawsuit alleged a violation of Title II of the ADA,[73] which prohibits disability discrimination by state and local governments and their programs (like Medicaid). The case reached the U.S. Supreme Court, where Justice Ruth Bader Ginsberg's majority opinion confirmed that "[u]njustified isolation ... is properly regarded as discrimination based on disability."[74] The opinion recognized that undue institutionalization simultaneously perpetuated stigma and prejudice against people with disabilities and severely diminished their ability to pursue "everyday life activities ... including family relations, social contacts, work options, economic independence, educational advancement, and cultural enrichment."[75] Articulating what, practically, a state had to do avoid violating Title II was trickier. If they were required to move some (but not all) disabled persons receiving state-funded services into community settings, states could face logistical and financial difficulties. Justice Ginsburg offered a nuanced (and ultimately ambiguous) standard for assessing whether the state had made the necessary "reasonable modifications" to its programs, by supplying an example: A state could show its compliance with the ADA "[i]f ... it had a comprehensive, effectively working plan for placing qualified persons with mental disabilities in less restrictive settings, and a waiting list that moved at a reasonable pace."[76]

Lois Curtis's and Elaine Wilson's lawsuit *Olmstead v. L.C. ex rel. Zimring* is sometimes called the *Brown v. Board of Education* for disability rights for its importance in decreasing the institutional segregation of people with disabilities. Justice Ginsburg's description of a "comprehensive, effectively working plan" has guided states' efforts to meet the ADA's so-called "community integration" mandate, as well as enforcement activities by disabled plaintiffs and the federal government. By branding unjustified institutionalization as illegal discrimination, *Olmstead*

---

[70] Terrence Ng et al., *Medicaid Home and Community-Based Services Programs: 2013 Data Update*, KAISER FAM. FOUND. REPORT (2016).

[71] Timothy Cook, *The Americans with Disabilities Act: The Move to Integration*, 64 TEMPLE L. REV. 393, 398 (1991).

[72] 42 U.S.C. § 12101.

[73] 42 U.S.C. § 12132.

[74] Olmstead v. L.C. ex rel. Zimring, 527 U.S. 581, 597 (1999).

[75] *Id.* at 602.

[76] *Id.* at 606.

motivated states to take advantage of the federal government's new Medicaid funding streams for HCBS.[77] By 2011, 80 percent of nonelderly Medicaid recipients with disabilities who were receiving LTSS lived in the community, as did 50 percent of elderly recipients with disabilities.[78] Progress has not been uniform, though. A 2020 report scored states' headway over the previous four years in providing long-term services and supports. It found half of the states increased their spending on HCBS relative to institutional care. But the gap between states providing the most support for HCBS and those providing the least grew wider, in part because some states decreased their HCBS spending.[79]

By 2017 the gradual, steady, and sometimes uneven movement away from institutional confinement of disabled people capable of living in the community seemed to reflect in a concrete way the sentiment of Martin Luther King, Jr., that "the arc of the moral universe is long, but it bends toward justice." Yet, Republican attempts in 2017 to fundamentally restructure Medicaid and slash its funding threatened to reverse that progress. To understand the threat, recall that states participating in Medicaid *must* cover care in nursing homes, whereas covering HCBS remains optional. That distinction explains why so many people with disabilities viewed the Republican proposal's projected $880 billion reduction in federal Medicaid spending as an existential threat to progress towards community integration. Optional services (like HCBS) would be natural targets for states desperate to find Medicaid savings in the face of federal cuts. A report from the Center on Budget and Policy Priorities (a nonpartisan research and policy institute) summed up the concern: "HCBS are a likely target if states must make substantial cuts due to federal funding shortfalls, because they spend more on optional HCBS than on any other optional benefit.... Some states could eliminate their HCBS programs altogether."[80] As a result, if enacted, the proposed changes to Medicaid would "risk a return to widespread institutionalization."[81]

[77] Sara Rosenbaum et al., *Olmstead v. L.C.: Implications for Medicaid and Other Publicly Funded Health Services*, 12 HEALTH MATRIX 93 (2002).

[78] Sowers et al., *supra* note 68.

[79] *Long-Term Services & Supports State Scorecard, Advancing Action, 2020 Scorecard Report: Preface*, http://www.longtermscorecard.org/2020-scorecard/preface, and *Major Findings*, http://www.longtermscorecard.org/2020-scorecard/major-findings#footnote6.

[80] Judith Solomon & Jessica Schubel, *Medicaid Cuts in House ACA Repeal Bill Would Limit Availability of Home- and Community-Based Services*, CENTER ON BUDGET AND POLICY PRIORITIES (2017), https://www.cbpp.org/research/health/medicaid-cuts-in-house-aca-repeal-bill-would-limit-availability-of-home-and.

[81] Rebecca Vallas et al., *5 Ways President Trump's Agenda Is a Disaster for People with Disabilities*, CENTER FOR AMERICAN PROGRESS (2017), https://www.americanprogress.org/issues/poverty/news/2017/03/08/427629/5-ways-president-trumps-agenda-disaster-people-disabilities.

6.4 A COMMON PROTEST TO PRESERVE MEDICAID

The changes to Medicaid proposed in 2017 spelled trouble for all persons enrolled in or eligible for the program.[82] Decreased federal funding and an end to the open-ended federal match of state Medicaid spending would leave all enrollees vulnerable to predicted cuts in covered benefits. In addition, finding providers would be a bigger challenge for enrollees if states reduced reimbursement. The disproportionate representation of Black people and people with disabilities among Medicaid enrollees, however, magnified concerns for these groups. Projected funding cuts could exacerbate the health disparities they already experienced. In addition, Black Americans were overrepresented in states that, for a combination of reasons, were less equipped to handle Medicaid funding cuts,[83] and the undoing of existing (and potential) Medicaid expansions would hit them harder than White Americans. For disabled Americans, the prospect of decimated federal funding for Medicaid raised the specter that states would slash funding for HCBS programs, forcing many out of their homes in the community and into institutions. Thus, disabled and Black Americans had both common and distinctive reasons for opposing draconian cuts to the Medicaid program and the repeal of the ACA.

These proposals did more than provoke political opposition; they unleashed moral outrage and a "massive popular mobilization."[84] Protesters showed up for weeks on end as the congressional debate went from simmer to boil. In their home districts, Republican congresspeople experienced "townhall hell," as constituents confronted them.[85] Large protests in Washington included acts of civil disobedience in the halls of Congress. In June 2017, about fifty disabled people were arrested when they staged a "die in" at Senator Mitch McConnell's office in the Capitol. Millions of Americans watched footage as police pulled disabled protestors from their wheelchairs and dragged them away.[86] Several weeks earlier, Reverend William Barber (who was then head of North Carolina's NAACP chapter and later became co-chair

---

[82] Julie Rovner, *Timeline: Despite GOP's Failure to Repeal Obamacare, the ACA Has Changed*, KAISER HEALTH NEWS (Apr. 5, 2018), https://khn.org/news/timeline-roadblocks-to-affordable-care-act-enrollment.

[83] Lola Fadulu, *The Republicans' Medicaid Cuts, if They Pass, Will Disproportionately Hurt Black Americans*, QUARTZ (June 29, 2017), https://qz.com/1016185/bcra-health-care-reform-the-republicans-medicaid-cuts-would-disproportionately-hurt-black-americans.

[84] Abbe R. Gluck & Thomas Scott-Railton, *Affordable Care Act Entrenchment*, 108 GEO. L.J. 495, 540 (2020).

[85] Jessica Taylor, *Anger Rises across the Country at GOP Congressional Town Halls*, NPR (Feb. 22, 2017), https://www.npr.org/2017/02/22/516527499/anger-rises-across-the-country-at-gop-congressional-town-halls.

[86] Jeff Stein, *"No Cuts to Medicaid!": Protesters in Wheelchairs Arrested after Release of Health Care Bill*, Vox (June 22, 2017), https://www.vox.com/policy-and-politics/2017/6/22/15855424/disability-protest-medicaid-mcconnell.

of the Poor People's Campaign) was among dozens of demonstrators arrested in Raleigh for protesting in favor of expanding Medicaid and preserving the ACA.[87]

Including fundamental restructuring of Medicaid in ACA repeal legislation was one of several tactical mistakes by Republicans that may have doomed their 2017 repeal efforts.[88] Medicaid went from being second-class health care in the eyes of many to the ACA's savior, as it "became the central talking point and sticking point of the entire debate over repeal and replace."[89] The predictable human impact of massive Medicaid cuts would have been felt widely and at very personal levels. "Republicans were pushing to restructure a 50-year-old program that covers more than 70 million Americans . . . . The consequences: more than $700 billion in federal spending cuts, versus current law, and a projected 15 million fewer enrollees."[90] Threats to Medicaid, combined with fears of losing guaranteed coverage and protections against preexisting condition exclusions, triggered sustained and effective activism by people of color and people with disabilities, who raised their voices alongside other opponents of the Republican proposals.[91] My research has not uncovered evidence that racial justice groups and disability rights organizations planned a joint strategy or coordinated their efforts. Yet the episode demonstrates the power of their actions, motivated by shared and distinctive interests in preserving and strengthening Medicaid.

6.5 THE NEXT ROUND: WORK REQUIREMENTS

Beating back attempts to repeal the ACA and restructure Medicaid was a temporary victory; it did not fully secure those programs' benefits for low-income Americans. Trump administration actions continued to feed states' appetites to restrict Medicaid eligibility at the margins. States' adoption of work requirements for their Medicaid programs posed special threats to access to care for disabled and Black Medicaid enrollees.

---

[87] Christina Sandidge, *Dozens Arrested after Health-Care Protest in North Carolina*, AP (May 30, 2017), https://apnews.com/article/77cd1e15e92940f29412a4a5a3b35b2e.

[88] Gregory Krieg, *Why the Republican Health Care Message Is Floundering*, CNN: POLITICS (July 8, 2017), https://www.cnn.com/2017/07/08/politics/republicans-health-care-messaging/index.html; Philip Bump, *As Long as the Republican Bill Cuts Medicaid Coverage, It's Likely to Be Unpopular*, WASH. POST (July 13, 2017), https://www.washingtonpost.com/news/politics/wp/2017/07/13/as-long-as-the-republican-bill-cuts-medicaid-coverage-its-likely-to-be-unpopular.

[89] Gluck & Scott-Railton, *supra* note 84, at 541.

[90] Dylan Scott & Sarah Cliff, *Why Obamacare Repeal Failed: And Why It Could Still Come Back*, VOX (July 31, 2017), https://www.vox.com/policy-and-politics/2017/7/31/16055960/why-obamacare-repeal-failed.

[91] Jennifer Flynn, *In the Fight to Save Health Care, the Heroes Ride on Wheelchairs – and Wear Pink*, NATION (Oct. 23, 2017), https://www.thenation.com/article/in-the-fight-to-save-healthcare-the-heroes-ride-on-wheelchairs-and-wear-pink.

Establishing employment-related conditions for receiving welfare benefits has long been a project of conservatives. "Welfare reform" enacted in 1996 subjected welfare recipients participating in the Temporary Aid to Needy Families (TANF) program to work requirements. Some governors argued for similar requirements in Medicaid, but for years the Centers for Medicare and Medicaid Services (CMS) refused to grant states' waiver applications seeking to implement work requirements.[92] In 2018, though, CMS approved Kentucky's waiver application requesting authority to condition Medicaid eligibility on meeting a "community engagement" requirement.[93] By the end of the Trump administration, CMS had approved work requirement waivers for eight states. Judicial challenges to three of those approvals succeeded in the lower courts, blocking their implementation, and in February 2021 the Biden administration informed states of its preliminary judgment that work requirements did not advance Medicaid's objectives, signaling its likely rescission of existing waivers.[94] As I write, Medicaid work requirements are thus off the table, but a future, conservative, administration could revive the policy.

Medicaid work requirements are dubious policy. The Trump administration claimed to support work requirements to assist states' "efforts to improve Medicaid enrollee health and well-being through incentivizing work and community engagement" and "to help individuals and families rise out of poverty and attain independence."[95] Experience with TANF work requirements, however, suggested Medicaid work requirements were unlikely to accomplish those goals. Many Medicaid enrollees already work. Most who don't work report that a family-related responsibility or a major impediment (like a physical health condition, addiction, or limited education) keeps them from holding a job. Expecting people in such circumstances to get and keep a job is unrealistic, at least without help from supportive services that state Medicaid agencies are not equipped to offer.[96] Many people receiving Medicaid rely on it to keep them healthy enough to be able to work, so, ironically, losing eligibility could decrease their employability.[97] Even people who find jobs in the

---

[92] HEATHER HAHN ET AL., WORK REQUIREMENTS IN SOCIAL SAFETY NET PROGRAMS 5 (Urban Inst. ed., 2017), https://www.urban.org/sites/default/files/publication/95566/work-requirements-social-safety-net-programs_4.pdf.

[93] Benjy Sarlin, *First-in-Nation Medicaid Work Requirements Approved for Kentucky*, NBC NEWS (Jan. 12, 2018), https://www.nbcnews.com/politics/white-house/first-nation-medicaid-work-requirements-approved-white-house-kentucky-n837281.

[94] *Medicaid Waiver Tracking: Approved and Pending Section 1115 Waivers by State*, KAISER FAM. FOUND. (Apr. 16, 2021), https://www.kff.org/medicaid/issue-brief/medicaid-waiver-tracker-approved-and-pending-section-1115-waivers-by-state/#Table2.

[95] Brian Neale, Dir., *Centers for Medicare & Medicaid Services, Letter to State Medicaid Directors on Opportunities to Promote Work and Community Engagement among Medicaid Beneficiaries* (Jan. 11, 2018).

[96] MaryBeth Musumeci & Julia Zur, *Medicaid Enrollees and Work Requirements: Lessons from the TANF Experience*, KAISER FAM. FOUND. 3 (2017), https://www.kff.org/medicaid/issue-brief/medicaid-enrollees-and-work-requirements-lessons-from-the-tanf-experience.

[97] *Id.* at 5–9. Hannah Katch et al., *Taking Medicaid Coverage Away from People Not Meeting Work Requirements Will Reduce Low-Income Families' Access to Care and Worsen Health*

wake of a work requirement are unlikely to "attain independence," since the jobs that Medicaid enrollees typically hold often do not offer health insurance. A study examining evidence from Arkansas's work requirement waiver bears out these points. Researchers found no evidence that employment rose among low-income adults in Arkansas as compared to three other states.[98] During the work requirement's implementation, more than 18,000 Arkansans lost their Medicaid coverage, often when they failed to meet online reporting requirements because they lacked a computer or internet access or because they were unaware of the need to report.[99]

Beyond these general drawbacks, work requirements pose distinctive threats to the coverage and well-being of people with disabilities and racial or ethnic minorities. The nature and seriousness of these threats somewhat depend on how a state crafts and implements work requirements, but several concerns deserve noting.

6.5.1 Black People and Work Requirements

"Welfare reform" initiatives often fall more harshly on Black people. Work requirements are no exception. Appeals to racist stereotypes ("Black people don't want to work") have activated political support for work requirements in contexts including cash welfare benefits, nutrition assistance, and Medicaid.[100] Some states even sought to implement work requirements in ways that directly disadvantaged Black residents. When they applied to the federal government for Medicaid waivers to permit them to implement work requirements, several states proposed exemptions from the requirement based on county unemployment rates. For example, Michigan's original proposal would have exempted Medicaid enrollees living in a county with an unemployment rate higher than 8.5 percent from being subject to a work requirement. The exemption ostensibly was to shield rural counties, which have fewer jobs and particular transportation challenges. Analyses revealed, however, that such exemptions would disproportionately favor White people.[101] Rural counties exempted from the work requirement are Whiter than more densely populated counties, where the requirement would kick people off Medicaid. In Michigan, counties with an unemployment rate above 10 percent were 75 percent to 90 percent

Outcomes, CTR. ON BUDGET & POL'Y PRIORITIES (2018), https://www.cbpp.org/sites/default/files/atoms/files/2-8-18health2.pdf.

[98] Benjamin D. Sommers et al., *Medicaid Work Requirements in Arkansas: Two-Year Impacts on Coverage, Employment, and Affordability of Care*, 39 HEALTH AFF. 1522 (2020).

[99] Houston Cofield, *The Medicaid Experiment in Arkansas: Thousands, Lost Coverage, Few Gained Jobs; Many Recipients Were Confused by Mandate, Had Technical Trouble Complying or Were Already Working*, WALL ST. J., Oct. 13, 2019.

[100] Bryce Covert, *The Not-So-Subtle Racism of Trump-Era "Welfare Reform,"* N.Y. TIMES (May 23, 2018), https://www.nytimes.com/2018/05/23/opinion/trump-welfare-reform-racism.html.

[101] Rachel Garfield et al., *Implications of Work Requirements in Medicaid: What Does the Data Say?*, KAISER FAM. FOUND. 11 (2018), https://www.kff.org/medicaid/issue-brief/implications-of-work-requirements-in-medicaid-what-does-the-data-say.

White.[102] Had it gone into effect, only 1.2 percent of the exemption's beneficiaries would have been Black, while Black enrollees constitute 23 percent of Michigan's Medicaid enrollment. After news stories publicized the racial disparity, Michigan eliminated the exemption from its proposal.[103]

Even without exemptions for high-unemployment counties, imposing work requirements for Medicaid eligibility would likely have an outsized negative effect on Black people. As a group, Black Americans face barriers to employment. Racial disparities in health, education, and incarceration all contribute to persistent gaps in White/Black employment rates.[104] Continuing discrimination is another likely contributor to racial disparities in employment outcomes.[105]

6.5.2 *People with Disabilities and Work Requirements*

Disabled people would also face greater harms from Medicaid work requirements. As with Black people, multiple impediments to employment are at play, including educational disparities and disproportionate incarceration rates. Despite the ADA's requirement that employers provide reasonable accommodations, many disabled people seeking employment still face biased attitudes and receive inadequate, if any, accommodations. The jobless rate for disabled people is much higher than it is for nondisabled people, and disabled people are more likely to be out of the labor force (meaning they do not seek employment).[106]

---

[102] Dylan Scott, *How Medicaid Work Requirements Can Exempt Rural Whites but Not Urban Blacks*, Vox (May 3, 2018), https://www.vox.com/policy-and-politics/2018/5/3/17315382/medicaid-work-requirements-michigan-race. Jeff Stein & Andrew Van Dam, *Michigan's GOP Has a Plan to Shield Some People from Medicaid Work Requirements*, WASH. POST (May 11, 2018), https://www.washingtonpost.com/news/wonk/wp/2018/05/11/michigans-gop-has-a-plan-to-shield-some-people-from-medicaid-work-requirements-theyre-overwhelmingly-white/.

[103] In comparison, Whites constitute 57 percent of Medicaid beneficiaries in Michigan, but would make up 85 percent of persons benefiting from the exemption. Alice Ollstein, *Trump Admin Poised to Give Rural Whites a Carve-Out on Medicaid Work Rules*, TALKING POINTS MEMO (May 14, 2018), https://talkingpointsmemo.com/dc/trump-admin-poised-to-give-rural-whites-a-carve-out-on-medicaid-work-rules. Amanda Michelle Gomez, *Michigan Scrapped Its Racist Medicaid Work Exemption. But It's Still Happening Elsewhere.*, THINKPROGRESS (May 24, 2018), https://thinkprogress.org/michigan-scrapped-its-racist-medicaid-work-exemption-but-its-still-happening-elsewhere-9a044d4ed9b2.

[104] Michael Massoglia, *Incarceration, Health, and Racial Disparities in Health*, 42 LAW. & SOC'Y REV. 275, 276–78 (2008); Janelle Jones, *Black Unemployment Is at Least Twice as High as White Unemployment at the National Level and in 12 States and D.C.*, ECON. POL'Y INST. (Oct. 30, 2018), https://www.epi.org/publication/2018q3_unemployment_state_race_ethnicity.

[105] Jhacova Williams & Valerie Wilson, *Black Workers Endure Persistent Racial Disparities in Employment Outcomes*, ECONOMIC POLICY INSTITUTE (Aug. 27, 2019), https://www.epi.org/publication/labor-day-2019-racial-disparities-in-employment.

[106] *Persons with a Disability: Labor Force Characteristics – 2020*, BUREAU OF LABOR STATISTICS (Feb. 24, 2021), https://www.bls.gov/news.release/pdf/disabl.pdf.

Proponents of Medicaid work requirements often defend them as targeting "able-bodied" adults and exempting people with disabilities, senior citizens, and pregnant women. Trump administration guidance clarified that work requirements could not apply to disabled persons receiving SSI and also directed states to include exemptions for "medically frail" persons.[107] But nearly 5 million disabled Medicaid enrollees do not receive SSI,[108] often because their impairments are not judged to produce total and permanent disability. Those Medicaid recipients can still experience significant functional limitations that make it hard to find and keep a job. Persons with mental illness or cognitive disabilities face special challenges. Employers are often ill equipped to accommodate sometimes fluctuating symptoms of mental illness, and Medicaid programs rarely provide the intensive employment supports that persons with mental or cognitive disabilities may need. Disproportionately high rates of criminal justice system involvement further diminish employability.

Nor would "medical frailty" exemptions reliably protect disabled people from losing Medicaid coverage. Trump administration guidance failed to specify how medical frailty should be determined and by whom, leaving states substantial discretion to flesh out the exemption. States could have chosen to turn to physicians to apply the exemption, reenacting the historical pattern of giving physician-gatekeepers power to control disabled people's access to needed benefits. Giving physicians the "keys" to Medicaid eligibility would have been particularly cruel for persons who lost coverage after failing to report employment. Without insurance, finding a doctor who would see them and document their medical frailty could have been nearly impossible.[109]

Medicaid work requirements thus represent another Medicaid policy issue where disabled people and Black people share common interests that could support collaborative advocacy and activism. The Biden administration's reprieve from work requirement implementation has been welcome, but its durability is uncertain. Conservative enthusiasm for work requirements and other policy initiatives to decrease the federal government's role in Medicaid and otherwise diminish the program are unlikely to dissipate. Medicaid thus is likely to remain common terrain on which Black people and disabled people fight to defend and advance their interests in health care access as a component of health equity.

---

[107] Neale, *supra* note 95, at 5–6.

[108] Center on Budget Pol'y & Priorities, *Taking Away Medicaid for Not Meeting Work Requirements Harms People with Disabilities* 2 (2020), https://www.cbpp.org/sites/default/files/atoms/files/1-26-18health.pdf.

[109] Milton C. Weinstein, *Should Physicians Be Gatekeepers of Medical Resources?*, 27 J. MED. ETHICS 268, 269 (2001). John Z. Ayanian et al., *Mitigating the Risks of Medicaid Work Requirements*, 379 N. ENG. J. MED. 803, 804 (2018).

7

Beyond Health Care

Social Determinants

7.1 SOCIAL DETERMINANTS OF HEALTH

Previous chapters examined how medical providers and the health care financing system have contributed to health inequities that Black people and disabled people in the United States encounter. But having health insurance and getting to see an unbiased, high quality doctor are not necessarily the most important contributors to promoting health and health equity, either for individuals or at the population level. More important are other determinants of health. These include individual behaviors like smoking, diet, and exercise and – critically – the social and physical environments that shape individual conduct.[1] To give one example: neighborhood safety and availability of parks or playgrounds nearby influence a person's ability to exercise conveniently and safely. Healthy behavior takes some individual initiative, but that initiative is far more likely when social and physical environments make healthy options available and easy to choose.[2]

7.1.1 *A Conceptual Framework*

Long part of public health's vocabulary, the phrase "social determinants of health" has entered mainstream discussions of health in recent years, signaling broader recognition that health is not simply a product of genetic endowment and medical care. The meaning attached to the phrase has evolved over time, and its usage today is not always consistent. The World Health Organization (WHO) describes "social

---

[1] Laura McGovern, *The Relative Contribution of Multiple Determinants to Health Outcomes*, HEALTH AFFAIRS HEALTH POLICY BRIEF (Aug. 21, 2014), https://www.healthaffairs.org/do/10 .1377/hpb20140821.404487/full; Samantha Artiga & Elizabeth Hinton, *Beyond Health Care: The Role of Social Determinants in Promoting Health and Health Equity*, KAISER FAM. FOUND. ISSUE BRIEF (May 2018).

[2] Paula Braveman & Susan Egerter, *Overcoming Obstacles to Health*, ROBERT WOOD JOHNSON FOUND. 9 (Feb. 2008).

determinants of health" as "the conditions in which people are born, grow, live, work and age."[3] That description is capacious, seeming to encompass much of human existence. To aid more precise thinking about social determinants, a conceptual framework adopted by the WHO divides them into two categories.[4] "Intermediary determinants" include things like living conditions, food availability, and psychosocial factors (like stress or discrimination). These provide the immediate context in which people go about their lives. "Structural determinants" are a step removed. They include things like government structures, public policies, and forces like racism and ableism. Structural determinants contribute to producing stratification in social status and conditions. They determine why some groups of people enjoy living in health-promoting conditions while other groups are consigned to health-harming conditions.[5]

This description of social determinants of health makes apparent that earlier chapters have already addressed some of them without using the label. Racism and ableism are structural determinants that show up in physician biases and in the "weathering" that Black patients experience from chronic exposure to discrimination (both intermediary determinants). And many discussions also include access to health care as an intermediary determinant.[6]

This chapter focuses on specific intermediary determinants in three realms: housing, education, and the criminal justice system. It explores how they operate to produce health inequity for Black people and people with disabilities. Close inspection reveals similarities in how those inequities are produced. It also reminds us that Blackness and disability as identities frequently overlap and that social factors' deleterious effects land with especial weight on persons who are both Black and disabled. In the process, the importance of intersectionality becomes highly visible.

7.1.2 *Poverty's Potency*

Poverty is a critical structural determinant of health and is central to the operation and interaction of multiple intermediary determinants. Both people with disabilities and Black people are disproportionately represented among people living in poverty

---

[3] World Health Organization, *Social Determinants of Health*, https://www.who.int/health-topics/social-determinants-of-health#tab=tab_1.

[4] World Health Organization, A Conceptual Framework for Action on the Social Determinants of Health 5–6 (2010), https://www.who.int/sdhconference/resources/ConceptualframeworkforactiononSDH_eng.pdf.

[5] Camara P. Jones draws a similar distinction between social determinants of health and social determinants of equity, with the latter playing a role analogous to the WHO's structural determinants. She uses "social determinants of equity" to refer to systems of power (like racism, ableism, and capitalism, among others) that "govern the distribution of resources and populations through decision-making structures, policies, practices, norms, and values." Camara P. Jones, *Systems of Power, Axes of Inequity: Parallels, Intersections, Braiding the Strands*, 52 Med. Care S71, S72 (2014).

[6] Lindsay Wiley, *Health Law as Social Justice*, 24 Cornell J.L. Pub. Pol'y 47 (2014).

in the United States. In 2019, the percentage of adults with a disability living in poverty (22.5 percent) vastly exceeded that of adults with no disability (8.4 percent).[7] Black people are more likely to live in poverty than are White people. According to Census Bureau data, in 2019 almost one in five Black people had incomes below the federal poverty level, compared to almost one in ten White people.[8] And a higher prevalence of many disabilities among Black people[9] means that, in an income-and-identity Venn diagram, the overlap among Blackness, disability, and poverty is substantial.

Poverty's intimate connections to other forms of insecurity and instability are easy to apprehend, making it a good launching pad from which to consider the intricate connections among social determinants of health. If your income is severely limited so are your opportunities to eat nutritious foods, attend a good school, and live in a safe neighborhood. Multiple social determinants may be tightly entangled in an individual's life, as well as in the lives of communities. For example, racial residential segregation leads to racially segregated schools. Predominantly minority schools often lack resources to provide social and developmental supports for their students, often leaving them to use suspensions and expulsions to try to manage student conduct. Punitive discipline is associated with disproportionate referral of students to the justice system compared with nonminority schools, a fact that contributes to mass incarceration of people of color. And determinants often interact in a bidirectional fashion.[10] Not only does the disruption of schooling make justice system involvement more likely; criminal conviction creates post-incarceration barriers to education and housing, as we will see.

Social determinants that harm health are parts of systems, not isolated problems.[11] Fully wrapping our collective head around the parallels between and intersections of social determinants for Black people and disabled persons would be a tall order, probably requiring its own book. My purpose here is more limited. This chapter's focus on specific intermediary determinants reveals headwinds that make good health seemingly unattainable. It also presents a question: Why are those metaphorical headwinds gusting through some neighborhoods and not others?

[7] *Income and Poverty in the United States: 2019*, https://www.census.gov/library/publications/2020/demo/p60–270.html. Census Bureau disability data come from three different surveys, all of which ask about six disability types: hearing difficulty, vision difficulty, cognitive difficulty, ambulatory difficulty, self-care difficulty, and independent living difficulty. The Bureau considers a respondent reporting any of the six disability types to have a disability. *U.S. Census Bureau, How Disability Data Are Collected from the American Community Survey*, https://www.census.gov/topics/health/disability/guidance/data-collection-acs.html.
[8] *Income and Poverty in the United States: 2019, supra* note 7.
[9] Nanette Goodman et al., *Financial Inequality: Disability, Race and Poverty in America*, NAT'L DISABILITY INST. (2019), https://www.nationaldisabilityinstitute.org/wp-content/uploads/2019/02/disability-race-poverty-in-america.pdf.
[10] McGovern, *supra* note 1, at 3.
[11] Emily A. Benfer, *Health Justice: A Framework (and Call to Action) for the Elimination of Health Inequity and Social Injustice*, 65 AM. U. L. REV. 275 (2015).

7.2 UNHEALTHY NEIGHBORHOODS

7.2.1 *Racial Segregation*

Two Metro stops, just miles apart from one another in Washington, D.C., tell a story. Residents living in the affluent, mostly White neighborhood near the Woodley Park stop have an average life expectancy of 89.4 years. The average for residents of the poor and mostly Black neighborhood adjacent to the St. Elizabeth's stop is 68.2 years.[12] This yawning gap is not unique. Findings like these are sometimes summed up in memorable (albeit oversimplified) proclamations that a person's ZIP code predicts health outcomes better than their genetic code.[13] Of course, the Postal Service' designations for letter carriers do not themselves affect residents' health. Rather, neighborhood-level variations in social determinants of health are the cause.

In short, place matters to health. Environmental factors at the neighborhood level affect individual health and are not evenly shared across communities.[14] Health-promoting amenities like walkable streets, parks for outdoor recreation, and sources for fresh and healthy foods are typically scarce in low-income neighborhoods. Health harms like polluted air and water, dangerous streets, and proximity to hazardous waste, by contrast, abound. The schools are under-resourced, the policing over-aggressive.

This negative balance of social determinants tends to be most pronounced in communities of concentrated poverty, where poverty is most pervasive, and where residents' complexions tend to be darker. In the early twenty-first century, the number of Americans living in extremely poor neighborhoods (where at least 40 percent of residents live below the federal poverty line) more than doubled. By the beginning of the century's second decade, one in four Black people lived in an extremely poor, distressed neighborhood, while only one in twenty Whites did.[15] Although concentrated poverty often evokes images of urban decay, poverty is also common in rural counties. In 2018, nearly 80 percent of high poverty counties (where 20 percent or more of residents lived below the federal poverty level) were rural counties. All the extreme poverty counties were rural, and they were

---

[12] Courtland Milloy, *The District's Racial and Income Divide Is Cutting Short Lives of Black Residents*, WASH. POST (May 14, 2019), https://www.washingtonpost.com/local/the-districts-racial-and-income-divide-is-cutting-short-the-lives-of-black-residents/2019/05/14/bb5f991a-765c-11e9-bd25-c989555e7766_story.html.

[13] See Garth N. Graham, *Why Your ZIP Code Matters More than Your Genetic Code: Promoting Healthy Outcomes from Mother to Child*, 11 BREASTFEEDING MED. 396 (2016).

[14] *Why Place Matters: Building a Movement for Healthy Communities*, POLICYLINK (2007), https://www.policylink.org/resources-tools/why-place-matters-building-the-movement-for-healthy-communities.

[15] Elizabeth Kneebone & Natalie Holmes, *U.S. Concentrated Poverty in the Wake of the Great Recession*, BROOKINGS INSTITUTION (2016), https://www.brookings.edu/research/u-s-concentrated-poverty-in-the-wake-of-the-great-recession/.

disproportionately located in areas (like Mississippi and South Dakota) with high non-White populations.[16]

Even as the country's population becomes more diverse, most Americans live in racially segregated neighborhoods.[17] And even middle-class Black Americans are more likely to live in neighborhoods where many of their neighbors are poor. Persistent segregation is the legacy of historically racist restrictive covenants, discriminatory zoning, mortgage discrimination, and redlining.[18] Despite de jure segregation's end a half century ago, a 2021 study found that between 1990 and 2019 racial segregation increased in over 80 percent of large metropolitan regions in the United States.[19] Racial segregation in housing also may be increasing in the suburbs and rural areas,[20] often encouraged by policies supporting "urban renewal" and gentrification.[21]

Racial residential segregation affects health via multiple pathways.[22] Highly segregated Black neighborhoods have few private primary care doctor practices, leaving residents to rely on resource-strapped safety net facilities for preventive health services.[23] And the impacts go much deeper than access to care. In 2001, David R. Williams and Chiquita Collins characterized segregation as "the cornerstone on which black-white disparities in health status have been built," contributing to disparities both by limiting socioeconomic mobility and by creating health-harming social and physical conditions in Black communities.[24] Racial residential segregation profoundly influences other social determinants of health, and recent studies connect it to specific negative health outcomes. Authors of a 2018 national study

[16] Tracey Farrigan, *Extreme Poverty Counties Found Solely in Rural Areas in 2018*, USDA ECO. RES. SERVICE (May 4, 2020), https://www.ers.usda.gov/amber-waves/2020/may/extreme-poverty-counties-found-solely-in-rural-areas-in-2018.

[17] Tracy Hadden Loh et al., *The Great Real Estate Reset*, BROOKINGS (Dec. 16, 2020), https://www.brookings.edu/essay/trend-1-separate-and-unequal-neighborhoods-are-sustaining-racial-and-economic-injustice-in-the-us/.

[18] RICHARD ROTHSTEIN, THE COLOR OF LAW: A FORGOTTEN HISTORY OF HOW OUR GOVERNMENT SEGREGATED AMERICA (2017); Ta-Nehesi Coates, *The Case for Reparations*, THE ATLANTIC (June 2014), https://www.theatlantic.com/magazine/archive/2014/06/the-case-for-reparations/361631.

[19] Stephen Menendian et al., *The Roots of Structural Racism: Twenty-First Century Racial Residential Segregation in the United States*, OTHERING & BELONGING INSTITUTE (June 21, 2021), https://belonging.berkeley.edu/roots-structural-racism-report.

[20] Scott Burris et al., *A Vision of Health Equity in Housing* 10–11 (2019), https://papers.ssrn.com/sol3/papers.cfm?abstract_id=3480628.

[21] Mindy Fullilove, *Root Shock: The Consequences of African American Dispossession*, 78 J. URB. HEALTH 72 (2001).

[22] David R. Williams et al., *Racism and Health: Evidence and Needed Research*, 40 ANN. REV. PUBLIC HEALTH 105, 107 (2019).

[23] Kellee White et al., *Elucidating the Role of Place in Health Care Disparities: The Example of Racial/Ethnic Residential Segregation*, 47 HEALTH SERV. RES. 1278 (2012).

[24] David R. Williams & Chiquita Collins, *Racial Residential Segregation: A Fundamental Cause of Racial Disparities in Health*, 116 PUB. HEALTH REPORTS 404 (2001). Later studies described in Williams (2019) bolster this description.

detected an association between levels of segregation and the odds of stillbirth, with Black women benefitting more than White women as segregation decreased. Their conclusion: Decreasing segregation could help narrow the racial disparity in still-birth rates.[25] A 2021 study found that higher levels of racial and socioeconomic segregation in a county predicted higher COVID-19 mortality rates.[26]

7.2.2 *Isolation's Harms for Black People and Disabled People*

Segregation "has never simply been about the sorting of people, but about the sorting of opportunity and the resources that shape life chances."[27] An insight from legal scholar john a. powell and researcher Stephen Menendian explains how the isolation associated with racial and economic segregation contributes to poor health outcomes and racial health disparities. Physical segregation enables forces of struc-tural racism to deprive predominantly Black neighborhoods of material goods needed for good health.[28] But perhaps as important is racial segregation's effect on access to social capital and resources. Living in a racially and economically diverse community offers access to social supports, decent schools, and job opportunities. By contrast, living in a high poverty, distressed neighborhood – a situation far more likely for Black Americans – increases social stresses, cuts off access to mainstream opportunities, and limits social mobility.[29]

Isolation and segregation of a different sort have characterized the living circum-stances of many people with disabilities in the United States. The long history of segregating disabled people includes the eugenics-era maintenance of "colonies" for the "feeble-minded," as well as mass confinement of disabled people in hospitals and other institutions well into the second half of the twentieth century. The deinstitutionalization movement that started in the 1950s eventually shuttered most state-run institutions for people with psychiatric or intellectual disabilities. But several dozen state-run institutions continue to operate,[30] and many disabled people reside in other congregate settings (like nursing homes or group homes) designed *only* for people with disabilities. These settings effectively segregate residents from

---

[25] Andrew D. Williams et al., *Racial Residential Segregation and Racial Disparities in Stillbirth in the United States*, 51 HEALTH & PLACE 208 (2018).

[26] Ahmad Khanijahani & Larisa Tomassoni, *Socioeconomic and Racial Segregation and COVID-19: Concentrated Disadvantage and Black Concentration in Association with COVID-19 Deaths in the USA*, J. RACIAL & ETHNIC HEALTH DISPARITIES (2021), https://doi.org/10.1007/s40615-021-00965-1.

[27] john a. powell & Stephen Menendian, *Segregation in the 21st Century*, 25 POVERTY AND RACE RESEARCH ACTION COUNCIL 17 (2016).

[28] Dayna Bowen Matthew, *On Charlottesville*, 105 VA. L. REV. 269, 327 (2019).

[29] Williams et al., *supra* note 22, at 108; Margery Austin Turner & Lynette A. Rawlings, *Overcoming Concentrated Poverty and Isolation: Lessons from Three HUD Demonstration Initiatives* 5, THE URBAN INSTITUTE (2005).

[30] *Home Is in the Community – with the Services to Thrive*, THE ARC, https://thearc.org/policy-advocacy/medicaid/medicaidcantwait/.

the broader community. And the tendency to site group homes close together has created "service-dependent ghettos," as some neighborhoods become identified as locations of congregate housing for people with cognitive or psychiatric disabilities.[31] Aside from residential segregation, businesses' failures to make their spaces fully accessible push people with disabilities out of public spaces.[32] And high incarceration rates, discussed below, also segregate disabled people from daily life in society.

Segregation of people with disabilities flows from structural apparati, policies, and prejudices that differ from those that have fed and still feed racial segregation. Yet the outcomes share an important feature. In both cases, isolation limits chances to develop intergroup connections and opportunities associated with mainstream society. While numerous health effects of racial segregation have been documented, connections between disability segregation and health (outside the context of COVID-19, discussed later) are less developed and need more investigation.

7.2.3 Barriers to Shelter: Affordability, Accessibility, and NIMBYism

Getting into and maintaining housing can be a struggle for people who are Black, disabled, or both. Trouble achieving stable housing can flow from a shortage of affordable and accessible housing options or from neighborhood resistance. The difficulty threatens the health of those for whom shelter is insecure or out of reach.

7.2.3.1 The Affordability Crunch

The number of households falling behind in their ability to pay for adequate housing and other needs has been growing. Many areas in the United States face a serious affordable housing shortage. In 2016, nearly 20 million renter households were "cost burdened," paying more than 30 percent of their annual income for rent and utilities.[33] And the percentage of very low-income renters who, without any government assistance, paid more than half their income for rent or lived in severely inadequate conditions increased by nearly 40 percent between 2005 and 2015.[34] Excess housing demand in those areas generates upward pressure on rents, exacerbating unaffordability.

---

[31] Philip T. Yanos, *Beyond "Landscapes of Despair": The Need for New Research on the Urban Environment, Sprawl, and the Community Integration of Persons with Severe Mental Illness*, 13 HEALTH PLACE 672 (2007).

[32] Dara Shifrer & Angela Frederick, *Disability at the Intersections*, 13 SOCIOLOGY COMPASS e12733 (2019).

[33] *National Low-Income Housing Coalition, the Gap: A Shortage of Affordable Homes* (Mar. 2018), https://reports.nlihc.org/sites/default/files/gap/Gap-Report_2018.pdf.

[34] See NICOLE ELSASSER WATSON ET AL., WORST CASE HOUSING NEEDS 2017 REPORT TO CONGRESS (2017), https://www.huduser.gov/portal/sites/default/files/pdf/Worst-Case-Housing-Needs.pdf.

Affordable housing advocates use terms like "cost-burdened" and "trade-offs" to describe how people who are hard put to afford shelter walk a financial tightrope. Folks paying a large fraction of a small income for a place to live know this as not having enough to go around. "Housing costs absorb more and more of my take home pay, so therefore I survive on less," wrote one person responding to HuffPost's call for readers' stories about housing affordability. "I eat once a day. I do not purchase new clothing or shoes unless absolutely required. My automobile is in need of significant repairs that I cannot afford."[35] Paying for housing forces some families to skimp on food, clothing, or medical care, with negative health effects. Constantly struggling to make ends meet causes chronic stress, itself an independent contributor to health problems including heart disease, obesity, accelerated cognitive decline, and mental health disorders. An unrelenting threat of eviction or foreclosure shadows daily life, accompanied by knowledge that a financial surprise or setback could tip an individual or family out of a dwelling and into homelessness.

7.2.3.2 Affordability and Accessibility for Black and Disabled People

Affordable housing shortages weigh more heavily on Black and Hispanic[36] renters, who are disproportionately likely to have extremely low incomes.[37] In documenting the housing travails of Milwaukee's poor residents, sociologist Matthew Desmond explicitly connects eviction to race: "If incarceration had come to define the lives of men from impoverished black neighborhoods, eviction was shaping the lives of women. Poor black men were locked up. Poor black women were locked out."[38] Desmond found that female renters in Milwaukee's poorest Black neighborhoods faced judicial evictions at a rate nine times higher than women in the city's poorest White neighborhoods. A maelstrom of further housing precarity, hasty moves into lower quality housing, or homelessness can follow in an eviction's wake, threatening the health of renters and their families. One study found that women who received an eviction notice while pregnant had higher rates of premature and low birthweight

---

[35] Michael Hobbes, *"I Eat Once a Day": The Untold Stories of the Housing Crisis*, HuffPost (Nov. 9, 2018), https://www.huffpost.com/entry/housing-crisis-reader-stories_n_5be0a09ce4b09 d43e321cedf?guccounter.

[36] The descriptors "Latino/a" (and its non-binary form, "Latinx") and "Hispanic" are sometimes used interchangeably, but their meanings vary. "Hispanic" refers to people from Spain or the Americas who are Spanish speaking or descendants of Spanish-speaking communities. "Latino," by contrast, describes persons with ancestry in Latin America. In this book, I follow the usage of the source that I am relying on.

[37] Burris et al., *supra* note 20.

[38] Matthew Desmond, Evicted: Poverty and Profit in the American City 98 (2016). Without separating out female renters, Desmond found that typically three-quarters of the people in Milwaukee's eviction court were Black. *Id.* at 97.

babies.[39] Communities with high eviction rates also suffer. High rates of residential turn over, a byproduct of housing unaffordability, cause harm to the entire community by disrupting social stability and cohesion.[40]

Housing unaffordability also burdens disabled people, who disproportionately live in poverty. Disabled adults who live on Supplemental Security Income (SSI) face a housing affordability gap in every state.[41] And some disabled people face the added hurdle of needing to find a place that is both affordable and accessible. The federal Fair Housing Act (FHA) creates accessibility requirements for private multifamily dwellings, but only for those first occupied after March 13, 1991.[42] The limited stock of affordable housing, however, is often in older structures not subject to the law's accessibility standards. A low-income disabled person who needs accessible housing thus faces a compounded challenge.

The health risks associated with housing precarity, described above, also affect people with disabilities. Some aspects of their risks, though, are distinctive. People with disabling mental illness face a heightened risk of homelessness if they do not receive supportive services, with about one in five homeless people in the United States having a severe mental illness.[43] For people who are chronically homeless, the prevalence of mental health disabilities and substance use disorders is likely much higher.[44] Difficulty finding affordable housing is not the only reason a person with a psychiatric disability may become homeless, but it magnifies other challenges to housing stability.

Institutional segregation is an alternative, often dreaded fate for some disabled people unable to find affordable and accessible housing. The ADA's "community integration" mandate means state programs like Medicaid that provide supportive services to people with disabilities must do so in the community when possible.[45] But Medicaid does not pay rent for independent housing; that responsibility is left to the individual, with whatever help might be available from low-income housing

[39] Gracie Himmelstein & Matthew Desmond, *Association of Eviction with Adverse Birth Outcomes among Women in Georgia, 2000–2016*, JAMA PEDIATRICS (Mar. 1, 2021), doi:10.1001/jamapediatrics.2020.6550.

[40] Burris et al., *supra* note 20, at 9–10.

[41] Gina Schaak et al., PRICED OUT: THE HOUSING CRISIS FOR PEOPLE WITH DISABILITIES, TECHNICAL ASSISTANCE COLLABORATIVE & CONSORTIUM FOR CITIZENS WITH DISABILITIES HOUSING TASK FORCE (2017).

[42] 42 U.S.C. § 3604(f)(3)(C).

[43] HUD, *HUD 2020 Continuum of Care Homeless Assistance Programs Homeless Populations and Subpopulations* 2 (2020), https://files.hudexchange.info/reports/published/CoC_PopSub_NatlTerrDC_2020.pdf.

[44] Heidi Schultheis, *Lack of Housing and Mental Health Disabilities Exacerbate One Another*, CENTER FOR AMERICAN PROGRESS (Nov. 20, 2018), https://www.americanprogress.org/issues/poverty/news/2018/11/20/461294/lack-housing-mental-health-disabilities-exacerbate-one-another. Doug Smith & Benjamin Oreskes, *Are Many Homeless People in L.A. Mentally Ill? New Findings Back the Public's Perception*, L.A. TIMES (Oct. 7, 2019), https://www.latimes.com/california/story/2019-10-07/homeless-population-mental-illness-disability.

[45] Olmstead v. L.C. ex rel. Zimring, 527 U.S. 581 (1999).

programs. Affordable housing programs may sometimes fail to address accessibility needs. For example, a federal lawsuit filed in 2018 alleged that the City of Chicago directed hundreds of millions of dollars of federal funding to private developers as part of its massive affordable housing program, but failed to make sure the resulting units would comply with the accessibility requirements of the ADA, Section 504 of the Rehabilitation Act, and the Fair Housing Act.[46] When failures like those alleged occur, finding affordable and accessible housing can prove to be insurmountable barriers for some people with disabilities, forcing them into undesired and segregated living situations.

7.2.3.3 Whose Back Yard?

Another shared antagonist in Black people's and disabled people's quest for integrated, affordable, and thus healthier, housing is NIMBYism (the acronym stands for "not in my backyard"). Despite fair housing laws prohibiting race and disability discrimination in housing, racial prejudice and disability bias block affordable housing development in some cases. Cities, landlords, neighborhood associations, and others may erect various types of impediments to affordable housing or independent living projects, including zoning ordinances, chronic nuisance regulations, neighborhood opposition, and lease restrictions. While objectors typically frame their "not in my backyard" concerns in neutral language about protecting property values or public safety, an undercurrent of bias is not hard to detect. In some cases, it's right on the surface.

When neighbors or local officials organize to block the opening of a group home for disabled people, disability's role is salient, even if the home's opponents assert allegedly neutral bases for their opposition. Though sometimes criticized by disability advocates as providing residents insufficient independence and integration, group homes are designed to provide the supports needed to enable people with cognitive, psychiatric, or physical disabilities to live in the community, outside of larger, more confining institutional settings. For example, after the operator of a group home for six men with disabilities faced mounting opposition from town residents, it sued elected officials in Cromwell, Connecticut, alleging they had violated the FHA and the ADA by stoking community opposition to the home's opening and challenging the operator's license and tax-exempt status.[47] In an order denying the defendant's motion for summary judgment, the trial court held that

---

[46] *Access Living Sues Chicago for Failing to Ensure Assisted Housing Is Accessible to People with Disabilities*, NATIONAL LOW INCOME HOUSING COALITION (May 21, 2018), https://nlihc.org/resource/access-living-sues-chicago-failing-ensure-assisted-housing-accessible-people-disabilities.

[47] *Gilead Suit Charges Cromwell for Opposition to Beleaguered Men's Group Home*, THE MIDDLETOWN PRESS (Aug. 11, 2017), https://www.middletownpress.com/news/article/Gilead-suit-charges-Cromwell-for-opposition-to-11753351.php.

town officials could be held individually liable for their discriminatory conduct and that punitive damages were potentially available.[48]

NIMBYist resistance to affordable housing developments more generally is also common and often racially tinged.[49] The dynamic between established neighborhood residents and advocates for their future low-income neighbors varies from place to place but usually follows a basic outline. When developers seek permits to construct multifamily affordable housing, established residents often raise objections that are practical (What about all the traffic? How will the school/the police/the fire department meet the increased need?) or financial (Will my property's value decrease?). Another common refrain is their desire to "protect" the neighborhood against incursion by new types of housing and new residents expected to alter the neighborhood's "character."

Appeals to neighborhood continuity and protection from outsiders have a long history of masking racially exclusionary motives. Some housing scholars argue that NIMBYists' objections reflect a purely rational desire to preserve the economic value of their home (many Americans' single largest investment). Others contend that this "rational self-interest" is inextricable from the history of racist policies and legal structures that supported White home ownership while excluding Black people from home ownership and desirable neighborhoods alike.[50]

Racial animosity or conscious prejudice doubtless motivates some opposition to affordable housing. Much of the resistance, however, likely flows from implicit biases. Researchers suggest that persons professing egalitarian commitments still may associate affordable housing with Blackness and a risk of crime, social disorder, and devalued homes. Such implicit biases may feed opposition to developing affordable housing outside of low-income areas.[51] Moreover, because historic discrimination and continuing structural exclusions have produced a trifecta of significant racial wealth gaps, racial residential segregation, and neighborhoods of concentrated poverty, stereotypes associating Blackness with crime and welfare

[48] Gilead Community Services, Inc. v. Town of Cromwell, 432 F. Supp. 3d 46 (D. Conn. 2019).

[49] A third type of land use often provoking a NIMBY response is the siting of hazardous industrial or storage uses. In these cases, the convergence of economic considerations and local politics typically leads to sitings near low-income, disproportionately non-White neighborhoods, a pattern that helped give rise to the Environmental Justice Movement.

[50] This debate is captured by recent works in the journal HOUSING POLICY DEBATE. Compare Robert W. Wassmer & Imaez Wahid, *Does the Likely Demographics of Affordable Housing Justify NIMBYism?*, 29 HOUSING POLICY DEBATE 343 (2019), with J. Rosie Tighe & Edward G. Goetz, *Comment on "Does the Likely Demographics of Affordable Housing Justify NIMBYism?"*, 29 HOUSING POLICY DEBATE 369 (2019).

[51] Jillian Olinger et al., *Challenging Race as Risk: How Implicit Bias Undermines Housing Opportunity in America – and What We Can Do about It*, KIRWAN INSTITUTE FOR THE STUDY OF RACE AND ETHNICITY (2017), http://kirwaninstitute.osu.edu/wp-content/uploads/2017/02/implicit-bias-housing.pdf.

dependency may be self-fulfilling.[52] This association is flawed, just as assertions that high tuberculosis rates among freed Black people following Emancipation were the result of their incapacity to care for themselves were flawed.[53] Urban studies scholars Rosie Tighe and Edward Goetz describe how those stereotypes undergird NIMBYist attitudes, reinforcing beliefs that "tenancy walks hand in hand with blackness, dependency, and vice, whereas homeownership fosters self-reliance, whiteness, and virtue."[54]

In sum, an inadequate supply of affordable, integrated housing negatively affects the health of Black people and disabled people . That shortage results not only from racist and ableist histories of segregation and exclusion but also from contemporary NIMBYist fondness for "public safety" or "neighborhood character."

7.3 HARSH EDUCATIONAL DISCIPLINE AND HEALTH

Unstable housing or living in an impoverished neighborhood can negatively affect one's health. It can also negatively affect the academic performance of school-aged children. When eviction or foreclosure forces a child's family to move, they may have to switch schools, which alone increases their risk of dropping out.[55] A move following eviction is often to a poorer neighborhood, with higher crime rates and fewer resources. Public schools in low-income areas are typically underfunded and often ill equipped to address the impediments to learning that housing instability, hunger, and lack of health care can all pose. And having parents forced to deal with housing precarity or the stresses of eviction can adversely affect a child's school readiness and performance.[56] Unaffordable housing's cascading effects on both health and education are unmistakable.

7.3.1 *Education's Influence on Health*

Education's influence on health has been established for decades. Empirical studies show an association between number of years of schooling and healthy lifespan.[57] Take one example: In 2005, a 25-year-old man who had graduated from high school

[52] L. Bobo & C.L. Zubrinsky, *Attitudes on Residential Integration: Perceived Status Differences, Mere In-group Preference or Racial Prejudice?*, 74 SOCIAL FORCES 883 (1996).

[53] This flawed association is discussed in Chapter 3.

[54] Tighe & Goetz, *supra* note 50, at 370.

[55] Megan Jula, *Eviction's Long Reach*, KNOWABLE MAG. (Sept. 23, 2020), https://knowablemagazine.org/article/society/2020/evictions-long-reach

[56] Abraham Gutman et al., *Health, Housing and the Law*, 22 NORTHEASTERN L. REV. 251, 261–62 (2019); Barbara Fedders, *Schooling at Risk*, 103 IOWA L. REV. 872, 884–86. (2018).

[57] Anna Zajacova & Elizabeth M. Lawrence, *The Relationships between Education and Health: Reducing Disparities through a Contextual Approach*, 39 ANN. REV. PUBLIC HEALTH 273 (2018).

could expect to live 11 to 15 years longer than a 25-year-old who had not.[58] The health penalty attached to less education is wide ranging: Poorer general health, more chronic conditions, and higher disability levels appear in both self-reporting and objective measures of health.[59] Numerous causal pathways appear to be at play, again showing the bidirectional influence of social determinants. For example, people with less education are more likely to dwell in low-income neighborhoods, which often have fewer health-promoting features and more health-destructive features.[60] For children with disabilities and Black children, disciplinary exclusion from school represents a shared pathway to poor educational outcomes and, thus, poorer health.

7.3.2 *Histories of de Jure Exclusion and Segregation*

Educational disadvantage has deep historical roots. Legal scholar Barbara Fedders describes the similarities in how public schools segregated Black children and disabled children or excluded them altogether.[61] Educating enslaved children was a criminal offense in many Southern states, and for nearly a century following Emancipation, many states segregated schools by race and left schools for Black students massively underfunded.[62] Students with disabilities experienced similar deprivation. States typically viewed disabled children as incapable of benefiting from education and their exclusion as necessary to permit orderly education of "normal" children. Whatever instruction disabled students received typically occurred in separate institutions or classrooms without resources adequate for an appropriate education.[63]

De jure racial and disability exclusion and segregation came to an end in the second half of the twentieth century. In 1954, *Brown v. Board of Education*[64] held that racially segregated public elementary schools violated the Fourteenth Amendment. No longer could states or local school districts enshrine racial segregation in official policy. After lawsuits inspired by *Brown* produced lower court rulings requiring states to provide a free public education to children with mental disabilities,[65] Congress passed the Education for All Handicapped Children Act (now

---

[58] Brian L. Rostron et al., *Education Reporting and Classification on Death Certificates in the United States*, 151 VITAL & HEALTH STATISTICS 1 (2010).

[59] Zajacova & Lawrence, *supra* note 57.

[60] *Why Education Matters to Health: Exploring the Causes*, VIRGINIA COMMONWEALTH UNIVERSITY CENTER ON SOCIETY AND HEALTH (2014), https://societyhealth.vcu.edu/work/the-projects/why-education-matters-to-health-exploring-the-causes.html.

[61] Fedders, *supra* note 56.

[62] *Id.* at 880–81.

[63] *Id.* at 882–83.

[64] 347 U.S. 483 (1954).

[65] P.A.R.C. v. Commonwealth of Pennsylvania, 334 F. Supp. 279 (E.D. Pa. 1972); Mills v. Bd. of Education, 348 F. Supp. 886 (D.D.C. 1972).

called the Individuals with Disabilities Education Act (IDEA)) in 1975.[66] The federal legislation ended de jure disability-based exclusion by mandating that children with disabilities receive a "free and appropriate public education" in the "least restrictive environment" appropriate to their needs.

7.3.3 *Excessive Discipline as a Mechanism of Segregation and Exclusion for Black and Disabled Students*

Despite these legal interventions, disabled and Black children's parallel histories have evolved into continuing patterns of de facto exclusion and segregation. Children who are Black or disabled (or both) disproportionately face exclusion when schools rely on excessive disciplinary measures or place "difficult" students in "alternative" schools. These practices negatively affect health outcomes for children subjected to them, contributing to health disparities.

7.3.3.1 Increased Use of Harsh Discipline and Surveillance

Schools' use of extreme and exclusionary discipline – measures like out-of-school suspensions, expulsions, and referrals to law enforcement – have increased dramatically in recent decades.[67] Rather than help students develop social and emotional skills equipping them to navigate school and life, such measures remove students from their classrooms. The upsurge in exclusionary discipline does not simply reflect an increase in serious student offenses; many schools rely on harsh disciplinary measures for seemingly trivial instances of disobedience, disrespect, and unruliness, behaviors that are within the bounds of developmental norms for children and teenagers. Starting in the 1990s, many schools adopted "zero tolerance" policies, which mandate punitive responses to defined categories of infractions without considering a student's behavior in context.[68] "Whether a student's misbehavior is serious, trivial, intentional, or accidental, the response in many districts is the same: exclusion from school. In fact, schools themselves report that minor misbehaviors, like disruption and disrespect, account for 95 percent of suspensions and expulsions."[69] Heightened surveillance of students in the wake of school shootings (for example, the use of metal detectors or security cameras) and an increased presence of police officers are associated with higher odds that even minor student

---

[66] 20 U.S.C. § 1412(a)(1)(A).

[67] Jason P. Nance, *Over-Disciplining Students, Racial Bias, and the School-to-Prison Pipeline*, 50 U. RICH. L. REV. 1063 (2016).

[68] Fedders, *supra* note 56.

[69] Derek W. Black, *The Constitutional Limit of Zero Tolerance in Schools*, 99 MINN. L. REV. 823, 825 (2015).

misconduct will lead to extreme discipline.[70] And, heightened surveillance occurs more often in schools serving primarily students of color.[71]

7.3.3.2 Disproportionate Impact on Black and Disabled Children

Schools' increased reliance on extreme discipline harms some groups of students more than others. Black children (especially boys), disabled children, and children from low-income families are disproportionately subjected to excessive and exclusionary discipline. Before they even enroll in kindergarten, Black children face a quadrupled risk of being suspended from preschool, and researchers have found an association between implicit bias among preschool teachers and suspension rates.[72] In 2019, the US Commission on Civil Rights issued a report on school discipline finding that Black students did not engage in disciplinable misconduct more frequently than their White classmates but were disciplined more often and more harshly.[73]

Low-income students who are Black are more likely than low-income children of other races to suffer childhood adversity (for example, experiencing abuse or neglect, witnessing violence, or living in a household with substance use problems).[74] Childhood trauma can contribute to learning difficulties and social and emotional disturbance, potentially leading to a child's being identified as having a disability.[75] Disruptive behavior may result from a child's disability but nonetheless lead to suspension or expulsion. Faced with a child whose disability is not readily apparent,

---

[70] Jason P. Nance, *Students, Police, and the School-to-Prison Pipeline*, 93 WASH. U. L. REV. 919 (2016).

[71] See Jason P. Nance, *Student Surveillance, Racial Inequalities, and Implicit Racial Bias*, 66 EMORY L.J. 765 (2017). Evidence also suggests that underfunded schools – which disproportionately enroll students of color – are more likely to implement harsh and exclusionary disciplinary policies. Christopher A. Mallett, *The School-to-Prison Pipeline: A Critical Review of the Punitive Paradigm Shift*, 33 CHILD & ADOLESCENT SOC. WORK J. 15 (2016); Sarah Mervosh, *How Much Wealthier Are White School Districts than Nonwhite Ones? $23 Billion, Report Says*, N.Y. TIMES (Feb. 27, 2019), https://www.nytimes.com/2019/02/27/education/school-districts-funding-white-minorities.html.

[72] LaWanda Wesley, *Exclusionary Discipline in Preschool: Young Black Boys' Lives Matter*, 8 J. AFRICAN AMERICAN MALES IN EDUCATION (2017), https://jaamejournal.scholasticahq.com/art icle/18489-exclusionary-discipline-in-preschool-young-black-boys-lives-matter.

[73] U.S. COMMISSION ON CIVIL RIGHTS, Transmittal Letter, in BEYOND SUSPENSIONS: EXAMINING SCHOOL DISCIPLINE POLICIES AND CONNECTIONS TO THE SCHOOL-TO-PRISON PIPELINE FOR STUDENTS OF COLOR WITH DISABILITIES (2019).

[74] *Adverse Childhood Experiences among U.S. Children*, CHILD & ADOLESCENT HEALTH MEASUREMENT INITIATIVE (Oct. 2017), https://www.cahmi.org/wp-content/uploads/2018/05/aces_fact_sheet.pdf.

[75] Sophia Miryam Schussler-Fiorenza, *Adverse Childhood Experiences, Disability, and Health-Risk Behaviors*, 26 POPULATION HEALTH MATTERS (2013), https://jdc.jefferson.edu/cgi/viewcontent.cgi?article=1852&context=hpn.

teachers or administrators may be prone to label the student a "problem" and default to disciplinary measures as a response.[76]

While being Black or disabled or poor increases the chances that a student will be suspended or expelled, students identified with more than one of these categories face the highest odds their education will be disrupted by extreme disciplinary measures. One report found that schoolchildren in Ohio who fell into more than one of those groups were ten times more likely to be suspended.[77] A heartbreaking study in one Florida county found that two out of every three Black boys who were poor and in special education were suspended at least once during the sixth grade.[78] The Civil Rights Commission concluded: "[T]he data on suspensions demonstrate that students with disabilities consistently face double the risk of getting suspended compared to their peers... [and] also show that students of color with disabilities face a significantly higher risk – year after year – for suspensions compared to white students with disabilities."[79]

7.3.3.3 Alternative Education Programs

Schools' adoption of zero tolerance policies also fueled growth in alternative education programs. These programs began in the 1960s as a more flexible learning environment for students who did not flourish in regular classrooms. Decades later, in some states they have become a dumping ground of sorts for students excluded from those classrooms pursuant to zero tolerance policies. For some students, involuntary assignment to an alternative school results from serious misconduct involving violence or drugs. Others find themselves transferred out of their regular

---

[76] Mariam Alnaim, *The Impact of Zero Tolerance Policy on Children with Disabilities*, 8 WORLD J. EDUCATION 1 (2018); Samantha Calero et al., *The Ruderman White Paper on the Problematization and Criminalization of Children and Young Adults with Non-Apparent Disabilities*, RUDERMAN FAM. FOUND. 3 (2017).

[77] Sarah Biehl, *Zero Tolerance and Exclusionary School Discipline Policies Harm Students and Contribute to the Cradle to Prison Pipeline*, CHILDREN'S DEFENSE FUND-OHIO 2 (2012).

[78] Linda M. Raffaele Mendez, *Predictors of Suspension and Negative School Outcomes: A Longitudinal Investigation*, 99 NEW DIRECTIONS FOR YOUTH DEV. 17, 31 (2003). The amplified disciplinary disadvantage connected to children's intersectionality (i.e., having multiple marginalized identities) connects to a robust, if disputed, scholarly dialogue on children's race and disability identification. Some scholars assert that Black children (and especially boys) are disproportionately likely to be labeled as having emotional or intellectual disabilities, whereas White children are more likely to be diagnosed with autism or learning disabilities. Jyoti Nanda, *The Construction and Criminalization of Disability in School Incarceration*, 9 COLUM. J. RACE & L. 265 (2019). Others argue that disproportionate labeling may flow more from socioeconomic status than race and may vary depending on the racial composition of a student's school, suggesting that school segregation may play a role; Todd E. Elder et al., *Segregation and Racial Gaps in Special Education*, 21 EDUCATION NEXT (2021), https://www .educationnext.org/segregation-racial-gaps-special-education-new-evidence-on-debate-over-dis proportionality/.

[79] U.S. COMMISSION ON CIVIL RIGHTS, *supra* note 73, at 71.

schools for far more modest (and often debatable) infractions like showing disregard for authority, using profanity, or truancy.[80] Some states and school districts tout alternative programs as designed to meet students' distinctive educational needs, when in reality some do little more than segregate students who have been disruptive.

Transfers are not limited to adolescents who get into trouble. Seth Murrell was a little boy – just four years old – when his preschool referred him to an alternative school that was part of the Georgia Network for Education and Therapeutic Support (GNETS). As a toddler Seth had been diagnosed with pervasive developmental delay, a diagnosis that later ripened into autism. His preschool teachers' frustration with their inability to control Seth's classroom behavior prompted his referral, but his new "school" lacked educational supports or specialized instruction appropriate for his disability. The GNETS school provided instruction for only about a half hour each day. Seth spent much of his day in "Cool Down, a desk facing a blank wall," often for behaviors associated with his disability. Most of the time, Seth's GNETS teachers had no specialized training in teaching students with autism. One teacher hit Seth multiple times when he was six years old.[81]

Seth Murrell is also Black. He embodies concerns that educational equity advocates have raised about alternative education programs. Allegations of disability and race discrimination in those programs have led to multiple investigations and lawsuits. After investigating the GNETS program that Seth Murrell was sent to, the US Department of Justice found that it effectively segregated students with behavior-related disabilities from their peers and provided education unequal to that received by other public school students.[82] Moreover, Georgia's alternative school system disproportionately enrolled Black children, especially boys; investigative reporting found there were two times as many Black boys among GNETS students as there were in Georgia's public schools generally. Some GNETS schools operate in run-down buildings that were once Jim Crow-era schools, helping to feed an impression of resegregation and punitive warehousing for Black children with disabilities.[83] This situation is not unique to Georgia.[84] As early as 2005, the Department of Education recognized that Black disabled students were "more likely to be educated in separate environments,"[85] and the federal government has investigated race and disability discrimination claims in alternative education programs in several states, including Massachusetts and Pennsylvania.

---

[80] Heather Vogell, *How Students Get Banished to Alternative Schools*, PROPUBLICA (Dec. 6, 2017).

[81] Rachel Aviv, *Georgia's Separate and Unequal Special-Education System*, NEW YORKER (Sept. 24, 2018).

[82] U.S. Dept. of Justice, Letter to Gov. Nathan Deal (July 15, 2015), https://www.ada.gov/olmstead/documents/gnets_lof.pdf.

[83] Aviv, *supra* note 81.

[84] Georgia is unique in having a statewide network of alternative programs, but not unique in its segregating practices.

[85] U.S. DEPT OF EDUCATION, 27TH ANNUAL REPORT TO CONGRESS ON THE IMPLEMENTATION OF THE INDIVIDUALS WITH DISABILITIES EDUCATION ACT, 2005, VOL. 1, 47–48 (2005).

But proving discrimination often is not easy. Beth Ferri, a scholar of race, disability, and gender, argues that failure to account for potential racial bias in the IDEA's "least restrictive environment" requirement has permitted the resurrection of racial segregation "under the guise of 'disability.'"[86] Fedders concurs, noting that contemporary alternative education programs "in important respects resemble the pre-civil rights era's separate and inferior educational settings for students of color and disabled students." More broadly, in Fedders' view, suspension, expulsions, and referrals to alternative programs reflect "an historical trope of the undeserving child" for whom education is unwarranted.[87]

7.3.4 *Health Impacts of Exclusionary Discipline*

So how do suspensions, expulsions, and transfers to alternative programs correlate with student health? Back in 2003 (and again in 2013) the American Academy of Pediatricians (AAP) issued a policy statement warning of the social, fiscal, and health impacts of excluding students from school in order to address misconduct.[88] According to the statement, students suspended out of school are more likely to get into fights, commit crimes, use illegal substances, and engage in sex. Put simply, being out of school increases a student's chances of getting into trouble. Moreover, the AAP warned that students suspended out of school are far more likely to drop out of high school, a decision associated with poor health outcomes. Recent research bears out those warnings. School connectedness (a student's feeling cared for at school) in adolescence is associated with health benefits lasting into adulthood. School connectedness operates as an inoculation of sorts, helping protect young people against various health hazards, including emotional distress and suicidal thoughts, committing or suffering physical violence, contracting a sexually transmitted infection, and substance misuse.[89]

Exclusionary discipline disrupts connectedness, leaving students feeling "silenced, undervalued, and misunderstood"[90] and depriving them (and their future adult selves) of the protective benefits of connectedness. The disproportionate use of such measures on Black students and disabled students drives home how excessive school discipline burdens the health of these students. Our society's feel-good narrative around education is that it provides a pathway for individual betterment and

---

[86] Aviv, *supra* note 81 (quoting Ferri).

[87] Fedders, *supra* note 56, at 875–76.

[88] Council on School Health, Out-of-School Suspension and Expulsion, 131 PEDIATRICS 131 (2013).

[89] Riley J. Steiner et al., *Adolescent Connectedness and Adult Health Outcomes*, 144 PEDIATRICS e20183766 (2019). *Centers for Disease Control and Prevention* "School Connectedness", https://www.cdc.gov/healthyyouth/protective/school_connectedness.htm.

[90] Sara Luster, *How Exclusionary Discipline Creates Disconnected Students*, NEA TODAY (July 19, 2018), https://www.nea.org/advocating-for-change/new-from-nea/how-exclusionary-discipline-creates-disconnected-students.

upward social mobility. "Get an education, and you can go far!" is the message. In reality, exclusionary discipline disproportionately pushes students who are Black or disabled or both out of school. Combined with their negative health impacts, schools' use of these excessive measures has the effect of enlarging existing health disparities.[91] Moreover, harshly punitive discipline functions as part of the school-to-prison pipeline by increasing the chances that students will become entangled in the criminal justice system, another arena where Black and disabled people are overrepresented.

7.4 CRIMINAL JUSTICE SYSTEM INVOLVEMENT

Imagine you have enrolled in a graduate program to become an evil genius. (Readers can decide which academic field is most likely to produce evil geniuses.) A required course for the program is titled "Exacerbating Health Disparities." Your final assignment for the course is to develop a mechanism for manipulating social determinants of health to negatively affect the health prospects of groups who already suffer health disparities. You are assigned Black people and people with disabilities as your specific target groups. Your professor tells you that, to get a good grade in the course, the mechanism you develop should:

- Function to further diminish the health prospects of the target groups;
- Operate in a manner that is legal and largely invisible to the public;
- Generate public support by invoking community safety;
- Leverage preexisting disadvantage and stigma among group members; and
- Harness the cascading effects of social determinants of health.

The assignment and the mechanism it contemplates sound nefarious. They might also sound mildly ridiculous were it not for the fact that a mechanism worthy of an A+ in the class is already operating. Collateral consequences of criminal conviction check all the boxes for the evil genius assignment. In so doing, they provide another illustration of similarities in the experiences of people who are Black, disabled, or both. After briefly examining disproportionate incarceration rates and the negative health impacts of incarceration, this section will explore how collateral consequences exacerbate health inequities.

7.4.1 *Disproportionate Incarceration Rates*

Compared to their share of the population overall, Black people and disabled people are overrepresented among persons confined in prisons and jails.[92] Black Americans,

---

[91] See Thalia Gonzalez et al., *Health Equity, School Discipline Reform, and Restorative Justice*, 47 J.L. MED. & ETHICS S2 47 (2019).

[92] Similarly, both Black people (particularly men) and disabled people are more likely to be victims of excessive police force. One study estimates that one-third to one-half of all people killed by law enforcement are people with disabilities. David M. Perry & Lawrence Carter-

who make up a mere 13 percent of the general population, constitute 40 percent of the people behind bars. In 2016, Black people were nearly six times as likely as White people to be incarcerated, with the disparity ballooning to nearly twelvefold if only 18- and 19-year-old males are considered.[93] People with disabilities are also over-represented among those confined to jails and prisons. Incarcerated people are about three to four times more likely to report having a disability compared to people who are not incarcerated.[94] About half of all people behind bars have a mental health condition.[95] Media reporting has brought the epidemic of mental illness in prisons to the public's attention; less well known is that other disabilities are also far more common among incarcerated people. According to the US Commission on Civil Rights, "Incarcerated people are twice as likely to have an intellectual disability, four to six times more likely to have a cognitive disability, twice as likely to have a mobility disorder, three to four times more likely to be blind or have a vision impairment, and two to three times more likely to have a hearing impairment."[96]

We must also recall that Blackness and disability are not neatly compartmental-ized identities but that they frequently intersect. A Department of Justice report found that in 2011–2012, 26 percent of Black prisoners (and 42 percent of multiracial prisoners) reported having at least one disability, as did 35 percent of Black jail inmates (and 55 percent of multiracial inmates).[97] Thus, although mass incarceration is most often described as locking up Black and Brown bodies, critical disability scholars argue that the intersection of race, class, and disability better defines the bodies subjected to mass incarceration.[98]

Long, *The Ruderman White Paper on Media Coverage of Law Enforcement Use of Force and Disability: A Media Study (2013–2015) and Overview*, RUDERMAN FAM. FOUND. (2016). Another found that the risk that Black men and boys will be killed by police is about 2.5 times that of White men and boys. Laura Santhanam, *After Ferguson, Black Men Still Face the Highest Risk of Being Killed by Police*, PBS NEWS HOUR (Aug. 9, 2019), https://www.pbs.org/newshour/health/after-ferguson-black-men-and-boys-still-face-the-highest-risk-of-being-killed-by-police.

[93] U.S. COMMISSION ON CIVIL RIGHTS, COLLATERAL CONSEQUENCES: THE CROSSROADS OF PUNISHMENT, REDEMPTION, AND THE EFFECTS ON COMMUNITIES, BRIEFING REPORT 20 (June 2019); Elizabeth Tobin Tyler & Bradley Brockmann, *Returning Home: Incarceration, Reentry, Stigma and the Perpetuation of Racial and Socioeconomic Health Inequity*, 45 J.L. MED. & ETHICS 545, 549 (2017).

[94] Rebecca Vallas, *Disabled Behind Bars: The Mass Incarceration of People with Disabilities in America's Jails and Prisons*, CENTER FOR AMERICAN PROGRESS 1–2 (2016).

[95] Doris J. James & Lauren E. Glaze, *Special Report: Mental Health Problems of Prison and Jail Inmates* 1, BUREAU OF JUSTICE STATISTICS (2006), https://www.bjs.gov/content/pub/pdf/mhppji.pdf.

[96] U.S. COMMISSION ON CIVIL RIGHTS, *supra* note 93, at 21.

[97] Jennifer Bronson & Marcus Berzofsky, *Disabilities among Prison and Jail Inmates, 2011–2012*, at 5, U.S. DEP'T OF JUSTICE, BUREAU OF JUSTICE STATISTICS (2015), https://www.bjs.gov/content/pub/pdf/dpji1112.pdf.

[98] Nirmala Erevelles, *Crippin' Jim Crow: Disability, Dis-Location, and the School-to-Prison Pipeline*, in DISABILITY INCARCERATED: IMPRISONMENT AND DISABILITY IN THE UNITED STATES AND CANADA 86 (Liat Ben-Moshe et al. eds., 2014).

Put simply, "[I]t is no mistake that poor disabled racialized bodies fill these spaces."[99]

7.4.2 *Incarceration's Health Impacts*

7.4.2.1 Health Impacts during Incarceration

In addition to depriving people of their liberty, incarceration regularly harms their health. "[T]he antithesis of a healthy setting"[100] is one public health researcher's description of the physical and social environment in prisons. Conditions are often crowded and unsanitary. Prison food produces high rates of foodborne illnesses and may be nutritionally deficient. Some inmates are given only limited opportunity to exercise. Transmission rates for infectious diseases are disastrous,[101] a fact driven home in 2020 when prisons emerged as COVID-19 hotspots. Verbal, physical, and sexual abuse by guards and other prisoners is endemic. The mental-health–wrecking isolation of solitary confinement[102] is regularly inflicted. These chronic stressors, alone or in combination, can negatively affect health.[103] Needed medical and mental health treatment may be inadequate or simply unavailable. In 2006, the federal government reported that only about one in three state prison inmates with mental health conditions received any treatment; the percentage was even lower in federal prisons.[104]

Little wonder, then, that conditions "inside" may aggravate health problems – particularly mental health problems – that prisoners had prior to incarceration and give rise to new ones. Research supporting definite causal relationships between incarceration and poor health outcomes is limited, partly because many incarcerated people faced health-harming conditions like poverty, limited education, and unemployment prior to incarceration.[105] For some groups (like Black men) incarceration may even have a limited protective effect, temporarily decreasing mortality and health risks. Explanations for that effect remain contested, but lower risks of violent

[99] Syrus Ware et al., It Can't Be Fixed Because It's Not Broken: Racism and Disability in the Prison Industrial Complex, in DISABILITY INCARCERATED: IMPRISONMENT AND DISABILITY IN THE UNITED STATES AND CANADA 178 (Liat Ben-Moshe et al. eds., 2014).

[100] Nick De Viggiani, *Unhealthy Prisons: Exploring Structural Determinants of Prison Health*, 29 SOCIOLOGY OF HEALTH AND ILLNESS 115 (2007).

[101] James Hamblin, *Mass Incarceration Is Making Infectious Diseases Worse*, THE ATLANTIC, July 18, 2016.

[102] Tyler & Brockmann, *supra* note 93; Joe Fassler & Claire Brown, *Prison Food Is Making U.S. Inmates Disproportionately Sick*, THE ATLANTIC, Dec. 27, 2017.

[103] Michael Massoglia & Brianna Remster, *Linkages Between Incarceration and Health*, 134 (Supp. 1) PUB. HEALTH REPORTS 8S, 10S (2019).

[104] James & Glaze, *supra* note 95, at 9–10.

[105] Christopher Wildeman & Emily A. Wang, *Mass Incarceration, Public Health, and Widening Inequality in the USA*, 389 THE LANCET 1464 (2017); Massoglia & Remster, *supra* note 103, at 9S.

or accidental death, less access to drugs and alcohol, and some (albeit limited) access to medical care may play roles.[106]

7.4.2.2 Post-Incarceration Health: Coverage and Access

Some of the most troubling health effects of incarceration follow release, potentially lasting far longer than time served and shortening the lives of former inmates.[107] When reentering their community, an incarcerated person with an acute or chronic health condition faces formidable health challenges. Incarcerated persons suffer many communicable diseases at rates significantly higher than the general population: rates of active tuberculosis are four times higher; rates of hepatitis C are nine to ten times higher; and rates of HIV infection are eight to nine times higher. Moreover, an estimated four out of five returning citizens have a chronic medical or psychiatric condition or substance use disorder.[108] Often they are released without a supply of medications or any appointments for follow-up care in the community,[109] magnifying the challenge of figuring out how to access primary care providers and follow a treatment regimen.[110]

Medicaid is the most likely source of health insurance coverage for returning citizens. The program cannot legally cover persons who are incarcerated, but a growing number of states are exploring ways to ensure that people otherwise eligible for Medicaid become covered immediately upon their release.[111] These initiatives are salutary, especially in states that have expanded Medicaid, where a large majority of newly released persons are eligible for the program simply based on their low income. In nonexpansion states, by contrast, many returning citizens remain ineligible for Medicaid either because of their childless status or their income.

Coverage alone does not ensure access to effective care. Prisons do not uniformly engage in discharge planning for inmates with health conditions. Most doctors are untrained in caring for formerly incarcerated persons and may hold implicit or explicit biases.[112] For their part, formerly incarcerated persons may view health care providers as authority figures to be avoided, or at least not trusted. Whatever the reasons, persons reentering society face a high risk of death, hospitalization, and deteriorating health outcomes after their release.[113]

---

[106] Wildeman & Wang, *supra* note 105, at 1467.
[107] *Id.* at 1468; Julia Acker et al., *Mass Incarceration Threatens Health Equity in America* 6, ROBERT WOOD JOHNSON FOUND. (2019).
[108] Jocelyn Guyer et al., *State Strategies for Establishing Connections to Health Care for Justice-Involved Populations: The Central Role of Medicaid*, COMMONWEALTH FUND, Jan. 11, 2019.
[109] Wildeman & Wang, *supra* note 105, at 1468.
[110] Lisa Puglisi et al., *Ethics Case: What Does Health Justice Look Like for People Returning from Incarceration?*, 19 AMA J. ETHICS 903 (2017).
[111] Guyer et al., *supra* note 108.
[112] Puglisi et al., *supra* note 110.
[113] *Id.*; Guyer et al., *supra* note 108.

7.4.2.3 Post-Incarceration Health: Collateral Consequences

Barriers to accessing medical care alone do not explain these outcomes. Persons reentering the community after being incarcerated face a surfeit of obstacles to putting their lives back together. One is stigma associated with ex-offender status, which for many returning citizens layers onto disadvantage that existed prior to incarceration. Social factors like housing and employment also play predictable roles, and collateral consequences of conviction powerfully influence those factors.

"Collateral consequences" refers to results of a criminal conviction that extend beyond the formal sentence and attach when a person reenters society. The phrase describes a gamut of restrictions and disqualifications that affect opportunities including voting, enlisting in the military, getting a job, finding a place to live, obtaining various licenses, and receiving public assistance.[114] Nationwide, more than 44,000 collateral consequences exist, creating barriers to community reintegration for the nearly two-thirds of a million people leaving state and federal prisons each year.[115] Considering the interaction of a few salient collateral consequences demonstrates their contribution to poor health.

EMPLOYMENT AND HOUSING Although numerous collateral consequences can have direct health sequelae, restrictions on employment and housing merit particular note.

Barriers to employment and earning a living make up the largest category of collateral consequences. These include legal restrictions on employers' hiring of persons with certain types of criminal convictions as well as on ex-offenders' ability to obtain a wide range of occupational licenses. In addition, a jobseeker who has been incarcerated is likely to run up against employer policies and practices that screen for prior convictions and widespread stigma associated with incarceration. Topping off these impediments, incarcerated people (in the aggregate) have starkly lower levels of educational attainment than the general population. They also often have limited work experience, limited social networks, and physical or mental conditions that limit their employability. These barriers help explain a finding from a 2018 Brookings Institution study that barely half of formerly incarcerated people reported any earnings in the year following their release.[116]

A criminal record also makes it hard to secure housing, whether subsidized or in the private market. Under federal law, certain types of criminal convictions (including illegal use of a controlled substance) prevent a person from living in subsidized housing. The restriction is not limited to persons named on the lease but extends to

---

[114] See generally Gabriel J. Chin, *Collateral Consequences of Criminal Conviction*, 18 CRIMINOLOGY, CRIM. JUST., L. & SOC'Y 1 (2017).

[115] U.S. COMMISSION ON CIVIL RIGHTS, *supra* note 93.

[116] *Id.* at 35–41.

all family members residing in the same household. That means that a person banned from living in subsidized housing cannot move in with family living there without risking their eviction. Public housing authorities also are permitted to refuse applicants based on a wider range of past criminal activity. The stigma of incarceration may shape private rental property owners' decisions as well. Higher rents, move-in costs, and credit checks often combine to put private housing financially out of reach for many returning citizens.[117]

Many reentrants returning to low-income communities face a shortage of affordable housing. This shortage, combined with housing-related collateral consequences, leaves formerly incarcerated persons particularly susceptible to housing insecurity and homelessness, with their attendant health risks. Men who have been incarcerated are more than twice as likely as men who have never been incarcerated to become homeless,[118] an event that elevates their risks of recidivism.

NEGATIVE SYNERGY AND SPILLOVER EFFECTS A "ton of bricks"[119] is one description of collateral consequences. They make it hard for persons reentering society to find employment and earn a living. Without earnings, searching for a place to live may be futile. (And, of course, unstable housing makes job searching more difficult.) Other collateral consequences may disqualify persons with a conviction from safety net programs like welfare and food stamps.[120] Collateral consequences combine with the stigma of ex-offender status to make reintegrating into the community uncommonly challenging for formerly incarcerated persons. These measures generate a negative synergy, "leaving [little] room for people with convictions to lead law-abiding lives"[121] and increasing the likelihood of reoffending and recidivism.[122] They give rise to health risks linked to housing and food insecurity, homelessness, and chronic stress. Research indicates that formerly incarcerated persons are more likely to suffer stress-related conditions like heart disease or hypertension[123] than persons never incarcerated.

This "ton of bricks" does not fall evenly across communities. Because Black people and people with disabilities experience disproportionate incarceration, they also endure a disproportionate share of collateral consequences. Simply tallying how many Black individuals and disabled individuals are subject to collateral consequences fails to fully convey the measures' adverse impact. Recall that these groups

---

[117] *Id.* at 60–75
[118] Massoglia & Remster, *supra* note 103, at 10S.
[119] Gabriel J. Chin, *Race, the War on Drugs, and Collateral Consequences of Criminal Conviction,* 6 J. GENDER RACE & JUST. 255, 255–56 (2002).
[120] U.S. COMMISSION ON CIVIL RIGHTS, *supra* note 93, at 76–85.
[121] Chin, *supra* note 114, at 2.
[122] Acker et al., *supra* note 107, at 11.
[123] Massoglia & Remster, *supra* note 103, at 10S.

(in comparison to White people and nondisabled people) are disproportionately disadvantaged financially and marginalized socially and politically, even without any taint of incarceration. If collateral consequences erect hurdles to reintegration, Black people and people with disabilities enter the racecourse with weights already strapped to them.[124] A "triple jeopardy" can result, where background levels of racism and ableism (manifested in disadvantage relating to employment, housing instability, and economic status) compound difficulties posed by collateral consequences and stigma.[125]

Finally, the deadweights created by collateral consequences do not drag down only the person convicted of a crime. Most obviously, children of formerly incarcerated persons and other family members experience them second hand, as predictors of poverty and poor mental and physical health. Neighborhoods can feel the crushing weight, too. Collateral consequences can harm the health of low-income neighborhoods that lose many residents to incarceration when those residents are released and return home. A direct health risk lies in the high rates of communicable diseases among returning citizens. Indirectly, the risks of unemployment, homelessness, and poor health that each neighbor returning from incarceration brings can magnify a distressed neighborhood's burden of stress. These "spillover effects" of laws and policies establishing collateral consequence thus further weaken an already frayed social fabric.[126] By making poor neighborhoods less healthy, collateral consequences may fuel growing health disparities involving both racial minorities and low-income groups, which include many disabled people.[127] And the spillage may spread even further. One study found that states with higher numbers of formerly incarcerated persons had poorer overall access to and quality of health care, even among people who were unlikely to be affected by incarceration personally.[128] Some have even reasoned that the United States' singularly high incarceration rates might help explain its poor international performance on population health measures.[129] Minimizing collateral consequences to measures empirically shown to improve public safety would lower barriers to reentry that formerly incarcerated persons face and have a salutary effect on their health[130] as well as the health of their communities.

---

[124] Tobin Tyler & Brockmann, *supra* note 93, at 551. Elizabeth Tobin Tyler and Bradley Brockmann characterize collateral consequences as a form of "legalized discrimination." U.S. COMMISSION ON CIVIL RIGHTS, *supra* note 93, at 21–22.

[125] Nicholas Freudenberg, *Adverse Effects of U.S. Jail and Prison Policies on the Health and Well-Being of Women of Color*, 92 AM. J. PUB. HEALTH 1895, 1896 (2002).

[126] Tyler & Brockmann, *supra* note 93, at 552–53; Freudenberg, *supra* note 125, at 1897.

[127] Wildeman & Wang, *supra* note 105, at 1468–69.

[128] Jason Schnittker et al., *The Institutional Effects of Incarceration: Spillovers from Criminal Justice to Health Care*, 93 MILBANK Q. 516 (2015).

[129] Wildeman & Wang, *supra* note 105, at 1470.

[130] Massoglia & Remster, *supra* note 103, at 12S; Chin, *supra* note 114, at 7.

7.5 WHY ARE SOCIAL FACTORS INEQUITABLY DISTRIBUTED?

Social factors like housing, education, and public safety measures can have either positive or negative effects on health. So, how do Black people and disabled people end up with more than their share of harmful influences?

"Population vulnerability is made, not born,"[131] is the answer provided by legal scholar Angela Harris and attorney Ayesha Pamukcu. In arguing for a civil right of health, they emphasize that uneven burdens of health harms are neither mere happenstance nor biologically based nor the simple product of individual choice. Instead, disadvantage has political origins and is traceable to systems of power and privilege. Because structural subordination shapes the social determinants of health, efforts to address persistent health disparities are pointless, unless public health advocates address their political and social root causes. Harris and Pamukcu suggest that public health advocates and civil rights advocates partner to challenge subordination and reduce health disparities.[132]

Legal scholar Daniel Dawes agrees that the political process (including voting, governing, and policy making) must be considered a determinant of health. He views political engagement and power as critical, human-driven connectors between structural forces like racism or ableism and the uneven distribution of social or environmental goods. Political processes are the mechanisms by which racism and ableism favor some groups and disfavor others.[133] According to Dawes, achieving progress towards health equity will require advocates to be more strategic and thoughtful in considering the interplay of political factors, commercial interests, structural racism, and other determinants of health.[134]

In conclusion, we see that effectively addressing health disparities experienced by Black people and disabled people will entail intervening to disrupt unjust distributions of protective and harmful social factors. And corrective measures addressing those inequitable distributions of social factors will require harnessing political processes and partnering among social justice and public health advocates. The outbreak of COVID-19 validated these arguments with withering force. The pandemic offers a case study in how political and social determinants produce devastating burdens of illness and death for disabled people and Black people, as Chapter 8 describes.

---

[131] Angela P. Harris & Aysha Pamukcu, *The Civil Rights of Health: A New Approach to Challenging Structural Inequality*, 67 UCLA L. REV. 758, 774 (2020).

[132] *Id.*

[133] DANIEL DAWES, THE POLITICAL DETERMINANTS OF HEALTH (2020).

[134] *Id.* at 167.

8

COVID Stories

8.1 COVID-19'S DISPARATE IMPACT

The unfolding of the COVID-19 pandemic provided the American public with a master class on health care inequality and how vulnerability to ill health is created. Black people and disabled people, along with folks in other marginalized communities, have suffered disproportionately from the coronavirus's ravages of sickness and death, as well as its economic burden.

Soon after the coronavirus shut down the United States economy, health equity experts began predicting that Black communities would be hit especially hard. "When it hits the fan, we're the ones that are going to suffer the most," physician Uché Blackstock warned.[1] Early tallies of cases and deaths rolling in from cities large and small bore out her warning. In Milwaukee, despite making up only 26 percent of the city's population, Black people suffered nearly half the city's coronavirus infections and 81 percent of its deaths, according to data reported in April 2020.[2] A funeral in Albany, Georgia, acted as a "super-spreader" event and left the sole hospital of a city that is almost three-quarters Black overwhelmed by patients suffering from an illness that its doctors had never seen before. Ninety percent or more of the resulting deaths were of Black people.[3] COVID-19 death rates in predominantly Black and Latinx neighborhoods in New York City exceeded those

[1] Julia Craven, *How Racial Health Disparities Will Play Out in the Pandemic*, SLATE (Mar. 30, 2020), https://slate.com/news-and-politics/2020/03/how-racial-health-disparities-will-play-out-in-the-coronavirus-pandemic.html.

[2] Akilah Johnson & Talia Buford, *Early Data Shows African Americans Have Contracted and Died of Coronavirus at an Alarming Rate*, PROPUBLICA (Apr. 3, 2020), https://www.propublica .org/article/early-data-shows-african-americans-have-contracted-and-died-of-coronavirus-at-an-alarming-rate.

[3] Haisten Willis & Vanessa Williams, *A Funeral Is Thought to Have Sparked a COVID-19 Outbreak in Albany, Georgia – and Led to Many More Funerals*, WASH. POST (Apr. 4, 2020), https://www.washingtonpost.com/politics/a-funeral-sparked-a-covid-19-outbreak–and-led-to-many-more-funerals/2020/04/03/546fa0cc-74e6-11ea-87da-77a8136c1a6d_story.html.

in mostly White neighborhoods a subway ride away by as much as fifteen times.[4] As the virus spread, similar scenarios emerged across the country.

For anyone familiar with how social factors produce racial health disparities, the stories were predictable. They flowed foreseeably from a confluence of economic, social, and political pathologies that left Black Americans especially vulnerable to contracting and dying from the virus. The reality that residents of many Black communities are unable to socially distance because they live in dense housing and travel by public transportation reflects the country's yawning racial gap in economic resources, attributable in part to histories of overt and structural discrimination in housing law and policies. A history of unequal educational investment helps explain why so many Black people work low-wage jobs as essential workers, which require contact with the public.[5] Such jobs often do not offer health coverage, leaving Black people less likely to have private health insurance and more likely to face financial barriers to accessing care.[6] The disproportionate prevalence among Black people of chronic health conditions like obesity, diabetes, hypertension, and chronic lung disease (all risk factors for severe or fatal COVID-19) can be traced to social determinants of health including stress, food insecurity, poverty, and environmental toxins.[7]

Compared to what has been documented for minority groups, COVID-19's disparate burden on disabled Americans has been less quantified because data collected and reported about cases and mortality have not systematically included disability. But we do have some evidence. Certainly, the tally of infections and deaths in nursing homes and group homes (discussed further below) showed the toll exacted on residents there, most of whom were disabled.[8] But the disparate impact

---

[4]   Maria Caspani & Jonathan Allen, *Coronavirus Deadliest in New York City's Black and Latino Neighborhoods, Data Show*, REUTERS (May 18, 2020), https://www.reuters.com/article/us-health-coronavirus-new-york-deaths/coronavirus-deadliest-in-new-york-citys-black-and-latino-neighborhoods-data-shows-idUSKBN22U32A.

[5]   Jennifer Abbasi, *Taking a Closer Look at COVID-19, Health Inequities, and Racism*, 324 JAMA 427, 427 (2020); PATRICIA J. WILLIAMS, The Endless Looping of Public Health and Scientific Racism, in ASSESSING LEGAL RESPONSES TO COVID-19, at 257, PUBLIC HEALTH LAW WATCH (Scott Burris et al. eds., 2020), https://static1.squarespace.com/static/5956e16e6b8f5b8c45f1c216/t/5f4d64825b2aa5391711e947/1598907525348/ClosingReflection_COVIDPolicyPlaybook-Aug2020.pdf.

[6]   Bobbi M. Bittker, *Racial and Ethnic Disparities in Employer-Sponsored Health Coverage*, ABA CIVIL RIGHTS AND SOCIAL JUSTICE (Sept. 8, 2020), https://www.americanbar.org/groups/crsj/publications/human_rightsmagazine_home/health-matters-in-elections/racial-and-ethnic-dis parities-in-employer-sponsored-health-coverage/#:~:text=According%20to%20a%202018%20analy sis,by%20employer%2Dsponsored%20health%20insurance.

[7]   Monica Webb Hooper et al., *COVID-19 and Racial/Ethnic Disparities*, 323 JAMA 2466, 2466 (2020).

[8]   COVID-19 Nursing Home Data, DATA.CMS.GOV, https://data.cms.gov/stories/s/COVID-19-Nursing-Home-Data/bkwz-xpvg (Feb. 28, 2021). Joseph Shapiro, *COVID-19 Infections and Deaths Are Higher among Those with Intellectual Disabilities*, NPR (June 9, 2020), https://www.npr.org/2020/06/09/872401607/covid-19-infections-and-deaths-are-higher-among-those-with-intellectual-disabili.

on disabled people was not confined to those living in congregate settings. Underlying health conditions contributed to the deaths of over nine in ten people who died from COVID-19. Many underlying conditions like asthma, diabetes, or heart disease can be considered disabilities if they substantially limit a person's functioning.[9] Having determined that Down syndrome is associated with immune dysfunction, pulmonary problems, and congenital heart failure, the CDC added it to the agency's list of those conditions that place COVID patients at risk of severe symptoms.[10] Little doubt exists that disabled people are among groups who have borne the worst of the pandemic's damage.[11]

Even less is known with certainty regarding COVID-19's impact on people who are both Black and disabled. Almost none of the reported data looks at the intersection of race and disability, making it impossible to precisely gauge the true scope of that impact. That said, Black people with disabilities have likely been exposed to the coronavirus at greater rates and suffered higher death rates than other Americans.[12]

At this writing it remains uncertain how and when the COVID-19 pandemic will end. Its innumerable stories can and should be told, from the lost lives and the personal bravery of health care and essential workers, to the harms of politicizing public health preparedness and response, to global interdependency. Many stories are still playing out and will demand volumes for their full telling. This chapter suggests how several subplots from the pandemic's early months illustrate present-day instances of devaluation, distrust, and socially and politically constructed vulnerability. This chapter's stories also underscore how persons who are both Black and disabled face amplified vulnerability in some settings.

8.2 RATIONING RESOURCES

This chapter's first pair of COVID stories involves disabled people and Black people getting the short end of the stick in terms of timely access to needed testing and care

---

[9] Travis Andersen, *CDC Says Most COVID-19 Deaths in US Involved Underlying Health Conditions*, BOSTON GLOBE (Aug. 31, 2020), https://www.bostonglobe.com/2020/08/31/metro/cdc-most-covid-19-deaths-us-involved-underlying-health-conditions. Other contributing conditions named by the CDC (like pneumonia, cardiac arrest, or an injury) were more transient or sudden and would not likely be considered disabilities.

[10] Zachary Mack, *The CDC Just Confirmed This Disorder Could Put You at Risk of Severe COVID*, BESTLIFE (Jan. 1, 2021), https://bestlifeonline.com/cdc-down-syndrome-covid.

[11] In the absence of US data regarding infections and deaths among people with disabilities, data from Britain's Office of National Statistics offers a sobering count. That office reported that from March to mid-July 2020, 59 percent of all COVID-19 deaths in England and Wales were of disabled people. *Coronavirus (COVID-19) Related Deaths by Disability Status, England and Wales: 2 March to 14 July 2020*, OFFICE FOR NAT'L STATISTICS (Sept. 18, 2020), https://www.ons.gov.uk/peoplepopulationandcommunity/birthsdeathsandmarriages/deaths/articles/coronaviruscovid19relateddeathsbydisabilitystatusenglandandwales/2marchto14july2020.

[12] Daniel Young, *Black, Disabled, and Uncounted*, NATIONAL HEALTH LAW PROGRAM (Aug. 7, 2020), https://healthlaw.org/black-disabled-and-uncounted.

for COVID-19 infections. Each group's story is distinctive, but they overlap significantly. The common thread is scarcity – of equipment, medications, hospital space, or physicians' attention. Some of the scarcity was actual; some of it was anticipated. Regardless, scarcity demands choosing how to allocate limited resources. And when some people needing resources are Black, or disabled, or both, they may justifiably worry about whether their allocations will be equitable. Given the histories examined in earlier chapters, it is obvious that equitable allocation was hardly a sure bet. Instead, medical devaluation of nonnormative bodies, implicit biases, and failures to address the expressed needs of disabled people and Black people reappear in these stories.

8.2.1 *Crisis Standards of Care and Disabled People*

As US government officials, scientists, and health professionals watched the early advances of COVID-19 internationally and tracked the growing number of domestic cases, one fact became clear. The scenario of a novel virus, one for which no one possessed immunity, presented a potentially breathtaking rate of transmission that threatened to result in health care systems being overwhelmed by critically ill patients. Specifically, seeing that the virus often attacked a patient's lungs, experts worried that the supply of life-sustaining mechanical ventilators might fail to meet a ballooning need. A concern that the supply of ventilators could fail to meet the need for them was not unfounded. Public messaging urged adoption of social distancing and other measures to "flatten the curve" and so avoid that frightening situation; at the same time, public and private discussions considered exactly how a limited supply of ventilators should be allocated among patients in need if in fact demand grew to outstrip supply.

As health professionals and policymakers grappled with the dawning threats from COVID-19, people with disabilities discerned two dire messages. First, for those with one or more of the chronic health conditions identified as risk factors for severe COVID-19, becoming infected posed a grave threat. Second, many disabled people feared that if they became seriously ill with COVID-19 they might be denied access to life-sustaining care.

8.2.1.1 Emergency Planning and Excluding Disabled People

Addressing a potential equipment shortage during a pandemic exemplifies the larger problem of a government's preparedness to address public health emergencies. Federal and state legislation directs public health and emergency officials to explicitly consider disabled people's needs when planning for public health emergencies, yet it provides scant guidance on the specific question of how to allocate medical resources in a widespread emergency. Public health agencies create plans – often referred to as "crisis standards of care" – to enhance their preparedness. That planning, however, does not typically include people with disabilities, and planners often fail to focus on distinct measures needed for disabled people during an emergency.[13] As a result, natural disasters like Hurricane Katrina, in New Orleans, or Hurricane Maria, in Puerto Rico, were especially devastating for people with disabilities. When it examined Katrina's impact, the National Council on Disability found that "a disproportionate number of the fatalities were people with disabilities" and discovered that American Red Cross shelters had a policy of excluding people with apparent disabilities.[14]

As the pandemic grew, states, health care systems, and medical societies quickly developed crisis standards of care to respond to a potential shortage of ventilators or other resources. Standards directing how scarce medical resources should be allocated commonly endorse a commitment to maximizing the number of patients who will benefit, often measured by projections of the number of lives saved.[15] These plans drew public attention as COVID-19 case counts rapidly escalated. For many people with disabilities, news of plans for triage triggered fears that their lives would be given low priority, that they would be sent to the back of the line for ventilators, if they were permitted to join the line at all. Some who regularly used a personal ventilator feared that, if they sought care for COVID-19, their ventilator might be confiscated and given to someone deemed a better bet for survival.[16] Disability advocates filed complaints with the Office of Civil Rights (OCR) at the federal Department of Health and Human Services (HHS), alleging that some crisis standards of care violated the Americans with Disabilities Act and Section 504 of the Rehabilitation Act.[17]

8.2.1.2 A 1990s Lesson from Oregon

This was not the first invocation of disability discrimination law to challenge a plan for rationing scarce medical resources. In the early 1990s, HHS rejected Oregon's application for a Medicaid waiver permitting it to implement a rationing scheme[18]

[13] Leslie Wolf & Wendy Hensel, *Playing God: The Legality of Plans Denying Scarce Resources to People with Disabilities in Public Health Emergencies*, 63 FLA. L. REV. 719 (2011).
[14] National Council on Disability, *The Impact of Hurricanes Katrina and Rita on People with Disabilities: A Look Back and Remaining Challenges* 3, 47 (2006), https://ncd.gov/publications/2006/aug072006.
[15] Ani B. Satz, *Healthcare as Eugenics*, in DISABILITY, HEALTH, LAW AND BIOETHICS 27–29 (I. Glenn Cohen et al. eds., Cambridge Univ. Press 2020).
[16] Joel Michael Reynolds et al., *Against Personal Ventilator Reallocation*, 30 CAMBRIDGE Q. HEALTHCARE ETHICS 272 (2021).
[17] Elizabeth Pendo, *Protecting the Rights and Wellbeing of People with Disabilities during the COVID-19 Pandemic*, St. Louis Univ. School of Law Scholarship Commons 2021, https://scholarship.law.slu.edu/cgi/viewcontent.cgi?article=1605&context=faculty.
[18] Letter from Louis W. Sullivan, Secretary of Health and Human Services, to Barbara Roberts, Governor of Oregon (Aug. 3, 1992) (with accompanying three-page "Analysis Under the Americans with Disabilities Act ('ADA') of the Oregon Reform Demonstration"), reprinted

within its Medicaid program. Oregon's goal was to limit payments for treatments that provided little benefit so it could use the Medicaid funds saved to cover a greater number of low-income residents. Eliminating low-value care would be accomplished by using "comparative benefit" to determine which services Medicaid would cover. Oregon employed an intricate set of methods for determining which treatments were beneficial; one was to conduct telephone surveys seeking input from Oregon's residents.[19]

Relying on the results of these surveys put Oregon's rationing plan into legal jeopardy. In rejecting Oregon's plan, HHS Secretary Louis Sullivan pointed out that incorporating public input and community values may have "quantifie(d) stereotypic assumptions" devaluing life with a disability. The concern was that the resulting ranking of treatments to determine what medical services Medicaid paid for may have discounted treatments that would save life but not return a patient to full functioning. Sullivan pointed to two specific instances where the prospect of disabilities appeared to place treatments so low on Oregon's prioritized list that they would not be covered. Alcoholic cirrhosis of the liver was ranked far below other cirrhosis. And treatments for extremely low birthweight babies would not be covered, while treatments for heavier babies would.[20] Sullivan didn't rule out the possibility of a nondiscriminatory rationing plan, though. Relying on a 1985 Supreme Court decision that applied Section 504 to Tennessee's Medicaid program,[21] Sullivan stated: "Oregon may consider, consistent with the ADA, any content neutral factor that does not take disability into account or that does not have a particular exclusionary effect on persons with disabilities."[22]

8.2.1.3 Ventilator Rationing and Disability Discrimination

This guidance on how to assess rationing schemes against claims of disability discrimination was on point as the OCR reviewed crisis standards of care nearly three decades after the rejection of Oregon's rationing plan. Some problems were easy to identify. For example, Alabama put out standards providing that "people with severe or profound intellectual disability are unlikely candidates for ventilator support."[23] Such exclusions or deprioritizations explicitly based on disability are clearly prohibited.

in Timothy B. Flanagan, *ADA Analyses of the Oregon Health Care Plan*, 9 Issues Law & Med. 397, 409 (1994).

[19] Michael J. Garland, Rationing in Public: Oregon's Priority-Setting Methodology, in Rationing America's Medical Care: The Oregon Plan and Beyond 37 (Martin A. Strosberg et al. eds., 1992).

[20] Philip G. Peters, *Health Care Rationing and Disability Rights*, 70 Ind. L.J. 491, 504 (1995).

[21] Alexander v. Choate, 469 U.S. 287 (1985).

[22] Letter from Louis Sullivan, *supra* note 18.

[23] Ari Ne'eman, *"I Will Not Apologize for My Needs,"* N.Y. Times (Mar. 23, 2020), https://www .nytimes.com/2020/03/23/opinion/coronavirus-ventilators-triage-disability.html.

In other cases, assessing whether guidelines for allocating ventilators would effectively exclude disabled people proved more challenging. After advocates filed a complaint about its allocation scheme, the Pennsylvania Department of Health revised its guidelines to state explicitly that allocation decisions must be based on an individualized assessment of each patient's condition (not simply the patient's diagnosis with a particular condition) and could not consider the patient's quality of life. From advocates' perspective, excluding quality of life considerations from allocation decisions is critical.[24] OCR accepted these changes as satisfactorily resolving the complaint against Pennsylvania,[25] but another aspect of the State's allocation framework still rankled disability advocates. Specifically, Pennsylvania (along with some other states) would still consider not only a patient's "near-term life expectancy" (basically an estimate of the patient's likelihood of surviving the current hospitalization) but also whether they had a medical prognosis of likely death within the five years that followed. Disability advocates insisted that any survival-related criteria for receiving treatment must be based on the patient's ability to survive the immediate health threat (here, COVID-19), not the projected likelihood of surviving other disability-related conditions over a longer timeframe.[26]

The legality of using a patient's projected five-year survival to ration treatments falls into a gray zone. It is unclear whether courts would find that denying ventilators to patients deemed unlikely to survive more than five years would have a "particular exclusionary effect" on disabled people. But it is troubling. The OCR's March 2020 bulletin on the applicability of antidiscrimination laws to allocation schemes states, "Our civil rights laws protect the equal dignity of every human life from ruthless utilitarianism."[27] Should policies that figured a patient's projected five-year survival into the decision of their access to a ventilator, so as to maximize the overall number of years of life saved, count as "ruthless"?

Even a restrained utilitarianism risks an endorsement of sentiments that view meeting the needs of disabled people as a hindrance to taking care of people who are "normal." "Any metric used for determining who should get limited resources will inevitably be drawn into a eugenics sinkhole," warned disability studies scholar

[24] Quality-Adjusted Life Years and the Devaluation of Life with Disability, National Council on Disability (Nov. 6 2019), https://ncd.gov/sites/default/files/NCD_Quality_Adjusted_Life_Report_508.pdf.

[25] *OCR Resolves Civil Rights Complaint against Pennsylvania after It Revises Its Pandemic Health Care Triaging Policies to Protect against Disability Discrimination*, HHS Press Office (Apr. 16, 2020), https://www.hhs.gov/about/news/2020/04/16/ocr-resolves-civil-rights-complaint-against-pennsylvania-after-it-revises-its-pandemic-health-care.html.

[26] Letter from David Carlson, Disability Rights Washington, to Roger Severino, Director, Office for Civil Rights, US Department of Health & Human Services 12 (Mar. 23, 2020), https://www.centerforpublicrep.org/wp-content/uploads/2020/03/OCR-Complaint_3-23-20-final.pdf.

[27] See Office for Civil Rights, Bulletin: Civil Rights, HIPAA, and the Coronavirus Disease 2019 (COVID-19), US Dep't Health & Human Servs. (Mar. 28, 2020), https://www.hhs.gov/sites/default/files/ocr-bulletin-3-28-20.pdf.

Lennard Davis.[28] Understanding the full scope of disabled people's apprehensiveness about COVID-19 crisis standards of care requires attention to the historic context of eugenics and many doctors' continued devaluation of the quality of disabled life.

A more egalitarian approach to allocating scarce resources in a pandemic health emergency commits to protecting persons already disadvantaged by prepandemic social and political decisions. We know that people with disabilities endure persistent economic and social disadvantages in American society, as well as disparities in health care and health status. In addition, as disability law scholar Sam Bagenstos points out, they are grossly underrepresented in both political roles and the medical profession. Bagenstos highlights that the feared scarcity of ventilators and medical resources was not a natural, inevitable event but rather the result of investment decisions made before the pandemic, decisions that disabled people had little voice in.[29] From this perspective, nondisabled people should not be able to use allocation policies to shield themselves from painful consequences of their political decisions failing either to maintain enough ventilators (or other resources) to meet everyone's needs or to take aggressive action to ramp up production and efficient distribution during the pandemic. Arguably, a rationing policy that takes five-year life expectancy into account lets nondisabled folks off the (worst) hook while placing much of the burden of their bad decisions on disabled people whose life expectancy is already limited.

8.2.2 *Informally Rationing Care for Disabled People*

Stories of informal rationing – denials of medical care apart from a formal crisis standard of care – emerged as well. One example is the story of Michael Hickson, which opened this book. Doctors in Hickson's case decided his treatment for COVID-19 should be discontinued; one doctor stated to Hickson's wife that no further treatment was warranted because Hickson (who had quadriplegia, blindness, and brain injuries) lacked "much of" a quality of life. A spokesperson for the hospital involved insisted that the decision to discontinue Hickson's treatment was not made because of limited hospital capacity.[30] Even assuming that denial's veracity, concerns regarding scarcity or anticipated scarcity may have shaped physicians' decisions.

---

[28] Lennard Davis, *In the Time of Pandemic, the Deep Structure of Biopower Is Laid Bare*, 47 CRITICAL INQUIRY S138 (2021).

[29] Sam Bagenstos, *Who Gets the Ventilator? Disability Discrimination in COVID-19 Medical-Rationing Protocols*, YALE L.J. FORUM (May 27, 2020), https://www.yalelawjournal.org/forum/who-gets-the-ventilator.

[30] Ariana Eunjung Cha, *Quadriplegic Man's Death from COVID-19 Spotlights Questions of Disability, Race and Family*, WASH. POST (July 6, 2020), https://www.washingtonpost.com/health/2020/07/05/coronavirus-disability-death.

8.2.2.1 Demanding DNRs from Disabled Patients

Biased views of the worth and quality of disabled people's lives seem especially likely to distort treatment decisions in conditions of actual or perceived scarcity. Investigative reporting in Oregon uncovered several stories of hospitals demanding the entry of do-not-resuscitate (DNR) orders for patients with intellectual disability and other disabilities who sought hospital admission during the COVID-19 pandemic. Some cases involved patients or their legal representatives being pressured to sign documents that would authorize denials of life-saving interventions. In one case, a hospital reportedly directed a group home to complete DNRs for all its residents in case they needed hospitalization.[31]

Lawyers at a disability rights advocacy group threatened to sue the hospital for disability discrimination. They also joined with other disability groups to file a complaint about Oregon's crisis standards of care with OCR. A state lawmaker became involved and successfully pushed legislation barring doctors from forcing patients to sign DNR orders as a condition of treatment or hospital admission. In addition, the Oregon Health Authority withdrew its crisis standards of care, acknowledging that failure to seek input from marginalized communities in their creation produced guidelines that risked operating in a discriminatory fashion.[32] This intervention – where legal advocacy motivated regulatory reexamination and state-level legislation – may offer a model for other efforts to address health inequities, as the concluding chapter will discuss.

Explicit or implicit bias in rationing scarce resources has not been disabled people's only concern in the pandemic. Hospitals' prohibitions on visitors disproportionately affected disabled people, who often rely on family members or assistants. Early in the pandemic, when public health messaging was rapidly evolving, many communications were not accessible to people who were deaf or hard of hearing. And once the vaccine rollout began, heavy reliance on inaccessible websites excluded persons with visual impairments. The list could go on, but questions of rationing present a notable parallel to Black people's experience in the pandemic.

8.2.3 *Black People: Indirect Rationing and Implicit Bias*

8.2.3.1 Impact of Crisis Standards of Care on Black People

Discussions about rationing early in the COVID-19 pandemic largely centered on implications for people with disabilities. In contrast to some direct references to

---

[31] Joseph Shapiro, *Oregon Hospitals Didn't Have Shortages. So Why Were Disabled People Denied Care?*, NPR (Dec. 21, 2020), https://www.npr.org/2020/12/21/946292119/oregon-hospitals-didnt-have-shortages-so-why-were-disabled-people-denied-care.

[32] *Id.*

disability, crisis standards of care did not refer to a patient's race as a factor relevant to allocating ventilators. The OCR's March 2020 guidance included a reminder that laws prohibiting discrimination based on race (along with disability and other factors) remained in effect as government officials and health care providers considered how best to allocate scarce resources, if needed.[33]

But Black people still worried that any rationing scheme would disfavor them indirectly, even if it did not single them out. OCR's guidance failed to note that disability generally is more prevalent among Black Americans than White Americans (a point the next chapter considers). As a result, when disabling preexisting health conditions or comorbidities trigger lower priority in a formal rationing system, Black people will feel an outsized impact. And legal scholar Patricia Williams pointed out that high COVID-19 death rates among Black Americans – in her words, "the perfect storm of collective mortality risk clustered by zip code and histories of real estate segregation" – meant Black people were more likely to face triage decisions.[34]

This tangled knot of comorbidities, disability, race, and socially diminished survivability surfaced as Massachusetts developed its crisis standards of care. In a letter to the governor, US Representative Ayanna Pressley raised concerns about the standards' incorporation of patients' comorbidities into allocation decisions: "We know communities of color are more likely to have comorbidities not because of any genetic predisposition, but due to the legacy of structural racism and inequality that has resulted in unequal access to affordable health care, safe and stable housing, and quality school and employment."[35] In response to advocacy by Pressley and others, the state's Department of Public Health removed consideration of medical conditions affecting long-term survival prospects from the guidelines. The change's stated goal was "to prevent unconscious bias against people of color, people with disabilities and other community members who are marginalized."[36]

The Sequential Organ Failure Assessment (SOFA) score is another component of most crisis standards of care that may disfavor Black Americans if applied indiscriminately, without attention to equity concerns. The SOFA score is a compilation of measures that track a patient's organ function or failure. Crisis standards of care rely on SOFA scores to indicate severity of illness and likelihood of survival. Some physicians attuned to health equity have argued that despite their facial objectivity,

---

[33] Office for Civil Rights, *supra* note 27.

[34] Williams, *supra* note 5, at 260.

[35] Emily Cleveland Manchanda, *Inequity in Crisis Standards of Care*, 383 NEW ENG. J. MED. e16 (1) (2020).

[36] *Pressley Says ICU, Ventilator Guidelines Negatively Affect Minorities and Wants Baker to Rescind Them*, WBUR (Apr. 14, 2020), https://www.wbur.org/commonhealth/2020/04/14/ ayanna-pressley-critical-care-state-guidance-governor-letter; *After Uproar, Mass. Revises Guidelines on Who Gets an ICU Bed or Ventilator amid COVID-19 Surge*, WBUR, https:// www.wbur.org/commonhealth/2020/04/20/mass-guidelines-ventilator-covid-coronavirus (Apr. 22, 2020).

SOFA scores have an inherent racial bias. Pointing to the "unjustly high prevalence of chronic kidney disease" among Black Americans, one group of physicians suggested revising the calculation of SOFA scores to limit the impact of kidney function on allocation decisions. To ensure that crisis standards of care do not compound harm visited on marginalized communities by the pandemic, they argue that "resource allocation criteria must be developed, revised, and implemented through an identity-conscious lens."[37]

8.2.3.2 Biased Decisions in COVID-19 Care

Unconscious bias can shape medical decisions about continuing treatment deemed to be of debatable benefit for specific patients, even when crisis standards of care are not invoked. Recall Michael Hickson; he was disabled and Black and his care was terminated. In writing about the hazards of triaging ill patients, Lennard Davis cautioned: "Race will factor in dramatically, and its combination with disability is an accelerant to any eugenic decision-making process."[38]

And even in cases where disability is not salient, medical decisions occur in the context of social and health care systems where disparities in health, opportunity, and resources abound. As three bioethicists reflected on that field's failure to address systemic injustices: "Questions of fair distribution don't suddenly appear at the bedside as novel issues of allocating ventilators; they are baked into the social fabric."[39]

With sad predictability, reports arose where COVID-19 patients' racial identity appeared to influence the care they received. Those experiences were not novel. Well before the pandemic, some Black patients experienced medical providers not listening to them, especially when they sought relief from pain. Well before the pandemic, Black patients in low-income areas have gone without medical resources needed to provide optimal care for their illnesses. Well before the pandemic, Black patients justifiably questioned whether to trust White doctors to make decisions in their best interests. The pandemic magnified all these concerns. High stress environments and conditions of uncertainty – like crowded clinics or emergency departments with staff responding to a highly infectious virus that isn't fully understood – are conditions ripe for implicit biases to operate.[40]

---

[37] Emily C. Cleveland Manchanda et al., *Racial Equity in Crisis Standards of Care – Reassuring Data or Reason for Concern?*, 4 JAMA NETWORK OPEN (2021), https://jamanetwork.com/journals/jamanetworkopen/fullarticle/2777677.

[38] Davis, *supra* note 28, at S140.

[39] Larry R. Churchill et al., *The Future of Bioethics: It Shouldn't Take a Pandemic*, 50 HASTINGS CENTER REP. 54 (May–June 2020).

[40] April Dembosky, *"All You Want Is to Be Believed"; The Impacts of Unconscious Bias in Health Care*, KAISER HEALTH NEWS (Oct. 1, 2020), https://khn.org/news/all-you-want-is-to-be-believed-the-impacts-of-unconscious-bias-in-health-care.

ACCESS TO TESTING Access to coronavirus testing is the starting point for examining the quality and amount of care that Black patients received. Ramping up COVID-19 testing availability posed a ubiquitous challenge in the pandemic's early months, and racial disparities in access to testing were apparent. Analysis of data regarding testing sites showed that ZIP codes where residents were predominantly (at least 75 percent) White had on average one testing site for every 14,500 people. That's hardly ample testing capacity, but it far exceeded the average of one site per 23,300 people in ZIP codes where, predominantly, people of color lived.[41] News accounts described Black patients with COVID-19 symptoms being unable to access testing and care. Rana Zoe Mungin, a 30-year-old Black teacher with asthma went to the hospital twice after she developed a fever but was not given a test. On her third trip, she was admitted and placed on a ventilator within hours. She later died from COVID-19. Her sister described an ambulance attendant discounting Mungin's need for care: "He tried to insinuate that she was having a panic attack, you know, and he was trying to really convince her not to go to the hospital."[42]

ACCESS TO APPROPRIATE TREATMENT FOR PATIENTS DIAGNOSED WITH COVID-19 In December 2020, another cell phone video and another death added Susan Moore's name to #SayHerName demands, along with Breonna Taylor, Sandra Bland, Michelle Cusseaux, and others. Taylor, Bland, and Cusseaux died at the hands of police or while in custody. Susan Moore died from COVID-19.[43] Moore was admitted to a suburban Indianapolis hospital with symptoms of COVID-19. She complained of pain and difficulty breathing and asked the White doctor treating her for medication to relieve the pain. When her doctor did not initially treat her pain, Susan Moore got the message. As she explained in a Facebook video she filmed in her hospital bed with an oxygen tube in her nose: "My doctor made me feel like I was a drug addict. . . . You have to show proof that you have something wrong with you, in order for you to get the medicine. I put forward, and I maintain: If I was white, I wouldn't have to go through that."[44]

So far the story is sadly unremarkable. Physicians' failure to adequately treat pain in Black patients is well documented. Moore's story garnered national attention because of the Facebook video she posted ... and because she was herself a physician. A person does not need a medical degree to know when they are in pain, but Dr. Moore knew her condition. She was equipped to express what she needed,

[41] Caitlin Owens & Andrew Witherspoon, *People of Color Have Less Access to Coronavirus Testing*, AXIOS (June 23, 2020), https://www.axios.com/minorities-coronavirus-testing-9a6397e4-a7e7-4077-bad2-bbd77fe5d1c2.html.

[42] Averi Harper, *COVID-19 Exposes Mistrust, Health Care Inequality Going Back Generations for African Americans*, ABC NEWS (Apr. 28, 2020), https://abcnews.go.com/Health/covid-19-exposes-mistrust-health-care-inequality-back/story?id=70370949.

[43] Aletha Maybank et al., *Say Her Name: Dr. Susan Moore*, WASH. POST (Dec. 26, 2020), https://www.washingtonpost.com/opinions/2020/12/26/say-her-name-dr-susan-moore.

[44] https://www.facebook.com/susan.moore.33671748/videos/3459156707536634.

and she knew how to advocate for herself. Still she was dismissed. The doctor suggested sending her home, prompting her to reflect, "[T]his is how Black people get killed. When you send them home and they don't know how to fight for themselves." Eventually, Moore received medications for her pain, after a test revealed new infiltrates in her lungs and lymphadenopathy. Her condition appeared to improve, and a few days later she was discharged home. Her condition quickly worsened, though, and she died less than three weeks later.

Susan Moore's case shows that education, knowledge, and professional stature do not reliably protect Black patients from having their health concerns disregarded by health care providers.[45] Self-advocacy is not a silver bullet guarding against dismissive attitudes. The outcry over this doctor's treatment grew when the CEO of the hospital where she was initially admitted tried to explain what happened by describing her as a "complex patient" and suggesting that hospital nurses "may have been intimidated" by Moore's demands for appropriate care. Racial justice advocates called the CEO's statement an instance of victim-blaming.[46] The CEO's description also suggests that stereotypes of Black people as dangerous or threatening were in play. It seems improbable that White male physician-patients' requests for appropriate care would be dismissed and that they would be threatened with being discharged.

Not being listened to by medical professionals is not unique to Black patients; nor is being treated as insubordinate. Other patients of color have reported similar experiences.[47] One Latina COVID-19 patient connected the dots between being treated dismissively at one hospital and poor outcomes for people of color in the pandemic: "Because when we go and seek care, if we are advocating for ourselves, we can be treated as insubordinate . . . and if we are not advocating for ourselves, we can be treated as invisible."[48]

Susan Moore's was not the only reported case where Black COVID-19 patients or their families believed that they were receiving less care than White patients. Recall Sarah Johnson's story from Chapter 4. Just twenty-three hours after being admitted to a hospital in New Orleans with COVID-19, the eighty-six-year-old retired nurse was sent home to die because hospital personnel said they couldn't do anything more for her. Johnson was one of about two dozen Black COVID-19 patients that ProPublica identified in New Orleans as having been discharged by hospitals while still ill. In many of those cases, patients' families reported that the hospital had

---

[45] John Eligon, *Black Doctor Dies of Covid-19 after Complaining of Racist Treatment*, N.Y. TIMES (Dec. 23, 2020), https://www.nytimes.com/2020/12/23/us/susan-moore-black-doctor-indiana .html?action=click&module=Top%20Stories&pgtype=Homepage.

[46] Sarah Polus, *Hospital CEO's Response to Black Doctor's COVID-19 Death Sparks Outrage*, THE HILL (Dec. 31, 2020), https://thehill.com/homenews/state-watch/532237-hospital-ceos-response-to-black-doctors-covid-death-sparks-outrage.

[47] Dembosky, *supra* note 40.

[48] *Id.*

pressured them to accept at-home hospice care for their loved ones. Sending dangerously ill coronavirus patients home to be cared for by untrained and unprotected family members was a departure from practices by hospitals nationally.[49]

SAFETY-NET CARE AND AVOIDING CARE COVID-19 racial disparities also connect to chronic resource constraints that safety net hospitals located in low-income communities of color typically face. Findings from a 2021 study suggested that higher COVID-19 death rates among hospitalized Black patients were associated with their disproportionate admission to hospitals with poor outcomes.[50] Accounts of hospitals in Chicago's South and West sides and in South Los Angeles portrayed thinly stretched staffing and an absence of state-of-the-art technology and medicines as limiting hospitals' ability to respond to gravely ill patients. Some symptomatic Black patients in Chicago preferred to drive to a hospital thirty minutes from their home rather than seek care at their neighborhood facility.[51] But transferring patients needing advanced technology to better resourced hospitals is not necessarily an option either, as some hospitals refuse to accept transfers of patients who are uninsured or covered by Medicaid.[52] In response to a *New York Times* article titled "Dying of Covid in a 'Separate and Unequal' L.A. Hospital," the CEO of Martin Luther King, Jr., Community Hospital in South Los Angeles took a broader view. She asserted that the fundamental problem was that coronavirus patients seeking care at her hospital live in communities that have been starved of resources: "A lifelong lack of access to health care drove disparate COVID-19 outcomes in South Los Angeles. And that lack of access is directly related to our nation's historic and continued underfunding of care for communities of color."[53]

Personal familiarity with having health concerns (either their own or friends' or family members') dismissed or discounted sometimes leads Black people to choose not to seek care, even when they need it. One Black woman explained why, despite experiencing body aches, chills and a fever, lethargy, and a dry cough (all COVID-19 symptoms), she didn't go to the hospital: "Black folk don't get treated well in

[49] Annie Waldman & Joshua Kaplan, *Sent Home to Die*, PROPUBLICA (Sept. 2, 2020), https://www.propublica.org/article/sent-home-to-die.

[50] David A. Asch et al., *Patient and Hospital Factors Associated with Difference in Mortality Rates among Black and White US Medicare Beneficiaries Hospitalized with COVID-19 Infection*, 4 JAMA NETWORK OPEN e2112842 (2021), https://jamanetwork.com/journals/jamanetworkopen/fullarticle/2781182.

[51] Duaa Eldeib, *The First 100: COVID-19 Took Black Lives First. It Didn't Have To*, PROPUBLICA ILLINOIS (May 9, 2020), https://features.propublica.org/chicago-first-deaths/covid-coronavirus-took-black-lives-first.

[52] Sheri Fink, *Dying of Covid in a 'Separate and Unequal' L.A. Hospital*, N.Y. TIMES (Feb. 9, 2021), https://www.nytimes.com/2021/02/08/us/covid-los-angeles.html.

[53] Elaine Batchlor, *Were COVID-19 Patients in the Wrong Hospital – or the Wrong Community? What Really Drove COVID-19 Outcomes in South Los Angeles*, HEALTH AFF. BLOG (May 9, 2021), https://222.healthaffairs.org/do/10.1377/hblog20210430.501118/full.

hospitals and so if I can stay at home and get better. . . . Why the hell am I going?"[54] Disbelief that seeking care will yield any benefit, combined with a distrust of health care workers, may be particularly strong among older Black Americans, who have experienced racism throughout their lives. Knowing that hospitals were isolating COVID-19 patients, shutting out family members who could act as advocates, could exacerbate that reluctance.[55] Some experts suggest this combination has played a role in excessive COVID-19 death rates among Black seniors: Black Americans aged 65 to 74 died of COVID-19 at five times the rate of White patients in the same age group.[56]

This accounting of racial equity issues that surfaced as the pandemic progressed is far from exhaustive. Questions about racial disproportionality in the distribution of pandemic aid funds, participation in vaccine trials, and vaccine access all arose, highlighting pervasive structural inequities in health care and public health systems. The next section considers two types of institutions where Black people, along with disabled people, were particularly vulnerable to coronavirus's ravages.

8.3 PRE-PANDEMIC POLICIES AND STRUCTURAL INEQUITY

Another COVID story is more properly thought of as a COVID history. This is the history that transpired decades before the virus ever appeared in humans: specifically, the record of choices leading to Black people's and disabled people's disproportionate representation both in nursing homes (particularly those hardest hit by COVID-19) and in prisons and jails. These institutions were among the worst hotspots early in the pandemic. Not by chance, the people consigned to them skewed dark-skinned and disabled as compared to the overall population. Building on points made in earlier chapters, the next sections unpack how the heightened vulnerability of incarcerated persons and persons residing in nursing homes to COVID-19's ravages was a predictable product of those choices.

8.3.1 Infecting Incarcerated People

Prisons and jails provided fertile ground for COVID-19 to take root in. Many factors were at play. Incarcerated persons typically live in tightly crowded spaces, making social distancing difficult. Few facilities have adequate personal protective equipment (PPE). About half of incarcerated persons faced increased COVID-19 risks by virtue of having one or more chronic diseases.[57]

---

[54] Harper, *supra* note 42.

[55] *Id.*

[56] Judith Graham, *Why Black Aging Matters, Too*, KAISER HEALTH NEWS (Sept. 3, 2020), https://khn.org/news/why-black-aging-matters-too.

[57] Brendan Saloner et al., *COVID-19 Cases and Deaths in Federal and State Prisons*, 324 JAMA 602 (2020); Matthew J. Akiyama et al., *Flattening the Curve for Incarcerated Populations – Covid-19 in Jails and Prisons*, 382 NEW ENG. J. MED. 2075, 2076 (2020).

Take root it did. Less than six months into the pandemic, more than twenty correctional institutions had reported more than 1,000 cases of COVID-19. Case rates in the prison population were estimated at 5.5 times as high as in the general population; death rates were 3 times as high.[58]

Elevated rates of sickness and death were not simply the result of people (many with risk factors for COVID-19) living in crowded conditions. Case and mortality counts also flowed from a history of disinvestment in health care provision for incarcerated persons. States' records in providing health care vary widely, but their overall record is abysmal. A frequent contributing factor is the choice to divert resources to for-profit correctional health care companies by contracting away public responsibility to meet incarcerated persons' medical needs. More than two-thirds of jails have engaged private companies to provide health care, as have most states. These companies seek to maximize profits and shareholder value, often by cutting staffing. Contract terms that reimburse the companies on a per-person basis or that require the correctional institution to pay a share of hospitalization costs can conflict with prisoners' interest in receiving timely and appropriate care.[59] This outsourcing of health care left many jails and prisons ill equipped to act quickly when COVID-19 cases started snowballing.

The United States surpasses all other countries in imprisoning its citizens.[60] But its impulse towards imprisonment does not apply evenly across its citizenry. Chapter 7 described how Black people and people with disabilities are sent to prisons and jails at rates far exceeding their representation in the population overall. In 2018, one in every three incarcerated persons was Black, compared to just under one in eight overall.[61] One in four Black prison and jail inmates surveyed in 2011–12 reported having at least one disability.[62] And rates of reporting some disability were three times higher among incarcerated persons generally than in the overall population. The multiples by which cognitive disabilities and serious mental illness exceeded overall rates were even greater.[63]

---

[58] Saloner et al., *supra* note 57. The death rate was adjusted to reflect that the proportion of people aged 65 or older is lower in prisons than in the general population.

[59] Steve Coll, *The Jail Healthcare Crisis*, NEW YORKER (Feb. 25, 2019). Increased reliance on for-profit companies for comprehensive operation of prisons and jails similarly contributes to unhealthy carceral environments. *Id.*

[60] Peter Wagner & Wanda Bertram, *"What Percent of the U.S. Is Incarcerated?" (and Other Ways to Measure Mass Incarceration)*, PRISON POLICY INITIATIVE (Jan. 16, 2020), https://www.prisonpolicy.org/blog/2020/01/16/percent-incarcerated.

[61] John Gramlich, *Black Imprisonment Rate in the United States Has Fallen by a Third Since 2006*, PEW RES. CTR. (May 6, 2020), https://www.pewresearch.org/fact-tank/2020/05/06/share-of-black-White-hispanic-americans-in-prison-2018-vs-2006.

[62] JENNIFER BRONSON ET AL., BUREAU OF JUSTICE STATISTICS, DISABILITIES AMONG PRISON AND JAIL INMATES, 2011–12 (Dec. 2015). Forty-two percent of multiracial prisoners reported having at least one disability.

[63] REBECCA VALLAS, DISABLED BEHIND BARS: THE MASS INCARCERATION OF PEOPLE WITH DISABILITIES IN AMERICA'S JAILS AND PRISONS, CTR. FOR AM. PROGRESS 1–2 (July 2016),

The overrepresentation of Black people and disabled people is also the product of public disinvestment choices. In the twentieth century's latter decades, "law and order" rhetoric replaced social spending on physical and human capital in poor communities. Police became the default responders for social problems that ranged from school discipline to mental health crises to substance abuse.[64] According to legal scholar Michelle Alexander, pervasive policing in poor urban neighborhoods of color is one way the criminal justice system exerts racial control, producing stark racial disparities in incarceration.[65]

Public disinvestment decisions and policing practices also contributed to hyper-incarceration of disabled people. A goal of the twentieth century deinstitutionaliza-tion movement was to end the confinement of people with disabilities, instead allowing them to reside in the community. States' failure to invest in community-based housing and supports for community living, however, left many disabled people without supports needed to manage their lives.[66] Without those supports, many became needlessly caught up in the criminal justice system.[67] Discriminatory policing of disabled people followed public disinvestment. Legal scholar Jamelia Morgan traces how skimping on community-based mental health, social supports, and affordable housing fed into discriminatory policing. In reviewing arrests for order maintenance or "quality of life" offenses like nuisance, loitering, or disorderly conduct, Morgan found disabled people experiencing mental distress were often involved. She argues such arrests overcriminalize conduct that poses no threat, but whose nonnormative nature makes nondisabled people feel uncomfortable. In this "mental distress-to-arrest pipeline," people land in jail because they act in a way typical of their disability.[68]

Today, three times as many people with mental health conditions are confined in prisons or jails as live in state mental hospitals.[69] Critical scholars describe the shift from confining disabled people in public treatment institutions to confining them in correctional institutions as "trans-institutionalization."[70] The decision of many states

https://www.americanprogress.org/issues/criminal-justice/reports/2016/07/18/141447/disabled-behind-bars.

[64] William Julius Wilson, *The Political and Economic Forces Shaping Concentrated Poverty*, 123 POL. SCI. Q. 555, 570 (2008–09).

[65] MICHELLE ALEXANDER, THE NEW JIM CROW: MASS INCARCERATION IN THE AGE OF COLORBLINDNESS (2010).

[66] Samuel R. Bagenstos, *The Past and Future of Deinstitutionalization Litigation*, 3 CARDOZO L. REV. 1, 3 (2012).

[67] John V. Jacobi, *Prison Health Public Health: Obligations and Opportunities*, 31 AM. J.L. & MED. 447, 452 (2005).

[68] Jamelia Morgan, *Policing under Disability Law*, 73 STAN. L. REV. 1401 (2020).

[69] Torrey E. Fuller et al., *More Mentally Ill Are in Jails and Prisons than Hospitals: A Survey of the States*, Treatment Advocacy Center (2010), https://www.treatmentadvocacycenter.org/storage/documents/final_jails_vhospitals_study.pdf.

[70] Laura I. Appleman, *Deviancy, Dependency, and Disability: The Forgotten History of Eugenics and Mass Incarceration*, 68 DUKE L.J. 417, 462 (2018).

not to invest in supporting the independence and integration of disabled people was not inevitable.

In sum, prisons and jails did not just "happen" to become COVID-19 hotspots. That outcome was no accident but rather the predictable result of a confluence of choices. The overrepresentation of Black people and disabled people in correctional institutions is the product of (dis)investment from social spending, particularly in poor communities of color. And decisions to leave inmates' medical needs up to private companies aggravated the ill effects of unhealthy living conditions in prisons and jails. The results included inadequate pandemic preparedness and high vulnerability to infection and severe disease among close-quartered Black people and disabled people.

8.3.2 *Nursing Homes "Like Tinderboxes"*

A remarkably similar story explains COVID-19's devastating impact on Black people and disabled people residing in nursing homes. Most nursing home residents are at considerable risk for COVID-19 because of age, health condition(s), or both. Residents typically receive hands-on personal care multiple times a day, requiring social proximity. The staff providing that care disproportionately live in low-income communities of color, where infection rates have been high. Few facilities had adequate personal protective equipment (PPE) at the start of the pandemic. For-profit chains that prioritize profit margins have come to dominate the industry.[71] These were among the reasons that led commentators in the *New England Journal of Medicine* to describe nursing homes as "like tinderboxes, ready to go up in flames with just a spark."[72]

The sparks of infection that landed in nursing homes didn't take long to produce a conflagration. A few months into the pandemic, more than 153,000 nursing home residents and workers had caught COVID-19, and 35 percent of total COVID-19 deaths in the United States were linked to nursing homes. By June 2020, that share climbed to 45 percent. In about half the states a majority of deaths were attributable to nursing homes.

The authors who compared nursing homes to tinderboxes pointed to "decades of neglect of long-term care policy" to explain the sorry state of affairs.[73] In other words, the COVID conflagration in nursing homes was not inevitable; it resulted from

---

[71] E. Tammy Kim, *This Is Why Nursing Homes Failed So Badly*, N.Y. Times (Dec. 31, 2020), https://www.nytimes.com/2020/12/31/opinion/sunday/covid-nursing-homes.html. Several of these factors also describe the situation of disabled people living in the community who receive support from direct care workers. Janette Dill et al., *Addressing Systemic Racial Inequity in the Health Care Workforce*, Health Aff. Blog (Sept. 10, 2020), https://www.healthaffairs.org/do/10.1377/hblog20200908.133196/full.

[72] Rachel M. Werner et al., *Long-Term Care Policy after COVID-19 – Solving the Nursing Home Crisis*, 383 New Eng. J. Med. 903, 903 (2020).

[73] *Id.*

decisions accreted over decades, decisions that valued some lives over others. And, as with prisons and jails, those decisions – while perhaps not overtly discriminatory – have had disparate negative effects for disabled people and Black people.

8.3.2.1 Ageism and Ableism at Play

Some of the disregard for the welfare of nursing home residents doubtless reflects ageism – prejudice and bias against people based on their age. Many nursing home residents are elderly, and ageism certainly helps explain why policymakers have not invested in ensuring that nursing homes are a safe place for residents in a pandemic. A chilling example of that ageism was evident in Texas Lieutenant Governor Dan Patrick's statement, early in the pandemic, that older Americans should accept the risk of infection and death in order to permit the economy to function without interruption.[74]

But a significant fraction of persons who live in nursing homes are minors or nonelderly adults.[75] Disability is the actual common denominator for most residents.[76] (Some nondisabled persons stay in a nursing home temporarily while recovering from an acute illness, surgery, or accident. By contrast, longer-term residents of nursing homes are disabled, perhaps as the result of aging, but not necessarily.) Simply portraying nursing home residents as old people obscures the reality that nursing homes' catastrophically high rates of COVID-19 illness and death have primarily affected disabled people. To disability activists, discussions of nursing home deaths that refer solely to older people without any mention of disability smack of ableism in their complete erasure of disability's overwhelming presence.[77]

Recall that for many disabled people residing in a nursing home is neither medically necessary nor desired. Chapter 6 explained that many people are forced to live in a nursing home because their state has not shifted sufficient funding to meet the demand for home and community-based services (HCBS). Recall as well that insufficient funding is traceable in part to Medicaid's structural preference for nursing homes (which states are required to cover) and that states' gradual progress in shifting funding to HCBS has been threatened by proposals to gut federal funding

[74] Jamie Knodel, *Texas Lt. Gov. Dan Patrick Suggests He, Other Seniors Willing to Die to Get Economy Going Again*, NBC NEWS (Mar. 24, 2020), https://www.nbcnews.com/news/us-news/texas-lt-gov-dan-patrick-suggests-he-other-seniors-willing-n1167341.

[75] Ashley Cleek, *Young, Disabled and Stuck in a Nursing Home for the Elderly*, AL JAZEERA ENGLISH (Oct. 2, 2013), http://america.aljazeera.com/articles/2013/10/2/young-disabled-andstuckinnursinghomes.html.

[76] Elaine K. Howley, *Nursing Home Facts and Statistics*, U.S. NEWS HEALTH (Nov. 2, 2020), https://health.usnews.com/health-news/best-nursing-homes/articles/nursing-home-facts-and-statistics#expert-sources.

[77] Attorney and activist Matthew Cortland made this point in a Tweet in April 2021, https://twitter.com/mattbc/status/1388258334923448322?cn=ZmxleGlibGVfcmVecw%3D%3D&refsrc=email.

for Medicaid. The upshot is that federal and state policy choices have forced many disabled people to reside in institutional settings prone to contagion.

8.3.2.2 Racial Segregation of Nursing Homes

In addition, people of color residing in nursing homes have suffered more severely during the pandemic. In its first six months, nursing homes with higher percentages of Black and Latinx residents were likelier to report at least one COVID-19 case. Death rates also tracked residents' complexions. The higher the percentage of Black patients in a facility the higher its death rate tended to be.[78] Using data available through early September 2020, a large analysis of nursing home deaths from COVID-19 found a death rate in majority-Black nursing homes over 20 percent higher than in majority-White homes. That disparity widened as the percentage of Black residents increased. Nursing homes where at least 70 percent of the residents were Black reported death rates about 40 percent higher than in facilities with mostly White residents.[79]

The simple fact that in some nursing homes over 70 percent of the residents are Black is remarkable, given that Black people make up only about 13 percent of the United States' population. It is indicative of a broader pattern of documented racial segregation within nursing homes.[80] Even as the overall population of nursing homes decreased in the decades following the *Olmstead* decision, the number of people of color living in nursing facilities grew.[81] Estimates indicate that Black older adults are overrepresented among nursing home residents nationally. One likely explanation relates to health: Older Black adults are generally in worse health than their White counterparts and more likely to need a higher level of care when they move from their homes. Another explanation is financial. Older Black adults are more likely to be low-income and rely on Medicaid, which pays for nursing home care, and less likely to have financial resources enabling them to choose the alternatives (like assisted-living facilities) that better-heeled White older adults enjoy.[82]

Segregation among nursing homes today follows a history of civil rights enforcement that has been perfunctory at best. Title VI of the Civil Rights Act of 1964

---

[78] *The Striking Racial Divide in How Covid-19 Has Hit Nursing Homes*, N.Y. TIMES (Sept. 10, 2020), https://nyti.ms/3e45iVv.

[79] See Sidnee King & Joel Jacobs, *Near Birthplace of Martin Luther King, Jr., a Predominantly Black Nursing Home Tries to Heal after Outbreak*, WASH. POST (Sept. 9, 2020), https://www.washingtonpost.com/business/2020/09/09/black-nursing-homes-coronavirus.

[80] David Barton Smith et al., *Separate and Unequal: Racial Segregation and Disparities in Quality across Nursing Homes*, 26 HEALTH AFF. 1448, 1448 (2007).

[81] Zhanlian Feng et al., *The Care Span: Growth of Racial and Ethnic Minorities in U.S. Nursing Homes Driven by Demographics and Possible Disparities in Options*, 30 HEALTH AFF. 1358 (2011).

[82] Meghan J. Morales & Stephanie A. Robert, *Black–White Disparities in Moves to Assisted Living and Nursing Homes among Older Medicare Beneficiaries*, 75 J. GERONTOLOGY, SERIES B, PSYCHOL. SCI. SOC. SCI. 1972 (2019).

prohibits racial discrimination by recipients of federal funding.[83] Any nursing home that receives payment from Medicaid (today by far the largest single payer for nursing home care in the United States) is subject to this prohibition. Title VI's potential force was evident in the late 1960s, when hospital desegregation was largely accomplished without much uproar. Hospitals desegregated to avoid losing federal payments they could receive for caring for enrollees in the then-new Medicare program.[84] Nursing homes, by contrast, have not faced that threat because the government's Title VI enforcement efforts in their industry were nothing more than a "half-hearted pro forma paper compliance effort that everyone understood was cosmetic."[85]

The reason for the enforcement differential is partly historical. In Title VI's early days, most nursing homes were small, often family-run establishments, and Medicaid paid for relatively few residents. As a result, operators could choose not to admit residents covered by Medicaid without risking a severe financial penalty. Over time, as Medicaid covered a larger percentage of people needing nursing home care, operators figured out ways to maximize their flexibility to admit Medicaid recipients to their facilities or refuse them. They learned they could certify or decertify individual beds (rather than the entire home) to participate in Medicaid and that they could revise those decisions as it suited them. Basically, operators learned that federal regulators would permit them to decide on a patient-by-patient basis whether to participate in Medicaid.

Nursing home operators typically gave Medicaid's low payment rates as their reason for preferring to fill beds with profitable, private-pay patients as much as they could. But having bed-level flexibility regarding Medicaid participation meant operators enjoyed broad discretion in deciding which patients to admit, with financial explanations likely hiding racial discrimination in some cases.[86] And the sizable overlap between disabled or elderly Black people and disabled or elderly people whose low income qualified them for Medicaid meant that even a sincere focus on maximizing profits would often produce a racially discriminatory effect.[87] For that reason, in Linton v. Tennessee a federal district court found a disparate impact violation of Title VI when the Tennessee Medicaid program permitted nursing homes to give preference to private-pay patients.[88] A Supreme Court decision subsequent to Linton, however, prevented private plaintiffs from suing to

[83] 42 U.S.C. § 2000d et seq.
[84] DAVID BARTON SMITH, HEALTH CARE DIVIDED: RACE AND HEALING A NATION 115 (1999).
[85] Id. at 246.
[86] Id. at 246–50.
[87] See Ruqaiijah Yearby, Is It Too Late for Title VI Enforcement? – Seeking Redemption of the Unequal United States' Long Term Care System through International Means, 9 DEPAUL J. HEALTH CARE L. 971, 989–91 (2005).
[88] Linton v. Tennessee, 779 F. Supp. 925 (M.D. Tenn. 1990).

enforce Title VI using a disparate impact theory.[89] *Linton* thus stands as an isolated exception to the general rule of Title VI nonenforcement against nursing homes.

8.3.2.3 Quality Disparities and Regulatory Inaction

Tepid Title VI enforcement has enabled abiding racial segregation in nursing homes, and that segregation is associated with quality disparities.[90] Prior to the pandemic, researchers found that facilities serving mostly Black or Latinx residents performed more poorly in the government's nursing home star rating system.[91] Full explanations for why majority-Black nursing homes have suffered higher death rates than majority-White homes during the pandemic await further research. One hypothesis is that the industry's racial segregation contributed to regulators' toleration of disparities among nursing homes with respect to quality and safety and that those disparities turned lethal during the pandemic.[92]

The prepandemic failure to vigorously enforce quality and safety standards against nursing homes generally helps explain why they were such fertile ground for the infection to spread. It was par for the course for many facilities to operate with inadequate levels of ill-trained, minimum wage staff and deficient infection control measures.[93] A government report found that from 2013 to 2017, more than four out of five nursing homes had received at least one citation for a deficiency relating to infection prevention. The deficiencies included things like a failure to isolate ill residents during an infectious disease outbreak and the failure by staff to consistently follow hand hygiene practices – failures that even members of the general public would today recognize as problems. The report also found that many facilities were repeat offenders with respect to infection-control measures. Nearly half received deficiency citations in multiple consecutive years.[94] In the years immediately preceding the pandemic, CMS eased up on imposing fines against nursing homes that violated safety standards and undid a mandate that facilities employ an infection preventionist at least part time.[95]

---

[89] *Alexander v. Sandoval*, 532 U.S. 275 (2001).

[90] Yue Li et al., *Deficiencies in Care at Nursing Homes and Racial/Ethnic Disparities Across Homes Fell, 2006–11*, 34 HEALTH AFF. 1139, 1139 (2015).

[91] *The Striking Racial Divide in How Covid-19 Has Hit Nursing Homes, supra* note 78.

[92] LaShyra T. Nolen et al., *How Foundational Moments in Medicaid's History Reinforced Rather than Eliminated Racial Health Disparities*, HEALTH AFF. BLOG (Sept. 1, 2020), https://www.healthaffairs.org/do/10.1377/hblog20200828.66111/full.

[93] Eric Carlson, Directing Attorney, Statement to House Select Subcommittee on the Coronavirus Crisis 1 (June 11, 2020), https://coronavirus.house.gov/sites/democrats.coronavirus.house.gov/files/2020.06.11%20Eric%20Carlson%20-%20Testimony.pdf.

[94] *GAO Infection Control Deficiencies Were Widespread and Persistent in Nursing Homes Prior to COVID-19 Pandemic*, GOV'T ACCOUNTABILITY OFF. (May 20, 2020), https://www.gao.gov/products/gao-20-576r.

[95] Debbie Cenziper et al., *As Pandemic Raged and Thousands Died, Government Regulators Cleared Most Nursing Homes of Infection-Control Violations*, WASH. POST (Oct. 29, 2020), https://www.washingtonpost.com/business/2020/10/29/nursing-home-deaths-fines.

Prior to the pandemic, nearly half of America's nursing homes had been cited repeatedly for deficient infection prevention and control practices. Rather than strengthen enforcement to address a chronic and pervasive problem, the Trump administration loosened the enforcement of rules they deemed "burdensome" to facility owners. This choice may have eased some burden on corporate nursing home chains, but it set the stage for a massive burden of sickness and death for nursing home residents. Several months into the pandemic, CMS acknowledged that large numbers of COVID-19 cases were more likely at facilities that performed poorly on quality inspections.[96] The association between facility quality and COVID-19 outbreaks requires further investigation as, overall, the evidence remains mixed.[97] It seems indisputable, however, that choices not to enforce (and even to weaken) standards created to safeguard the well-being of disabled nursing home residents elevated the interests of facility owners over disabled people's lives and health.

8.4 CONCLUSION

In conclusion, COVID-19's devastating impact on disabled people forced to reside in nursing homes, with worse impacts on facilities having larger proportions of Black residents, was neither unpredictable nor unpreventable. Instead, as legal scholar Nina Kohn concludes: "[T]he skyrocketing death rates in nursing homes are ... a predictable consequence of the failure to enforce federal regulations, gaps in regulatory requirements for facilities, and policies that steered vulnerable [persons] into these institutions in the first place."[98]

The same point applies to COVID-19's impact on incarcerated persons, who are disproportionately Black or disabled or both. That so many Black people and disabled people are incarcerated and so many disabled people live in nursing homes is no accident. These realities were not inevitable; they reflect the cumulative impact of social and political choices, not genetic or physiological predispositions. They illustrate the operation of political determinants of health, to use Daniel Dawes' phrase.[99] And those political determinants placed disabled people and Black people confined to such institutions squarely in the crosshairs of the pandemic's fury.

---

[96] Carlson, *supra* note 93.

[97] Priya Chidambaram et al., *Racial and Ethnic Disparities in COVID-19 Cases and Deaths in Nursing Homes*, KAISER FAM. FOUND. (Oct. 27, 2020), https://www.kff.org/coronavirus-covid-19/issue-brief/racial-and-ethnic-disparities-in-covid-19-cases-and-deaths-in-nursing-homes.

[98] Nina A. Kohn, *Nursing Homes, COVID-19, and the Consequences of Regulatory Failure*, GEO. L.J. ONLINE (2021), https://www.law.georgetown.edu/georgetown-law-journal/glj-online/glj-online-vol-110/nursing-homes-covid-19-and-the-consequences-of-regulatory-failure.

[99] DANIEL DAWES, THE POLITICAL DETERMINANTS OF HEALTH (2020).

9

The Busy, Troubled Intersection of Blackness and Disability

9.1 BLACKNESS AND DISABILITY: AN INTERSECTION WITH HEAVY TRAFFIC

The rates at which Black people, disabled people, and disabled Black people have borne the brunt of suffering and death in the COVID-19 pandemic have made structural inequities visible. They also drive home the need to pay attention to and think more comprehensively about the lives of people who are both Black and disabled, who live at the intersection of race and disability: How are their experiences of the world different from and similar to those of nondisabled Black people and disabled White people?

Better understanding is not the only benefit that putting a focus on race-disability intersectionality offers. It also can lay the groundwork for building alliances between social movements. In the decades since Kimberlé Crenshaw birthed the concept, intersectionality's "insistence on examining the dynamics of difference and sameness has played a major role in facilitating consideration of gender, race, and other axes of power in a wide range of political discussions and academic disciplines."[1] The idea of intersectionality has spread from the context to which it was originally applied (what Black women experience) to examining the experiences of other people with multiple marginalized identities, including sexual orientation, gender identity, and immigrant status. The question of how race (specifically Blackness) and disability overlap in people's lives has been explored less, particularly in health-related fields.

9.1.1 *Disability's Greater Prevalence among Black People*

In the US, disability is typically more prevalent among Black people than it is among Whites. There are, however, caveats to this broad point and the ones that follow.

---

[1] Sumi Cho et al., *Toward a Field of Intersectionality Studies: Theory, Applications, and Praxis*, 38 SIGNS 785, 787 (2013).

Varying methods for defining and measuring disability as well as the absence of systematic data collection regarding disability make difficult the drawing of confident conclusions about disability's prevalence.[2] In addition, to be counted as disabled by researchers, a person must first be diagnosed as disabled. Greater barriers to care that Black people experience may limit or delay receiving a diagnosis, a point considered further below. Provider biases may shape the diagnosis made, especially with behavioral health conditions. For example, evidence is growing that young people of color, as compared with White youth, are more likely to be diagnosed with a disruptive behavior disorder and less likely to be diagnosed with ADHD, a disparity that raises a "concern that unconscious biases may play a role in diagnostic decision-making."[3]

Caveats acknowledged, the data indicate the following: Disability is generally (but not always) more prevalent among Black populations than among White non-Hispanic, Hispanic/Latino, and Asian populations.[4] For example, results of a national survey showed a higher prevalence of physical disability (the most common type of disability) and vision problems among Black Americans compared to White Americans; the latter group, however, had a higher prevalence of hearing problems. Black people are overrepresented among adults with intellectual disabilities, whereas mental illness is more prevalent among non-Hispanic White people.[5] Another way of classifying disability looks at "complex activity limitations," or how an impairment affects a person's ability to fully conduct social roles like working, keeping house, socializing, and caring for oneself. Researchers have found that Black Americans have the highest prevalence of complex activity limitations.[6] Across groups, women are more likely than men to experience disability, and disability's prevalence increases with advancing age.[7]

9.1.2 *Accelerated Disablement among Black People*

Disability's higher prevalence among older people is unsurprising. Far more troubling is evidence indicating that experiences of being Black in the United States are associated with, and may cause, more rapid aging and disablement. One study

---

[2] Silvia Yee et al., *Compounded Disparities: Health Equity at the Intersection of Disability, Race, and Ethnicity* (2017), https://dredf.org/wp-content/uploads/2018/01/Compounded-Disparities-Intersection-of-Disabilities-Race-and-Ethnicity.pdf.

[3] Matthew C. Fadus et al., *Unconscious Bias and the Diagnosis of Disruptive Behavior Disorders and ADHD in African American and Hispanic Youth*, 44 ACADEMIC PSYCH. 95 (2020).

[4] *Id.* at 10–19.

[5] *Id.* at 16–17.

[6] Brian W. Ward & Jeannine S. Schiller, *Prevalence of Complex Activity Limitations among Racial/Ethnic Groups and Hispanic Subgroups of Adults: United States, 2003–2009*, 73 NCHS DATA BRIEF 1 (2011).

[7] David F. Warner & Tyson H. Brown, *Understanding How Race/Ethnicity and Gender Define Age-Trajectories of Disability: An Intersectionality Approach*, 72 SOC. SCI. & MED. 1236, 1238 (2011).

focusing on Black women found that they "experience a trajectory of accelerated disablement."[8] National survey data show that, at least after the age of 50, "the prevalence of physical disability for African Americans/blacks in any given age group was similar to the prevalence for non-Hispanic whites who were 10 years older."[9] Additional research bolsters the conclusion that Black people face a greater risk of disablement over time than White people.[10]

The higher prevalence of some incidence of disability among Black people, as compared to White people, signals that the intersection of Blackness and disability is an especially crowded one. Among Black Americans, disabled people are over-represented compared to the overall population. And among people with disabil-ities, Black people are overrepresented. So, it is puzzling that interest in this intersection has only recently begun to flourish. What explains this lack of attention?

9.2 RACE AND DISABILITY: FROM "COMPARE AND CONTRAST" TO INTERSECTIONALITY

9.2.1 *Drawing Analogies*

As critical race theorists elaborated Crenshaw's insights, they generally paid little attention to disability as an axis of intersectionality. As late as 2019, sociologists Angela Frederick and Dara Shifrer referred to disability as "an uncharted area of intersectionality research, particularly in the discipline of sociology."[11] Of course, advocates, scholars, and even courts recognized parallels between race and disability in discussions of discrimination and segregation. In a case involving the denial of a zoning permit for a group home for persons with mental disabilities, Justice Thurgood Marshall explicitly drew the parallel: "A regime of state-mandated segre-gation and degradation [of persons with mental disabilities] ... emerged that in its virulence and bigotry rivaled, and indeed paralleled, the worst excesses of Jim Crow."[12]

For years this "compare and contrast" or analogical approach tended to dominate discussions bringing together race and disability. Disability advocates and scholars bolstered claims to disability civil rights by highlighting how disability

[8] *Id.* at 1236.
[9] Yee et al., *supra* note 2, at 16 (citing J. Holmes et al., *Aging Differently: Physical Limitations among Adults Aged 50 Years and Over: United States, 2001–2007*, 20 NCHS DATA BRIEF 2 (2009).
[10] Carlos F. Mendes de Leon et al., *Black–White Differences in Risk of Becoming Disabled and Recovering from Disability in Old Age: A Longitudinal Analysis of Two EPESE Populations*, 145 AM. J. EPIDEMIOLOGY 488, 495 (1997).
[11] Angela Frederick & Dara Shifrer, *Race and Disability: From Analogy to Intersectionality*, 5 SOCIOLOGY OF RACE & ETHNICITY 200, 200 (2019).
[12] City of Cleburne v. Cleburne Living Ctr., 473 U.S. 432, 462 (1985) (Marshall, J., concurring in part and dissenting in part).

discrimination was in many ways like racial discrimination. This analogy helped fuel formation of a "minority model" of disability, which promoted a shared political identity for people with varying disabilities.[13] Drawing the analogy helped spread support for disability rights by engaging the imagination of nondisabled people who were more familiar with the harms visited by racial discrimination.

9.2.1.1 Disability Essentialism and the "Oppression Olympics"

The analogical approach to race and disability also had negative effects, though. Frederick and Shifrer argue that it contributed to a form of "disability essentialism," in which discrimination based on disability can be isolated from other types of oppression that disabled people endure and remedied simply by the creation of antidiscrimination rights. Chris Bell, a Black disability studies scholar, captured this mentality in recounting a remark by a disabled conference attendee: "Being disabled is just like being black, ... society should stop hating us and give us our rights."[14] This disability essentialism effectively centered the experiences and interests of middle-class White people with disabilities while marginalizing and erasing the distinctively layered experiences of disabled people of color.[15] The presumption is that legal rights effectively addressing disability discrimination will correct for any stigma and bias that White disabled people encounter. By contrast, even with effective disability discrimination laws, Black disabled people would still be Black and would still face discrimination and relegation to lower rungs of society on that basis.

In addition, making a claim that the effects of ableism are like those of racism, while treating disability and racism as separate categories, may descend into a debate over which group has it worse. This exercise is known to scholars as comparative subordination and colloquially known as the "oppression Olympics."[16] Such comparisons risk spurring competition – for resources and political advantage – among marginalized groups who view politics as a zero-sum game.[17] Thus, despite comparisons' potential value in prompting new perspectives and increasing understanding, analogical reasoning alone is of limited value and even poses risks. Complementary attention to how race and disability intersect in people's lives is necessary to appreciate the fullness and complexity of combined disadvantage from racism and ableism.[18]

---

[13] Frederick & Shifrer, *supra* note 11, at 202.
[14] Chris Bell, Introducing White Disability Studies: A Modest Proposal, in The Disability Studies Reader 275 (Lennard J. Davis ed., 2d ed. 2006).
[15] Frederick & Shifrer, *supra* note 11, at 201.
[16] Jasmine E. Harris, *Reckoning with Race and Disability*, 130 Yale L.J. Forum 916, 921 (2021); Hajer Al-Faham et al. credit Elizabeth Martinez with first using the term "oppression Olympics." Hajer Al-Faham et al., *Intersectionality: From Theory to Practice*, 15 Ann. Rev. Law & Soc. Sci. 247, 259 n.2 (2019).
[17] Hajer Al-Faham et al., *supra* note 16, at 259.
[18] Beth Ribet, *Surfacing Disability through a Critical Race Theoretical Paradigm*, 2 Geo. J.L. Mod. Critical Race Perspectives 209 (2010).

9.2.2 *Exploring the Intersections of Blackness and Disability*

Important work has begun teasing out what the intersections of race and disability look like, their significance in people's lives, and their connection to social issues more broadly. But the work is not straightforward. Empirical research investigating the intersection of race and disability "overlays nuance onto complexity."[19] Nonetheless, a rich dialogue combining both empirical and theoretical work is underway in some fields. A sense of this dialogue's richness may be obtained through a brief look at some of its projects.

The education realm offers perhaps the most developed work plumbing the intersection of race and disability. Under the banner of DisCrit, a cadre of scholars has applied disability critical race theory to issues including the disproportionate representation of students of color in special education, disparities in educational outcomes for disabled students of color, and the school-to-prison pipeline.[20] Scholars investigating the intersection of critical prison studies and disability studies enlarge our understanding of "incarceration" to take in other settings – like nursing homes and psychiatric hospitals – used to confine diverse bodies.[21] A variety of projects falling under the umbrella of cultural studies considers Black and disabled bodies as "an invitation to rethink embodiment and representation" in literature, music, and the visual arts.[22]

Race–disability intersectional work has begun flowering in legal scholarship as well.[23] Scholars have interrogated how courts' approaches to policing of disabled people implicitly incorporates a medical model of disability,[24] and they have examined how police disproportionately use excessive force against mentally ill people of color.[25] Katherine Prez has explored how grassroots organizing by Latinx disabled

[19] GLENN T. FUJIURA & CARLOS DRAZEN, "Ways of Seeing" in Race and Disability Research, in RACE, CULTURE, AND DISABILITY: REHABILITATION SCIENCE AND PRACTICE 23 (Fabricio E. Balcazar et al. eds., 2010).

[20] Subini Ancy Annamma et al., *Disability Critical Race Theory: Exploring the Intersectional Lineage, Emergence, and Futures of DisCrit in Education*, 42 REV. RES. EDUC. 46 (2018).

[21] LIAT BEN-MOSHE ET AL. (EDS.), DISABILITY INCARCERATED: IMPRISONMENT AND DISABILITY IN THE UNITED STATES AND CANADA x (2014).

[22] CHRIS BELL, Introduction: Doing Representational Detective Work, in BLACKNESS AND DISABILITY: CRITICAL EXAMINATIONS AND CULTURAL INTERVENTIONS 4 (Christopher M. Bell ed., 2011).

[23] Legal scholar Kimani Paul-Emile takes a different tack by arguing that, under conditions of White supremacy in the United States, "blackness [can be] understood as disabling in many contexts." Kimani Paul-Emile, *Blackness as Disability?*, 106 GEO. L.J. 293, 299 (2018). She describes her purpose as "more conceptual than doctrinal," using disability law to reframe how the law might better address structural racial inequality. Paul-Emile's argument has historical antecedents in "the underlying premise of eugenics . . . that race is in itself a kind of disability, and that race/disability must be bred out or eliminated." Ribet, *supra* note 18, at 213–14.

[24] Jamelia N. Morgan, *Policing under Disability Law*, 73 STAN. L. REV. 1401 (2021).

[25] Camille Nelson, *Racializing Disability, Disabling Race: Policing Race and Mental Status*, 15 BERKELEY J. CRIM. L. 1 (2010).

people offers an intersectional perspective for countering immigration policies that favor nondisabled bodies.[26] Ann McGinley and Frank Rudy Cooper considered whether students who live in a predominantly minority community and who experience disabling childhood trauma might form an "intersectional cohort" of class-action plaintiffs in order to seek remedies offered by disability law.[27] Alice Abrokwa has extended Crenshaw's insights regarding workplace discrimination to claims brought by workers who are Black and disabled.[28] And legal scholars Jamelia Morgan and Jasmine Harris have begun sketching contours of a more comprehensive application of a race–disability lens to American law, aiming to develop more robust protections for disabled people of color.[29]

In sum, theoretical work on race–disability intersectionality is gathering steam in the twenty-first century. Scholarship that simply compares race and disability as two discrete categories no longer seems adequate. Woven through these explorations and interrogations of the intersection of race and disability is a common thread: the recognition that ableism and racism are closely intertwined and mutually reinforcing in valorizing particular types of bodies (White and nondisabled) as they heap disadvantage (political, economic, social, and physical) on bodies deviating from this norm.[30] The result: Black people (and people of color generally) with disabilities face especially steep uphill grades when navigating the world.

Given the documented health disparities experienced by Black Americans and disabled Americans, one might expect researchers and scholars to have explored health care access and health outcomes of people who are both Black and disabled. Remarkably, however, limited empirical and even less theoretical work applying an intersectional lens has been done in health-related fields. Also scarce are attempts within social medicine and public health to make sense of the disproportionate incidence of disablement among Black Americans.

9.3 INTERSECTING HEALTH DISPARITIES

Until recently, inquiry into how race and disability interact to affect health care access, quality of health care received, and health outcomes has lagged.[31] Few

---

[26] Katherine Pérez, *A Critical Race and Disability Legal Studies Approach to Immigration Law and Policy*, UCLA L. REV.: L. MEETS WORLD (Feb. 2019), https://www.uclalawreview.org/a-critical-race-and-disability-legal-studies-approach-to-immigration-law-and-policy.

[27] Ann C. McGinley & Frank Rudy Cooper, *Intersectional Cohorts, Dis/Ability, and Class Actions*, 47 FORDHAM URB. L.J. 293 (2020).

[28] Alice Abrokwa, *"When They Enter, We All Enter": Opening the Door to Intersectional Discrimination Claims Based on Race and Disability*, 24 MICH. J. RACE & L. 15 (2018).

[29] JAMELIA MORGAN, *Toward a DisCrit Approach to American Law*, in DISCRIT EXPANDED: INQUIRIES, REVERBERATIONS & RUPTURES (Annamma et al. eds., 2021); Harris, *supra* note 16.

[30] Ribet, *supra* note 18; Morgan, *supra* note 29.

[31] See Jana J. Peterson-Besse et al., *Barriers to Health Care among People with Disabilities Who Are Members of Underserved Racial/Ethnic Groups: A Scoping Review of the Literature*, 52 MED. CARE (Supp. III) S51, S60 (2014); Tawara D. Goode et al., *Parallel Tracks: Reflections on*

studies of racial health disparities address how having a disability might compound racial disadvantage; nor did many investigations of disability health disparities consider the impact of disabled people's race or ethnicity.[32] Little attention has focused on health-related inequities experienced by people who are Black and disabled. Nor have researchers focused on how those health equity concerns connect to and reinforce intersectional injustice in domains like education and criminal justice. Intuitively, it makes sense to hypothesize that persons who have two (or more) identities often associated with worse health or health care face compounded health disadvantage. But effective intervention – whether at patient or policy level – to address this disadvantage requires more than intuition; it requires understanding the problem's precise nature, along with its causes and contours. Hence, accelerating the pace of research on race–disability intersectional health disparities ought to be a priority.

9.3.1 *What Little We Know*

Appearing primarily in the public health literature, nascent research explored how various permutations of race, disability, and other sociodemographic factors interact in populations.[33] A summary of several types of studies in this area offers a sense of what little we know.[34]

9.3.1.1 Health Care Use and Diagnosis

Some studies examine how simultaneously identifying with a racial or ethnic minority group and being disabled affects health care usage. For example, one study focused on people with a nonsevere disability and, within that group, found racial and ethnic disparities existed in overall health, total annual health care visits, and percentage of people reporting not having visited a doctor during the year.[35] Another study examined surveys of working-age adults, focusing on responses indicating unmet medical needs and absence of a usual source of care. This study confounded

---

the Need for Collaborative Health Disparities Research on Race/Ethnicity and Disability, 52 MED. CARE (Supp. III) S3 (2014).

[32] Willi Horner-Johnson et al., *Promoting a New Research Agenda: Health Disparities Research at the Intersection of Disability, Race, and Ethnicity*, 52 MED. CARE (Supp. III) S1, S1 (2014)

[33] *Id.* at S2; Peterson-Besse et al., *supra* note 31, at S52.

[34] My summary of the research is brief and not comprehensive. The fullest accounting of this research is in a report commissioned by the National Academies of Sciences, Engineering, and Medicine in 2017. See Yee et al., *supra* note 2.

[35] Stephen P. Gulley et al., *Difference, Disparity & Disability: A Comparison of Health, Insurance Coverage and Health Service Use on the Basis of Race/Ethnicity among U.S. Adults with Disabilities, 2006–2008*, 52 MED. CARE (Supp. III) S9 (2014). These researchers found fewer racial/ethnic disparities among persons with more severe disabilities.

researchers' expectations by producing little evidence of "interaction or additive effects of disability and race/ethnicity" with respect to those items.[36]

Some investigations of potentially compounding effects of race and disability have focused more narrowly on specific disabilities or specific health care services. Two studies, for example, examined receipt of mammograms by women with intellectual disabilities and deaf women. They found that Black women with either disability were significantly less likely to have mammograms than similarly disabled White women.[37] Other research found that families of Black and Latinx children with autism faced greater challenges in accessing high quality care than did families of White children.[38]

Medical validation of disability is often needed for accessing care or benefits, and Black people can have a harder time achieving that validation. Accurate diagnosis of subtle or complex disabling conditions (for example, multiple sclerosis or autism) often require clinicians to listen attentively to and carefully observe patients; access to a specialist may also be required.[39] For Black people these features of patient care can be elusive because of either physicians' implicit biases or higher likelihood of being covered by Medicaid.

Delayed diagnoses of autism among Black children is an example. One study of children covered by Medicaid found that Black children were 2.6 times less likely than White children to be diagnosed with autism the first time they visited a specialist.[40] Focusing just on a large cohort of Black children, a 2020 study found significant delays in diagnoses of autism spectrum disorder (ASD). Specifically, it took three years on average from parents' first sharing concerns about their child's developmental progress with a professional for an ASD diagnosis to be made. In addition, nearly half of the parents in the study had to visit multiple providers before their child was diagnosed with ASD, and nearly a third identified not being able to access providers as contributing to the delay.[41] Commentary on the study characterized its findings as "suggestive of structural racism leading to inequity."[42] Structures potentially connected to delayed diagnoses include Black families' disproportionate

---

[36] Willi Horner-Johnson & Konrad Dobbertin, *Usual Source of Care and Unmet Health Care Needs: Interaction of Disability with Race and Ethnicity*, 52 MED. CARE 40 (2014).

[37] Yee et al., *supra* note 2, at 70–71.

[38] Sandra Magana et al., *Racial and Ethnic Disparities in Quality of Health Care among Children with Autism and Other Developmental Disabilities*, 50 INTELLECTUAL & DEVELOPMENTAL DISABILITIES 287, 287–88 (2012).

[39] LISA IEZZONI, WHEN WALKING FAILS: MOBILITY PROBLEMS OF ADULTS WITH CHRONIC CONDITIONS (2003).

[40] David S. Mandell et al., *Disparities in Diagnoses Received Prior to a Diagnosis of Autism Spectrum Disorder*, 37 J. AUTISM DEVELOPMENTAL DISORDERS 1795 (2007).

[41] John N. Constantino et al., *Timing of the Diagnosis of Autism in African American Children*, 146 PEDIATRICS e20193629 (2020).

[42] Sarabeth Broder-Fingert et al., *Structural Racism and Autism*, 146 PEDIATRICS e2020015420 (2020).

reliance on Medicaid (with its low reimbursement rates for diagnostic services) and the paucity of Black pediatricians who specialize in neurodevelopment.[43]

9.3.1.2 Health Status and Outcomes

Intersecting race and disability may bode poorly for health status and outcomes as well.[44] Researchers have found that adults from medically underserved racial or ethnic groups were more likely to report being in fair to poor health or experiencing worsening health over the previous year if they were also disabled, as compared either to their nondisabled counterparts or to White people with disabilities.[45] Compounded disparities with respect to poor physical and oral health and unmet medical needs have also been identified among Black and Hispanic children with disabilities.[46] One research team found that Latinx and Black adults with intellectual or developmental disability (IDD) had worse health outcomes compared to White adults with IDD. They also found that Latinx and Black adults with IDD experienced worse health outcomes compared to nondisabled adults from the same racial and ethnic group.[47] In short, being both intellectually disabled and Black or Latinx was associated with worse outcomes than having either one of those identities alone.

9.3.1.3 Mechanisms of Compounded Disadvantage and Providers' Role

It is not surprising that having more than one identity associated with disadvantage amplifies negative outcomes. The precise mechanisms by which doubly marginalized status produces compounded effects, however, remains largely unexplored.[48] Socioeconomic and environmental factors influencing health doubtless play a leading role. Factors relating to health care providers likely do as well. We know from Chapter 2 that negative attitudes, stereotypes, and biases among some providers can contribute to health disparities for Black people and disabled people. Such mindsets can affect treatment recommendations and alienate patients. Focus groups of disabled people from underserved minority groups provide qualitative evidence of

---

[43] *Id.* Of the families involved in the Constantino study, nearly half (46 percent) had public health insurance, which was most likely Medicaid. The commentary reported that only 2 percent of neurodevelopmental or developmental-behavioral pediatricians were Black.

[44] Rachel Blick et al., Ohio Disability & Health Program, The Double Burden: Health Disparities among People of Color Living with Disabilities 1 (2015).

[45] Gulley et al., *supra* note 35; Yee et al., *supra* note 2, at 69.

[46] Ilhom Akobirshoev et al., *The Compounding Effect of Race/Ethnicity and Disability Status on Children's Health and Health Care by Geography in the United States*, 58 Med. Care 1059 (2020). The researchers also found a disparity with respect to problems in paying medical bills.

[47] Sandra Magana et al., *Racial and Ethnic Health Disparities Among People with Intellectual and Developmental Disabilities*, 54 Intellectual & Developmental Disabilities 161, 168 (2016).

[48] Yee et al., *supra* note 2, at 76.

how racial stereotypes, ableist attitudes, and ignorance about caring for people with disabilities combine to affect clinical care.[49] And one study of adults with IDD living in the community found that, among Black and Latinx respondents, "distrust toward health professionals was one of the top reasons for not having a primary care provider and for delaying and foregoing [sic] care."[50] Scant effort, however, has been devoted to quantitatively assessing provider attitudes towards patients who are both disabled and in a marginalized racial group.[51]

Currently, any attempt to grasp the existence and extent of intersectional health disparities for people who are Black and disabled is like trying to use a weak flashlight to inventory the contents of a darkened room. Too much remains obscured to permit a clear assessment of the situation. The faint outlines visible under the weak beam of extant research are not encouraging, however. More empirical study is needed, as is attention to voices of people in whose lives race and disability intersect. What we know suggests that, at least in some areas, Black disabled people face more formidable access barriers and endure worse health outcomes than Black people who are not disabled or disabled people who are not Black. And, of course, both Black Americans and disabled Americans experience health disparities compared to nondisabled White Americans.

9.4 CRITICALLY APPROACHING DISPROPORTIONATE DISABLEMENT AMONG BLACK PEOPLE

Expanding knowledge about how race–disability intersections affect health is complicated. Much of the progress in understanding how society has constructed race and disability has entailed pushing back against the significance of bodily distinctiveness, rejecting ideas that Black bodies and disabled bodies are deviant or inferior. But bodies are the sites on which a considerable portion of race–disability intersections are created. Recall the points above about the higher prevalence of disability and accelerated disablement among Black people. Much disability is created either by injury to or gradual degradation of bodies, a phenomenon warranting further inquiry. Thinking about why disability is more prevalent among Black people can also help make sense of tensions existing between racial civil rights activists and disability rights advocates.

---

[49] *Id.* at 73–74.

[50] Henan Li et al., *Racial and Ethnic Disparities in Perceived Barriers to Health Care among U.S. Adults with Intellectual and Developmental Disabilities*, 59 INTELLECTUAL & DEVELOPMENTAL DISABILITIES 84, 89 (2021).

[51] Yee et al., *supra* note 2, at 47. A volume on race, disability, and culture in rehabilitation practice views the question largely through a cultural competency lens, emphasizing the need for practitioners who serve "culturally diverse individuals with disabilities" to avoid interpersonal discrimination. FABRICIO BALCAZAR, Introduction: Examining the Nexus of Race, Culture, and Disability, in RACE, CULTURE, AND DISABILITY: REHABILITATION SCIENCE AND PRACTICE 23 (Fabricio E. Balcazar et al. eds., 2010).

9.4.1 *Race as a Determinant of Disability?*

Considering the interaction of social and environmental factors, discrimination, and unequal treatment in the health care system, higher rates of disability among Black people are predictable. These elevated rates reflect what social epidemiologist Nancy Krieger calls "the cumulative embodiment of multiple types of discrimination, deprivation, and other harmful exposures."[52] Living in poverty, not receiving quality education, suffering exposure to stressful or dangerous workplace conditions, or residing in neighborhoods marred by toxic exposures or chronic violence: all these make experiencing disability more likely, especially as a person ages.[53] For some people, incarceration has disabling impacts.[54] Black Americans disproportionately experience these conditions,[55] and chronic exposure to systemic and interpersonal racism pervasive in American society adds a dose of "weathering." Black patients' receipt of delayed, biased, or lower quality medical care can also produce disabling outcomes.[56] We can think of all these as social determinants of disability, much as we saw in Chapter 7 how social determinants affect health.[57]

Higher risks of disablement are not limited to adults. Researchers have found that disability is also more prevalent among Black children than their White counterparts.[58] Black children in America are more likely to be born too small and to mothers receiving too little prenatal care. They are more likely to live in racially

---

[52] Nancy Krieger, *Methods for the Scientific Study of Discrimination and Health: An Ecosocial Approach*, 102 Am. J. Pub. Health 936, 942 (2012).

[53] Gopal K. Singh & Sue C. Lin, *Marked Ethnic, Nativity, and Socioeconomic Disparities in Disability and Health Insurance among U.S. Children and Adults: The 2008–2010 American Community Survey*, 2013 Biomed Res. Int'l 1–2 (2013) (finding that socioeconomic differences accounted for 60.2 percent of racial/ethnic variations in disability among children and 89.7 percent among adults).

[54] Syrus Ware et al., It Can't Be Fixed Because It's Not Broken: Racism and Disability in the Prison Industrial Complex, in Disability Incarcerated: Imprisonment and Disability in the United States and Canada 164 (Liat Ben-Moshe et al. eds., 2014).

[55] Singh & Lin, *supra* note 53; Seth A. Seabury, *Racial and Ethnic Differences in the Frequency of Workplace Injuries and the Prevalence of Work-Related Disability*, 36 Health Aff. 266, 271 (2017); Warner & Brown, *supra* note 7, at 1; Kenzie Latham, *Progressive and Accelerated Disability Onset by Race/Ethnicity and Education among Late Midlife and Older Adults*, 24 J. Aging Health 1320, 1323 (2012); T. Brown & R. Thorpe, *Race/Ethnicity, Stress, Mobility Limitations and Disability among Older Men*, 56 Gerontologist (Supp. III) 591 (2016); Carlos Siordia, *Disability Prevalence According to a Class, Race, and Sex (CSR) Hypothesis*, 2 J. Racial Ethnic Health Disparities 303, 304 (2015); Roland J. Thorpe et al., *Racial Disparities in Disability among Older Adults: Findings from the Exploring Health Disparities in Integrated Communities Study*, 26 J. Aging Health 1261, 1261 (Dec. 2014).

[56] David A. Ansell, The Death Gap: How Inequality Kills 130–31 (2017).

[57] See generally Regina Fiorati & Valeria Meirelles Carril Elui, *Social Determinants of Health, Inequality and Social Inclusion among People with Disabilities*, 23 Revista Latino-Am. Enfermagem 329 (2015); Gregor Wolbring, *People with Disabilities and Social Determinants of Health Discourses*, 102 Can. J. Pub. Health 317 (2011); Rashmi Goyat et al., *Racial/Ethnic Disparities in Disability Prevalence*, 3 J. Racial Ethnic Health Disparities 635, 642 (2016).

[58] Yee et al., *supra* note 2, at 18–19.

segregated and impoverished neighborhoods and to encounter environmental toxins, unsafe housing, neighborhood violence, and inadequate health care. Flint, Michigan, provides an example. The city's decision to switch its drinking water supply from Detroit's water supply to the Flint River in 2013 exposed residents to dangerously high levels of lead. For nearly a year and a half, families in Flint (which is 57 percent Black) drank, cooked with, and bathed in water contaminated by lead. The percentage of Flint's children with blood-lead levels known to impede brain development nearly doubled after the water supply switch. In some neighborhoods, it nearly tripled.[59] Increased disability among Flint's children followed predictably. In 2019, one in five children entering its public schools had disabilities qualifying them for special education services, up from fewer than one in seven in 2012–13.[60]

In sum, Black children are less likely to avoid disablement during their early development, just as Black youths and young adults suffer more potentially disabling urban gun violence,[61] and Black adults are more likely to become disabled before they reach old age.

9.4.2 *Emergent Disability*

The idea that social structures create disability is not novel. Since the 1990s, scholars of disability have recognized that a growing share of disability results from impairments that are created or imposed rather than occurring "naturally" or "accidentally." Katherine Seelman and Sean Sweeney called it an "expanding or new universe of disability."[62] They recognized violence, substance abuse, inadequate prenatal care and low birthweight, environmental exposure to toxins, and injuries as contributing to this expanding universe, and poverty as the most common denominator (or "primary screening indicator" in their words). Other scholars have dubbed the growing number of disabilities found in communities experiencing poverty and disadvantage "emergent disability."[63] Emergent disability can arise quickly and dramatically, with gun violence in an impoverished neighborhood or with a workplace injury suffered by a person with limited education whose work opportunities are limited to dangerous jobs. Emergent disability can also materialize gradually, as when lack of access to a healthy diet contributes to obesity or diabetes or the stresses of discrimination give rise to hypertension. When a person's exposure to COVID-19

[59] Melissa Denchak, *Flint Water Crisis: Everything You Need to Know*, NRDC (Nov. 8, 2018), https://www.nrdc.org/stories/flint-water-crisis-everything-you-need-know.

[60] Corey Mitchell, *In Flint, Schools Overwhelmed by Special Ed. Needs in Aftermath of Lead Crisis*, EDUCATION WEEK (Aug. 28, 2019), https://www.edweek.org/ew/articles/2019/08/28/special-ed-concerns-loom-large-after-flint.html?cmp=soc-edit-tw.

[61] Katherine A. Fowler et al., *Firearm Injuries in the United States*, 79 PREVENTIVE MED. 5 (2015).

[62] Katherine Seelman & Sean Sweeney, *The Changing Universe of Disability*, 95 AM. REHAB. 2 (1995).

[63] See, e.g., Ribet, *supra* note 18.

resulted from inequitable living, working, or transportation arrangements, any long-term disabling aftereffects will be identifiable as an emergent disability.

A growing body of research examines how experiencing racism – both interpersonal discrimination and structural racism – affects health.[64] A plausible hypothesis predicts that experiencing ableism produces similar ill health effects as experiencing racism. Recent research has found a relationship between experiencing ableist microaggressions (for example, joking that a disabled person is "lucky" because they have a disabled parking permit) and worse mental health outcomes.[65] Negative impacts on physical health seem likely as well. Ensuring that one's own needs for support are met (for example, hiring assistants, seeking accommodations, and finding accessible establishments) is itself hard work; disabled people are also expected to do the emotional labor of managing other people's emotions and social expectations relating to their disability.[66] Experiencing both racism and ableism simultaneously or sequentially can be predicted to multiply negative health effects. Much more work is needed to "[capture] the meaning of being exposed to both racism and ableism together and separately over time."[67]

9.4.3 *Emergent Disability's Implications for Justice*

The concept of emergent disability makes readily discernible the connections of earlier and more prevalent disability among Black Americans to health injustice. It suggests that experiences of being Black heighten one's risk of disablement. Camara Jones describes race (along with other axes of inequity) as a *risk marker*, or an identifier of "how opportunity is structured and value is assigned in our society."[68] This characterization comports with critical scholars' insistence that uneven distributions of opportunity and deprivation are not matters of happenstance. Nor are they "natural" occurrences. They are not "just the way the world is." Heightened risk of disability links to larger questions of social justice and equality for disabled people

---

[64] This research is described in Chapter 2.

[65] Shanna K. Kattari, *Ableist Microaggressions and the Mental Health of Disabled Adults*, 56 COMMUNITY MENTAL HEALTH J. 1170 (2020).

[66] Amy Gaeta, *Cripping Emotional Labor: A Field Guide*, DISABILITY VISIBILITY PROJECT BLOG (June 3, 2019), https://disabilityvisibilityproject.com/2019/06/03/cripping-emotional-labor-a-field-guide.

[67] CHRISTOPHER B. KEY, Conclusion: How Race, Culture, and Disability Intersect: Pragmatic and Generative Perspectives, in RACE, CULTURE, AND DISABILITY: REHABILITATION SCIENCE AND PRACTICE 23 (Fabricio E. Balcazar et al. eds., 2010).

[68] Camara P. Jones, *Systems of Power, Axes of Inequity: Parallels, Intersections, Braiding the Strands*, 10 MED. CARE (Supp. 3), S71, S73 (Oct. 2014). In *Blackness as Disability?*, Kimani Paul-Emile makes the related but distinctive point that Blackness is disabling not in the sense of causing impairment but in the sense of preventing full participation in society. Paul-Emile, *supra* note 23.

and people of color.[69] "Embodied inequality" is Nancy Krieger's phrase for describing discrimination's impact on bodies.[70]

Emergent disability also complicates the social model of disability by emphasizing that unjust structures do not simply create or tolerate barriers to inclusion for people who already have some impairment; they also create impairments. It "adds a more materialist dimension to the social model . . . reveal[ing] how the inequitable structure of society produces concrete physical and mental impairments that affect an individual's life chances."[71] The wedding of disability and low socioeconomic status in a mutually reinforcing relationship[72] means a disabled person (and their offspring) faces a heightened risk of acquiring (further) disability. Black Americans also face unequal risk of unnecessary disability across their life course. Beth Ribet makes the point succinctly: "[D]isability is not simply racially charged, but often racially generated."[73] And disproportionate disablement in turn magnifies barriers to upward social mobility for individuals and communities.[74]

Once we understand many disabilities as products of exploitative and unjust social and economic structures, we can make out the state's role in creating, supporting, or enabling those structures. That understanding also attributes responsibility for some share of individual disability to an economy that glorifies free markets.[75] Placing responsibility for emergent disability on the state and market economy aligns with the work of critical race and feminist scholars who identify racial, gender, and class oppression as rooted in state policies and capitalist structures.[76] From a public health perspective, epidemiologist Carlos Siordia describes this interplay as "systematic relegation to different social strata [that] becomes *embodied inequality* when it is manifested" as health disparities.[77]

From a critical vantage point, growing economic inequality in the United States surfaces as a leading indicator predicting increasing levels of emergent disability. Income and wealth gaps in general have widened over the past half century in the United States; the gap in wealth between the richest and the least well-off families more than doubled between 1989 and 2016. Black families' income, specifically, failed to rebound following the Great Recession as compared to White families.[78] As the rich get richer, the poor get poorer, and those in the middle class get left behind,

[69] Jennifer Pokempner & Dorothy E. Roberts, *Poverty, Welfare Reform, and the Meaning of Disability*, 62 Ohio St. L.J. 425, 457–58 (2001).

[70] Krieger, *supra* note 52, at 936.

[71] Pokempner & Roberts, *supra* note 69, at 427.

[72] Siordia, *supra* note 55.

[73] Ribet, *supra* note 18, at 241.

[74] Pokempner & Roberts, *supra* note 69.

[75] *Id.* at 458.

[76] For example, Beth Ribet has described these disabilities as arising from "injuries and deprivations rooted in racial and class oppression." Ribet, *supra* note 18, at 211.

[77] Siordia, *supra* note 55, at 304.

[78] Katherine Schaeffer, *6 Facts about Economic Inequality in the U.S.*, Pew Res. Ctr. (Feb. 7, 2020), https://www.pewresearch.org/fact-tank/2020/02/07/6-facts-about-economic-inequality-in-the-u-s.

it is foreseeable that an increasing number of people will acquire disabilities through privation or dangerous conditions. Emergent disability helps explain increasing levels of disability in the United States. It also augurs that the face of disability will grow increasingly Black or Brown. In sum, Black Americans' unequal risk of becoming disabled is tied closely to economic and social inequalities that are products of racism.

9.4.4 *Emergent Disability Meets Disability Pride, and Other Sources of Tension*

Viewing Black people's overrepresentation among people with disabilities as an outgrowth of racial injustice can help us understand the at times fraught relationship between movements for racial justice and for disability rights. The concept of emergent disability pushes against some tenets of the dominant disability rights movement, tenets described as "coded white."[79] Chapter 3 discusses prenatal screening for disability and selective pregnancy termination as an example of practices that view disabled life as something bad, something to be prevented. It also suggests that health professionals and society have encouraged that view, either explicitly or implicitly. For that reason, many disability rights scholars and advocates view prenatal screening for disability as a contemporary incarnation of eugenic thinking.[80] This is just one example of the disability rights community's more general discomfort with public health campaigns that stigmatize disability in an effort to prevent it. Some campaigns (for example, messaging to discourage drunk driving) "have played upon emotions of fear generated by possible disability to advocate desired health practices."[81] Disabled people often hear the message that disability is a bad thing to be avoided, even eliminated. Rejecting that message, the "mainstream" disability rights movement instead has worked to eliminate the stigma and disadvantage that has long accompanied being disabled. The cultivation and endorsement of "disability pride" is meant to replace disability shame.

Disability pride encourages people with varying disabilities to value their common identity as disabled people. It draws inspiration from other "pride" movements, like Black Pride and LGBT Pride. But disabled activists of color have criticized disability pride events as being dominated by White disabled people and erasing experiences of non-White disabled people.[82] More relevant to the current discussion, appeals to disability pride may simply miss the mark in cases of emergent

---

[79] Frederick & Shifrer, *supra* note 11, at 210.

[80] Gareth M. Thomas & Barbara Katz Rothman, *Keeping the Backdoor to Eugenics Ajar?: Disability and the Future of Prenatal Screening*, 18 AMA J. ETHICS 406 (2016).

[81] Katharine Hayward, *A Slowly Evolving Paradigm of Disability in Public Health Education*, 24 DISABILITY STUD. Q. 1 (2004).

[82] Carrie Elizabeth Mulderink, *The Emergence, Importance of #DisabilityTooWhite Hashtag*, 40 DISABILITY STUD. Q. (2020), http://dx.doi.org/10.18061/dsq.v40i2.6484.

disability. Disability pride may be a bitter pill to swallow for a mother in Flint, Michigan, whose child has been intellectually disabled by lead poisoning. Or for the resident of a poor urban neighborhood left with paraplegia by a bullet. Or for the middle-aged Black woman who lost a foot to amputation because she lacked health insurance and her diabetes was not properly managed. When a person's impairment (how their mind or body varies from some norm) is spawned from unjust social structures, pride seems an unsuitable response.

Some scholars have noted emergent disability's challenge to disability pride and other aspects of the "mainstream" disability rights movement. Disability's increasingly close tracking of social inequality may "[transform] the very nature of disability."[83] And, critically, identifying unjust social structures as *causes* of disability reveals that legal rights that attach only to existing disability cannot accomplish full justice.[84] Disability rights narratives that fail to address racial and economic justice concerns are inadequate. Talk about disability pride and disability as "mere difference" rather than "bad difference"[85] runs the risk of obscuring that emergent disability is a product of oppression falling most heavily on darker and poorer bodies.

In addition, promoting disability pride via parades and other events doesn't adequately reckon with historical reasons that many Black people have attached especial stigma to disability. For centuries, dominant White society has associated Blackness with biological inferiority, incapacity, and disability. Black people's supposed inferiority supplied White people with arguments for enslaving, disenfranchising, and oppressing Black people. To counter that false narrative, disability "became the category against which racial minority groups had to distance themselves to make claims to citizenship rights."[86] Seeking to avoid further stigmatization and discrimination, some Black people with disabling impairments hesitate to identify themselves as having a disability.[87]

Actor Chadwick Boseman's death from colon cancer is again illustrative. Legal scholar Jasmine Harris points to a hostile exchange on Twitter that commenced when the Black Disability Collective referred proudly to Boseman as a Black man with a disability. Some people of color objected to that characterization, scolding the Black Disability Collective for a perceived affront to Boseman's power and stature. The implicit message of those who objected to Boseman being identified as disabled was that such a label diminished him, that being called disabled marked

---

[83] Pokempner & Roberts, *supra* note 69, at 431.

[84] Beth Ribet, *Emergent Disability and the Limits of Equality: A Critical Reading of the UN Convention on the Rights of Persons with Disabilities*, 14 YALE HUMAN RIGHTS & DEVELOPMENT L.J. 101, 114 (2011).

[85] The "mere difference" versus "bad difference" distinction is discussed in Chapter 3 and comes from ELIZABETH BARNES, THE MINORITY BODY: A THEORY OF DISABILITY (2016).

[86] Frederick & Shifrer, *supra* note 11, at 207.

[87] Harris, *supra* note 16, at 929; Ola Ojewumi, *Why Black History Month Needs to Feature the Stories of the Disabled*, NBC NEWS (Feb. 28, 2021), https://www.nbcnews.com/think/opinion/why-black-history-month-needs-feature-stories-disabled-ncna1259029.

Boseman as weak. The Collective's tweeted response to the objection minced no words: "So many of y'all hate disabled people so much that you're deeply uncomfortable with Chadwick Boseman being referred to as disabled and his experiences being discussed through a disability lens. Cancer is a disability. Unpack your discomfort with this."[88]

The history of White supremacists' attribution of disability to Black people as a mechanism for oppressing them illuminates how the "mainstream" disability rights movement's readiness to embrace disability pride reflects an assumption that White people's experience of disability is the experience that matters. That assumption may reflect an ignorance of or indifference to the historical weaponization of disability against Black people. It may not reflect an understanding that Black people's disabilities disproportionately arise from unjust origins. Whatever the explanation, the alienation produced among Black people who have some disability is the same.

Recognizing that unjust social, environmental, and economic structures produce disability in ways that especially burden poor people and Black people thus stands in tension with some aspects of traditional advocacy for disability civil rights. Perhaps that tension helps explain why the Movement for Black Lives initially paid minimal attention to Black lives' intersection with disability, as compared to other axes of subordination. The critique of Disability Studies as tending to whitewash the history and experience of disability includes a claim that the field has paid little heed to the intersectional lives of disabled Black people. As part of that critique, disability studies scholar Chris Bell issued a proposal to recognize "White Disability Studies." Bell's proposal highlights that many White disabled people remain unaware of the privilege that attaches to their racial identity.[89] They fail to grasp that their proclaimed goal – the enforcement of legal rights against disability discrimination – does not fully address the subordination that Black disabled people live with.

Other reasons may also help explain the lack of affinity between racial civil rights and disability civil rights. Some scholars employ critical race theory's concept of triangulation to explain the distance between the movements as reflecting efforts by each movement to best the other in achieving closer proximity to nondisabled Whiteness.[90] Another explanation operates at the individual level, where for some disabled Black people their identity as being Black supersedes any identification as being disabled. Lack of understanding and ally-ship between the movements can make life more challenging for disabled Black people trying to navigate the world. Disabled Black activist Angel Love Miles writes of the painful experience as a college student at an historically black college or university (HBCU) of having her request to have a lecture moved to a wheelchair accessible venue denied.

---

[88] Harris, *supra* note 16, at 943.

[89] BELL, *supra* note 14.

[90] ERIC MILLER, Policing Disability, in DIS/ABILITY IN MEDIA, LAW AND HISTORY: INTERSECTIONAL, EMBODIED AND SOCIALLY CONSTRUCTED? (Micky Lee et al. eds. 2022).

Administrators called her request unreasonable because it would unfairly inconvenience everyone else.[91]

9.5 DISABILITY JUSTICE AND INTERSECTIONAL ACTIVISM

The often arms-length postures of the dominant disability rights and racial justice movements helps explain why research on intersectional health disparities remains overshadowed by single-axis (race *or* disability) research and policy initiatives. But intersectional race–disability advocacy is proliferating in other settings. Much of the initiative to foreground Black disabled intersectional lives has come from activists and artists giving voice to their lived experience. A growing chorus of artists and activists who are people of color and disabled are demanding that social movements center their perspectives, not marginalize them.[92] Groups like the Harriet Tubman Collective (a group of Black organizers who are deaf or disabled) seek to make plain how social justice movements have failed to pay attention to intersections of race and disability. The Collective called out Black Lives Matter for initially failing to mention disability in its public commitment to raise up voices of "the most marginalized Black people."[93]

In addition, justice-oriented organizations led by disabled people of color take a broad and inclusive view of the work of intersectional activism. The Disability Justice Collective describes its work as "centering the lives and leadership of disabled people of color, Trans*, queer, poverty class folks and all brilliance from the margins."[94] Similarly, the mission of the Sins Invalid ("disability justice performance project") is to "incubate and celebrate artists with disabilities, centralizing artists of color and LGBTQ/gender-variant artists as communities who have been historically marginalized."[95] These descriptions evince a commitment not simply to expand from "single-axis" to "dual-axis" thinking, but to embrace fully the multiple dimensions of lived identities as sources of knowledge, power, and beauty.

Reflecting the reality that conventional street-level protests may be inaccessible or otherwise infeasible for activists with some disability, social media platforms have been central to race–disability intersectional activism.[96] For example, Vilissa Thompson, an activist who identifies as a disabled person of color, created the

---

[91] Angel Love Miles, *Disability: What Have Black People Got to Do with It?*, BLACK PERSPECTIVES (Apr. 22, 2020), https://www.aaihs.org/disability-whats-black-people-got-to-do-with-it-angel-love-miles.

[92] Subini Ancy Annamma et al., *Disability Critical Race Theory: Exploring the Intersectional Lineage, Emergence, and Potential Futures of DisCrit in Education*, 42 REV. RES. EDUC. 46, 50 (2018).

[93] Frederick & Shifrer, *supra* note 11, at 209.

[94] Disability Justice Collective, https://www.littleglobe.org/portfolio/disability-justice-collective.

[95] Sins Invalid, MISSION & VISION, https://www.sinsinvalid.org/mission.

[96] Mulderink, *supra* note 82.

hashtag #DisabilityTooWhite in 2016 to call out the disability rights movement's failure to include people of color with disabilities and their perspectives in its activism and their lack of representation in the media.[97] Thompson and other advocates claim a movement for disability *justice*, not simply disability *rights*. They contend that focusing solely on legal rights to address the exclusion of disabled people is most likely to address the single-axis disadvantage experienced by disabled White people and leave unaddressed the social and economic harms experienced by disabled people of color. The reframing that occurs when experiences of multiply marginalized persons are intentionally centered is itself a transformative process.[98]

The call for a movement that advances disability justice as inseparable from racial justice gained considerable traction as the COVID-19 pandemic laid bare how structural inequities disproportionately sickened and killed people who were Black or disabled or both. In 2021, noted antiracist scholar and activist Ibram X. Kendi invited noted disability justice leader Rebecca Cokley to a conversation on his podcast, Be Antiracist. After a rich discussion of the shared roots and common manifestations of racism and ableism in the United States, Kendi concluded, "It is pretty apparent to me that one cannot be antiracist while still being ableist, [and] you can't be anti-ableist unless you're also striving to be antiracist." To which Cokley replied: "It is such an opportunity for greater solidarity, greater learning, greater co-conspiratorship."[99]

Amplifying the voices of persons living at the intersection of minoritized racial identity, disability, and other marginalized identities serves to deepen understanding of the intimate connections between experiences of injustice too often seen as separate. Those subjective accounts, though, are not enough. They must be augmented by empirical research investigating the existence and origins of intersectional health disparities. Simply amassing empirical evidence of intersectional disparities will not resolve historical tensions between movements, to be sure. But developing that evidence is a crucial step towards building bridges between movements. As James Baldwin is often quoted as saying: "Not everything that is faced can be changed, but nothing can be changed until it is faced." Scholars have ample room to engage in conceptual work fleshing out the meaning of and potential remedies for these layered injustices. And what about health professionals? They still have a way to go to eradicate single-axis racism and ableism from patients'

---

[97] *Id.*; Sarah Bahovec, *Confronting the Whitewashing of Disability: Interview with #DisabilityTooWhite Creator Vilissa Thompson*, HUFFINGTON POST (Dec. 6, 2017), https://www.huffpost.com/entry/confronting-the-whitewash_b_10574994. Other hashtags include #DisabilityRightsinBlack and #BlackDisabledLivesMatter.

[98] Harris, *supra* note 16, at 934.

[99] *Ableism & Racism: Roots of the Same Tree*, Be Antiracist, Ibram X. Kendi podcast (June 8, 2021), https://podcasts.apple.com/us/podcast/ableism-racism-roots-of-the-same-tree/id1564144316?i=1000524608715.

experiences. Ensuring that disabled Black patients receive care comparable to nondisabled White patients will be a heavy, but necessary, lift. The concluding chapter argues that attention to intersectional perspectives is beneficial, indeed imperative, for any effort to address the health injustices that Black and disabled people in the United States continue to endure.

10

Conclusion

The Payoff for Health Justice

10.1 INTERSECTIONALITY'S VALUE

10.1.1 *Intersectionality as Common Sense*

Few people, if they paused to reflect on the question, would disagree with the idea that various aspects of a person's identity have a bearing on their experiences in the world. There are differences in how a person of twenty-five years versus one of sixty-five years mediates a dispute, trains to run a marathon, or walks into a dance club. Completing a graduate degree versus dropping out of high school affects the opportunities a person has when applying for a job or running for office. Identifying as a woman, a man, or neither will affect a person's experience of serving in the military, seeking a job promotion, or being the primary caregiver for young children (at least in many locales). Most of these variations in experience have little to do with persons' biological differences. Instead, they grow out of social environments and others' expectations. To the identifiers of age, education, and gender suggested above, we can add race, disability, immigrant status, sexual orientation, and other markers of identity. And it is the intersection of those multiple various aspects of a person's identity, combined with personal choices and life experiences, that make each person distinctive and shape each person's experience.

The body is not entirely irrelevant, either. Each person wakes up and inhabits their body throughout the day. Conditions such as chronic pain, blindness, or quadriplegia affect one's experience. Black bodies may receive an imprint from racism and discrimination, and they are disproportionately likely to become disabled. Most academic work regarding intersectionality has taken place in the social sciences and law, but social epidemiologist Nancy Krieger's work provides a public health perspective on bodies' role in intersectionality. In describing how effects of unjust social structures are "embodied" by persons subjected to racism, ableism, and other isms, Krieger does not speak figuratively or theoretically. Instead, she refers to "how we literally incorporate, biologically, the material (biophysical) and social world in which we live."[1] Krieger's point means that structures and practices of both racism and ableism can affect the physical being of a person who is both Black and disabled – an individual corporeal representation of the "cumulative embodiment of multiple types of discrimination, deprivation, and other harmful exposures."[2]

In short, one does not need to be a critical theorist to understand intersectionality, in both its social and bodily dimensions. Simply reflecting on one's own experience – and using a bit of imagination (or study) to consider the experiences of others who have a different configuration of identities – should be enough to grasp the concept. Black feminist writer, activist, and cancer survivor Audre Lorde said, "There is no such thing as a single-issue struggle because we do not lead single-issue lives."[3] To adapt her point somewhat, single-axis thinking or single-axis organizing may occur, but there are no single-axis–embodied people.

10.1.2 *Intersectionality as a Moral Matter*

Acknowledging that what a person encounters as they wend their way through life varies depending on their social and bodily identities also offers an important moral insight. Others have argued persuasively, relying on multiple ethical theories, that racial (and other) health disparities are morally wrong. Those arguments are not repeated here. Instead, my emphasis is on the moral importance of intersectionality in considering disparities.

At its core, the choice to emphasize intersectionality is a moral commitment. Justice-promoting initiatives that fail to consider intersectional lives risk leaving behind persons who face multiple sources of disadvantage, those who are often most marginalized. A concrete example lies in assertions that the "mainstream" disability rights movement's focus on establishing legal rights against discrimination ignores the material harms that many Black disabled people endure. Ending disability discrimination (if indeed that could be accomplished) may not appreciably improve the life of a disabled person who endures the effects of poverty and structural racism. Similarly, "mainstream" Black activism has paid limited attention to the distinctive forms of disadvantage that disabled Black people face. Foregrounding intersectional perspectives reconfigures philosophical arguments that, to be just, any inequality in the distribution of resources must benefit the worst

---

[1] Nancy Krieger, *Measures of Racism, Sexism, Heterosexism, and Gender Binarism for Health Equity Research: From Structural Injustice to Embodied Harm – An Ecosocial Analysis*, 41 ANN. REV. PUB. HEALTH 37, 47 (2020).

[2] Nancy Krieger, *Methods for the Scientific Study of Discrimination and Health: An Ecosocial Approach*, 102 AM. J. PUB. HEALTH 936, 941–42 (2012).

[3] (1982) Audre Lorde, *"Learning from the 60s"*, BLACKPAST (Aug. 12, 2012), https://www.blackpast .org/african-american-history/1982-audre-lorde-learning-60s. In the same address, she also said, "By seeing who the we is, we learn to use our energies with greater precision against our enemies rather than against ourselves."

off – those with the worst baseline position.[4] Ijeoma Oluo puts it plainly in *So You Want to Talk about Race*:

Intersectionality helps ensure that fewer people are left behind and that our efforts to do better for some do not make things far worse for others. Intersectionality helps us stay true to our values of justice and equality by helping to keep our privilege from getting in our way. Intersectionality makes our systems more effective and more fair.[5]

10.1.3 *Intersectionality and Expanding Social Justice Frames*

In referring to the need to keep "our privilege from getting in our way," Oluo highlights a core observation about intersectionality's value to advocacy and social movements. Social justice movements – including those committed to antiracism and disability rights – have not always adopted intersectional perspectives. Oluo suggests this failure is due to activists' inattentiveness to privilege *within* social justice movements, resulting in their tendency to devote attention to the most privileged and well-represented people within a movement.[6] Keen awareness of disadvantage based on one aspect of personal identity may block recognition of relative privilege on a different axis.[7] Again, to make this more concrete, a racial justice activist highly attuned to their own disadvantage in a racial hierarchy may not consider the privilege attached to their lack of disability. Or a disability rights advocate, while highly aware of the stigma and barriers that disabled people face, may be oblivious to their particular privilege as a White person. As a result, multiply disadvantaged persons can be marginalized within social justice movements.

Centering the multiple facets of each person's identity may help mitigate this intramovement marginalization. Kimberlé Crenshaw encourages us to view "organized identity groups . . . [as] potential coalitions waiting to be formed."[8] Applied in the context of race and disability, this approach calls for Blackness to be understood as a coalition of disabled and nondisabled Black people and for disability to be understood as a coalition of White and Black disabled people, along with other disabled people of color. This reconceptualization moves disabled Black people away from the periphery of both antiracism movements and disability rights movements and resituates them centrally, at the point of overlap between two groups. Centering intersectional lives in this fashion opens an opportunity for "transformative coalition building in social movements" by simultaneously disrupting settled

---

[4] This is a simplification of John Rawls' "difference principle." JULIAN LAMONT & CHRISTI FAVOR, Distributive Justice, in THE STANFORD ENCYCLOPEDIA OF PHILOSOPHY (Edward N. Zalta ed., Winter 2017), https://plato.stanford.edu/archives/win2017/entries/justice-distributive.

[5] IJEOMA OLUO, SO YOU WANT TO TALK ABOUT RACE 77–78 (2018).

[6] *Id.* at 76.

[7] Camara P. Jones, *Systems of Power, Axes of Inequity: Parallels, Intersections, Braiding the Strands*, 10 MED. CARE (Supp. 3), S71, S74 (Oct. 2014).

[8] Kimberlé Crenshaw, *Mapping the Margins: Intersectionality, Identity Politics, and Violence against Women of Color*, 43 STAN. L. REV. 1241, 1299 (1991).

conceptions of privilege within social movements and helping those movements transcend a competitive zero-sum game approach to politics.[9]

In other words, foregrounding the lives of people who are both Black and disabled does not narrow the focus to movement subsets defined by bodily characteristics, like physical or mental impairments and traits read as Black. Instead, it prompts recognition of movements' shared objectives and beliefs.[10] It enlarges the number of people who feel included in a movement, and it can engender more expansive understandings of what justice requires. It holds the potential to unleash "convergent strength... in terms of expanding advocacy agendas, integrating research agendas, and sharing successful policy strategies."[11]

As a practical matter, this "convergent strength" could take many forms. Most modestly, simply increasing recognition (among each movement's leadership and rank and file) that disabled Black people live with multiple forms of marginalization would be a first step. Regular and explicit acknowledgement that a substantial number of people are Black *and* disabled could help prompt greater conversation and understanding about those persons' distinctive experiences of injustice. Deeper understanding could pave the way for increased communication regarding planned advocacy and activism, which in turn could permit cooperation, coordination, or even collaboration between antiracist and antiableist movements.

10.2 CROSS-MOVEMENT COLLABORATIONS: CHALLENGES AND TWO EXAMPLES

Collaborations across social movements can be generative. They can generate power in increased numbers, to be sure, but they can also generate new thinking or fresh frameworks for approaching problems. Historian Robin D. G. Kelley referred to collective social movements as "incubators of new knowledge."[12]

If building cross-movement alliances were simple and easy, however, those alliances would be more prevalent. Intersectional politics can be messy, and unreflective adoption of an intersectional lens can oversimplify the experience and meaning of intersectional identities.[13] Nirmala Erevelles, a scholar studying race-and-disability intersectionality in education, warns that "very real painful antagonisms [may] keep disrupting any easy possibility of alliance."[14] The previous chapter

---

[9] Hajer Al-Faham et al., *Intersectionality: From Theory to Practice*, 15 ANN. REV. L. & SOC. SCI. 247, 259–60 (2019).

[10] *Id.* at 260.

[11] Jones, *supra* note 7, at S74.

[12] ROBIN D.G. KELLEY, FREEDOM DREAMS: THE BLACK RACIAL IMAGINATION 8 (2002).

[13] Carrie Elizabeth Mulderink, *The Emergence, Importance of #DisabilityTooWhite Hashtag*, 40 DISABILITY STUD. Q. (2020), http://dx.doi.org/10.18061/dsq.v40i2.6484.

[14] NIRMALA EREVELLES, Crippin' Jim Crow: Disability, Dis-Location, and the School-to-Prison Pipeline, in DISABILITY INCARCERATED: IMPRISONMENT AND DISABILITY IN THE UNITED STATES AND CANADA 84 (Liat Ben-Moshe et al. eds., 2014).

talked about how Black people may feel pressure to distance themselves from identifying as disabled to avoid taking on further stigma. The commonness among Black people of emergent disabilities, with their origin in oppressive conditions, may also discourage Black people from connecting with groups celebrating a disability identity. And disability activists may be so committed to rights accomplished through legislative victories like the ADA that they hesitate to acknowledge how some disabled people benefit little from those victories.

These cross-movement alliances are not unheard of. But creating and sustaining them takes work, patience, and humility. Two examples of intersectional cooperation and alliance-building offer some lessons.

10.2.1 Section 504 Protest

In 1977, disabled people, with support from the Black Panther Party based in Oakland, occupied a federal government building in San Francisco. The protests' purpose was to pressure the federal department of Health, Education, and Welfare (HEW)[15] to issue strong regulations implementing Section 504 of the Rehabilitation Act of 1973. Section 504 broke new ground by prohibiting recipients of federal funding from discriminating based on handicap. But that prohibition was of limited value without forceful regulations implementing it.

English and Disability Studies scholar Susan Schweik unspools the story of the weeks-long sit-in and the role that support from the Black Panthers played in its success.[16] Her account describes the role of a single person, Bradley Lomax, in engaging the Panthers' support for the demonstration. Lomax was Black and disabled, and he had been active within both movements. Even prior to the Section 504 sit-in, his commitments combined "revolutionary black nationalism and disability power."[17] By some accounts, it was Lomax's participation in the sit-in that assured the Black Panthers' steadfast support of a mostly White group of people demonstrating for disability rights. That support included sustenance in its most vital form. The Panthers delivered food to participants throughout the sit-in, sometimes relying on a sympathetic guard to permit them access when the government tried to prevent it.[18]

From Schweik's account, the Panthers' meal deliveries to the disabled protesters do not appear to have been part of a long-term, strategic plan for leveraging

---

[15] HEW was the predecessor to today's cabinet-level Department of Education and Department of Health and Human Services. When the separate Department of Education was created in 1979, HEW was renamed.

[16] Susan Schweik, *Lomax's Matrix: Disability, Solidarity, and the Black Power of 504*, at 31 DISABILITY STUD. Q. 1 (2011).

[17] *Id.*

[18] The Panthers' support also included covering the sit-in and endorsing its goals in the Black Panther newspaper.

movement intersectionality. Nor did they reflect any kind of deep disability consciousness within the Black Panther Party.[19] The support was more organic in
nature, and it was but one example of assistance the demonstrators received from
a coalition of allies, including gay men, labor organizations, a nearby urban church,
and the Chicano group Mission Rebels. Yet support from this range of groups was
not unprecedented. Many protesters – the "disabled queers, disabled radical black
activists, disabled Chicanas and so on [who] took part in occupying"[20] the HEW
building – lived intersectional lives. And some of them had pursued disability
activism within the other movements they affiliated with. As an example, Schweik
describes Lomax's earlier solicitation of support from the Black Panther Party for a
center for independent living in East Oakland. This description supports the idea
that centering intersectional lives and advocacy within movements – for example,
lifting up disabled people within the Movement for Black Lives or validating the
experiences of Black people within disability advocacy efforts – can help link
movements to expand their reach and power.

In thinking more broadly about collective social movements, however, Schweik
concludes that the disability rights/Black Panthers alliance during the Section 504
sit-in does not demonstrate the Panthers' full solidarity with the disability rights
movement. For Schweik, solidarity implies "clear-cut relations between social
bodies, political agents and cultural identities that are fully formed, perpetually
intact, [and] active in ways we can easily track."[21] Instead, she views the sit-in
alliance as more fluid and situational in nature. Because it depended in no small
part on one person's intersectional activism, it was not a durable foundation for
ongoing cross-movement activism.

10.2.2 A Carefully Engineered Bridge between Reproductive Justice and Disability Rights Activists

A contrasting example of a more deliberately developed race/disability alliance is
found in a coalition-building process that brought together advocates for women of
color and Indigenous women, reproductive rights and justice, and disability rights,
groups among which suspicions and tension have existed.[22] Women of color
founded the Reproductive Justice (RJ) movement because they were dissatisfied
with how the largely White-led reproductive rights movement focused on abortion
rights, sidelining issues like contraceptive rights and the right to have children,
which were important to women of color. Disability rights advocates, some of whom

---

[19] Schweik does note, however, that the demonstration benefited from "extraordinarily effective
strategic planning" by its leadership. *Id.*

[20] *Id.*

[21] *Id.*

[22] Dorothy Roberts & Sujatha Jesudason, *Movement Intersectionality: The Case of Race, Gender,
Disability, and Genetic Technologies*, 10 Du Bois Rev. 313 (2013).

found disability-based abortions to reflect deeply ableist views, at times clashed with reproductive rights advocates who rejected any questioning of a woman's reasons for choosing an abortion. These groups had issues with each other's preexisting advocacy agendas; they were not an easy audience for building cross-movement alliances.

Dorothy Roberts and Sujatha Jesudason write about a multi-stage coalition-building process among these groups as a case study. Their contention is that an intersectional framework permits activists from different groups first to confront their differences openly and honestly, and then to identify how their experiences were similar and what values they shared. The process began with a national convening of women of color and Indigenous women (some of whom had disability) from seven reproductive rights and justice organizations to discuss reproductive and genetic technologies. Over the course of two days, the women identified and articulated a set of shared perspectives and values regarding genetic technologies. The next stage expanded the discussion to include disability rights leaders. A series of five roundtable conversations between disability rights and reproductive justice advocates started by highlighting each participant's multiple identities (for example, race, ability, class, sexual orientation, and immigration) and concluded with defining a set of shared values. A commitment to recognizing and respecting the multiple dimensions of each participant's identity proved critical to building bridges between the two movements: "Rather than erasing our identities for the sake of coalition, we learn[ed] from each other's perspective to understand how systems of privilege and disadvantage operate together and, therefore, to be better equipped to dismantle them."[23]

Appreciating how the same interacting power hierarchies (or "matrix of domination"[24]) generate disadvantages for different groups can nourish a sense of common purpose. Academic theorists from diverse disciplines are increasingly addressing "the complex intertwining of ableism and anti-Black racism."[25] On the ground, adopting deliberate processes that draw out participants' recognition of their own multidimensional experiences can make plain the confluence of oppressive structural forces like racism and ableism. Carefully elucidating shared concerns and understanding distinctive concerns can build trust that enables intersectional organizing, allowing activist groups to identify and expand their common ground rather than to splinter into ever smaller subgroups. This process reveals how struggles often understood as separate are in reality linked.[26]

This is not all just feel-good talk. The processes described by Roberts and Jesudason laid the groundwork for disability rights advocates and reproductive rights

---

[23] *Id.* at 316.

[24] Patricia Hill Collins, Black Feminist Thought: Knowledge, Consciousness and the Politics of Empowerment 18 (2d ed. 1999).

[25] Joel Michael Reynolds, *Disability and White Supremacy*, 10 Crit. Phil. of Race 48 (2022).

[26] Roberts & Jesudason, *supra* note 22, at 322–23.

advocates to collaborate on specific policy projects. These included projects relating to passage and implementation of the Prenatally and Postnatally Diagnosed Conditions Awareness Act, which recommends that a woman who receive a diagnosis (either prenatally or after giving birth) that her baby has Down syndrome or other condition receive education and support regarding parenting a child with a disability. Overcoming the initial suspicion of reproductive rights groups regarding the proposed legislation (largely because it was sponsored by a vocal opponent of abortion rights), five disability rights and reproductive health organizations built on the earlier cross-movement discussions to craft a joint statement in support of the legislation. The groups also worked together to influence the law's implementation to ensure that it would not demonize either disability or women's reproductive decision making.[27]

10.2.3 *Some Lessons for Intersectional Movement Building*

A deliberately crafted intersectional approach to building cross-movement alliances offers some advantages. Identifying common values provides a foundation for developing a shared advocacy agenda, coordinating strategies, and acting collectively.[28] It increases numbers and broadens networks of support. Coordination among movements not known for joining forces can supply a tactical advantage, upending settled expectations and tactics of defenders of entrenched power structures.[29] And even if advocacy groups representing different interests or identities do not always find common ground on a particular policy issue, a cross-movement approach will make it harder for power structures to pit activist groups against one another.

A more profound lesson also emerges from the coalition-building process that Roberts and Jesudason describe. A process that reveals the commonalities among people subject to interlocking systems of oppression – while still acknowledging and reflecting on how their experiences diverge – can cultivate solidarity.[30] According to philosopher Carol Gould, solidarity goes beyond simply being helpful to someone seen as like oneself to include collective work by people who share an interest in overcoming structural injustice.[31] Solidarity among groups goes beyond feelings and

---

[27] *Id.* at 323.

[28] *Id.* at 319.

[29] Sherrilyn Ifill et al., A Perilous Path: Talking Race, Inequality, and the Law 79 (2018) ("Being able to make the connections to the way in which oppression works similarly across different boundaries, really can allow you to do your finest work. And it confuses the enemy. It really confuses the other side.").

[30] Roberts & Jesudason, *supra* note 22, at 313.

[31] Carol C. Gould, *Solidarity and the Problem of Structural Injustice in Healthcare*, 32 Bioethics 541 (2018).

orients toward action, without needing to entail erasure of a group's distinctive concerns or coordination of action on every issue.[32]

The value of greater collaboration between groups advocating against anti-Black racism and against ableism is not a new idea. The previous chapter described some groups already doing this challenging and soul-nourishing work. By illuminating similarities in health inequities endured by disabled people and Black people and highlighting the unjustly high prevalence of disability among Black people, this book seeks to foster greater solidarity between advocates for racial justice and for disability justice. It means to contribute stones for constructing a foundation for cross-alliance collective action. The following pages suggest some specific targets for collective action that promotes a shared vision of health equity for Black and disabled people.

10.3 TARGETS FOR INTERSECTIONAL ADVOCACY

The variety of health inequities experienced intersectionally or similarly by Black people and disabled people offers numerous potential targets for cross-alliance advocacy efforts. One could imagine collaborative efforts to ensure reproductive autonomy or to disrupt the school-to-prison pipeline. My goal here is not to identify the "right" target or to provide a playbook that sets out the "best" targets but simply to identify three potential targets as examples. The book began by pointing out how health inequity flows from causes operating at interpersonal and institutional levels as well as from social determinants of health. Now it suggests targets roughly corresponding to each of those dimensions, and for each it highlights a particular policy change to advance both racial and disability health justice. The purpose is to stimulate productive discussion and engagement by the two social movements. And while the focus here is on policies advancing health justice for Black people, disabled people, and Black disabled people, one could expect achieving these policy changes to advance health justice more broadly as well.

10.3.1 *Transforming Medical Mindsets*

This book describes many instances where physicians' mindsets – their biases, beliefs, and predilections – have resulted in actions harming Black patients and disabled patients. Sometimes those actions have reflected overt racial or disability bias. More often, at least in the twenty-first century, those harmful actions reflect implicit bias, widely held stereotypes, misinformation, lack of perspective, or lack of education. All these scenarios still lead to worse outcomes for patients. Too often, doctors fixate on a patient's race or disability rather than consider a situation holistically; or they fail to listen as carefully to patients who are Black, disabled, or

---

[32] *Id.* at 546.

both; or they view those patients as somehow less competent, less able to make good decisions and less likely to comply with a medical plan. Too often, doctors fail to craft treatment plans that account for health-affecting social factors, including the pervasive racism and ableism those patients live with. While achieving health justice will require reforms well beyond the doctor-patient encounter, that encounter still matters. Advocacy relating to transforming physicians' mindsets is a target that racial and disability health justice advocates may be able to coalesce around. Together, they could demand an answer to the question: How can doctors learn to value and understand bodies and minds that vary from norms of abledness and Whiteness and to respect the patients who live in them?

An obvious mechanism for transforming mindsets is education. Advocates could target medical school accreditation standards as the site where educational advocacy could have maximum leverage. The accrediting body for US medical schools is the Liaison Committee on Medical Education (LCME), which sets standards medical schools must meet to achieve or retain accreditation. Each standard is accompanied by a set of elements that specify the variables the LCME will examine in determining whether a medical school has satisfied the standard. Over the past decades, the LCME has added language regarding the need for diversity in the medical profession. It has also addressed the need for medical students to develop cultural competency and to learn about health care disparities.[33] The 2021 version of Standard 7 on "Curricular Content" includes Element 7.6 on "Cultural Competence and Health Care Disparities." It calls on medical school faculty to ensure that medical students have curricular "opportunities ... to learn to recognize and appropriately address biases in themselves, in others, and in the health care delivery process." It further calls for the curriculum to include content about the following: basic principles of cultural competency; health care disparities' impacts on all populations and possible ways to eliminate disparities; the "diverse manner in which people perceive health and illness and respond to various symptoms, diseases, and treatments"; and the "knowledge, skills, and core professional attributes needed to provide effective care in a multidimensional and diverse society."[34]

This Element shows that the LCME recognizes that medical schools must prepare their students to practice medicine in a culture that is diverse and wracked by health disparities. As it stands, however, the Element will not meaningfully help transform medical mindsets. It is too weak. It merely requires medical schools provide opportunities for students to learn about biases and to include content regarding cultural competence, among other things. It does not require students to complete specific requirements or establish specific competencies. It is also too

[33] Norma E. Wagoner et al., The Role of Accreditation in Increasing Racial and Ethnic Diversity in the Health Professions, in In the Nation's Compelling Interest: Ensuring Diversity in the Health-Care Workforce (Brian D. Smedley et al. eds., 2004).

[34] LCME, *Functions and Structure of Medical School: Standards for Accreditation of Medical Education Programs Leading to the MD Degree* (Mar. 2021).

watered down. It utterly fails to mention structural factors like racism or ableism or social determinants of health that contribute to health and health care disparities.

Racial justice and disability justice advocates could join forces to persuade the LCME to strengthen this Element by incorporating explicitly antiracist and anti-ableist perspectives in its accreditation standards. Those groups' "wish lists" for medical education may not be entirely congruent, but they likely share much common ground. And an intersectional alliance will ensure no patients are left behind. Focusing solely on incorporating antiracism in medical education may produce doctors who are attuned to their own racial biases and the way racism affects patient health, but who remain ignorant of the parallel effects of ableism. Conversely, simply incorporating antiableist content may leave newly minted doctors uneducated about the role racism plays in producing ill health. In either case, patients will be left behind, including patients who are both disabled and Black.

Advocates don't have to start from scratch. The murder of George Floyd and shocking racial disparities in the COVID-19 pandemic have accelerated discussions of antiracist medical education. Physicians and public health professionals have argued that medical schools and post-graduate training programs should equip every clinician, in every role, to address racism by including "mastering the health effects of structural racism" as a required professional medical competency. And, they argue, "licensing, accreditation, and qualifying procedures should test this know-ledge as an essential professional competency."[35] A Viewpoint in *The Lancet* medical journal calls for medical education to replace race-based medicine (which uses race as a shortcut in clinical decision making) with race-conscious medicine (which "emphasises racism, rather than race, as a key determinant of illness and health").[36] A *New England Journal of Medicine* editorial argued for the importance of diagnosing and treating systemic racism, urging:

> It is time to reimagine the medical interaction and the doctor-patient relationship, recommitting ourselves to the quiet work of doctoring and building trust with individual patients. We can become more conscious of our biases when we care for minority patients and push ourselves to go the extra mile. Even if we can't change the social determinants of health for any individual patient in any given encounter, we can think more seriously about how they affect what the patient can and can't do, tailor the patient's care accordingly, and show that we're invested.[37]

Agitation for incorporating disability-conscious and antiableist principles and perspectives as an integral part of medical education may have been less prominent

---

[35] Rachel R. Hardeman et al., *Stolen Breaths*, 383 NEW ENG. J. MED. 197 (2020).
[36] Jessica P. Cerdena, *From Race-Based to Race-Conscious Medicine: How Anti-Racist Uprising Call Us to Act*, 396 THE LANCET 1125 (2020).
[37] Michele K. Evans et al., *Diagnosing and Treating Systemic Racism*, 383 NEW ENG. J. MED. 274 (2020).

in the past few years. But it is not new,[38] and some medical schools have incorporated antiableist content.[39] Disability Studies scholar Joel Reynolds argues that clinicians need to understand how the problem of ableism distorts understandings of how patients live their lives with disabilities and leads to worse care for patients.[40]

Advocacy aimed at transforming medical mindsets could go beyond medical school accreditation standards. It could also address post-graduate training programs, lobby state medical licensing boards, and argue for federal standards that apply to providers participating in Medicare and Medicaid. Such advocacy will no doubt provoke pushback; legislation in some states prohibiting the teaching of Critical Race Theory in public education is evidence of that certainty. In seeking to advance such measures, however, advocacy groups could seek support from the American Medical Association (AMA) so as to benefit from its political muscle. That typically staid organization and its flagship journal *JAMA* have in the past shied away from acknowledging racism within health care as a cause of disparities. A leading patient safety advocate describes being told by *JAMA*'s editor in 2015 that the journal would not publish an article with the word "racism" in its title, because doing so would result in "losing readers."[41] The AMA now claims to recognize the need to name and target anti-Black racism. In 2021, it published a strategic plan for incorporating antiracism into its operations and programs; the plan also recognizes the need to address oppression experienced by people with disabilities.[42] Whether the AMA will follow through remains to be seen, but activists could offer it an opportunity to put its weight behind concrete steps.

10.3.2 *Centering Equity in Medicaid Provider Payments*

Health care access and financing are another dimension where racial justice and disability justice advocates might target justice-promoting policy changes. Third-party payment for health-related services implicates access by influencing what care is provided, who provides it, where it is provided, and who receives it. Insurers' payments not only protect patients (at least in theory) from bearing the full cost of

---

[38] Tom Shakespeare & Ira Kleine, *Educating Health Professionals about Disability: A Review of Interventions*, 2 HEALTH & SOC. CARE EDUC. 20 (2013).

[39] Hannah Borowsky et al., *Disability and Ableism in Medicine: A Curriculum for Medical Students*, 17 MEDEDPORTAL 11073 (2021), https://www.mededportal.org/doi/10.15766/mep_2374-8265.11073.

[40] Joel Michael Reynolds, Three Things Clinicians Should Know about Disability, 20 AMA J. ETHICS E1181 (2018), https://journalofethics.ama-assn.org/article/three-things-clinicians-should-know-about-disability/2018-12.

[41] Ron Wyatt, *Opinion: The Health-Care Industry Doesn't Want to Talk about This Single Word*, WASH. POST (Apr. 5, 2021), https://www.washingtonpost.com/opinions/2021/04/05/health-care-racism-medicine.

[42] Joyce Frieden, *AMA Releases Plan for Fighting Racism – Starting with Itself*, MEDPAGE TODAY (May 11, 2021), https://www.medpagetoday.com/publichealthpolicy/ethics/92534.

needed care, they also act as a secure source of income for providers. As such, health care financing through insurance deeply implicates a wide range of equity issues involving access to care, quality of care, and even the types of services available.

Because Black people and disabled people disproportionately receive insurance coverage through Medicaid, that program offers an important policy lever for increasing health equity. Perhaps most obviously, expanding Medicaid eligibility to increase the number of low-income people covered can benefit both groups. And legal reforms to require states to include additional services among their covered benefits could help each group. For example, making coverage of home and community-based services a mandatory benefit (rather than simply an optional benefit) would generate more funding for disabled people to access services and supports that would allow them to live in the community. Similarly, advocates are lobbying to require Medicaid to pay for doulas (trained nonmedical professionals who support women before, during, and after births) as one strategy for addressing devastating maternal mortality rates among Black women.[43] And some states have obtained federal approval to experiment with using Medicaid funds to pay not simply for medical care but also for some health-related social needs. As part of North Carolina's goal of "buying health, not just health care," the state's Medicaid program is paying for services relating to housing, food, transportation, and interpersonal violence/toxic stress.[44] Black people and people with disabilities could likely find common ground from which to advocate for expanding Medicaid's covered benefits to help address these social needs.

A less obvious but vitally important potential target for intersectional advocacy is the way Medicaid programs pay providers. Following the lead of the Medicare program, some states have begun incorporating value-based payment models into their Medicaid programs. The goal of value-based reimbursement (also referred to as "pay for performance") is to pay providers in a fashion that encourages them to provide high value care (meaning care that is high quality *and* efficiently delivered). It stands in contrast to traditional fee-for-service models, which pay separately for each service rendered, encouraging doctors and hospitals to provide *more* services.

It's hard to argue with the idea of encouraging high value care. But implementing value-based reimbursement methods may pose risks to Medicaid enrollees who experience particular social disadvantages or medically complex conditions. Because Black people and disabled people are overrepresented in these categories,

---

[43] Cara B. Safon et al., *Doula Care Saves Lives, Improves Equity, and Empowers Mothers. State Medicaid Programs Should Pay for It*, HEALTH AFF. BLOG (May 26, 2021), https://www.healthaffairs.org/do/10.1377/hblog20210525.295915/full.

[44] Mandy Cohen et al., *Buying Health, Not Just Health Care: North Carolina's Pilot Effort*, COMMONWEALTH FUND BLOG (Jan. 27, 2020), https://www.commonwealthfund.org/blog/2020/putting-price-social-services-north-carolinas-pilot-effort.

ignoring the risks places them in harm's way.[45] Two types of risks in particular need attention.

First, pay-for-performance approaches commonly attempt to value improvements in patients' health, often by financially rewarding providers whose patients enjoy good health outcomes and penalizing those whose patients have undesirable outcomes. So that they can be applied across a broad range of patients, models often use a limited number of objective markers of good outcomes (like controlling blood sugar levels in persons with diabetes) or poor outcomes (like death within ninety days after a specific type of surgery). Using fixed performance measures like these, however, incentivizes providers to avoid caring for patients who are less likely to achieve the targeted outcomes. To continue the example of diabetes care, persons who are homeless or have other stressful social circumstances face especial challenges in managing their own diabetes by obtaining the equipment and medications for adhering to an insulin regimen, monitoring their blood glucose levels, managing their diet, and exercising.[46] Compared to other patients in less challenging circumstances, they are not likely to control their blood sugar levels. If providers cherry pick patients, Medicaid enrollees who are disabled, Black, or both – because they disproportionately face adverse social and environmental conditions or have multiple medical conditions – are likely to face increased barriers to accessing care.[47]

To address this problem, some value-based reimbursement systems incorporate risk adjustment measures. These measures adjust how provider payments are calculated to account for differences in patient health and other risk factors, with the goal of eliminating any penalty that providers whose patients have multiple chronic conditions or environmental health challenges would otherwise face. The point is to enable accurate comparisons of providers' performance even if their patients are sicker or poorer than average. Designing risk adjustment methods that accomplish this goal, however, is complex and expensive.[48] In addition, adjusting payment for "riskier" patients threatens to pathologize race and disability as the problem (rather than structural forces like racism and ableism).[49] Entirely satisfactory risk adjustment methods remain elusive.

Another concern is that pay-for-performance measures could have a "reverse Robin Hood" effect,[50] leading resource-rich providers to grow richer and resource-poor providers to grow poorer. The latter category includes traditional safety-net

---

[45] Karen E. Joynt Maddox, *Financial Incentives and Vulnerable Populations – Will Alternative Payment Models Help or Hurt?*, 378 NEW ENG. J. MED. 977, 977–78 (2018).

[46] Janice Constance & Joanne M. Lusher, *Diabetes Management Interventions for Homeless Adults: A Systematic Review*, 65 INT'L J. PUB. HEALTH 1773 (2020).

[47] Maddox, *supra* note 46.

[48] *Id.* at 978.

[49] Ayotomiwa Ojo et al., *Value-Based Health Care Must Value Black Lives*, HEALTH AFF. BLOG (Sept. 3, 2020), https://www.healthaffairs.org/do/10.1377/hblog20200831.419320/full.

[50] Austin B. Frakt & Ashish K. Jha, *Face the Facts: We Need to Change the Way We Do Pay for Performance*, 168 ANNALS INTERNAL MED. 237, 291 (2018).

providers serving disadvantaged populations. These providers operate on a proverbial shoestring. Resource constraints limit their ability to ramp up investments in health information technology, case management, and other services needed to adapt successfully to value-based reimbursement. Early federal pay-for-performance programs tended to be zero-sum games, where bonuses were offset by penalties.[51] The zero-sum approach effectively rewards those providers who can meet value benchmarks at the expense of those who cannot. Safety-net providers are ill-equipped to adapt to new expectations, so zero-sum, value-based reimbursement schemes may easily end up punishing those who serve Medicaid enrollees, with their penalties funding richer, more adaptable institutions.[52]

Value-based reimbursement's unintended consequences – whether for Medicaid recipients or for providers traditionally serving them – are not necessarily insurmountable. Adaptations could potentially address these concerns. (In designing reimbursement methods, the devil truly is in the details. But for purposes of identifying targets for cross-movement advocacy and to keep this discussion from getting bogged down, general points should suffice.) Performance benchmarks could be designed to incentivize *improving* each patient's health rather than a patient's attaining an absolute health standard. An improvement-based standard could make patients in poorer health attractive to providers because they have more room to improve![53] Alternatively, Medicaid programs could incorporate benchmarks that reward providers who succeed in narrowing specific health disparities across a larger population. For example, Medicaid might pay managed care systems a bonus if they reduce racial disparities in cancer screenings among their patients.

The point here is not to get into the weeds of Medicaid value-based reimbursement design but to flag the challenges (and opportunities) for creating and implementing methods that advance health equity rather than exacerbate health inequity. A basic starting point is for any state Medicaid program that considers incorporating pay for performance to explicitly include progress towards greater equity as part of the performance it rewards. And to the extent that state reimbursement innovations require federal approval, the federal government should require states to identify equity as a central goal and include specific, measurable equity-enhancing targets. These basic points seem like ones that racial justice advocates and disability justice advocates could agree on. Whether by targeting administrators at the federal Centers for Medicare and Medicaid Services or educating and agitating state policy makers, intersectional advocacy could have an effect.

---

[51] Eric T. Roberts et al., *The Value-Based Payment Modifier: Program Outcomes and Implications for Disparities*, 168 ANNALS INTERNAL MED. 255, 256 (2018).

[52] *Id.*; Rita Rubin, *How Value-Based Medicare Payments Exacerbate Health Care Disparities*, 319 JAMA 968, 968 (2018).

[53] Maddox, *supra* note 46, at 979.

10.3.3 *Social Determinants of Health: Single-Family Zoning Policies*

Interventions targeting the doctor-patient relationship and health care access, standing alone, cannot fully achieve health justice. Significant progress toward that goal will require addressing social determinants of health and structural forces producing inequity (like racism and ableism). Examples of social determinant targets that might garner intersectional support from racial justice and disability justice advocates include policies eliminating or restricting exclusionary school discipline or cutting back the number of collateral consequences that make it difficult to reintegrate into society after incarceration. The advocacy target suggested here is local zoning laws.

Unaffordable and inaccessible housing has deleterious effects on the health of low-income people who are Black, disabled, or both, as described in Chapter 7. From adding to burdens of stress, to forcing trade-offs with other health-related needs, to increasing evictions and rates of homelessness and institutionalization, housing unaffordability and inaccessibility are health crises that hurt some groups of people worse than others.

Numerous factors contribute to the problem; one is the prevalence of single-family zoning rules in many cities. These policies create barriers to home ownership for people unable to afford the purchase of a single-family home. They also constrain the stock of rental units in neighborhoods that are desirable because of their location, schools, or other amenities. Originating during the early twentieth century, single-family zoning rules were a part of a web of housing laws and policies that operated as tools of racial exclusion, contributing to enduring racial segregation.[54] Single-family zoning rules also affect the likelihood of disabled people living in the community by hindering the development of group homes or other multiunit dwellings designed for people with disabilities.[55] More broadly, these rules stifle development of new multiunit dwellings that would be subject to the Fair Housing Act and its accessibility guidelines. With these exclusionary effects, single-family zoning laws may support NIMBYist preferences.

In 2020, Minneapolis became the first major city in the United States to eliminate single-family zoning throughout its neighborhoods. The move responded to a housing shortage and affordability problems generally, but it also was explicitly equity driven. Two years earlier, in 2018, Minneapolis had been ranked as having the lowest Black home ownership rate among more than 100 cities. Its city council

---

[54] RICHARD ROTHSTEIN, THE COLOR OF LAW: A FORGOTTEN HISTORY OF HOW OUR GOVERNMENT SEGREGATED AMERICA (2017).

[55] While federal laws (the Fair Housing Act and the ADA) restrict local government's ability to use zoning regulations to regulate where group homes can be operated, in some cases local opposition compels group home operators to pursue legal action in order to establish a group home.

adopted the single-family zoning ban as part of a comprehensive twenty-year plan for the city's growth and development. The change was possible partly as the result of engaged advocacy to elect progressive city council members who supported housing policy reform. Also important was a commitment that local Yes in My Backyard (YIMBY) activist groups made to community outreach. Over two years and countless meetings, planners reached out to diverse groups – including the disability community and people of color – to seek their input and engagement.[56]

Though the first city to act, Minneapolis is not alone in considering how eliminating or restricting single-family zoning policies could address housing affordability and equity. Action is also possible at the state level. In 2019, Oregon passed a law requiring cities of over 10,000 residents to permit duplexes in single-family zoned areas.[57] The federal government could also influence local governments to weaken single-family zoning rules by creating financial incentives for doing so. The *New York Times* editorial board urged the federal government, as part of a broader urban policy agenda, to "require communities that want federal funding for roads and other infrastructure to allow the development of denser, more affordable housing."[58] President Joe Biden's infrastructure plan took a similar tack, offering grants and tax credits to cities that change zoning laws to increase affordability and equity.[59]

An active and potentially productive debate about equitable affordable housing is underway across the country. In addition to ending single-family zoning, it encompasses policy innovations like inclusionary zoning laws. These laws encourage or require developers to include affordable units as part of new developments in low-poverty areas.[60] Affordable accessible housing shortages carry significant public health implications, particularly for Black people and people with disabilities. Those groups have common interests in eliminating single-family zoning. Because authority around zoning laws resides primarily at the local level, this issue is one where intersectional advocacy could have a meaningful impact on local council races. And local initiatives offer a proving ground for a fledgling reform's impact.

---

[56] Kathleen McCormick, *Rezoning History: Influential Minneapolis Policy Shift Links Affordability, Equity*, Land Lines 8 (Jan. 2020).

[57] Laurel Wamsley, *Oregon Legislature Votes to Essentially Ban Single-Family Zoning*, NPR (July 1, 2019), https://www.npr.org/2019/07/01/737798440/oregon-legislature-votes-to-essentially-ban-single-family-zoning.

[58] Editorial Board, *The Cities We Need*, N.Y. Times (May 11, 2020), https://www.nytimes.com/2020/05/11/opinion/sunday/coronavirus-us-cities-inequality.html.

[59] Romina Ruiz-Goiriena, *Biden's Infrastructure Plan Calls for Cities to Limit Single-Family Zoning and Instead Build Affordable Housing*, USA Today (Apr. 14, 2021), https://www.usatoday.com/in-depth/news/nation/2021/04/14/zoning-biden-infrastructure-bill-would-curb-single-family-housing/7097434002.

[60] David Tuller, *Housing and Health: The Role of Inclusionary Zoning*, Health Aff. Health Policy Brief (June 7, 2018), https://www.healthaffairs.org/do/10.1377/hpb20180313.668759/full.

10.4 HEALTH JUSTICE IS GOOD FOR EVERYONE

These three policy targets suggest opportunities for cross-movement collaboration between anti-Black racism advocates and disability justice advocates. No doubt other useful targets exist as well. The point is that, despite the distance that has often existed between these movements, areas of common concern and values exist relating to health.

The time is opportune to recognize shared concerns and values and act on them. Activists are already at work building networks committed to intersectional inclusivity and action, building up the people power critical to social justice movements. A growing number of scholars across disciplines are exploring the intersection of Blackness and disability, providing tools for discerning intersectional concerns and perspectives on their importance. As I write, the United States has just endured over a year in which Black people and disabled people (along with other marginalized groups) were disproportionately sickened and killed by a brutal pandemic.

This book seeks to increase appreciation of Black people's and disabled people's shared concerns relating specifically to health, a topic that has been underexamined. The specific goal in doing so is to contribute knowledge and understanding useful in establishing a foundation for building cross-movement, intersectional alliances to further health equity. The motivating spirit is Congressman John Lewis's posthumously published exhortation: "When you see something that is not right, you must say something. You must do something.... Continue to build union between movements ... because we must put away our willingness to profit from the exploitation of others."[61]

While the book focuses on health justice for people who are Black, disabled, or both, achieving policy objectives like the ones suggested offers potential benefit for advancing health justice more broadly. Most health-equity promoting interventions – even if targeted to address injustice experienced by a particular group – are readily adaptable to provide broader progress toward equitable health outcomes.

Nor does promoting health justice for Black people, disabled people, and others who experience health disparities necessarily entail harming persons in groups that have already been living relatively longer and healthier lives. In her bestselling book *The Sum of Us: What Racism Costs Everyone and How We Can Prosper Together*, Heather McGhee argues that zero-sum thinking, when it comes to social issues, is simply erroneous. Using example after example (including the Medicaid expansion), she makes the case that it is not necessary for White people to lose something for Black people to participate fully and equally in American society.[62] To be sure, remedying structural inequities and the other factors contributing to

[61] John Lewis, *Together, You Can Redeem the Soul of Our Nation*, N.Y. TIMES (July 30, 2020), https://www.nytimes.com/2020/07/30/opinion/john-lewis-civil-rights-america.html.

[62] HEATHER MCGHEE, THE SUM OF US: WHAT RACISM COSTS EVERYONE AND HOW WE CAN PROSPER TOGETHER (2021).

health disparities will not be costless, which is why conservative and moneyed forces incessantly promote racially divisive, zero-sum narratives. However, even those forces are limited in their ability to retreat to their castles and pull up their drawbridges. Nobel-winning economist Joseph Stiglitz makes the point: "The top 1 percent have the best houses, the best educations, the best doctors, and the best lifestyles, but there is one thing that money doesn't seem to have bought: an understanding that their fate is bound up with how the other 99 percent live."[63]

This point is perhaps nowhere truer than when it comes to health. Studies find an association across societies between increased inequality in wealth and overall worse health outcomes. More egalitarian societies, by contrast, tend to be healthier.[64] We know from the COVID-19 pandemic that although poorer, darker-skinned and disabled people have sickened and died at higher rates, wealthy, White, abled people have not been spared. America should learn from the pandemic that "structural inequality threatens the health of our entire population, not just the health of the poor."[65] To adapt an often-quoted warning, health injustice anywhere is a threat to health everywhere.

That cautionary point can also be framed more positively: Health justice is good for everyone. Racial justice and disability justice activists are rightly motivated to improve the health prospects and lives of the people they care about most. But one thing we've learned from the successes of the disability rights movement is that numerous modifications called for by the ADA do not benefit only disabled people. Indeed, nondisabled people end up benefiting from curb cuts and closed captioning, to give two examples. The so-called "curb cut effect" describes the more general phenomenon of laws or programs designed specifically to benefit vulnerable groups ultimately benefiting society more broadly.[66] As this book draws to a close, we might ask: Which health-related curb cut effects could flow from a more equitable health care system and society?

Perhaps we should think of health justice as posing a Universal Design challenge. Heather McGhee makes the point that designing social programs to achieve greater inclusion and equality helps everyone. Universal Design applies an analogous philosophy to product design, reflecting the principle that an environment should be designed to meet the needs of all people using it. It applies to physical buildings, but also to products and services broadly. Universal Design seeks to make products as

---

[63] Joseph E. Stiglitz, The Price of Inequality: How Today's Divided Society Endangers Our Future (2012).

[64] Richard Wilkinson & Kate Pickett, The Spirit Level: Why Greater Equality Makes Societies Stronger 73–87 (2009).

[65] Dayna Bowen Matthew, *Structural Inequality: The Real COVID-19 Threat to America's Health and How Strengthening the Affordable Care Act Can Help*, 108 Geo. L.J. 1679, 1680 (2020).

[66] Angela Glover Blackwell, *The Curb-Cut Effect*, Stan. Soc. Innovation Rev. 28 (Winter 2017).

inclusive as possible, without diminishing anyone's experience of using the product.[67]

Admittedly, addressing the health effects of structural inequity is far more complex and challenging than cutting curbs. Pursuing policies to ensure that *all* members of our society have the opportunity to enjoy good health and long lives will require interventions targeting groups that currently fall the furthest short of that ideal. But targeted interventions that move those groups toward health equity can move us all toward a healthier society. Health justice is good for us all.

---

[67] *10 Things to Know about UD*, CENTRE FOR EXCELLENCE IN UNIVERSAL DESIGN, http://universaldesign.ie/what-is-universal-design/the-10-things-to-know-about-ud/10-things-to-know-about-ud.html.

Index

CPSIA information can be obtained
at www.ICGtesting.com
Printed in the USA
LVHW050233080123
736639LV00008B/550